Paid to Care

Joe R. and Teresa Lozano Long Series in
Latin American and Latino Art and Culture

Paid to Care

*Domestic Workers in Contemporary
Latin American Culture*

RACHEL RANDALL

University of Texas Press ◆ *Austin*

Chapter 2 draws on material previously published in "'Eu não sou o meu pai!': Deception, Intimacy and Adolescence in (the) *Casa grande*" in *New Visions of Adolescence in Contemporary Latin American Cinema* (2018), 101–126, and is reprinted here with the permission of Palgrave Macmillan. Chapter 3 draws on material previously published in "'It is very difficult to like and to love, but not to be respected or valued': Maids and Nannies in Contemporary Brazilian Documentary" in *Journal of Romance Studies* 18 (2): 275–300, and is reprinted here with the permission of Liverpool University Press.

Copyright © 2024 by the University of Texas Press
All rights reserved
Printed in the United States of America
First edition, 2024

Requests for permission to reproduce material from this work should be sent to:
    Permissions
    University of Texas Press
    P.O. Box 7819
    Austin, TX 78713-7819
    utpress.utexas.edu

♾ The paper used in this book meets the minimum requirements of ANSI/NISO Z39.48-1992 (R1997) (Permanence of Paper).

LIBRARY OF CONGRESS CATALOGING-IN-PUBLICATION DATA

Names: Randall, Rachel, 1988– author.
Title: Paid to care : domestic workers in contemporary Latin American culture / Rachel Randall.
Description: First edition. | Austin : University of Texas Press, 2023. | Includes bibliographical references, filmographies, and index.
    Identifiers: LCCN 2023020744
    ISBN 978-1-4773-2770-8 (cloth)
    ISBN 978-1-4773-2771-5 (pdf)
    ISBN 978-1-4773-2772-2 (epub)
Subjects: LCSH: Household employees in motion pictures. | Household employees in literature. | Household employees--Latin America--Social conditions. | Motion pictures--Latin America. | Documentary films--Latin America. | Digital media--Latin America. | LCGFT: Filmographies.
Classification: LCC HD8039.D52 L388 2023 | DDC 305.5/62098--dc23/ eng/20230720
LC record available at https://lccn.loc.gov/2023020744

doi:10.7560/327708

For Daniel and Arthur

Contents

Acknowledgments   *ix*

Introduction   *1*

CHAPTER 1. Paid Domestic Workers' Testimonios in Latin America   *37*

CHAPTER 2. Labors of Love? Live-in Domestic Workers in Latin American Fiction Film   *87*

CHAPTER 3. Immaterial Labors: Spectral Domestic Workers in Brazilian and Argentine Documentary   *131*

CHAPTER 4. Domestic Workers in the Digital Domain   *183*

Conclusion   *217*

APPENDIX 1. Latin American Testimonios Exploring (Paid) Domestic Work and Published in the Late Twentieth and Early Twenty-First Centuries   *227*

APPENDIX 2. Filmography: Latin American Fiction Films Released since 2000 That Feature Paid Domestic Workers in Key Roles   *229*

APPENDIX 3. Filmography: Contemporary Latin American Documentaries That Focus on Paid Domestic or Care Workers   *233*

APPENDIX 4. Filmography: Other Films and Television Shows Mentioned in Text   *235*

Notes   *237*
References   *253*
Index   *277*

Acknowledgments

I MUST BEGIN by thanking the Leverhulme Trust, whose support of this research project, through a Leverhulme Early Career Fellowship (ECF-2016-400) at the Universities of Oxford and Bristol, gave me the time and space to work on this book. The ideas behind the project began to take shape in early 2016 while I was working at the University of Leeds, and I am grateful to colleagues in the Department of Spanish, Portuguese, and Latin American Studies who provided initial feedback on my plans. I am particularly thankful to Joey Whitfield for his support when I was drafting my Leverhulme proposal.

My research into representations of paid domestic workers in post-dictatorship Latin American culture benefited enormously from the time I spent at the University of Oxford between 2016 and 2018. I am particularly grateful for the help and feedback provided by colleagues in the Sub-faculty of Portuguese and especially for the guidance of my mentor, Claire Williams, whose reading recommendations and encouragement were invaluable.

Since I embarked on the research for this project, I have been lucky to participate in various academic networks and events dedicated to paid domestic workers in Latin America (and related topics). I am grateful to the Red de Investigación sobre Trabajo del Hogar en América Latina (Domestic Workers in Latin America Research Network or RITHAL) and its founder, Erynn Masi de Casanova. Through the network, I have been able to participate in conference panels and roundtables with fellow researchers including Sônia Roncador and María Julia Rossi. I am grateful to them and to Rosario Fernández and Rebekah Pite for their feedback on earlier drafts of sections of this manuscript. The ideas developed in this book also benefited from a double panel on cordiality and intimacy in Brazilian culture organized by Stephanie Dennison and supported by the European Network of Brazilianists Working in Cultural Analysis (REBRAC) at the Association of British

X ACKNOWLEDGMENTS

and Irish Lusitanists (ABIL) Conference in 2017 in Sheffield, England, as well as from a panel exploring domestic work in Latin America that was co-organized with my wonderful friend Megan Ryburn at the Latin American Studies Association (LASA) Congress in Lima, Peru, in 2017.

I owe a huge debt of gratitude to my colleagues at the University of Bristol in the Department of Hispanic, Portuguese, and Latin American Studies, including Matthew Brown, who patiently gave me feedback on drafts of these chapters and discussed the book's overall structure with me, and Jo Crow, who provided such useful comments on my introduction. I am also grateful to Paul Merchant, Ed King, Paco Romero Salvado, James Hawkey, Rebecca Kosick, Bethan Fisk, José Lingna Nafafe, and Miguel Garcia Lopez for all their support, suggestions, and encouragement.

In addition, I would like to thank those who agreed to be interviewed for this project and whose answers hugely enriched the analysis I was able to develop in chapter 1. They include Elena Poniatowska, who kindly spoke to me about her prologue to *Se necesita muchacha*, and Cristina Goutet's friends and colleagues, Angelica Alvarez Velarde and Isabel Baufumé, in Cusco, Peru. I would also like to thank the staff at the Biblioteca Bartolomé de las Casas and the Cinemateca Brasileira for their help while I was on research trips in Cusco, Peru, and São Paulo, Brazil, as well as Rizoma Films and The Match Factory GmBH for supplying me with a copy of the film *Los dueños*. Finally, I would like to thank the reviewers of this manuscript and my acquiring editor at the University of Texas Press, Kerry Webb, for her patience.

My utmost gratitude goes to all the family and friends who have supported me during the lengthy process of researching, drafting, and editing this book. Lucy Bollington, your detailed feedback on the chapters of this manuscript has left an imprint on these pages. Edila Mandur Thomaz, thank you for patiently keeping and posting so many books and films to me. Liz and Ed Randall, as always, I am hugely grateful for your unending support. Finally, Daniel Mandur Thomaz, thank you for all your love and continuous encouragement, and thank you to our son, Arthur Alberto Randall Thomaz, who joined us not long after I submitted the full manuscript of this book.

My greatest wish is that *Paid to Care* inspires readers to listen to and reflect on the stories of paid domestic and care workers across the globe, people whose contributions are often undervalued, underacknowledged, and underpaid.

Paid to Care

Introduction

RIO DE JANEIRO: CITY OF SPLENDOUR ([1936] 2016) is a documentary short made by the US filmmaker James A. FitzPatrick as part of his travelogue series *Traveltalks* (1930–1955). In one of the documentary's sequences, a young Afro-Brazilian woman wearing a domestic worker's uniform sits on a bench next to Copacabana Beach while a White child in a swimsuit lounges on her lap. The Afro-Brazilian woman, who is likely the child's nanny, stares back into the camera's lens when she realizes she is being filmed in a way that suggests both her curiosity and her refusal to serve as a passive object of the filmmaker's gaze. She then turns away, ignoring the camera until the child on her lap becomes aware of it and pushes her on the shoulder, insisting that she turn back to look. A painful irony is provoked as this footage is juxtaposed with the film's extradiegetic commentary. The narrator remarks that in Latin America, "the color of one's skin does not always determine one's social standing; as a matter of fact, the racial color line seems to be so thinly drawn that it has become a haven of toleration for all races." FitzPatrick's misreading of this scene is perhaps not so surprising, particularly coming from the United States prior to the civil rights movement.[1] Furthermore, the misconception that Brazil and other Latin American countries constitute racial democracies forms a part both of international portrayals of these nations and of their own self-narrativization. Sociohistorical and cultural depictions of and discourses about wet nurses, and later paid domestic workers, have been used to shore up this fiction.

Since the 1980s, however, a wave of Latin American cultural texts that are the product of direct collaborations with or close personal relationships to paid domestic workers have begun to challenge and critique this myth of racial democracy, while in some cases simultaneously invoking an ambivalent, postcolonial nostalgia for intimate relationships to paid domestic

2 PAID TO CARE

Figure 0.1. An Afro-Brazilian woman with a White child sitting on her lap, *Rio de Janeiro: City of Splendour* (dir. FitzPatrick, 1936, Metro-Goldwyn-Mayer)

employees or deploying well-known cultural stereotypes about them. All the cultural representations analyzed in this book, then, draw either on the personal experiences of paid domestic workers or on intimate relationships to domestic employees; sometimes they constitute a mixture of both.

This analysis focuses on literary *testimonios*,[2] fiction and documentary films, and digital culture. Around half (nine) of these works were made in Brazil, with the other half originating in Argentina (two), Chile (one), Mexico (two), Peru (two), and Uruguay (one). All of them were created either during or after these countries' transitions from periods of authoritarian rule to democracy (1980–2020). They include testimonios that have been shaped by paid domestic workers' experiences of unionization in the 1980s, such as Ana Gutiérrez's (1983) *Se necesita muchacha* (Maid wanted)[3] and Lenira Carvalho's (1982) "Só a gente que vive é que sabe" (Only those who live it can understand). They also include testimonios that clamor for domestic workers' rights to be respected today, such as Preta-Rara's (2019) *Eu, empregada doméstica* (I, domestic worker), a collection featuring stories originally shared on the eponymous Facebook page. The following analysis also addresses critically acclaimed films such as *Roma* (Cuarón 2018), *Que horas ela volta?* (When is she coming home?) (Muylaert 2015; *The Second Mother*), *La nana* (Silva 2009; *The Maid*), and *Santiago* (Salles 2007). I refer to these works as cultural representations because they are texts that employ systems of signifiers in order to construct meaning and transmit it (Hall 1997); in many cases, these texts also self-reflexively intervene in debates about who is represented and how, and they trouble traditional distinctions between intellectual or artistic production, labor, and activism.

The films and visual artworks analyzed are all inspired by close, affective ties to current or former domestic workers; this means that they are often framed by middle- or upper-class directorial perspectives, which they nonetheless simultaneously interrogate in many cases by drawing on a variety of techniques. The testimonios discussed endeavor to serve as a platform for domestic workers' own voices to be heard, although their form, content, and promotion are also mediated by gatekeepers, including scribes, academics, publishers, a social media influencer, and in one case, an employer herself. The interplay between artist (or content creator) and subject in all the works analyzed in this book enables them to evoke and interrogate the power relationships between bosses and domestic employees. Consequently, they foreground the complex ethical issues surrounding the depiction of subaltern figures that relate to consent, mediation, and appropriation. These themes are a central concern in this book, as they have been within Latin American studies, cultural studies, and visual studies more broadly.

My focus on these kinds of personal or co-produced cultural representations of paid domestic workers permits an analysis of an element of paid domestic and care relationships that makes them particularly difficult to regulate and account for in economic terms: their affective dimension. On the one hand, close, personal ties between employer-families and domestic workers underlie the senses of intimacy and indebtedness that have motivated the moving filmic portrayals produced by so many of the directors whose works are analyzed here. On the other hand, the works discussed also painfully attest to the negative impacts that these labor relationships have had on so many domestic workers' own personal lives by circumscribing their freedom in ways that have limited their ability to form autonomous romantic relationships or families of their own. Many of the films I address powerfully evoke this emotional paradox through their portrayals of live-in domestic workers and the relationship between employees and their employers' children, in particular. I argue that the difficulty of accounting for the affective (or immaterial) products of paid domestic work culminates in depictions of spectral or ghostly paid domestic employees in several of the representations analyzed here. They evoke the ways in which domestic work (and reproductive labor, more broadly) haunts the capitalist economic models that have never properly accounted for it while also alluding to the ways in which paid domestic labor relationships in Latin America are shaped by the legacy of colonialism and slavery.

The Historical Development of Paid Domestic Work in Colonial Latin America

Domestic service and domestic slavery were prevalent across Latin America throughout the colonial period, and the characteristics that these forms of labor developed during that time continue to mark the nature of paid domestic employment in the region today, including the ways in which it is gendered, racialized, and underpaid. As Elizabeth Kuznesof (1989, 17–20) argues, following Spanish colonization, the patriarchal household became the central vector of social control, and domestic servants and slaves were present in almost all Spanish houses, including the homes of *encomenderos* (settlers who were granted land and laborers by the Spanish Crown) and those houses belonging to merchants and artisans. Studies of sixteenth-century towns in Mexico, Peru, and Chile indicate that colonial Spanish households (or *casas pobladas*) included anywhere from one to more than forty domestic servants (Kuznesof 1989, 20).

The home was the most important arena for female labor in the colonial era, and domestic service was the major wage-earning employment option for women, especially those who were young and unmarried, as Susan Migden Socolow (2015, 127) points out. Tasks undertaken ranged from cleaning and cooking to childcare, including wet-nursing, and making items for domestic consumption (127–128). The racial background of women in domestic service in colonial Latin America varied according to the period and the region, but throughout the sixteenth, seventeenth, and eighteenth centuries, domestic service was a sector that included Indigenous peoples, *mestiza* and *mulata* (mixed-race) individuals, freed African slaves, and European immigrants (Kuznesof 1989, 20; Migden Socolow 2015, 127). Working-class European women were often indentured to an employer already living in the colonies or accompanied the employer traveling to settle in colonial Spanish America (Kuznesof 1989, 19).

Domestic servants commonly received a significant proportion of their wages "in-kind" in the form of food and accommodation (Migden Socolow 2015, 127). In-kind payment is a characteristic of domestic service that has undermined attempts to regulate paid domestic work and to implement those workers' legal rights and that still does so even today. Following the abolition of the enslavement of Indigenous peoples and the attempt to end the *encomienda* system in 1542, both free and enslaved Africans and Afro-descendant people became an even more important part of the domestic labor force in Spanish America (Kuznesof 1989, 21). By the end of the seventeenth century, while servants of Spanish descent tended to hold overseeing or housekeeping jobs, "servile" domestic chores were increasingly being performed by Indigenous and mestiza or mulata women, as well as free and enslaved Black women (Migden Socolow 2015, 127).

In Brazil, much as in colonial Spanish America, the patriarchal homestead, or *casa grande* (master's house), was central to the functioning of the Portuguese colonial enterprise, and domestic slaves and servants were integral to its upkeep. The relationship between the European descendant landowners and their families and the predominantly African and Afrodescendant slaves and servants who labored for them both in their homes and on the sixteenth- and seventeenth-century sugar plantations concentrated in the Northeast has been documented in Gilberto Freyre's ([1933] 2003) well-known and much-criticized *Casa grande & senzala* (*The Masters and the Slaves*). The predominance of enslaved Africans in colonial households, as compared to Indigenous peoples, is a result of the fact that Brazil received almost half of the twelve million African captives who were transported to the Americas between 1492 and the 1860s (Schwartz 2011, 160; Marques 2019, 1). However, the casa grande was not the only form of colonial household; domestic slaves and servants were also present in smaller homes (Algranti 1997). The legacy of the enslavement of African peoples in Brazil continues to be acute, in part because Brazil was the last country in the Western world to abolish the practice, doing so in 1888, a fact that marks many cultural depictions of, and testimonios by, paid domestic workers in Brazil. Today, over 90 percent of domestic workers in the country are women, and the majority are Black women (Cornwall et al. 2013, 149).

Sexual exploitation of domestic slaves was frequently the result of a colonial system that viewed enslaved individuals as property. Any children born to an enslaved woman automatically belonged to her "master." This principle functioned as an incentive for slave owners and their sons to impregnate female slaves, with or without their consent, because doing so could increase the former's wealth and the size of their workforce (Freyre 2003, 456; Migden Socolow 2015, 142–143). Spanish men similarly targeted Indigenous servants in Spanish American households for extramarital sex (Terraciano 2011, 136). Many of the mestizo offspring resulting from those relationships were then raised in the colonial household and treated as servants themselves (Kuznesof 1989, 21). In addition, it was common for African, Afro-descendant, or Indigenous women who had given birth to be employed (or enslaved) subsequently as wet nurses to their master's children—whether or not their own offspring survived (Migden Socolow 2015, 128, 143).

Paid Domestic Work in Post-Independence Latin America

In the nineteenth century, although employment options for women in Latin America expanded, domestic service continued to absorb "a substantial proportion of female labor" (Kuznesof 1989, 24). For Afro-descendant women in particular, the end of slave labor across the Americas culminated with them (and their descendants) taking up paid service positions, the only jobs available because of both the scarcity of employment options and the consequence of the racialized assumption that servitude was the "natural" destiny for most Black and mulatto women in postslavery society (Roncador 2014, 6; da Cunha 2007, 377–418). For example, in Rio de Janeiro in the 1870s, women working as servants represented about 16 percent of the total urban population (Lauderdale Graham 1989, 69). The private home was considered a safe and reputable place for a woman to work. It was therefore common for homeless or impoverished women and orphaned, abandoned, or poor children, in particular girls, to be placed into domestic service with "respectable" families (Kuznesof 1989, 24). This practice was both incentivized and ignored by various state governments in Latin America at different moments throughout the nineteenth and early twentieth centuries (Allemandi 2015, 33; Guy 2002, 154; Poblete 2015, 5–6).

Recent studies have indicated that, in various countries in Latin America, minors continue to be employed as domestic workers despite laws prohibiting it (Blofield 2012, 25; Silva Santisteban 2007). In Latin America in 2012, an estimated two million children continued to work as domestic employees, the vast majority of them girls (Blofield 2012, 25). Relatively little attention has been paid to this issue, particularly when compared to the spotlight that has been shined on the stories of predominantly male "street children" in Latin American media and culture, even though female child labor is a reality that has marked the histories and portrayals of paid domestic work examined here.

Female child labor has also shaped the traditional conflation of domestic service and surrogate daughterhood that has often impeded domestic workers from achieving "domestic sovereignty" or from "imagining them[-selves] as wives and mothers" (Milanich 2005, 13). Delia Dutra (2017, 350) traces this issue back to a nineteenth-century Latin American conception of the family, when this unit was viewed as comprising the employer-family and their domestic servants. Servants could have their own children, but they and their offspring were not considered to constitute a family because they did not possess the entire extended family structure and because they enjoyed very little time or space to themselves (350–351).

The worker's status as an appendage of the employer-family has translated into an architectural phenomenon that persists in the design of many Latin American homes today: the servants' quarters or the maid's room. Edja Trigueiro and Viviane Cunha's (2015) analysis of the dwellings occupied by live-in domestic workers in Brazil, for example, attests to the enduring influence of the Portuguese-style colonial homestead both on the layout of urban houses (or *sobrados*) in the post-independence period (from 1822 onward) and on the design of homes and apartments across the country in the twentieth and early twenty-first centuries. While nearly all the key rooms and areas in Brazilian homes have been reshuffled in terms of positioning, becoming more or less accessible to other parts of the house or to the outside over time, rooms or areas "occupied by servants span centuries of nearly unaltered spatial segregation" (Trigueiro and Cunha 2015, 118). In the colonial period, the slave quarters (*senzalas*) were separate from the main house (casa grande); this separation continued in nineteenth-century urban *sobrados*, where domestic employees tended to be accommodated in outbuildings that often also comprised a laundry or a garage (122). In the twentieth century, most homes and apartments were designed so that they included a small service area or maid's room, which was generally separated from the family areas and accessible only through the kitchen (124). When there was a second door into the service area, it was usually a designated "service entrance" to the home, which provided access via a utility corridor (121). In this design, when the kitchen door was closed, the family area gained independence from the service area.

In the early twenty-first century, some home designs or remodels omit the maid's room, which is probably attributable both to the increasing popularity of hourly paid, as opposed to live-in, domestic workers and to changing attitudes toward privacy. In Brazil, for instance, fewer than 3 percent of domestic workers reported residing with their employers in 2012, while by 2015, the proportion had dropped further to just over 1.5 percent (Institute for Applied Economic Research 2016, 24). Nonetheless, recent studies show that service areas continue to be maintained in many homes across Brazil and that service areas are usually diminutive in size, located in the hottest area of the house, and often lack windows (Trigueiro and Cunha 2015, 130).

Many of the films analyzed in this book draw on the capacity of cinema to reconstruct and depict middle- and upper-class domestic spaces in order to play on the continuing presence and significance of the maid's room or service quarters across Latin America, to the extent that this specific domestic space has become a cinematic trope. Films utilize mise-en-scène

8 PAID TO CARE

to dramatize the spatial relationships between the areas of the home and to foreground the power dynamics that characterize postcolonial paid domestic labor relations, particularly by emphasizing the dichotomy between the employer's power, freedom, and public (or professional) life and the small, dark spaces that are portrayed as an attempt to imprison live-in domestic workers and limit their opportunities for independence. A bourgeois fear of working-class invasion, crime, and contamination is also evoked through the relationship between these segregated spaces, usually with the depiction of fortress-like middle- and upper-class homes that are owned by bosses obsessed with security. The figure of the paid domestic worker has become associated with these fears ever since workers began moving en masse out of employer-family homes to other parts of the city in the late nineteenth and early twentieth centuries (Roncador 2007, 130).

Despite the mistreatment and abuse of female domestic servants and slaves, they nonetheless began to be celebrated and romanticized as foundational figures in modernist discourses of the nation during the first half of the twentieth century. Afro-descendant or Indigenous wet nurses in particular were seized upon as powerful symbols of the culturally and racially mixed nations that many Latin American countries projected themselves as being. Freyre's (2003, 367) infamous description of the African or Afro-Brazilian wet nurse, or *mãe preta* (black mammy), is one of the best-known examples. His emphasis on the physical connection to the wet nurse who suckles her young, White charges and rocks them to sleep has been used to foreground the idea of a unifying "milk kinship" between this emblematic pair, which has also been deployed by other influential Brazilian modernist writers (Roncador 2014, 72).[4] The mãe preta was venerated to such an extent in the early twentieth century that she was often cited in newspapers run by Afro-Brazilian people as a symbol "not just of the sacrifices that black people had made for Brazil, but also of the powerful ways in which Euro- and Afro-Brazilians were linked in a common destiny" (Andrews 1991, 215). Campaigns to erect a monument in the mãe preta's honor also gained support in both Rio de Janeiro and São Paulo in the 1920s; one was inaugurated in São Paulo in 1955 (Roncador 2014, 83; L. Shaw 2018, 14). Kimberly Cleveland (2019) notes the lasting impact of Freyre's discourse on visual art from the late nineteenth to the early twenty-first century, stating that the African or Afro-descendant wet nurse is the only enslaved figure who continues to be referenced in contemporary visual culture and in discussions about race relations in Brazil.

In some ways a counterpart to Freyre's (2003) modernist celebration of racial and cultural mixing in Brazil, *La raza cósmica* (The cosmic race), by the Mexican philosopher and politician José Vasconcelos ([1925] 2017), celebrates the fusion of European, African, and Indigenous influences across Latin America due to the nature of Spanish colonization, and the book identifies the creation of a new mestizo race as the region's great strength (in contrast to the United States). The significance of this mixing is explored in well-known, semiautobiographical Mexican works from the twentieth century that portray the relationship between the artist (or upper-class more broadly) and domestic servants, such as in Rosario Castellanos's 1957 novel *Balún-Canán* (The nine guardians) and in Frida Kahlo's 1937 painting *Mi nana y yo* (My nurse and I), which depicts the artist suckling at her Indigenous nurse's breast. Although these works are undoubtedly critical of the violent nature of colonization and of its impact on Indigenous peoples, their focuses on the corporeal availability of, and intimacy with, dark-skinned wet nurses or nannies are suggestive of the tendency to reduce these women to their physical bodies, which is reinforced by a racialized association of them with animality or a lack of humanity.

In Latin American popular culture, the wet nurse functions as a clear counterpart to the sexualized figure of the young mixed-race domestic worker whose body is also symbolically associated with miscegenation. Peter Wade (2013, 189) explains that young *chola* (mixed-race Indigenous) and *mulata* (mixed-race Afro-descendant) women are also viewed as "transitional figures" in Latin American ideologies where *mestizaje* or *mestiçagem* (mixture) is considered "the basis of society." Their sexualization results from an eroticized view of these women's "hybridity," which is characterized by a racialized animality that is nonetheless considered to be tempered by "whitening" and modernizing influences (189). Their strong historical association with being of service to the dominant class has reinforced an image of sexual desirability and availability that continues to burden paid domestic workers today.

The proximity of the figures of the sexualized young mixed-race domestic worker and the maternal Indigenous wet nurse or nanny to their European descendant employer-family betrays the strategic nature of their deployments in narratives that ultimately reveal a desire to whiten and modernize the nation (or region) via mixing with European influences. These discourses nonetheless implicitly consign Indigenous peoples and cultures to the past, as Vasconcelos (2017) does in his book *La raza cósmica*. Freyre's (2003) romanticized depiction of the sexual and maternal domestic relationships between the landowner's family and their Afro-descendant domestic slaves and servants has also been criticized for masking intimate forms of abuse that hark back to the colonial period and continue to extend into the present. In his seminal text, *Raízes do Brasil (Roots of Brazil)*, Sérgio Buarque de Holanda ([1936] 2014, 176) sheds light on the nature and implications of these intimate power dynamics when he writes about the predominance of personal or familial relations in modern Brazilian society, even within the public or political realm, which he views as a consequence of the country's prevailing patriarchal, postcolonial, and rural culture. He argues that "cordiality" (coming from *cordis*, meaning "of the heart") is a defining element of Brazilian national culture and character. It describes an abhorrence of distant or formal relationships and a drive to impose intimate ones that could as easily be characterized by affection as by aggression (178–180). Jean Franco's (2013, 5, 9) analysis of the roots of contemporary violence across Latin America resonates with that of Holanda when she observes that, in many nations, there has been civility for the privileged few and ill treatment for the impoverished masses, particularly for Indigenous populations and the descendants of enslaved peoples, who suffer both because the mentality and practice of conquest extended well into the twentieth century and because there are many areas that remain cut off from contemporary legal restraints (5, 9). Franco adds that various myths have been concocted to conceal the violent path that modernizing forces have forged.

The cultural representations analyzed in this book reproduce and rewrite the complex and contradictory foundational narratives identified here. They demonstrate how paid domestic labor relations have had a profound impact on the formation of Latin American society and culture, not only because they are integral to the organization of so many domestic spaces and have contributed to the development of emotional attachments between the offspring of the middle and upper classes and their working-class, often dark-skinned, employees, but also because they transcend the sphere of the home by reflecting and shaping broader socioeconomic and political relationships.

Domestic Workers' Struggles for Rights in the Twentieth and Twenty-First Centuries

By the mid-twentieth century, labor laws in all Latin American countries included chapters that outlined the rights and duties of paid domestic workers, and all of them granted this group of employees "fewer rights and benefits than other workers" (Blofield 2012, 28). The labor codes reflected the demands, interests, and perspectives of employers and predominantly male politicians. Merike Blofield (50) notes that the laws established regimes of "servant subservience" in which domestic workers were "always available, outside of sleep," to serve their bosses. This practice reflects a historical and legal tendency to treat paid domestic labor as an exceptional form of work. Differential legal treatment on the issue of working hours is particularly illustrative in this respect. While the maximum number of weekly working hours was capped at either forty-four hours or forty-eight hours throughout Latin America in the 1980s, the maximum hours were significantly longer for domestic workers. In Mexico, it was simply specified that domestic employees should have "enough time off to rest and eat," while in Brazil, the maximum number of working hours was unlimited; in both cases, this was interpreted as allowing for a sixteen-hour workday (29). Labor codes in Peru and Uruguay in the 1980s also permitted workdays of up to sixteen hours (amounting to ninety-six hours per week), while in Argentina and Chile, domestic employees could be asked to work up to seventy-two hours per week, which was twenty-four hours more than other kinds of workers (29).

Although initial attempts to organize and improve domestic employees' working conditions had taken place in the 1930s and 1940s, the transition from dictatorship to democracy in many Latin American countries in the late 1970s, 1980s, and early 1990s bolstered these efforts (Blofield 2012, 50). These attempts were also crucially supported by the Catholic Church and, in particular, by Young Catholic Workers organizations, known as Juventud Obrera Católica/Juventude Operária Católica, or JOCs for short, which had branches across Latin America (Chaney and Garcia Castro 1989, 10). In their outlook, the JOCs adhered to Catholic liberation theology, which combines a class-based Marxist analysis with Christianity's compassion for the poor. Elizabeth Hutchinson's 2010 (67) study of domestic workers' organizations in Cold War Chile examines the pioneering efforts of that country's JOC, which was the first to formally mobilize household workers through the establishment of the Federation of Household Employees (Federación de Empleadas de Casa Particular) during the 1940s. Similar organizations supported by JOCs were later replicated in Brazil, Mexico, Peru, and Uruguay (Hutchinson 2010, 72; Blofield 2012, 144). The crucial impact of these kinds of organizations is discussed in chapter 1, which analyzes literary testimonios published in the 1980s in Brazil and Peru that explore the experiences of domestic workers who were involved in processes of unionization and who were deeply influenced by either liberation theology or a branch of the JOC.

Nascent domestic workers' organizations in the 1980s began to join with clerical and secular allies to demand recognition of their members as *trabajadoras* or *trabalhadoras* (workers) with rights. The organizations repudiated the use of terms such as *muchacha* (young girl or maid) and *criada* (servant or maid). "Criada" comes from the verb *criar*, which in both Spanish and Portuguese means "to bring up" or "to raise," that is, to bring up or raise a child.[5] These names are suggestive of attempts both to infantilize domestic workers and to define them as "almost" members of an employer-family, which have contributed to the informality that has characterized the profession. Domestic workers' unions in the region have also rejected the terms *empleada doméstica* or *empregada doméstica* (domestic employee). In Spanish, the names *trabajadora (remunerada) del hogar* or *trabajadora de casa particular* ([paid] worker of the home) are favored because they avoid the use of the term *doméstica* and its relationship to the word *domesticada* (domesticated), which could carry the implication that employees are expected to demonstrate obedience and become "domesticated" within their employers' bourgeois households (de Casanova 2015, 42–43). In Portuguese, *trabalhadora doméstica* (domestic worker) now tends to be used by domestic workers' organizations rather than *empregada doméstica*, although both are often shortened in informal speech to *doméstica*.[6] All the terms so far discussed are provided with their feminine endings in Spanish and Portuguese to reflect the fact that the majority of paid domestic workers are women, but the words can also be used in their masculine forms to refer to male employees.

Names for paid domestic workers that are rooted in coloniality, informality, and intimate power hierarchies have persisted despite the efforts of domestic workers' organizations to change nomenclature. Their proliferation indicates the many different types of work and tasks that paid domestic employees in the region undertake. In Spanish, the names vary according to country and have changed over time, but a few examples, including some used in works analyzed in this book, are *empleada puertas adentro* (live-in domestic worker), *empleada puertas afuera* (live-out domestic worker),[7] *asesora del hogar* (domestic worker), *nana* (maid or nanny), *niñera* (nanny or childcare worker), *cocinera* (cook), *mucama* (servant, maid, or housekeeper), and *sirvienta* (servant). In Brazil, *empregada doméstica* is often, though not always, used to refer to a live-in domestic worker, while the terms *diarista* or *faxineira* denote hourly paid, live-out employees or cleaners. *Babá* is a term used for a nanny or childcare worker, and *cozinheira* is used for a cook. *Secretária do lar* is infrequently used to mean housekeeper or domestic worker more generally. Except where I am quoting directly or translating from a text or film that uses a different term, I have chosen to refer to these workers as (paid) domestic workers or employees because these terms most closely approximate those used in Spanish and Portuguese by domestic workers' organizations. "Domestic worker" is the term that continues to be used by the United Nations' International Labour Organization (ILO) to describe the profession.

Despite the efforts of paid domestic workers' unions in Latin America throughout the twentieth and early twenty-first centuries, the path toward equal rights reform has not been smooth, and progress has often been painfully slow. This is partly because Latin America exhibits some of the world's highest income inequalities, which have created both the demand for paid domestic labor and a steady supply of potential employees (Blofield 2012, 2). These dynamics place paid domestic workers in a precarious position, which has compounded the additional problem that these employees can be difficult to mobilize and unionize because of the draining and often isolated nature of their work in employers' private homes.

In Brazil, the 1943 Labor Code explicitly excluded domestic workers from general labor rights, and throughout the 1970s, 1980s, 1990s, and early in the first decade of the twenty-first century, rights reform was piecemeal (Blofield 2012, 44). In 1972, the Brazilian military regime conceded the rights to paid vacation and to social security to domestic workers (44). During the democratic transition in the late 1980s, the new constitution in 1988 gave domestic workers the rights to a minimum wage, thirty days advance notice of dismissal, one day off a week, maternity leave for 120 days, five days of paternity leave, and an extra third of the minimum salary before taking holidays (Cornwall et al. 2013, 150). In 2006, further fractional reforms prevented employers from making in-kind discounts to salaries and gave workers the right to double pay for working on holidays, among other measures. Equal rights reform was finally achieved in 2013 by a constitutional amendment, known as the PEC das domésticas, approved during former president Dilma Rousseff's 2011–2016 Workers' Party (PT) government. The PEC has been referred to as the *segunda abolição da escravatura*, or second abolition of slavery (CartaCapital 2013). The amendment's legal application was specified in the Lei Complementar No. 150 in 2015 (Acciari 2018a). The law aims to bring paid domestic workers' rights in line with those rights enjoyed by other kinds of workers by limiting their working hours to eight per day and forty-four hours per week, guaranteeing them overtime pay, and introducing the requirement that employers pay a proportion of their employee's salary into a severance fund designed to protect domestic workers in cases of unfair dismissal (Presidência da república 2015). Rousseff was ousted from the presidency before completing her second term by impeachment proceedings that have been viewed as a form of "lawfare" that culminated in a soft coup (Baird 2017). She was replaced by her vice president, Michel Temer, who pushed through labor reforms that affect many kinds of employees besides domestic workers and that allow for the possibility of extending the length of the maximum working day. The reforms also enable agreements reached between employers and employees to take precedence over legislation in certain cases and encourage the use of outsourcing, a practice that can obfuscate who an employee's real employer is, thus making it more difficult to identify and combat instances of modern slavery (Magalhães 2017; Senado Notícias 2019). In 2017, for example, a group of migrant domestic employees from the Philippines were found to have been deprived of both food and rest while working sixteen-hour days for families living in São Paulo: the workers had been contracted by an agency called Global Talent (Locatelli 2017).

Despite those issues, Brazil ratified the ILO's (2011) "Domestic Workers Convention No. 189" in 2018. The convention, which was originally adopted by the ILO in 2011, recognizes the significant contribution that domestic workers make to the global economy and sets out provisions designed to address the specific forms of discrimination or exploitation that domestic workers often face on the basis of age, gender, and immigration status. The articles in the convention that establish that domestic workers should benefit from the same rights and protections as other kinds of workers are Article 10 for working hours, overtime compensation, rest, and annual leave; Article 11 for a national minimum wage entitlement; and Article 14 for social security protection, including maternity (ILO 2011). Louisa Acciari (2018a) argues that, while the ILO has been determinative in creating an international political opportunity for the domestic workers' movement, Convention No. 189 "has its roots in the global South" and specifically in the work of Latin American domestic workers' unions.[8] In 1988, leaders of domestic workers' associations from several countries united in Bogotá, Colombia, to form the first regional domestic workers' organization in the world: the Confederation of Domestic Workers of Latin America and the Caribbean, or CONLACTRAHO (Goldsmith 2013, 234). The CONLACTRAHO has been collaborating with the ILO since the first decade of the twenty-first century and pushing for a dedicated convention on domestic work since 2005 (Acciari 2018a). Additionally, CONLACTRAHO members participated in the ILO's ninety-ninth and one hundredth International Labour Conferences in 2010 and 2011, respectively, and attended meetings where Convention No. 189 was discussed and approved (Goldsmith 2013, 233). As of January 2023, over half (eighteen) of the thirty-five countries that have ratified Convention No. 189 are Latin American or Caribbean (ILO, n.d.).[9]

The important part that these countries have played in both shaping and adopting the convention can also be explained by the high proportion of people in the region involved in paid domestic work, which includes 14.6 percent of all working women in Latin America (Valenzuela and Velasco 2019). The occupation employs between eleven and eighteen million individuals in both Latin America and the Caribbean, of whom 93 percent are women and 77.5 percent work informally (ECLAC 2020). In Brazil alone, over six million people are employed in the sector, which makes it the country with the largest population of paid domestic workers in the world (Wentzel 2018).

Latin America's leading role in the international struggle to improve paid domestic workers' rights is best illustrated by the case of Uruguay, which in 2021 became the first nation in the world to ratify the ILO's Domestic Workers Convention No. 189 (Human Rights Watch 2012). Uruguay's national-level achievement of equal rights reform for paid domestic workers came even earlier, in 2006. Prior to this, however, Uruguay's domestic labor laws were characterized by exclusions. In 1950, for example, domestic workers were given the right to be included in social security pensions, but were excluded from health and unemployment insurance (Trezza de Piñeyro 2001, 117–127). Additionally, the minimum wage for domestic workers was set by an executive decree that permitted wage reductions of up to 20 percent if food, accommodation, or other material "benefits" had been accrued by employees in the course of their labor (Blofield 2012, 108). A bill that would have granted domestic workers equal rights was submitted to the Uruguayan Congress in 1990 and was eventually approved in a plenary vote in the House in 1996, though it was repeatedly postponed when it reached the Senate and died in commission (7–8). However, in 2005 and following the election victory of the left-wing coalition Frente Amplio (Broad Front), the Uruguayan government initiated equal rights reform, which was quickly approved as Ley 18.065 (Asamblea General de la República Oriental del Uruguay 2006). Since then, paid domestic workers in Uruguay have had the right to an eight-hour working day and cannot be excluded from the rights afforded to other workers (Blofield 2012, 34).

In Peru, a bill to reform domestic workers' rights was initially submitted to the Congress in 1980 and made no progress (Blofield 2012, 45). President Alberto Fujimori (1990–2000) subsequently stalled the bill throughout the following decade (66). Partial reform achieved in 2003 under the Ley de Trabajadores del Hogar (Law No. 27896) granted paid domestic workers access to some labor rights, including fifteen days of vacation (half the amount given to other workers), an eight-hour workday, one day off a week, two annual bonus payments, and severance pay; the law did not guarantee rights to social security or to receive the minimum wage (Pérez and Gandolfi 2020, 79; Blofield 2012, 34). Peruvian paid domestic workers have suffered from intersectional forms of discrimination: the vast majority of them are women from low-income backgrounds who are predominantly of Andean Indigenous origin, and many have migrated from rural to urban areas (Pérez and Llanos 2017). Leda M. Pérez and Andrea Gandolfi (2020, 79) estimate that the partial reform of 2003 granted paid domestic workers only around 50 percent of the rights given to other dependent employees. However, in September 2020, Law 27896 (2003) was overturned following Peru's ratification of ILO Convention No. 189 in 2018, and a new law, No. 31047, was introduced that complies with all the stipulations made in the ILO Convention (Pérez and Gandolfi 2020, 82).

In Argentina, although the 1960s brought an acknowledgment by some influential members of the middle class, including journalists, that domestic employees were professional workers (Pite 2011, 128), they remained excluded from many of the rights and protections enjoyed by others throughout the late twentieth and early twenty-first centuries, including the rights to severance pay and to maternity leave (Pereyra 2019; Blofield 2012, 32). By 2010, paid domestic workers were still granted only about two-thirds of the paid vacation time to which other workers were entitled, and room and board could also be included in a paid domestic worker's salary, although it could not be deducted from the sector's executive-decreed minimum wage, which tended to be set at a lower level than the national minimum wage for workers in general (Blofield 2012, 31–32). In March of the same year, however, former president Cristina Fernández de Kirchner (2007–2015) initiated the process of equal rights reform in anticipation of upcoming ILO meetings where the issue of domestic workers' rights would be discussed (135). A resulting bill was passed in 2013: Law 26.844, which entitled paid domestic workers to maternity leave, a month of paid holidays, and insurance; additionally, the law established a commission for the collective bargaining of wages and working conditions in the sector (Pereyra 2019; Romero 2021). In March 2014, Argentina ratified ILO Convention No. 189.

In Chile, following the transition to democracy after the end of General Augusto Pinochet's military dictatorship (1973–1990), rights reforms for the domestic worker sector throughout the 1990s and the first decade of the twenty-first century were particularly piecemeal in the face of strong conservative opposition (Blofield 2012, 8). Reforms in 1990 and 1998 granted domestic workers severance pay and maternity leave, respectively, both entitlements from which they had previously been excluded (33). Under the first administration of former president Michelle Bachelet (2006–2010), two legal reforms regarding paid domestic workers were passed. First, her government proposed a gradual equalization of wages for paid domestic workers, with the aim of increasing wages from 75 percent to 100 percent of the national minimum wage by 2011. Second, in 2009, live-in paid domestic workers were granted the right to take a vacation on national holidays (121–122). In 2015, a new domestic labor law (No. 20.786) came fully into force, and Chile ratified ILO Convention No. 189 the same year, during Bachelet's second presidential term (2014–2018). The new legislation responded to the calls of domestic workers' unions for their members to be defined as *trabajadoras de casa particular* (private household workers), rather than as *nanas*, a term that risks masking the employee's condition as a worker (Fernández 2018, 55). In addition, the new law finally reduced domestic employees' maximum working hours from seventy-two to forty-five (55). Many Chilean paid domestic workers have migrated internally from poorer rural locations to more affluent urban areas in search of employment, although increasingly, Peruvian women have also traveled to Chile, in particular to Santiago, to work as paid domestic employees, where they often suffer racist and classist discrimination (Staab and Maher 2006).

In Mexico, until very recently, paid domestic work was characterized by "a complete lack of regulation" (Blofield 2012, 30). Throughout the twentieth century and well into the twenty-first century, domestic workers were excluded from social security programs obligatory for other kinds of employees and from the right to a vacation. The minimum wage for the sector was set by the executive, and half of the employee's salary could be received in-kind. Domestic workers were also mandated to show respect toward their bosses, who, in turn, were supposed to refrain from mistreating them (37). The monumental public impact of the Mexican film *Roma* (2018), which centers on the adversities faced by a domestic worker in Mexico City in the early 1970s, created a transformative opportunity to reform paid domestic workers' legal rights in the country, which is discussed in more detail in chapter 2. The film's influence was largely due to the high profile of its director, Alfonso Cuarón, who is renowned internationally both for his Spanish-language films and for his success in Hollywood, including *Gravity* (2013). *Roma* garnered further worldwide attention due to a Netflix distribution model, and the film won various prizes at the 2019 Academy Awards. Soon after, the president of Mexico, Andrés Manuel López Obrador, announced that his administration was working toward the ratification of ILO Convention No. 189 (Excélsior 2019), which was achieved in July 2020. Cuarón mobilized the interest piqued by *Roma* to champion the cause of paid domestic workers both via social media and by collaborating directly with domestic workers' organizations in Mexico. In February 2019, not long after the film's release, the Instituto Mexicano del Seguro Social (Mexican Social Security Institute or IMSS) launched a pilot program to incorporate paid domestic workers into the social security system, a program that provides these workers access to healthcare, among other provisions, and that is obligatory for other kinds of employees. The director of the IMSS thanked the team behind the film *Roma* for their support of the pilot program and recognized the work undertaken by domestic workers' organizations in the country over many years (Forbes Staff 2019). Also in 2019, Mexico's federal labor and social security laws were amended to grant domestic workers paid holidays and a maximum eight-hour working day (Santiago Páramo 2020, 37). It is clear that the backing of well-known figures, such as Cuarón, is crucial when advocating for the improvement of paid domestic workers' legal rights, because once the issue has achieved visibility, legislators have a difficult time avoiding reform (Blofield 2012, 56). In addition, rights reform throughout Latin America has consistently been helped by the election of left-wing or center-left governments, notably in the cases of Mexico, Brazil, Uruguay, Argentina, and Chile. And in three of those cases, the administrations were also led by women presidents: Bachelet in Chile, Kirchner in Argentina, and Rousseff in Brazil.

The Continuing Impacts of Informality, Covid-19, and Cultural Prejudice

Unfortunately, while rights reform is crucial, it does not remedy many of the problems faced by paid domestic workers in Latin America. Various scholars have noted that the high rates of informality that characterize the sector make it difficult to ensure that these workers can access the full gamut of rights and protections that they have been granted (Blofield 2012, 68; Pereyra 2019). For example, a report published by the ILO on the initial effects of the constitutional amendment on domestic work in Brazil found that the amendment had had the most noticeable impact for monthly paid workers (*mensalistas*) because of a movement toward the shortening of their working day and a greater number having signed work booklets that formally registered them as workers; however, for the high proportion of informal, hourly paid diaristas, the amendment's effects were negligible (Institute for Applied Economic Research 2016, 52). Legally, employers in Brazil have no obligations toward paid domestic workers who labor for less than three days per week in a single household (54). Furthermore, in situations where a paid domestic worker should be officially registered or entitled to specific rights, implementation is challenging to monitor, even when attempted by government agencies, because the work is undertaken within the private space of a home and because bosses commonly avoid declaring that they have an employee (de Casanova 2015, 41; Pereyra 2019).

The difficulties associated with informality were aggravated by the onset of the Covid-19 pandemic in Latin America in 2020. In greater numbers than in other sectors, paid domestic workers saw their hours reduced or lost their jobs entirely. Data from the second quarter of 2020 shows the number of domestic workers fell by 25 to 50 percent in most Latin American and Caribbean countries, and by 70 percent in Peru, compared to pre-pandemic employment levels (UN 2021). From a survey carried out in Lima and Callao, Peru, during the pandemic, Pérez and Gandolfi (2020, 80) found that 86 percent of domestic workers indicated that they were not working and 82 percent were not receiving any public aid. In Brazil, many hourly paid domestic workers reported being let go suddenly without any salary; these workers were generally unable to access the Brazilian government's emergency financial package benefits, which were available only to formally registered workers (Guimarães and Gragnani 2020). In Argentina, while the government imposed a period of compulsory social isolation for everyone except essential workers in March 2020, self-employed and informal workers were entitled to economic support, but most migrant domestic workers in the country could not access the entitlements, in some cases because they did not have the two years of permanent residence required to collect the aid (Romero 2021).

At the same time, paid domestic workers were among the most vulnerable to the virus because of the nature of their labor, which brings them into close contact with their employers. The dangers of this were illustrated when it was confirmed that Cleonice Gonçalves, a sixty-three-year-old domestic worker who suffered from comorbidities, had become Rio de Janeiro's first coronavirus-related death (G1 Rio 2020). When she fell ill on March 16, 2020, she was working at her boss's apartment in the affluent neighborhood of Leblon. Her employer had just returned from a trip to Italy, where Covid-19 had been rapidly spreading, and she did not advise Gonçalves that she was feeling unwell (Simões 2020). Gonçalves's family called a taxi to bring her from the state capital to her hometown sixty miles away. It took her two hours to arrive. She entered the hospital the same evening and died the next day. Her employer, who tested positive for Covid-19, later recovered (Conde 2020, 242). Gonçalves's story illustrates the ways in which the virus exacerbated existing class- and race-related inequalities regarding mobility, housing, healthcare, and income security. Indeed, across Latin

America, many domestic employees were compelled to continue working either out of economic necessity or because they were classified as essential workers, a move made by some employers in Argentina and a number of states in Brazil to oblige paid domestic workers to continue working despite the risks (Sobreira 2020; Romero 2021). For live-out domestic employees, traveling to their employers' homes often necessitates long journeys on public transport, which would have contributed further to their exposure. At the same time, live-in domestic workers reported having been confined to their employers' residences and not permitted to return to their own houses or families for extended periods due to their bosses' fears of contamination (Romero 2021; Santiago Páramo 2020). Domestic workers in Peru launched a campaign supported by the ILO in May 2020 to highlight both domestic workers' health and safety concerns and the financial precarity faced by so many because of the pandemic. It was entitled "Tu casa también es un centro de trabajo. Convenio No. 189 de la OIT es vigente" (ILO 2020; Your home is also a place of work. ILO Convention 189 is in force). All these issues are addressed in *Nuestras voces cuentan* (Our voices count), a digital collection of testimonios that describes domestic workers' experiences in Mexico during the pandemic and which is discussed in chapter 4 (Santiago Páramo 2020).

To ensure that paid domestic workers are treated well and that their rights are respected, amending labor laws is not enough: a cultural transformation is also necessary to change behavior, particularly within the home. Cultural representations, such as those analyzed in this book, can contribute to processes of self-reflection and consciousness-raising because they have the potential to denaturalize racialized, gendered, and classed assumptions about who should be doing domestic work and about how paid domestic workers can be treated. Various recent incidents in the countries whose cultural productions are the focus of this study illustrate that ingrained social attitudes about paid domestic workers are often slow to shift. In 2007, human rights activists in Peru denounced attempts to restrict domestic employees' use of Playa de Asia, a beach favored by Lima's elite, by allowing them to swim only after dusk or by stopping them from being there altogether (*El Universo* 2007). In 2012, internet users in Chile called for a protest in response to the classist rules implemented in a gated community in Santiago's north zone that prevented domestic workers from walking through the area on foot because of security concerns (Bustamente 2012). In 2020, Brazil's economy minister, Paulo Guedes, also expressed prejudices about access to "elite" or "consumer" spaces when he bemoaned the consequences of the US dollar's fall in value in relation to the Brazilian real because the devaluation allowed everyone, even paid domestic workers, to travel to Disneyland, which he described as "uma festa danada" (a bloody mess), a statement that attracted substantial criticism (Caram 2020). In 2014, there was public outcry in Chile when the musician Ana Tijoux revealed that a group in the audience during her performance attempted to insult her by yelling "cara de nana" (Cooperativa.cl 2014; maid face). Tijoux's mother, the sociologist María Emilia Tijoux, later explained that the incident provided an insight into the country's racist and classist national imaginary, which strongly associates domestic workers with Indigenous features (Vargas Rojas 2014).

It is clear, then, that paid domestic workers and their families have been seized upon as key figures in public sociocultural debates surrounding social mobility, inequality, and race. During the wave of antigovernment protests that engulfed Brazil in the lead-up to former president Rousseff's impeachment in August 2016, a photograph circulated widely on social media showing the vice president of Rio de Janeiro's Flamengo football club and his wife on a protest accompanied by their children, who were being pushed in a stroller by the family's "Sunday maid" (*Correio Braziliense* 2016).[10] While the family was dressed in Brazil's national colors, their employee, Maria Angélica Lima, was identifiable by her plain white clothes, the uniform that many employers oblige domestic workers to wear.[11] The shot caused online consternation because the image was held up as proof of the privileged socioeconomic provenance of many of those who occupied the streets to call for the end of the Workers' Party administration. The anti-PT sentiment expressed through that wave of protests was informed by the consequences that the party's programs had had for Brazilian society since the initial election of former president Luiz Inácio Lula da Silva in 2003. PT policies allowed more than thirty million Brazilians to enter the consumer economy, which represented an enormous redistribution of income and privilege that shook the structures buttressing Brazil's social divide (de Luca 2017, 204). As Tiago de Luca (2017, 204) explains, class conflict was fueled by the entry of lower middle-class consumers into spaces such as shopping malls, airports, and universities, which had previously been reserved for the wealthy. The reactions sparked by the changes helped to prepare the ground for the political polarization that has riven the country ever since and that contributed to the election of the far-right populist Jair Bolsonaro, who assumed the presidency in 2019. At a demonstration in April 2018 against the imprisonment of former president Lula on charges that have since been annulled, and at a protest in May 2019 criticizing the cuts to funding for public universities made during Bolsonaro's administration, demonstrators have been photographed holding up signs that invoke the positive impact that the PT's introduction of quotas for public university admissions has had for Afro-descendant people and for people from working-class backgrounds, namely the children of paid domestic workers. The way in which the children of paid domestic workers have been deployed as symbols for (a lack of) social mobility is discussed in chapters 2 and 4 in the analysis of Anna Muylaert's film *Que horas ela volta?* (When is she coming home?) and in the testimonios shared on Preta-Rara's Facebook page "Eu empregada doméstica" (I domestic worker), respectively.

Cultural representations themselves constitute responses to, and are involved in shaping, public debates surrounding paid domestic workers, as will be shown by the analysis undertaken throughout my book. This becomes particularly clear in chapter 4, which explores contemporary digital culture, including a graphic novel entitled *Confinada*, by Leandro Assis and Triscila Oliveira (2020), and visual art on Instagram by Cristiano Suarez (2020a, 2020b). Both these works satirize the treatment of paid domestic workers by their employers during the Covid-19 pandemic. The impact of fiction films is also notable given the national and international discussions provoked by films such as *Roma*, *Que horas ela volta?*, *Casa grande* (Barbosa 2014; The master's house), and *La nana*, which are addressed in chapter 2.

Theorizing Reproductive and Affective Labor

In recent years, numerous sociological studies have explored the phenomenon of transnational migrant domestic work undertaken, in particular, by women from the Global South who labor in the Global North (B. Anderson 2000; Hondagneu-Sotelo 2001; Ehrenreich and Hochschild 2003; Cox 2006; Pyle 2006; Gutiérrez-Rodríguez 2010). A couple of edited volumes have linked the characteristics of this employment explicitly to the legacy of colonization and the impact of neocolonialism today (Hoerder et al. 2015; Haskins and Lowrie 2015). Transnational global care chains are not a strong theme in the cultural representations I analyze in this book; instead, I tend to focus on paid domestic workers' experiences of internal, rural-to-urban migration, which reflect patterns of mobility within Latin America throughout the twentieth century. Nonetheless, this body of scholarship, and a burgeoning body of ethnographic studies of paid domestic labor within Latin America,[12] has helped to shape the theoretical framework I use when analyzing the characteristics of paid domestic labor and the challenges that these workers face. My approach is also strongly molded by my analysis in chapter 1 of the insights gleaned from paid domestic workers' own literary testimonios.[13] The insights provided by the scholarly literature and the testimonios of domestic workers (in particular, by those of organizers) often mutually reinforce each other; however, here I draw on the former body of work to shed light on the categorization of paid domestic work as a form of reproductive or affective labor and as a type of care work, all of which are concepts pertinent to an understanding of the analysis undertaken in this book.

As Jocelyn Olcott (2011, 3) explains, the terms "domestic work" and "reproductive labor" have often been used interchangeably, although they have subtly different meanings. Reproductive labor encompasses a range of duties linked to the processes of socializing, maintaining, and reproducing the workforce, for example, biological reproduction (such as childbearing, child-rearing, surrogacy, and wet-nursing), social reproduction (including socialization and education), and maintaining forms of community (through hospitality or charitable work). Domestic labor has been treated as a form of reproductive labor, though it is often understood in a narrower sense as referring to specific household tasks, such as cooking, cleaning, and child-rearing.

Within both classical and Marxist economic theory, reproductive labor has been viewed as "unproductive" or "non-productive" labor, which, in contrast to forms of "productive labor," does not create "surplus value," that is, it does not add value to a particular product or service (Staples 2007; Hoerder et al. 2015, 5–6; Marçal 2016). In other words, unpaid domestic work is viewed as having "use-value" but not "exchange-value," because "its products are designed to serve the immediate basic needs of their producers"; they are not destined to be sold as commodities on the market, where their value would also be defined, and potentially increased, by the dynamics of trade (Gutiérrez-Rodríguez 2010, 90). Even when domestic work is remunerated, its individual products do not tend to form the basis for its valuation; for example, a bath run for a child is not viewed as a commodity to which an individual price tag is attached (90).

Instead, the value attributed to paid domestic work is socially and culturally codified. Its devaluation is a result of the association of paid domestic work with unpaid domestic labor and with the naturalization of both as "women's work" or the type of labor undertaken for free by a housewife so that her husband can go out to earn a wage. As Pierette Hondagneu-Sotelo (2001, 9) has noted, "paid domestic work is distinctive not in being the worst job of all, but in being regarded as something other than employment." As such, this categorization has meant that domestic labor, often labeled a service because of the nature of the tasks it involves, could then be discarded from traditional forms of accounting, economic analysis, and remuneration, which saves the state, and society more broadly, reproduction costs (Hoerder et al. 2015, 6). For example, Bridget Anderson (2000, 21–22) notes that household production was omitted from the system of national accounts in the UK in 1993 on the justification that household services have "limited repercussions for the rest of the economy"; in 1997, however, the UK Office for National Statistics attempted to produce a "Household Satellite account," which thoroughly undermined the 1993 justification by finding that "depending on how one values domestic work, in the UK it accounts for between 40% and 120% of GDP."

The ideological division between public and private spheres has also contributed to the production of domestic labor as nonwork. The location of domestic work within the domain of the private household means that the work has been regarded as an extension of kinship, or as a labor of love, rather than as a form of employment ruled by contractual obligations (Hoerder et al. 2015, 6; Romero and Pérez 2015, 185). This sentiment has made it particularly difficult for paid domestic workers to win the same legal labor protections that other kinds of workers have and to ensure that their rights are respected once granted. In sum, the classical distinctions between the public and private spheres, and between productive and reproductive work, have been perpetuated in the service of patriarchy, capitalism, and neocolonialism. These ideological dichotomies are the focus of narratives analyzed in this book, and these narratives interrogate the real impacts they have on individuals' lives, in particular, on the experiences of domestic workers.

In reality, both paid and unpaid domestic work undoubtedly produce surplus value. First, the reproduction of both the current and future workforce depends on them. Employees cannot work if they are not fed, washed, or clothed. If they are not raised, educated, and cared for, children will not be available to replace workers in the labor market. Second, the remittances sent by increasing numbers of migrant domestic workers to their families and communities-of-origin help to sustain those societies' balances of payments and are invested in housing and education, among other areas, thereby undoubtedly adding value (Hoerder et al. 2015, 18–19). Third, the labor of paid domestic and childcare workers has enabled the entry of other women into the salaried workforce (B. Anderson 2000; MacDonald 2010; Ally 2015). As Bridget Anderson (2003, 106) has pointed out, the delegation of domestic and care work to paid employees has constituted a strategy to avoid or manage gender and generational conflict over these responsibilities in employer-families. While, in the second half of the twentieth century, feminists agitated for women's entry into paid employment outside the home "as a material and symbolic resistance against the patriarchy," the rise of paid domestic work "exposed the unfinished sexual revolution that this entailed" (Ally 2015, 48). Primarily upper- and middle-class White women have used their race and class privilege to "buy their way out of the gendered responsibility for domestic labour," which has, in turn, been displaced onto working-class, and increasingly migrant or darker-skinned, women (48).

The class- and race-related divisions engendered by this relationship reverberate throughout the cultural representations analyzed in this book, which consequently adopts an intersectional approach when considering how multiple characteristics frequently overlap to compound the marginalization or exploitation of paid domestic workers. These factors include race, gender, class, age, citizenship, regional or national origin, and level of education (Romero and Pérez 2015, 173; Brites 2014, 63). While Kimberlé Crenshaw's (1989) research on intersectionality has popularized the concept in the United States, my approach is also inspired by the testimonio of the Indigenous descendant Bolivian community organizer Domitila Barrios de Chúngara (Viezzer [1977] 1999) and by the works of Afro-Brazilian feminist intellectuals, such as Lélia Gonzalez (1984), whose texts provided pioneering insights into the intersections of racism, sexism, and classism in Latin American societies at an even earlier stage. Gonzalez (224) explores the pernicious impacts that the intersection of race- and gender-related forms of oppression have on the lives of Afro-Brazilian women by interrogating the origins of their dominant representation in the national imaginary as "*mulata, domética e mãe preta*" (mulattas, maids, and black mammies).[14] She traces these stereotypes back to the figure of the Afro-Brazilian *mucama* (house slave or servant), who was treated by the European descendant landowner as a sexual object and was thereby converted into both the origin of racial mixing in Brazil and a model of service and self-sacrifice (230).

Encarnación Gutiérrez-Rodríguez (2010, 14–15) argues that to conceive more fully the intrinsic value produced by paid domestic labor, we must depart from the concept of "affective value." Although the products of domestic work are often physical, their value also lies in the emotions, feelings, and relationships that they create or enable. When a domestic worker enters a household, "she immediately becomes part of a network of energetic and affective relations"; the worker may be involved in managing intrafamilial relationships or in cleaning or rearranging objects to create a hygienic, pleasant living environment (131). For example, by relieving middle- and upper-class women of the need to do the dirty work of cleaning their own toilets, the negative affects associated with such tasks become displaced onto the domestic worker (137), who is viewed, moreover, as the "most suitable" person to carry them out because of the ways in which her body is classed, racialized, and dehumanized (Pinho 2015). Consequently, the domestic worker becomes aligned with dirt, waste, and the abject in ways that resonate throughout, and are critiqued in, the cultural representations examined in this book. By contrast, the employer is distanced from the feminized role of servicer and the polluting effects such proximity can have on her class- or race-related status, or both; she is free to devote herself to providing only the emotional or moral support associated with motherhood and femininity (Cox 2016, 104–110; B. Anderson 2003, 105–106).

The physical and affective power of domestic work, including the way that this power flows into both the individual reproduction of the household and society as a whole, is reflected neither in the social and cultural codification of domestic work nor by traditional Marxist economic measurements such as use-value or exchange-value (Gutiérrez-Rodríguez 2010, 14, 140–141). This means that domestic labor remains underappreciated and undervalued in social and economic terms. Gutiérrez-Rodríguez (2010) acknowledges that affective value is difficult to quantify because its products (feelings, emotions, and energies) are often intangible or immaterial. Furthermore, Michael Hardt and Antonio Negri (2004, 111) note that when someone perceives they are selling their ability to produce certain emotions or to create human relationships, this can feel "extremely alienating," in part because affective labor is a form of "living labor" (146). This means it has a biopolitical quality that emerges from the immediate pulses of social life and from the vital character of being human (Gutiérrez-Rodríguez 2010, 14, 89, 139–140; Hardt and Negri 2004, 146–147).

A sense of alienation may also be produced by the traditional distinction made between labor and love. As Viviana Zelizer (2009, 1–3) observes, there is a common perception that the economy corrupts intimate relations, including those that develop between family members or within a household. Zelizer (179–180) attributes the affective, intimate, immaterial quality of care work and domestic work to an avoidance of explicit discussions about the financial conditions of the contracts of migrant Latin American and Latinx domestic workers who are employed in the United States and who are often given perks, such as new clothing, special trips, and meals out, to strengthen the sense of kin-like ties between them and their employer-family. Domestic workers themselves, including the organizer Lenira Carvalho (1982), whose testimonio is analyzed in chapter 1, have identified the ways in which the "purchase of intimacy" (to borrow Zelizer's term) sets their labor apart from other occupations and creates challenges. Romero and Pérez (2015, 185), by contrast, argue that it is best not to strategically invoke the "unique" quality of domestic and care work, because doing so undermines the struggle by many of those who undertake it to be seen primarily as *workers* who deserve fair wages, labor regulation, and protection.

Nonetheless, the emotional ties and affective products that characterize paid domestic labor are a complex reality that cannot be ignored. As Jurema Brites (2014, 64, 66) has found, affectionate ties in Brazil are frequently expressed in the gossip shared between employer and paid domestic employee, in the exchange of extra-wage payments and services outside of any contract, and in the close bonds developed between workers and children. Employees often consider the benefits that can be reaped from these personal relationships to be advantageous, even though they are ultimately characterized by an "emotional ambiguity" that does not impede, and even bolsters, the hierarchical system that distinguishes bosses from workers (64–65). The thorny issues surrounding capital's co-optation of the biopolitical and affective products of domestic labor, which are undervalued within traditional economic models and perceived as difficult to quantify because of both their association with love and intimacy and their frequent intangibility, can be addressed only by introducing new mechanisms of value or by overhauling the capitalist system.

Domestic Workers in Latin American Cultural Production: An Overview of the Field

The prevalence of paid domestic workers in global cultural production, both old and new, confirms their symbolic importance in imaginaries of the family and the nation even outside Latin America. This is illustrated by the success of Bong Joon-ho's *Parasite* (2019), for example, which focuses on the relationships between a wealthy employer-family and their various employees. In 2020, *Parasite* was the first foreign-language film to win the Oscar for Best Picture, just one year after *Roma*, with a narrative centered on a domestic worker protagonist, had been touted to achieve the feat, although it ultimately lost out to *Green Book* (Farrelly 2018).

The plasticity of the figures of governess, servant, maid, butler, and nanny has enabled them to be deployed to create a variety of different effects. In the films *The Help* (Taylor 2011) and *The White Tiger* (Bahrani 2021), the interpersonal relations between mistresses and paid domestic workers and between an employer-family and a servant are depicted to explore the broader race- and class-related divisions that shattered the national contexts of the United States during the civil rights movement and of a modern-day India beleaguered by the caste system. The popular UK television series *Downton Abbey* (Fellowes 2010–2015) similarly depends on the exploration of the intersections between the lives of those upstairs and of those below-stairs in a stately home belonging to a decadent British aristocratic family in the early twentieth century. The series' romanticization of class relations appears designed to soothe social tensions much as does *The Help*, in which the African American domestic workers' experiences are filtered through the writing of a "benevolent" White protagonist. The hit films *Mary Poppins* (Stevenson 1964), *The Sound of Music* (Wise 1965), and *Mrs. Doubtfire* (Columbus 1993) all deploy eccentric governess, nanny, and housekeeper characters who enter their employers' homes to enchant their bosses' children in ways that begin to remedy profound emotional imbalances or interpersonal problems at the heart of the family. The recent novel *Lullaby*, by Leïla Slimani (2018), and the film *Parasite,* invert the aforementioned dynamics by deploying domestic worker characters who uncannily infiltrate or invade the bourgeois home and family, thereby invoking middle- and upper-class fears surrounding the contaminating potential of the working class. In *Lullaby*, the infiltration culminates in the nanny's murderous attack on her employers' young children.

The figure of the inhuman employee-infiltrator has also been central within Latin American film and literature, as discussed in chapter 2. One of the best-known invocations can be found in Clarice Lispector's *A paixão segundo G. H.* (1964; *The Passion According to G. H.*), a foundational novel within the canon of cultural representations of paid domestic workers in Latin America. In the novel, the narrator, who refers to herself as "G. H." for *género humano* (humankind), enters the room of her recently departed domestic worker, Janair, and sees a series of etchings on the wall depicting a man, a woman, and a dog; G. H. also finds a cockroach. The dog and cockroach function as symbols of the servant class that unsettle the narrator, who eventually feels driven to ingest the liquid that the cockroach's body exudes in what Jean Franco (1999, 58) has called "a parody of Christian communion." The novel thereby interrogates the foundations of G. H.'s privileged existence by foregrounding the idea that all forms of life are equal (58). María Julia Rossi (2018, 123) has explored G. H.'s shock upon entering Janair's vacant room and finding that her former employee has left an indelible imprint on it. Janair's marks of her independence and capacity for self-expression haunt G. H., and Janair is thereby converted into "una máquina que está permanentemente produciendo fantasías" (126; a machine that is permanently creating fantasies). This conversion constitutes a gesture that undermines the perceived distinctions between employer and employee because the fantasies engendered by Janair's etchings can be interpreted as a reflection of G. H.'s own activities as a sculptor. Thus, the novel alludes to the creative inspiration that domestic workers have provided for artists, as well as to the possible parallels between artistic and domestic work, which are both addressed as forms of immaterial labor in my analysis of a series of Argentine and Brazilian documentaries in chapter 3.

This book engages in dialogue with the ideas developed in key works that examine artistic representations of paid domestic workers in Latin American cultural production that have been published in recent years, including those that attest to the influence of Lispector's writing. Sonia Roncador's (2014) pioneering *Domestic Servants in Literature and Testimony in Brazil, 1889–1999* examines a variety of different texts, including housekeeping manuals, literary works, chronicles, and testimonios, to chart the changes in the ways domestic workers have been represented in the Brazilian cultural imaginary from the late nineteenth century up to the end of the twentieth century. Roncador (2, 21) notes that, despite their "emergence as major literary tropes" in texts involved in the elaboration, negotiation, or contestation of modernity, the representation of domestic workers is "a neglected topic" in Latin American cultural history and criticism. Roncador's study confirms the importance of relationships to domestic workers in the thought and writing of Clarice Lispector, which become a means of ethical self-examination for the author, by exploring the different attitudes she expressed toward them in the newspaper columns and chronicles that she published in the mid-twentieth century. Roncador's analysis of the emergence of various literary testimonios (co)authored by Brazilian domestic workers in the 1980s constitutes a key reference in chapter 1 of this book, which examines similar texts published in other Latin American countries as well.

María Julia Rossi's *Ficciones de emancipación* (2020) interrogates the depiction of domestic service in the works of the well-known Latin American women writers Victoria Ocampo, Rosario Castellanos, Silvina Ocampo, Elena Garro, and Clarice Lispector. Rossi's (17) argument that the "sovereign" voices and gestures of domestic workers are recognized for their creative potential in the fiction of the latter three authors has informed my understanding of Lispector's influential writing and my own analysis of *Las dependencias* (1999), a documentary by the Argentine filmmaker Lucrecia Martel that explores the creative inspiration Silvina Ocampo's domestic employees provided for the author.

Moving beyond the field of literary studies, the volume *Los de abajo* (Those below stairs), edited by María Julia Rossi and Lucía Campanella

(2018), skillfully brings together analyses of Latin American literary, visual, and cinematic works that center on the figure of the domestic worker from the nineteenth, twentieth, and twenty-first centuries. My analysis in chapter 4 resonates with two contributions in this edited volume that signal the links between artistic and domestic work as precarious forms of labor: Julia Kratje's examination of the film *Réimon* (Moreno 2014) and Lucía Campanella's analysis of performances by the Brazilian artist Millena Lízia.

In the arena of television, film, and popular culture, several scholars have analyzed the role of Latin American *telenovelas* in deploying stereotyped domestic worker characters from the mid-twentieth century onward that tended to reaffirm the racist, sexist, and classist codes associated with these employees and their experiences (Durin and Vázquez 2013; Melo 2016, 8; Oliveira 2020, 147–149). A well-known example is *Simplemente María* (Simply Maria), a Peruvian telenovela that was broadcast between 1969 and 1971 in several Latin American countries and that has been repeatedly remade. The protagonist, a rural-to-urban migrant, is initially employed as a domestic worker, but she transcends her circumstances by learning how to sew and eventually becoming a successful fashion designer; she later marries her teacher and becomes the employer of a domestic worker herself in a narrative that appealed to the desire, among spectators from comparable backgrounds, to see Indigenous descendant migrant women like María "better" themselves and their circumstances (Durin and Vázquez 2013, 31–32, 41).[15] Sofia Rios (2015, 229–230) and Maurício Sellmann Oliveira (2020, 148–149) identify a similar penchant for Cinderella stories or rags-to-riches narratives featuring paid domestic workers who marry out of poverty in Brazilian and Mexican telenovelas (and popular films), particularly in those produced throughout the second half of the twentieth century. Both note, however, that these fairy-tale heroines tend to be light-skinned and to conform to European standards of beauty, in spite of the fact that the majority of paid domestic workers in Brazil are Black, while in Mexico, most paid domestic workers come from Indigenous or rural backgrounds, or both (Rios 2015, 225; Oliveira 2020, 149).

Oliveira (2020, 149) argues that, although the "whitening" of paid domestic labor has begun to change in more recent Brazilian telenovelas, when Afro-Brazilian domestic employees are depicted, these characters play on the fantasy of the "sensual housemaid" who arouses the desires of the boss's son. The pernicious trope of the "randy maid" (*empregada hipersexualizada*) can nonetheless be traced back much further in Brazilian popular culture to the *pornochanchadas* (sexual comedies) of the 1960s and 1970s, and to films such as *Como é boa nossa empregada* (How good our maid is), a 1973 production by Victor di Mello and Ismar Porto (Dennison and Shaw 2004, 158–163).[16] The tendency to deploy domestic workers as comedic stock characters in popular culture is also illustrated by the long career of Mexican actor María Elena Velasco, known as *la india María* (the Indian Maria), who consistently portrayed a domestic worker (Rohrer 2017, 20).

Since 2000, paid domestic workers depicted in Latin American cinema have received more in-depth treatment, which can be attributed in part to changing social dynamics, including a greater awareness of these employees' improved labor rights. As discussed in chapters 2 and 3, an increasing number of films have taken domestic workers as their protagonists, often in an attempt to empower them or to endow them with a greater level of agency. This is not to say that these films never play on stereotypes, or that the domestic workers depicted in them hold ultimate power over their representations. Nonetheless, the collaborative nature of the films analyzed in this book contributes to the complexity of their portrayals and, in the case of the documentaries analyzed, enables them to meditate more openly on the power dynamics inherent to representations of the Other.

The boom in films focusing on paid domestic workers has been accompanied by a rich seam of film criticism that has recently begun to burgeon. Deborah Shaw (2017, 124) has argued that this wave of filmmaking constitutes a new "thematic genre" in her insightful analysis of domestic employees in *La mujer sin cabeza* (Martel 2008; *The Headless Woman*) and *El niño pez* (Puenzo 2009; *The Fish Child*). The works are nonetheless so generically diverse, drawing on conventions from horror, noir, social comedy, historical drama, performative documentary, found-footage filmmaking, and even musicals,[17] that what ultimately unites them is their topic, sociopolitical critique, or certain tropes. The films certainly constitute a cultural phenomenon, and their prevalence, in my view, owes to the fact that they enable filmmakers to condense and explore multiple concerns surrounding race-, class-, and gender-based inequalities in rapidly changing societies, but to do so all within the reconstructed space of the home, which is expedient when making a production on a limited budget.

Elizabeth Osborne and Sofía Ruiz-Alfaro's (2020) edited volume *Domestic Labor in Twenty-First Century Latin American Cinema* is a marvelous resource that brings together analyses of a number of key, primarily fictional, works, which have begun to define the new canon of domestic worker films, including *Domésticas—O filme* (Meirelles and Olival 2001; Maids—The film), *Casa grande, Cama adentro* (Gaggero 2004; *Live-in Maid*), *Que horas ela volta?*, *La nana*, *La teta asustada* (Llosa 2009; *The Milk of Sorrow*), and *Hilda* (Clariond 2014). Osborne and Ruiz-Alfaro's

(2020) introduction briefly addresses the more recent film *Roma*, which was released not long before the volume was published and which has also been the subject of short-form online analysis in the wake of its awards success (see Tierney and Cosentino 2018; de Casanova 2019). Karina Vázquez's (2014) article offers a particularly rich and early analysis of the Chilean film *La nana* and focuses on the emancipatory significance of the protagonist's movement outside of the home at the film's conclusion. By contrast, María Mercedes Vázquez Vázquez (2019, 162–203) has argued that these kinds of films are ultimately framed by privileged directorial perspectives despite their focus on domestic worker protagonists, and she has termed them *cine clasemediero* (middle-class cinema).

Within Brazilian film criticism, Mariana Souto's (2019) book *Infiltrados e invasores* (Infiltrators and invaders) makes an important contribution to the analysis of class relations on screen by examining the wave of productions that have focused on domestic employer-employee relations, such as *Que horas ela volta?*, *Babás* (Lins 2010; Nannies), *Santiago*, and *Doméstica* (Mascaro 2012). Gustavo Procopio Furtado (2019) has acknowledged how important the theme has become by dedicating a chapter of his book on contemporary Brazilian documentary to an analysis of the ways in which *Babás*, *Santiago*, and *Doméstica* rework the "home mode." Other important references include articles, chapters, and a master's thesis exploring the Brazilian films previously mentioned, together with the works of Pernambucan director Kleber Mendonça Filho, by Tiago de Luca (2017), Francianne Velho (2017), Lúcia Sá (2018), and Stephanie Dennison (2018).

Chapter Outline

In the pages to follow, I build on these existing analyses by comparing literary testimonios, fiction and documentary films, and digital culture artifacts that center on the experiences of paid domestic workers and that were, in many cases, produced by or in collaboration with these employees. Chapter 1 maps out the ways in which both paid and unpaid domestic labor resonate throughout the genre of Latin American women's testimonios by analyzing the treatment of these themes in the foundational texts: *Me llamo Rigoberta Menchú y así me nació la conciencia* (Burgos 1998; *I, Rigoberta Menchú*) and *"Si me permiten hablar . . .": Testimonio de Domitila una mujer de las minas de Bolivia* (Viezzer 1999; *"Let Me Speak . . .": Testimony of Domitila, a Woman of the Bolivian Mines*). Chapter 1 then examines a range of testimonios focusing on the lives of paid domestic workers, specifically from Brazil, Peru, and Uruguay, that were published in the 1980s.

The analysis distinguishes between texts that tend to focus on the *testimonialistas'* individual struggles, including *Diário de Bitita* (de Jesus [1986] 2014; *Bitita's Diary*), an understudied work by the well-known Afro-Brazilian author Carolina Maria de Jesus, and two testimonios that are resolutely collective publications on the level of both form and content: Lenira Carvalho's "Só a gente que vive é que sabe" (1982) and Ana Gutiérrez's *Se necesita muchacha* (1983) along with its earlier, 1982 iteration, *Basta: Testimonios* (Enough: Testimonies). These testimonios contain some of the earliest insights provided by domestic workers themselves into processes of unionization. Elsa M. Chaney and Mary Garcia Castro confirm the significance of *Se necesita muchacha* when they write in their own ground-breaking text, *Muchachas No More* (1989, 9), that they are presenting the first information on organizations established by domestic workers themselves in Latin America, notwithstanding the work of Ana Gutiérrez. This chapter remedies the surprising dearth of scholarship on Gutiérrez's volume by incorporating the insights provided by interviews I undertook with friends and colleagues of Gutiérrez—a pseudonym employed by the French academic Cristina Goutet, former adviser to the Cusco Union of Household Workers. None of the testimonios can abrogate the ethical concerns that plague projects in which middle- or upper-class or academic scribes mediate the voices of subaltern subjects; however, these issues enable chapter 1 to tackle theoretical and ethical concerns regarding representation that are pertinent to this study. Ultimately, I argue that the testimonios represent an underused resource in the study of domestic workers' struggles, unionization, and representation. The chapter draws on the insights the testimonios collectively generate to elaborate a theoretical framework that contributes to the analysis undertaken throughout the remainder of the book.

Chapter 2 focuses on the critically acclaimed fiction films *La nana, Casa grande, Que horas ela volta?*, and *Roma*, which exemplify the broader wave of twenty-first-century Latin American productions featuring paid domestic workers in central roles. The directors of all four films have openly discussed either that they recorded these productions in their own childhood homes or that the films are semiautobiographical and were inspired by affective ties to current or former paid domestic workers, including, in some cases, to the individuals employed to help raise the filmmakers themselves. Consequently, these films are imbued with a sense of emotional indebtedness to paid domestic workers whose labor resulted in personal sacrifices that are difficult to recompense. Ultimately, the works are characterized by a level of ambivalence that sees them both pay homage to domestic employees but also risk reinforcing foundational myths that rely on the subjugation of the racial and gender Other (the live-in maid or second mother) so that the modern, mestizo (mixed-race) nation-state can be forged. The use of abject and bestial imagery to criticize the dehumanization that live-in domestic work entails enables me to connect the films with Lispector's foundational text, *A paixão segundo G. H.*, as well as with a spate of lesser-known Brazilian films that feature paid domestic workers in key roles and draw on elements of both comedy and horror to critique the vampirism characteristic of middle- and upper-class exploitation of the working class, including *Trabalhar cansa* (Rojas and Dutra 2011; *Hard Labor*), *As boas maneiras* (Rojas and Dutra 2017; *Good Manners*), and *O clube dos canibais* (Parente 2018; *The Cannibal Club*).

Chapter 3 examines contemporary Latin American documentaries that are the product of artists' and employers' collaborations with current or former paid domestic workers. It posits that all the documentaries analyzed are characterized by the depiction of spectral (or ghostly) domestic employees precisely because paid domestic work, and forms of immaterial or "unproductive" labor more broadly, have not been properly accounted for by traditional, capitalistic economic models. The first part of the analysis focuses on Martel's *Las dependencias* (1999; *The outbuildings*) but also makes reference to *Santiago* and the Argentine fiction film *Réimon*. These films' slow, haunting sequences, and emphases on performance, contribute to their interrogation of the wildly differing economic values and cultural capital that are attributed to paid domestic work when compared to artistic or intellectual labors, despite the fact that all these forms of labor are characterized by the creation of immaterial products. Martel's defamiliarizing use of sound in *Las dependencias* gestures toward the ways in which real domestic workers supported, inspired, and consequently haunted Argentine author Silvina Ocampo's literary work. Its use of sound serves to unite the made-for-television documentary with Martel's later fiction films, including *La niña santa* (2004; *The Holy Girl*) and *Zama* (2017), which are also briefly discussed. The second part of the chapter returns to an analysis of *Santiago*, which is compared with two other Brazilian documentaries that bear the marks of its influence: *Babás* and *Doméstica*. All three depict paid domestic workers who are filmed by their previous employers or by their current or former employers' children. While elements of the documentaries betray a nostalgic yearning for the intimate relationships that have been permitted by forms of live-in domestic service, these films also simultaneously undertake a critical exploration of the ways in which contemporary domestic labor relationships are haunted by the legacy of Brazil's slave-owning past, namely by reflecting on their own filmic forms. The focus on different domestic spaces allows the documentaries to be compared to other recent Brazilian films that portray relationships between domestic employers and employees in homes that function as allegorical locations, either by displaying postcolonial characteristics or by appearing temporally out-of-sync with their settings, including Marco Dutra and Caetano Gotardo's *Todos os mortos* (2020; *All the Dead Ones*), Kleber Mendonça Filho's *Recife frio* (2009; *Cold Tropics*), *O som ao redor* (2012; *Neighboring Sounds*), *Aquarius* (2016), and *Bacurau* (2019).

Chapter 4 returns to the topic of paid domestic workers' testimonios to explore how the genre has evolved in the age of social media. It compares the Afro-Brazilian rapper and influencer Preta-Rara's (2016) Facebook page, "Eu empregada doméstica" (I domestic worker), with the Peruvian artist Daniela Ortiz's (2010) physical and virtual exhibition *97 empleadas domésticas* (97 domestic workers). While Preta-Rara's project uses Facebook as a platform to share the stories of current and former domestic workers and their friends and relatives (a selection of which were published as a book in 2019), Daniela Ortiz approaches the social networking site as an archival resource and trawls through it to appropriate photographs posted by upper-class, Lima-based families. Each image included in her exhibition features at least one domestic employee in the background or at the edges of the frame. Both works enact powerful critiques of the continuing coloniality of paid domestic labor relations in the region, while Preta-Rara's page constitutes an important element in the struggle to challenge historical forms of discrimination and exploitation in Brazil. However, the artists' methods also raise questions about the ethics of appropriation in the social media era, most notably in the case of *97 empleadas domésticas*. The fact that their creative forms of activism rely on the Facebook platform compounds the ethical concerns discussed in the chapter, because the platform's business model is predicated on the imperative to share personal data (including images or narratives pertaining to others), which is then harvested by third parties for financial gain. The chapter briefly compares these two works with the collaborative transmedia exhibition *Mucamas* (2010; Hotel maids), by the well-known Argentine artist Lola Arias, which focuses on hotel cleaners rather than on paid domestic workers but adopts similar techniques and aesthetics to shed light on the forms of exploitation and invisibilization faced by employees who are also involved in a form of care work designed to produce specific affects. Finally, the chapter closes by tracing the connections between these three projects and other works of digital artivism that have addressed the challenges faced by paid domestic employees during the Covid-19 pandemic. These include a second collection of digital testimonios from Mexico, *Nuestras voces cuentan*, and a Brazilian graphic novel entitled *Confinada* (Assis and Oliveira 2020; Confined), which was published on Instagram.

In sum, this book shows how cultural productions from Latin American countries have been mobilized to advocate for the improvement and respect of paid domestic workers' rights, particularly when these employees have faced acute challenges. These objectives are evident in the testimonios of paid domestic workers from Brazil, Peru, and Uruguay that were published in the 1980s during the struggle for equal rights reform and, more recently, in the wave of digital artivism that has raised awareness of the ways in which the Covid-19 pandemic has put paid domestic workers' lives and livelihoods at risk. This book draws on the insights proffered by paid domestic workers' testimonios to analyze the striking interest in these figures that has characterized Latin American cinema since the beginning of this millennium. Fiction and documentary films from Argentina, Brazil, Chile, and Mexico that have all been shaped by, or are based on, real-life relationships to paid domestic employees simultaneously rework and regurgitate familial and national founding narratives that seize on domestic workers as symbols of the region's mestizaje or mestiçagem, while also critiquing the stark class-, race-, and gender-based inequalities that continue to mark Latin American societies. These films' narratives and mise-en-scènes are shown to undermine the notion that paid domestic work is not productive of surplus value in economic terms. Instead, the perceived difficulties of recompensing the huge affective contributions that these workers make to their employer-families (namely via their relationships to their bosses' children) in late capitalist, postcolonial contexts result in the portrayal of spectral or ghostly paid domestic employees, especially in the documentaries analyzed. Ultimately, the ways in which all the works I examine wrestle with power hierarchies both at the level of content and at the level of their creation (between scribe and testimonialista, artist and subject, or employer and employee) mean that they either evoke or explicitly address the ethical complexities that recur when depicting subaltern figures. Finally, I have written this book with an awareness that I am a researcher from the Global North whose experiences—like those of the artists, directors, and scribes discussed here—remain at a distance from those of the workers portrayed in the cultural representations analyzed.

CHAPTER 1

Paid Domestic Workers' Testimonios in Latin America

"Women's work" and paid domestic labor are significant concerns in Latin American women's testimonios published throughout the second half of the twentieth century and the beginning of the twenty-first century,[1] but these themes have yet to be thoroughly explored in the scholarly literature about the testimonio genre.[2] After tracing the ways both paid and unpaid domestic labor resonate as concerns throughout the foundational testimonios of Rigoberta Menchú and Domitila Barrios de Chúngara, this chapter will concentrate its analysis on five testimonios that center on histories of paid domestic work: *Ai de vós! Diário de uma doméstica* (da Silva 1983; Woe unto you! A maid's diary), *Diário de Bitita* (de Jesus [1986] 2014; *Bitita's Diary*), *La niña, el chocolate, el huevo duro* (Caraballo 1987; The girl, the chocolate, the boiled egg), "Só a gente que vive é que sabe: Depoimento de uma doméstica" (Carvalho 1982; Only those who live it can understand: Testimony of a domestic worker), and *Se necesita muchacha* (Gutiérrez 1983; Maid wanted). All five testimonios were written or recorded by women who worked as domestic employees for significant periods. They were published in the early to mid-1980s, when their countries of origin (Brazil, Peru, and Uruguay) were transitioning from dictatorship to democracy. This was also a moment when Latin American women began to emerge as protagonists in grassroots movements.

My analysis distinguishes Lenira Carvalho's (1982) "Só a gente que vive é que sabe" and Ana Gutiérrez's (1983) *Se necesita muchacha* from the other three testimonios because the histories of union activism that shaped the former convert them into resolutely collective publications. Carvalho's and Gutiérrez's texts serve three functions: to establish and elaborate syndicalist identities, to contest domestic workers' exploitation and marginalization, and to garner visibility and sympathy for future domestic workers' rights reform. These two works represent some of the earliest insights into the associations and organizations of paid domestic workers in Latin America. By contrast, the testimonios of Ramona Caraballo, Francisca Souza da Silva, and Carolina Maria de Jesus focus more on their individual biographies, although they also contain elements of social criticism and valuable insights into the live-in domestic worker's condition.

In this chapter, I interrogate the nature of the relationships between the testimonial subjects and the employers, academics, and authors who helped to publish and promote the texts, and I ultimately demonstrate that all the testimonios are influenced, in differing ways, by Christian precepts. Finally, I draw on the knowledge these testimonios collectively produce to outline a theoretical framework that will be used throughout the rest of this book to analyze paid domestic workers' cultural representations and their struggles to contest, influence, or control them.

Domestic Workers in Latin America (1950s–1990s): Rights and Unionization

Many of the subjects whose testimonios are examined in this chapter entered domestic service in the mid-twentieth century,[3] at a moment when the demand for domestic workers increased throughout Latin America because women began joining the paid workforce in greater numbers (Kuznesof 1989, 29). By this time, labor codes in countries across the region outlined the rights of paid domestic employees; however, as discussed in more detail in my introduction, the codes all treated domestic work as "exceptional" and did not grant these employees rights that were equal to the rights enjoyed by other kinds of workers (Blofield 2012, 28). In the 1980s, when the testimonios analyzed in this chapter were published, the demand for paid domestic work contracted when the decade's debt crises impacted many of the region's economies (Blofield 2012, 23). The crises depressed wages and compounded difficulties in defending paid domestic workers' labor rights (Bunster and Chaney 1985, 30–31; Prates 1989, 272). Nonetheless, during the same decade, authoritarian regimes began to cede power to democratically elected governments, which provided an opportunity for paid domestic workers to organize and demand equal labor rights.[4]

Throughout the region, nascent domestic workers' organizations were often supported by different branches of the Catholic Church (Blofield 2012, 144), including the Young Catholic Workers (Juventud Obrera Católica/Juventude Operária Católica, or JOCs), which was an offshoot of the Catholic Action movement (Hutchinson 2010, 67). The first JOC was a radical Catholic youth organization that originated in Belgium in

1912 and was founded by Canon Joesph Cardijn, who began to work first with domestic employees and later with other sectors of the working class (Goldsmith 1989, 230; Zotti 1990, 387). The JOCs relied heavily on a "Catholic liberationist rhetoric" (Hutchinson 2010, 88), which was particularly popular in Latin America in the 1970s. Carvalho's and Gutiérrez's collective testimonios attest to the importance of Catholic Base Communities and liberation theology in shaping and supporting the nascent domestic workers' unions that emerged in Peru and Brazil (and across Latin America) in the 1970s and 1980s.

The path toward equal rights reform for paid domestic workers has nonetheless been long and arduous. Deep class divides, which are often reinforced by divisions based on gender, ethnicity, and/or race, make demands for equal labor rights challenging to achieve, even in a stable democratic and economic environment (Blofield 2012, 23). In her analysis of paid domestic workers' struggles for equal rights in Latin America, Blofield (2012, 56) argues that the key strategies that advocates of reform must adopt include organizing, recruiting allies, and garnering visibility for the issue in order to force it onto the political agenda. The testimonios analyzed in this chapter, especially those produced by Carvalho and Gutiérrez, not only formed a crucial element of reform strategies but also represented a reaction to the abysmal conditions domestic workers faced in the 1980s. Perhaps even more important, the two texts still have the potential to influence cultural attitudes toward paid domestic work and the treatment of workers. A change in culture is crucial if paid domestic workers' rights are to be respected. Even after improvements to their legal entitlements, the practical enforcement of labor codes continues to be a challenge (Chaney and Garcia Castro 1989, 5; de Casanova 2015, 41).

The Genre of Testimonio in Latin America

Latin American testimonios originate from firsthand experience of social or political injustice, which is often retold in the first person. The accounts attest to life experiences that have been characterized by a marginalization shared by others; consequently, testimonios are either explicitly or implicitly collective (Bartow 2008, 504). The process of recording, compiling, editing, and publishing testimonial literature varies among publications, as will be shown in the cases of the five texts to be discussed. It is common, however, either for authors to write their own testimonios (and be supported in publishing it by individuals with literary or cultural connections) or for subjects to record their stories for a writer, academic, journalist, or ethnographer, who then transcribes, edits, and publishes their conversations. Doris Sommer (1988, 117–118) notes that the oral quality of the testimonial subjects' narratives is usually "unmistakeable," even in the "polished versions that reach us." The editor or publisher often preserves this oral characteristic to foreground the authenticity and veracity of the subject's account. This recourse to orality distinguishes testimonial literature from autobiography, which is a genre that originates in "the lives of privileged men who stand out as individuals and whose experience is not necessarily meant to represent others" (Bartow 2008, 504). In her discussion of testimonial literature, Sommer's (1988, 118) analysis hinges on the contrast between autobiography and testimonio: the former "strains to produce a personal and distinctive *style* as part of the individuation process," and the latter "strives to preserve or to renew an interpersonal *rhetoric.*"

Testimonio's potential to serve as a vehicle for resistance to subjugation, through its articulation of collective solidarity (among members of a particular community, with an academic interviewer, or with readers), allowed the genre to flourish starting in the mid-1960s. The explosion in testimonial writing during that decade has been attributed to the triumph of the Cuban Revolution (Bartow 2008, 506; Sommer 1988, 114–115). After Cuba's principal cultural institution, the Casa de las Américas, created an award for testimonial literature in 1970, testimonio, with its emphasis on popular experiences, gained widespread recognition as a genre (Yúdice 1991, 25–26; Sommer 1988, 115). The award has been viewed as a "contestatory" move, one that helped erode the "boom" canon of Latin American literature that "cultivated self-referentiality, simulation, and poststructuralist écriture" (Yúdice 1991, 25–26). Consequently, some writers, journalists, and anthropologists "left their writing desks to become scribes" (Sommer 1988, 114). They acknowledged that the people whose causes they advocated, who did not enjoy a similar level of privilege, were also the subjects, not merely the objects, of national history (Sommer 1988, 114).

According to Sommer (1988, 114), women writers "stood to gain the most" from the new genre because they could address their own marginalization by helping to portray other women as workers, militants, and strategists. Unsurprisingly, the majority of women's testimonios in Latin America are based on interviews that have been transcribed or promoted by other women (Bartow 2008, 504), as is the case of the texts discussed in this chapter. Many of these testimonios' subjects are impoverished, Afro-descendant women or Indigenous women who had not previously had access to such a public platform from which they could voice their concerns.

Rigoberta Menchú's *Me llamo Rigoberta Menchú y así me nació la conciencia* (Burgos 1998; first published in 1983 and commonly called *I, Rigoberta Menchú*) is the best-known and most contentious example of the testimonio genre.[5] Menchú, who is a Quiché Maya from Guatemala, related her people's struggles to the Venezuelan anthropologist Elizabeth Burgos in 1982. During the Guatemalan Civil War, from 1960 to 1996, Menchú's community had been targeted both by the military and by big landowners who attempted to dispossess them of their lands (Burgos 1998). In 1979, Menchú began to act as the leader of an Indigenous peoples' organization, the Comité de Unidad Campesina (Committee for Peasant Unity) (Burgos 1998, 187). Her testimonio has been the source of controversy following research into the veracity of specific claims made by Menchú (Stoll 1999). As John Beverley (1999, 65, 178) points out, the epistemological and ethical authority of testimonial narratives is contingent on the belief that they are a faithful representation of a personal experience that usually involves repression, poverty, or a struggle for survival.[6] Nonetheless, Beverley (1999, 74) criticizes David Stoll's (1999) renowned attack on the trustworthiness of Menchú's account by suggesting that it reveals Stoll's desire that Menchú should serve simply as a "native informant." Beverley (1999, 74) states that "what seems to bother Stoll above all is that Menchú *has* an ideological agenda."

The negative impact that paid domestic work has had on Indigenous peoples in Guatemala marks Menchú's family history as well as her own biography. Menchú states that her grandmother worked as a servant for a wealthy man and was eventually obliged to give away (*regalar*) her son, Menchú's father, to do unpaid labor for a different family because she was unable to earn enough to afford food and board for all three of her children (Burgos 1998, 23). When Menchú's father grew older and began doing paid work on plantations, he helped his mother leave the post where she had been forced to become her employer's mistress (23). The risks for Indigenous women that are posed by entering paid domestic work, and consequently being compelled into prostitution, are also highlighted later in the testimonio (102, 120–121). Menchú herself undertook paid domestic work on two occasions; first for a period while living in Guatemala City when she was still a child and again when she went into hiding in a nunnery because of her persecution by the army (116–127, 264). One chapter of her testimonio, entitled "Sirvienta en la capital" (Servant in the capital), is dedicated to the humiliations, privations, and exploitations she endured on the first occasion. It is an episode of her life that, she states, she will never forget and that contributed to her alienation from her own community's struggles for a short time (127, 148).

Another well-known example of the testimonio genre is Domitila Barrios de Chúngara's *"Si me permiten hablar . . .": Testimonio de Domitila una mujer de las minas de Bolivia* (Viezzer 1999; first published in 1977; *"Let Me Speak . . .": Testimony of Domitila, a Woman of the Bolivian Mines*). It recounts Chúngara's participation in organizing women in a Bolivian mining community through the Comité de Amas de Casa de la Mina Siglo XX (Housewives' Committee of the Siglo XX Mine) in the 1960s and 1970s. Chúngara, who was an Indigenous descendant woman,[7] related her experiences to the Brazilian sociologist Moema Viezzer. Chúngara states that the paucity of her husband's mining salary usually means that they are not able to employ domestic help or to cover all their household expenses (Viezzer 1999, 32, 34). Consequently, she is compelled to supplement his income by making and selling *salteñas* (pasties) in the street every day, like the wives of many other local miners (2013, 357). Along with this, Chúngara assumes responsibilities for various arduous domestic tasks, including childcare, grocery shopping, cooking, doing the laundry by hand, and making clothes, which are too expensive for them to purchase ready-made (32–34). She concludes that

> todo esto muestra bien claro cómo al minero doblemente lo explotan, ¿no? Porque, dándole tan poco salario, la mujer tiene que hacer mucho más cosas en el hogar. Y es una obra gratuita que le estamos haciendo al patrón, finalmente, ¿no? Y [. . .] no solamente la explotan a su compañera, sino que hay veces que hasta los hijos. Porque los quehaceres en el hogar son tantos que hasta a las wawas las hacemos trabajar [. . .]. Pero, a pesar de todo lo que hacemos, todavía hay la idea de que las mujeres no realizan ningún trabajo, porque no aportan económicamente al hogar, que solamente trabaja el esposo porque él sí percibe un salario. (34–35)[8]

> All of this clearly shows how the miner is doubly exploited, doesn't it? Because, by giving him such a low salary, his wife has to do many more things at home. And, in the end, this is work that we are doing for free for the boss, isn't it? And [. . .] sometimes they aren't just exploiting his partner, but also his children, because there are so many domestic tasks that we even have to get the kids to work [. . .]. But, despite everything that we do, there is still this idea that women don't do any work, because they don't contribute economically to the household, that only the husband works because he does receive a salary.

Chúngara's comments illustrate that various forms of labor power are dependent on reproductive domestic labor. Nonetheless, domestic work has been economically undervalued in relation to other forms of labor that are viewed as productive, which has meant that reproductive labor has been socially and culturally undervalued too.

Although not the principal theme of Menchú's or Chúngara's narrative, "women's work," and more specifically paid domestic labor, reverberates throughout these foundational testimonios. Indeed, Chúngara thinks of the housewives' struggle principally as one of class but also as one of gender; it is a consequence of the housewives being allied with, but also subservient to, the miners (their husbands). Menchú, by contrast, views her community's marginalization primarily as a result of racism, colonialism, and US imperialism. She argues against the establishment of women-only organizations while recognizing that her status as a community leader prevents her from feeling able to have a family and children because she would not be able to dedicate herself sufficiently to both tasks (Burgos 1998, 247–248, 251). Consequently, she implicitly acknowledges the *doble jornada* (double shift) expected of women to which Chúngara explicitly refers.

Despite Menchú's and Chúngara's discussions of both paid and unpaid domestic labor and their impacts on working-class Indigenous or Indigenous descendant women, this theme has generally not been the focus of critical analyses of their texts, and many other testimonios that center on histories of domestic service from Latin America have received little attention. This is perhaps a result of the limited distribution of the latter, particularly outside Latin America. Notably, however, Roncador (2014, 153–188) has analyzed several Brazilian testimonios by domestic workers and comments (156) that this "sizeable body of subaltern testimonios has yet to be acknowledged in a number of Brazilian research institutions and public archives" but that these texts "carry immeasurable cultural and historical value" because of "the dearth of materials engaged with the political struggle of domestic servants in Brazil, as well as the ever-extant paradigm of denying social agency to the servant class." Raquel Roman-Morfin (2015, 56) addresses *Se necesita muchacha* in her PhD dissertation, commenting that, at present, it appears that the testimonios themselves have received no critical attention, while the renowned Mexican author Elena Poniatowska's prologue to it has received limited analysis. Even *Diário de Bitita* remains largely ignored in critical studies of the well-known Brazilian author Carolina Maria de Jesus's oeuvre (Moreira 2009, 65).

This chapter represents an effort to redress these gaps. Its contribution lies in its comparison of paid domestic workers' testimonios from across

PAID TO CARE

Latin America and in its examination of the ways that they provide an insight into the process of subjectification and "coming-to-consciousness," bear witness to exploitative labor practices, and aim to gain collective political ground and to reflect on the representation of paid domestic workers in popular culture.

The Role of Mediators in Testimonios of Domestic Work: Employers, Academics, and Authors

The challenge that the editors of testimonios about paid domestic work faced in securing contracts for their publications, and in promoting them, is illustrated by the fact that two of the texts mentioned here first appeared outside their countries of origin.[9] *Se necesita muchacha* (Gutiérrez 1983), which was published in Mexico, is much better known internationally than its original Peruvian edition, *Basta: Testimonios* (STHC 1982; Enough: Testimonios). This attests to the subaltern status of the subjects whose voices these books channel and to the existence of a larger market for these kinds of texts abroad.

A recurrent strategy used to bolster sales of testimonios about domestic work was the inclusion of a prologue or an introduction authored by a well-known public figure. These usually champion the "authentic" social insights provided by, and the aesthetic qualities of, the testimonio to follow. The critical and commercial success enjoyed by da Silva's *Ai de vós!* (1983), for instance, can partly be attributed to the inclusion of an introduction by the well-known writer and memorialist Pedro Nava, and partly to the testimonio's publication by the prestigious Civilização Brasileira (Roncador 2014, 181). Two editions of the text were published in one year; it was also translated into German and reviewed in widely read magazines and newspapers, and the author was interviewed on television (181). Roncador (182) notes that all this sets it apart from other Brazilian testimonios of domestic service, including *Testemunha de uma vida* (Basseti 1987; Witness of a life) and *Ilhota* (Z. Barbosa 1993), which did not enjoy the same levels of success. *Ilhota* was published once, with a distribution of one thousand copies, whereas three thousand copies of *Ai de vós!* were distributed (182).

In his introduction to da Silva's testimonio, Nava lauds her writing as "cheio de talento e força, cheio de um primitivismo igual ao da pintura do Douanier Rousseau" (da Silva 1983, 8; brimming with talent and strength, full of a primitivism akin to the paintings of the Douanier Rousseau). On one level, Nava's comparison of da Silva's prose with the work of French postimpressionist painter Henri Rousseau endeavors to elevate the aesthetic status of her writing. On another level, it is problematic that Nava explicitly likens what da Silva represents in her testimonio (her life, work, and family) to the paintings of an artist who is best known for his depictions of jungle scenes featuring wild animals. As well as emphasizing that da Silva's work is primitivistic, Nava also insists that her narrative is important because she is autochthonous to the class that she describes. It becomes clear that the invocation of the authenticity of da Silva's testimonio, and of her membership of an oppressed class, is a crucial marketing strategy. A page of da Silva's handwritten manuscript is even reproduced on the back cover of the edition, as Roncador (2014, 160) notes.

Despite being the book's author, da Silva did not select the book's title or its cover image.[10] Da Silva's employer, Ivna Mendes de Moraes Duvivier, reveals in her preface that she chose the title *Ai de vós!* (da Silva 1983, 11), translated as "Woe unto you!," which is likely a biblical reference to the following passage from the Gospel of Matthew:

> Woe unto you, scribes and Pharisees, hypocrites! for ye pay tithe of mint and anise and cumin, and have omitted the weightier matters of the law, judgment, mercy and faith: these ought ye to have done, and not to leave the other undone. [. . .]
>
> Woe unto you, scribes and Pharisees, hypocrites! for ye make clean the outside of the cup and of the platter, but within they are full of extortion and excess. (Matt. 23: 23, 25, AV)

According to Duvivier, the image reproduced on the front cover of da Silva's testimonio functions as an allusion to the title: it depicts the hand of the pope (da Silva 1983, 11). This accusatory title implicitly attributes the blame for da Silva's mistreatment to the wealthy and, perhaps more directly, to her former bosses, who are described as hypocritical and exploitative. It is a title that also potentially betrays a sense of middle-class or elite guilt regarding relationships to domestic workers. Beverley (1999, 73) argues that testimonios of this kind conform to a "romanticizing victimization,"[11] which tends to "confirm the Christian narrative of suffering and redemption that underlies colonial or imperialist domination." In practice, this romanticizing victimization leads toward benevolent paternalism rather than effective solidarity or the articulation of a new political program.

In her testimonio, da Silva (1983, 131) states that it was her employer, Duvivier, who made her write her life story, and she describes Duvivier as *minha fada-madrinha* (130; my fairy godmother), adding that her employer has given both her and her children valuable guidance and support. Da Silva states that "Não é só para mim que tem essa compreensão, é geral, com todos" (131; It isn't only toward me that she is understanding, she is like this with everyone). Ivna Duvivier's grandson, Gregório Duvivier, who is a member of the famous Brazilian comedy group Porta dos Fundos (The Back Door), has published a biographical sketch of his grandmother that is dedicated to her memory. In a chronicle that first appeared in his column in the *Folha de São Paulo* newspaper, and later in his collection *Caviar é uma ova*, Duvivier (2016, 46) says that his grandmother studied sociology in college in the 1930s, had three children, and cultivated adoptive relationships with numerous others, some of whom lived on the streets and whom she taught to play chess or encouraged to follow their artistic passions. Nonetheless, he laments some of his grandmother's political convictions.

In her preface to *Ai de vós!*, Ivna Duvivier states that the text "resultou de conversas esporádicas com uma empregada" (da Silva 1983, 11; resulted from sporadic conversations with a maid). Duvivier subsequently provided da Silva with a notebook so that she could write down her own memories, which Duvivier later typed up. Duvivier insists, though, that she always respected "a redação original, apesar de pequenas coreções *e da omissão de certas passagens prejudicais à coesão da narrativa, ou repetitivas e sem maior importância*" (11 [my emphasis]; the original composition, notwithstanding small corrections *and the omission of certain passages that undermined the narrative's cohesion, or that were repetitive and did not have greater importance*). Duvivier's declaration represents an attempt to limit the impression that she had too much control over da Silva's narrative, even though Duvivier's contacts clearly played a crucial role in the testimonio's publication and relative commercial success. She also had an influence on the way the book was edited, produced, and marketed as an authentic testimonio of a domestic worker and member of an oppressed class, a statement that would have struck a chord with guilt-stricken middle- or upper-class readers. Gayatri Spivak (1988, 292) warns of the dangers of such an approach, which involves "the first-world intellectual masquerading as the absent nonrepresenter who lets the oppressed speak for themselves." Duvivier's representation of herself as "transparent," or her normalization of her own positionality, necessarily entails an othering of the subaltern subject of study, as Spivak suggests (275).

By contrast, the political and pedagogical agendas that motivated Ana Gutiérrez and Beatriz Costa's involvement in helping to produce *Se necesita muchacha* (or *Basta*) and "Só a gente que vive é que sabe," respectively, are much more apparent.[12] Focusing on interventions in *Se necesita muchacha*, Ana Gutiérrez is a pseudonym used by Cristina Goutet (Silva Santisteban

2007).[13] Gutiérrez/Goutet spent three years collecting the oral testimonios included in the publication (Gutiérrez 1983, 94), which is dedicated to the memory of Egidia Laime, a domestic worker who founded the Sindicato de Trabajadoras del Hogar del Cusco, or STHC (Cusco Union of Household Workers) and died soon afterward.[14]

Gutiérrez (1983, 92) writes in *Se necesita muchacha* that the STHC was established in April 1972, but the STHC website states that it was founded in October 1971.[15] Both sources concur that the organization received official recognition from the Peruvian state in July 1972 (Gutiérrez 1983, 92; STHC, n.d.).[16] The discrepancy could possibly be attributed to Gutiérrez's choice to not disclose in *Se necesita muchacha* that the group had been holding clandestine meetings since 1971 because Peru had been under military rule. The STHC was one of the founding members of the Confederación Latinoamericana y del Caribe de Trabajadoras del Hogar (Latin American and Caribbean Confederation of Household Workers), which held its first meeting in March 1988 in Bogotá, Colombia (STHC, n.d.).[17]

The testimonios included in *Se necesita muchacha* are preceded by Gutiérrez's (Goutet's) introduction (1983, 89–98) and a seventy-nine-page prologue by the acclaimed Mexican author Elena Poniatowska (1983, 7–86). During my interviews with Angelica Alvarez Velarde and Isabel Baufumé on January 10, 2019, in Cusco, Peru, I learned that Goutet was a French mathematician and academic employed at the Universidad Nacional de San Antonio Abad del Cusco. She spent her childhood and much of her adolescence in Peru because of her father's employment in the country. After completing her degree in France and working in Paris, she returned to Peru, where she devoted time, effort, and her own funds to the establishment and maintenance of the STHC, as did the organization's other early members. On the union's website (STHC, n.d.), which features a photograph of Goutet, she is described as having served as an adviser for over thirty consecutive years, and the publication of *Se necesita muchacha* is mentioned as one of the union's crowning achievements. Elsa M. Chaney and Mary Garcia Castro (1989, 9) confirm the significance of *Se necesita muchacha* when they write in their own groundbreaking text, *Muchachas No More*, that they are presenting the first information on organizations established by domestic workers in Latin America "aside from the pioneering work of Gutiérrez." The dearth of scholarship on *Se necesita muchacha* is thus all the more surprising.

During my interview, Baufumé suggested that in collecting and publishing the testimonios that constitute *Se necesita muchacha*, Goutet was responding to an initiative supported by various members of the STHC.

In her introduction, Gutiérrez (1983, 94) states that the tragic death of the Cusco Union's founder, Egidia Laime, compelled all her companions to undertake the task of producing the volume. It is difficult to ascertain whether Gutiérrez alone collected and recorded the testimonios, although her introduction suggests that she was deeply involved in the process. Gutiérrez also reveals that the testimonios had a clear objective, and she implies that this was agreed collectively when stating the following:

> Se acordó que cada una contara sencillamente su vida y cómo llegó a ser empleada, insistiendo en las dos rupturas, ejes de estas vidas: la primera le arranca a su familia y a su medio, reduciendo su horizonte a la casa de la patrona. La segunda la vincula al Sindicato, ensanchando su conciencia a la dimensión de su clase. (1983, 95)

> It was agreed that each individual would recount their life story in simple terms, including how they became a maid, with a focus on two breaks, or turning points, in their lives: the first rips them from their family and environment, limiting their horizons to their mistress's home. The second connects them to the Union, broadening their consciousness to include an awareness of their class.

Clearly, the testimonial subjects were encouraged to focus on specific topics, but it is not possible to determine whether the person recording their testimonios asked them questions or made comments to which they responded. If questions were posed, we do not know how these were phrased or whether they were the same in all cases. Gutiérrez's (1983, 94) introduction also suggests that there is no difference, other than in changes to individuals' names and to the names of some places, between the recorded testimonios and the published text.[18] However, if there was an interaction between the testimonial subject and an interviewer, the latter's comments have been omitted from the printed text. A close textual analysis suggests that comments made by Gutiérrez, or someone else involved in the recording process, may have had an influence on the shape and direction the testimonios took. In one testimonio (230), Fátima moves abruptly from providing a detailed description of a sandwich business that she has started (including its financial viability) to reflecting on the behavior of men toward her, which implies that she may have been prompted by a question or a comment from an interlocutor. Joanna Bartow (2008, 505) notes that until quite recently, it was typical for the editor or transcriber of a mediated testimonio to eliminate his or her questions "to create a seamless monologue." Nonetheless, this tendency is beginning to change, with recent testimonios including questions, acknowledging the presence of others, and even incorporating the interviewer's thoughts as the conversation develops (505).[19] Such texts emphasize collaboration and "strive for greater transparency" regarding any influence that the relationship between the subject and interviewer might have had on the finished text (505).

Although any questions or comments made by Gutiérrez (or another interviewer) have been eliminated in *Se necesita muchacha*, substantial explanatory footnotes are frequently included in the body of the subjects' testimonios. The footnotes contextualize the testimonios and explain specific terminology employed by the workers (Gutiérrez 1983, 109–110, 125–126, 313), which reveals a concern about whether the women's experiences will be fully comprehended by readers. It seems likely that these footnotes were authored by Gutiérrez, given that her introduction implies that she has taken on the roles of editor and coordinator of the text. The footnotes allow for reflections on the similarities between different testimonios, thereby revealing an impulse toward the theorization of the domestic worker's condition, which can also be traced in Gutiérrez's introduction.

Most important, however, the introduction and footnotes shed light, perhaps inadvertently, on the influence that Gutiérrez and the union have had on the domestic workers' perspectives. This correlation begins to align the book with more recent testimonial texts that endeavor to provide an insight into the relationship between the different parties involved in their creation, including the positionality of the editor/interviewer. In the first part of *Se necesita muchacha* (Gutiérrez 1983, 137), when the domestic worker Tomasa recounts her transition to a new home where she works for an employer who treats her well, a response to her claim appears in a footnote, which begins "¿puede existir un buen patrón?" (can a good boss exist?). The footnote continues with the following:

> En ausencia de una visión crítica, se podría fácilmente confundir bueno con paternalista. La dependencia afectiva frente a los patrones es a veces la fuente de mucha explotación. [. . .] Tomasa se ha "hallado" donde su patrona. Esta expresión tiene fuertes implicaciones para las que no son conscientes todavía: ya no sienten la necesidad de cambiar algo en su vida y menos en esta sociedad. [. . .] Para mantener a su empleada en su casa, la patrona dispone de dos medios: presionarla, o lograr que se halle, lo cual es al fin y al cabo otra forma de presión. Más bien, la que se ha conocido el Sindicato ya entiende que la lucha no se dirige contra su patrona como persona, sino contra toda una clase social y un sistema. (138)

> In the absence of a critical perspective, it is easy to confuse good with paternalistic. Emotional dependence on bosses is often the root of much exploitation. [. . .] Tomasa has begun to feel "at home" with her mistress. This expression has huge implications for those who have not yet developed a consciousness: they no longer feel the need to change anything in their lives and even less so in society. [. . .] To keep her maid in her employ, the mistress has two options: to pressure her, or to make her feel at home, which ultimately, is another form of pressure. On the contrary, those who have become involved with the Union understand that the battle will not be waged against their boss as an individual, but rather against an entire social class and system.

Ultimately, this intervention reveals an inconsistency at the heart of this testimonial project, because in her introduction, Gutiérrez (1983, 95) states that "no se ha querido hacer de este libro la expresión de la posición del Sindicato" (the intention was not to make this book an expression of the Union's position). The same statement is made in the introduction to *Basta* (STHC 1982, 23), which nonetheless includes a photograph of the Cusco Union members at a demonstration holding up signs that demand an eight-hour workday and one day off per week.

It appears that *Se necesita muchacha*'s Mexican publishing house, Fondo de Cultura Económica, believed that the book's sales and visibility would benefit if the book was championed by a well-known figure, the Mexican journalist and author Elena Poniatowska. A section of her lengthy "Presentación al lector mexicano" is reproduced on the back cover of the edition (Gutiérrez 1983; Presentation to the Mexican reader). Her prologue is followed by a caveat inside the volume: "Este Prólogo fue pedido expresamente a la autora por el Editor y no refleja necesariamente los pareceres del Sindicato (N. del E.)" (86; This Prologue was expressly requested from the author by the publisher and does not necessarily reflect the opinions held by the Union [editor's note]). The earlier version of the collection, *Basta* (STHC 1982), instead includes a short prologue authored by Domitila Barrios de Chúngara (17–18). The choice to include a prologue by Chúngara seems particularly apt given her own indigeneity, her involvement in the organization of women in a mining community in Bolivia, and the concerns that she expressed about "women's work" in "*Si me permiten hablar . . .*". The fact that Chúngara's prologue and a quotation from her on *Basta*'s cover flap have been replaced by Poniatowska's text in *Se necesita muchacha*, which was envisaged as the "international" version of the collection, demonstrates

Figure 1.1. Photograph of STHC demonstration (Sindicato de Trabajadoras del Hogar del Cusco, *Basta: Testimonios* [Cusco, Peru: Bartolomé de las Casas, 1982]). Copyright owner unknown.

the way in which market forces can result in the subaltern being silenced. Poniatowska, who is by her own admission a privileged European descendant author, nonetheless cites Chúngara's concerns about the limitations of "international feminism" in her own prologue (Poniatowska 1983, 57–58). A quotation from "*Si me permiten hablar . . .*" also features as an epigraph in *Se necesita muchacha*: it introduces the heavily union-influenced testimonios in the second part of the book (Gutiérrez 1983, 211).

One can assume that *Basta*'s limited circulation led Goutet to seek to republish the volume elsewhere so that it would be accessible to a wider readership. Based on what Alvarez Velarde told me during my interview with her in 2019, *Basta* was printed first in Cusco and then in Lima in 1982; no further copies of it appear to have been produced. By contrast, three thousand copies of Gutiérrez's *Se necesita muchacha* were produced on its first print run in Mexico City, and it was reprinted in 1993. The testimonios were also translated from Spanish and Quechua into French by Gutiérrez and published as *On demande une bonne* (a literal translation of *Se necesita muchacha*) in Paris in 1982.[20] There are some differences between the two Spanish editions: the pseudonyms attached to the testimonios in *Basta* have been altered in *Se necesita muchacha*, as has the order in which the testimonios appear, and two of the testimonios included in *Basta* (given by Fortu-

52 PAID TO CARE

nata and Ernestina) have been replaced by two different ones in *Se necesita muchacha* (provided by Dominga and Guadalupe).[21]

Elena Poniatowska's Prologue to *Se necesita muchacha*

Poniatowska's dedication to recuperating and disseminating the perspectives of marginalized individuals through interviews and testimonios probably led to her involvement in the publication of *Se necesita muchacha*.[22] As Roman-Morfin (2017, 57) has noted, attempting to give "'voice' to those who have been historically silenced" has been a defining characteristic of Poniatowska's career as a writer and has led her to reflect on the lives of Indigenous women in various ways. In her prologue, Poniatowska endeavors to shed a critical light on the injustices faced specifically by young, Indigenous, female domestic workers in both Mexico and Peru, including by focusing on the ways that they are exploited and emotionally manipulated by their employers (Poniatowska 1983, 59–62). She does so by piecing together some of the most powerful quotations from the testimonios collected in *Se necesita muchacha*. This includes a section where Poniatowska lists the numerous passages in which workers describe the severe physical abuse they have been subjected to (23–26). For example, Fortunata describes being beaten "como burro" (like a donkey) after having been blamed for the loss of one thousand *soles* (25). She continues: "He gritado, entonces me han metido caca de perro en la boca [. . .]. Cuando me he desmayado, me han echado un balde de agua. Todo maltratado, verde estaba mi cuerpo" (25; I screamed, so they put dog poo in my mouth [. . .]. When I had fainted, they threw a bucket of water over me. My body was completely battered and bruised). Poniatowska's strategy thus relies on emphasizing visceral moments in the testimonios that enrage the testimonial subject and the reader. In Beverley's words (1999, 73), these are moments in testimonios where "the experience of the Real breaks through the repetitious passivity of witnessing."

Poniatowska's prologue affords its greatest insights when its author reflects on the racialization of domestic work, which is a reality that unites both the Peruvian and Mexican contexts and thus lends to her comparative analysis. She describes the domestic workers' rapid alienation from their own communities and traditions after moving to the city for work (Poniatowska 1983, 12), which leaves them even more vulnerable and isolated. Poniatowska then focuses on the young women's physical appearance. She evokes their indigeneity as she imagines a group of young domestic workers on a Sunday, their only day off, standing on a street corner (15). She includes a description of their strong, white teeth, which she suggests are "dientes de Popul Vuh, dientes de América Latina" (15; teeth from the Popul Vuh, teeth of Latin America).[23] In a section of her text that she incorporated later when it was published in a separate collection of essays, Poniatowska adds:

> Todas son totonacas, mazahuas, mixtecas, chontales, otomíes, mazatecas, choles, purépechas. Todas son indígenas. [. . .] México, Bolivia, Perú, Guatemala, El Salvador, Honduras, los países de población indígena son surtidores de sirvientes y de artesanía popular. Hace casi quinientos años que su situación es la misma. (1994, 119)

> All of them are Totonacs, Mazahuas, Mixtecos, Chontal Maya, Otomi, Mazatecos, Ch'ol Maya, Tarascans. All of them are Indigenous. [. . .] Mexico, Bolivia, Peru, Guatemala, El Salvador, Honduras, the countries with Indigenous populations are suppliers of servants and folk art. The situation has been the same for almost five hundred years.

Poniatowska thus frames domestic workers' exploitation as an issue of Indigenous peoples' oppression. This framing is reflective of reality, but may also be tactical, given that her prologue was designed to increase the visibility of the Peruvian workers' testimonios and to raise awareness of the injustices faced by domestic employees in Mexico. As Blofield (2012, 61) argues, presenting the struggle for these workers' rights as an Indigenous peoples' issue can mean that the message resonates with a broader audience, particularly in countries with a majority, or large minority, Indigenous population. Furthermore, by reflecting on the subjugation of domestic workers in Mexico and Peru, Poniatowska sheds light more broadly on the discrimination faced by Indigenous people, who are viewed as "out-of-sync" with the process of nation-building in Mexico, because they do not form part of the "imagined community" of mestizos that has become associated with Mexican identity and modernity (Roman-Morfin 2015, 83–84).

When Poniatowska republished her prologue in 1994, she also included portraits of anonymous Indigenous women within her text. Underneath the photographs, captions that read "Emilia o Isabel" (Emilia or Isabel) (153) and "Ascensión o Romanita" (Ascención or Romanita) (149) emphasize that the women could represent any Indigenous domestic worker. Almost in spite of herself, Poniatowska's scathing critique and determination to foreground the violent injustices to which domestic workers are subject risk

54 PAID TO CARE

slipping into a process of othering them. The captioned portraits imply that the women are interchangeable. This, together with the somewhat exoticizing descriptions of their physical appearance, creates a "distancing effect," as Roman-Morfin (2015, 77) has similarly argued, because their anonymity verges on becoming a "reductive sign."

When I interviewed Poniatowska by phone on November 27, 2018, she stated that she had never been to Peru when she wrote the prologue and that she was not familiar with the members of the Cusco Union. She revealed that it was her love for Jesusa Palancares, the protagonist of her 1969 novel *Hasta no verte Jesús mío* (2016; *Here's to You, Jesusa!*), that motivated her to write such a lengthy prologue for *Se necesita muchacha*. Jesusa Palancares's character is based on the testimonio of Josefina Bórquez, an impoverished woman who could not read or write and who recounted her life story to Poniatowska (D. Shaw 1996, 191).[24] Palancares spent some of her life employed as a domestic worker in the early twentieth century (Poniatowska 1983, 64). In her prologue to *Se necesita muchacha*, Poniatowska laments that Palancares was never able to remain a member of

> una organización clasista, que cuenta entre sus propósitos el de dar a sus miembros la explicación de esta situación inferior que es de orden estructural; económica y social. Jesusa nunca pudo salir de su visión individual, nunca se percibió a sí misma como miembro de una clase social—la clase trabajadora, motor de la historia—y por lo tanto ya no pudo dejar de atribuir su situación inferior a su propia incapacidad: "soy la misma basura que usted ve, a la que el perro le echa una miada y se va," conclusión que la agobia y nos agobia también. (79)

> a class-based organization among whose objectives is that of providing its members with a structural, economic and social explanation for their inferior situation. Jesusa could never move past her individual perspective, she never saw herself as a member of a social class—the working class, the motor of history—and therefore she could not stop attributing her inferior situation to her own lack of ability: "I am the same piece of rubbish that you see, that the dog wees on and leaves," a conclusion that weighs her down and weighs us down too.

Poniatowska contrasts Palancares's outlook, as well as her isolation and feelings of victimization, with the solidarity expressed in the testimonios shared in *Se necesita muchacha*.

The indignation that permeates Poniatowska's text appears to be, at least in part, a product of guilt, provoked both by her relationship to Palancares and by her own privilege. She reflects on her relationship to her family's domestic employees when she was a child. She mentions Magdalena Castillo, who was seventeen, and just a few years older than the author, when she began to work as a nanny to Poniatowska and her sister. Poniatowska admits that "nos dió su vida" (she gave us her life), adding that Castillo never married so as not to leave them (Poniatowska 1983, 63). She criticizes the unfair, traditional division of academic and manual labor, yet Poniatowska acknowledges in the following that, as an adult, the labor of paid domestic workers has permitted her intellectual development and production:

> Mientras yo escribo, María en la cocina, calienta la leche para darles de desayunar a mis hijos. De mí dirán después que qué buen prólogo (o qué malo) que qué inteligente o qué bestia peluda, pero de un modo o de otro, estaré en el candelero dizque cultural. María problablemente se encuentre de nuevo frente a la estufa, abriendo el gas, no para meter su cabeza dentro del horno como Sylvia Plath (lo cual ya es un privilegio de la clase dominante), sino vigilando la olla de leche que hierve, para darles a los niños el desayuno número 17159374628430000. (55)

> While I write, María in the kitchen heats up the milk to feed my children breakfast. Afterward they will say of me, "what a good prologue" (or "what a bad prologue"), "how intelligent," or "what a stupid idiot," but one way or another I will be in the so-called cultural spotlight. María probably finds herself once more in front of the stove, turning on the gas, but not to put her head in the oven like Sylvia Plath (which in itself is a privilege of the ruling class), but rather keeping an eye on the pan of milk that is boiling, to feed my children breakfast number 17159374628430000.

She laments, bitterly, that guilt serves no one (67) and is disapproving of hypocritical leftist intellectuals who rely on domestic workers but do nothing to improve their lot (54, 67).

Poniatowska has stated that other Mexican writers consider her "la cocinera, la barrendera, la criada que está limpiando los escusados de la gran casa de la literatura" (Schuessler 2017; the cook, the street sweeper, the maid who is cleaning the toilets in the great house of literature). This declaration, together with her reflections on her difference from the Indigenous women whose stories she is interpreting, indicates that she considers herself to be both an "insider" and an "outsider," as well as someone who straddles the so-called high and low cultural spheres. She does not view herself simplistically as a "transparent mediator" (Roman-Morfin 2015, 78), given that she recognizes, and struggles with, the privilege that has allowed her to benefit from paid domestic labor. Her prologue acknowledges, to borrow Beverley's terms (1999, 82), that, although it is possible to "enter into relations of understanding and solidarity" with the testimonial project, it is not hers "in any immediate sense" and in fact it structurally implies "a contradiction with [her] own position of relative privilege and authority in the global system."

Poniatowska's prologue, like Gutiérrez's footnotes, thus begins to foreshadow the inclusion and interrogation of the position of the author, filmmaker, interviewer, or intellectual, who is also often a beneficiary of paid domestic help, in more recent domestic workers' testimonios, including the self-reflexive film documentaries and digital productions that I discuss in chapters 3 and 4. This is crucial not only to acknowledge the dialogical reality of domestic employer-employee relationships but also because the domestic workers' "collaborators" (i.e., Gutiérrez, Poniatowska, and Duvivier) are those who have the most influence over the process of a cultural work's creation and distribution. Acknowledging this does not, of course, resolve all the ethical complexities that arise from these attempts to enable the subaltern's voice to be heard, as the example of Poniatowska's prologue demonstrates. The distinct nature of the relationships between the testimonial subjects and editors documented here gains expression in the form and ideological content of the testimonios themselves.

Ambivalence and the Individual in Domestic Workers' Testimonios: Caraballo, da Silva, and de Jesus

Ramona Caraballo was inspired to record her memories of her life and experiences as a domestic worker while she was recovering from an operation and following the irrevocable breakdown of her relationship with her mother (Caraballo 1987, 117, 122). She was born in 1942 and grew up in Achar, a rural area in the Tacuarembó Department in Uruguay. Her testimonio, *La niña, el chocolate, el huevo duro*, recounts her experience of being terribly mistreated as a child while she was shuttled between different employers (12–20). She was accused of theft by one *patrona* (female boss) and subsequently attempted suicide (30–32). At eighteen she found secure employment working as a cook in an affluent household in Montevideo, together with her sister (53). Nonetheless, she became pregnant when a romantic relationship left her vulnerable to manipulation (59). She was subsequently rushed to the hospital after an unsuccessful abortion attempt; while there, she was told that she had syphilis (60–61). The diagnosis, which Caraballo later learned was mistaken (88–89), resulted in the loss of her job (61–62). Caraballo's life while pregnant was extremely turbulent, but once her daughter was born, she again managed to find secure employment (99) and eventually rented her own room (103).

According to Oscar Brando (1997, 15) and Mabel Moraña (2013, 140), Caraballo's testimonio was edited by Álvaro Barros Lémez. Moraña (2013, 140) suggests that Barros organized the publication in order to document the life choices of a working-class woman and the survival strategies that she is forced to improvise in an environment that offers her few alternatives. The resulting manuscript was published in Uruguay by Monte Sexto. Unusually, Barros's name is entirely absent from the first edition of the book; the front and back covers feature childish drawings of a girl and a train, perhaps to underscore the element of Caraballo's story that the editor or publisher considered most shocking: that she was sent away by her mother at just four years old to reside in a home in Montevideo where she was trained for future domestic service (Caraballo 1987, 7). It has been difficult to garner further information about Barros's relationship to Caraballo, and acquiring a copy of the book was a challenge.[25] These difficulties could be a product of the historical context in which the book was published. Brando (1997, 17) notes that the text was produced during the Uruguayan democratic recomposition, a time when cultural industries were strongly selective and subject to strict controls, which "impide que ciertas formas testimoniales (digamos, Ramona Caraballo) puedan desenvolverse" (prevented certain forms of testimonio [including Ramona Caraballo's] from flourishing).

Ai de vós! Diário de uma doméstica is the testimonio of Francisca Souza da Silva (1983); it records her experiences of domestic work as a child, adolescent, and young adult. Da Silva was born in 1943 in a rural area of the municipality of Campos in the north of Rio de Janeiro state. She opens *Ai de vós!* by reflecting on the illness and death of her father, to whom she was deeply attached (13–16). When she was six years old, her mother placed her with an abusive employer who beat her and forced her to fetch the family's water each day in a pail or a can, which she carried on top of her head (22–23). Subsequently, da Silva was unofficially adopted by a wealthy woman who was kind to her (35); however, when she was ten, her mother removed her from that situation and sent her to Rio de Janeiro city to work for a different family that treated her badly (26). As a teenager in Rio, da Silva worked for various families, often for short periods of time, usually leaving because she suffered mistreatment or sexual abuse. At thirteen or fourteen, she had the opportunity to attend school (28), which is presumably where she became literate and was thus later able to write down her memories herself. While living with her sister's friend, da Silva met a man called Leo, who raped her (45). Like Caraballo, da Silva then entered a romantic relationship characterized by manipulation and deceit; she and Leo had two children together (60). After a second abusive relationship and having two more children, da Silva became homeless and was forced to sleep on the street (96). She had no one to help her look after her children, so she was unable to find work. At the end of her testimonio, da Silva states that her situation has improved, in part as a result of her positive relationship with her current boss, Ivna Duvivier (130–131).

De Jesus's (1986) testimonio, *Diário de Bitita*, pertains to an earlier period than do Caraballo's and da Silva's. De Jesus was born in Sacramento, Minas Gerais, in 1914, just twenty-six years after the abolition of slavery in Brazil (Moreira 2009, 69). The testimonio's title incorporates the author's childhood nickname, Bitita, because the text contains her memories of her childhood, adolescence, and youth up until 1937, the year she migrated to the city of São Paulo to work as a domestic employee (69–70). Before her death, de Jesus is believed to have handed two notebooks that contained her handwritten story to a Brazilian journalist, Clélia Pisa (Alves 2014, 11). Together with two French journalists, Pisa edited the testimonio manuscript, which was published in France in 1982, after de Jesus's death and under the title *Journal de Bitita* (11). Four years later, the book was published in Brazil in Portuguese (11). It has been confirmed that the texts published as *Diário de Bitita* match the original manuscripts de Jesus wrote in Portuguese; the book is not a retranslation from French into Portuguese (Moreira 2009, 69). The concern provoked by this issue attests to the importance placed on the authenticity of testimonio.

De Jesus won widespread recognition before she died for *Quarto de despejo* ([1960] 2021; The garbage room), which was based on the diaries she had written as an adult while living in Canindé, one of São Paulo's favelas. Daniel da Silva Moreira (2009, 65) emphasizes that de Jesus's book was seized upon as a symbol of the struggle against the injustices of Brazilian society at that moment. Nonetheless, her subsequent books did not receive the same level of attention, undoubtedly as a consequence of Brazil's changing sociopolitical context, which saw the populism of the early 1960s replaced by a military coup and dictatorship (66). Despite her disappointment, de Jesus continued to write after moving from São

Paulo to a rural *sítio* (farm). Moreira (68) suggests that de Jesus wrote and remembered as a form of resistance to the wave of criticism that she had received during the brief period in which she had enjoyed the status of a successful writer. The way in which she memorializes her childhood in *Diário de Bitita* betrays a desire for resistance because she reflects on her precocious love of reading and on her aptitude for critical thinking, in spite of her difficult material circumstances and the little formal education she received (de Jesus, 127–129, 133).

Early in her testimonio, de Jesus (2014, 13) reveals that she does not know the identity of her biological father; her closest and most supportive male relative was her maternal grandfather, who died when she was young (123–124). During de Jesus's childhood, her mother worked as a washerwoman (25), both in a domestic setting and in brothels (31, 83). Sometimes, de Jesus was taken by her mother to her workplace, and occasionally, she was left with a family member. Her first direct experience of domestic service appears to have taken place as a child after moving with her mother and stepfather to the countryside, where they worked the land (131). She helped the landowner's wife clean her house, for which she hoped to be paid or given a new dress, which she never received (137). Later, as an adolescent, de Jesus entered paid domestic service independently in the city (141). However, she was often not properly remunerated (144, 148). Like Caraballo, de Jesus was also wrongly accused of theft; a priest, who was a relative of one of her employers, claimed that she had stolen a hundred thousand *réis* from him, and she was imprisoned. The priest later found his money in a cigarette case (146). De Jesus's employment, which ranged from working as a cook and a washerwoman to acting as a nanny, became particularly erratic after she developed some recurring wounds on her legs that she was unable to treat (151). Her situation improved after finding work at a "Santa Casa" (religious institution) where she cooked for the nuns and was able to consult their recipe book (199–200). Of all three testimonios discussed so far, de Jesus's undertakes the most extensive sociohistorical critique and develops a clear class- and race-based consciousness, which distinguishes her text from da Silva's and Caraballo's.

However, on a limited number of occasions, a veiled desire for collective solidarity can be detected in da Silva's testimonio. First, when she finds that she cannot rely on her family during her time of need (much as does de Jesus [2014, 163–169]), da Silva (1983, 108) writes, "os peores pedaços de meu caminho percorri sosinha" (I traveled the worst parts of my journey alone). She concludes, "eu não encontrei amor [...] e não quero, porque não acredito em amor e sim em solidariedade humana de algumas pessoas" (99;

I have not found love [. . .] and I do not wish to, because I do not believe in love but rather in human solidarity from some people). Second, at the end of her narrative, da Silva (131) briefly wonders what will become of other vulnerable girls and women from impoverished rural and urban areas who will have experiences similar to her own. This thought suggests an increase "in political awareness and interest in other defenceless girls through her engagement in self-writing," as Roncador observes (2014, 183). Nonetheless, da Silva's thought is immediately preceded by a declaration, made in religious terms, that she hopes her book will be "a *minha* salvação. Queira Deus que assim seja" (1983, 131 [my emphasis]; *my* salvation. God willing). Similarly, Caraballo's (1987, 13) testimonio does not display the clear development of a political or class consciousness, although she does reflect on the difficulties of being a woman and hopes that others will not have to suffer the same experiences that she did. Carlos Badessich (1992, 414) suggests that Caraballo's attitude toward her misfortunes is shaped by the traditional Catholic precept that life itself is suffering, as is da Silva's. Caraballo does not come to the conclusion that her experience is the result of socioeconomic factors that shape her condition as an impoverished woman and domestic worker (414).

In her analysis of Brazilian domestic worker testimonios that have not been influenced by the involvement of an interviewer with a particularly strong political agenda, Roncador (2014, 182) observes an ideological ambivalence in which the testimonialistas (the subjects of the testimonios) defend their own class interests but also "align themselves with the values and class/gender ideologies of their mistresses." This alignment expresses itself through the writers' or subjects' vested interests in winning "the personal respect of their public" rather than in "fostering solidarity for a political cause or a communal situation of distress" (182). Roncador (185) posits that such an alignment is one rationale for da Silva's abundant and graphic depictions of her sexual abuse and rape, which contest popular representations of domestic workers as easy sexual targets and represent an attempt to uphold bourgeois standards of sexual morality and femininity. In Caraballo's, da Silva's and de Jesus's testimonios, respectability is often deployed as a form of social control, and bosses use the quality to negatively stereotype domestic workers' *purported* laziness, untrustworthiness, and lack of moral and sexual rectitude. Such use provides a rationale for de Jesus's and Caraballo's strong negative reactions to accusations of theft, as well as for da Silva's breakdown following her misdiagnosis with a sexually transmitted disease.

Roncador (2014, 179) broadly aligns de Jesus's writing with da Silva's, and she suggests that in *Quarto de despejo*, de Jesus offers a realistic portrait of the favela in which she lived without questioning stereotypical images of favela dwellers. De Jesus also occasionally regurgitates the discourse of her oppressors in *Diário de Bitita*, as when she calls all Black men drunken brawlers (55). Despite this occasional ambivalence, de Jesus's consistent concern for, and critical reflections on, Brazil's Afro-Brazilian community distinguishes her testimonio from da Silva's and Caraballo's works, which nonetheless do offer vital insights into domestic workers' exploitation. The unevenness of the narrative style in *Diário de Bitita* can, at least in part, be accounted for by de Jesus's attempts to invoke her childhood voice while looking back on her past as an adult with a firmer sociopolitical viewpoint.

When de Jesus was a child, a key figure in her development of a race-centered critical consciousness was Manoel Nogueira (de Jesus 2014, 55), whom she describes as a "mulato" who was literate and who read passages of the newspaper to residents in her community. From him, de Jesus (39, 48, 52, 56) learned of the ideas expounded by the Brazilian politician and intellectual Ruy Barbosa, an abolitionist who argued for the right of Afro-Brazilians to receive a school education. Her memories of Nogueira and of Ruy Barbosa's discourse often preempt the explicitly historical passages of her testimonio, when she reflects on the legacy of slavery in Brazil. De Jesus (30) comments that "a maioria dos negros era analfabeta. Já haviam perdido a fé nos predominadores e em si próprios" (the majority of Black people were illiterate. They had already lost faith in the dominant class and in themselves), and later she emphasizes that "os negros foram escravizados durante quase 400 anos" (Black people were enslaved for almost 400 years). She also implies that there is a need for collective action, specifically when reflecting on Getúlio Vargas's revolution of the wealthy in 1930; she suggests that it should be "nos" (160; us), the poor, who should be rising up instead. Furthermore, despite apparently not having been involved in the organization or unionization of domestic employees (later in life she worked as a *catadora de papéis* [paper collector] rather than as a domestic worker), de Jesus links domestic workers' struggles to race-, gender-, and class-based discrimination rooted in slavery and colonization. She explains that

> se o filho do padrão espancasse o filho da cozinheira, ela não podia reclamar para não perder o emprego. Mas se a cozinheira tinha filha, pobre negrinha. O filho da patroa a utilizaria para o seu noviciado sexual. Meninas que ainda estavam pensando nas bonecas, nas cirandas e cirandinhas eram brutalizadas pelos filhos do senhor Peireira, Moreira, Oliveira, e outros porqueiras que vieram de além-mar. (38)

62 PAID TO CARE

If the master's son were to hit the cook's son, she [the cook] could not complain so as not to lose her job. But if the cook had a daughter, poor little Black girl. The boss's son would use her for his sexual initiation. Girls who were still interested in dolls and playing ring-around-the-rosy were brutalized by the sons of Pereira, Moreira, Oliveira, and other awful individuals who came from across the Atlantic.

Collective Testimonios of Paid Domestic Work: Carvalho and *Se necesita muchacha*

In contrast to the testimonios introduced so far, Lenira Carvalho's (1982) "Só a gente que vive é que sabe: Depoimento de uma doméstica" and Ana Gutiérrez's (1983) *Se necesita muchacha* are resolutely collective publications in terms of their content, their form, and their paths to publication. These two works employ differing strategies to link themselves explicitly to domestic workers' broader struggles to organize and to unionize in various Latin American countries throughout the 1970s and 1980s. Carvalho's (1982, 7) testimonio was recorded on tape in March 1982, and the published version retains the markers of its orality. The text is the product of Carvalho's encounter with Beatriz Costa (Roncador 2014, 163), who produced the testimonio because of its pedagogical potential and who published it as part of the series *Cadernos de educação popular* (Popular education textbooks). The objective of the series was to use testimonio as a tool to disseminate knowledge developed by those who suffered from political and economic oppression in order to increase readers' abilities "to discern and reject the rules of domination," which constituted an educational approach inspired by Paulo Freire's *Pedagogy of the Oppressed* (Roncador 2014, 163).

"Só a gente que vive é que sabe" opens with a brief description of Carvalho's childhood and relates the circumstances in which she entered domestic service (Carvalho 1982, 9). She declares, "sou filha de doméstica e de mãe solteira [. . .] eu nunca tive [. . .] pai, nunca tive casa" (9; I am the daughter of a domestic worker and of a single mother [. . .] I never had [. . .] a father, I never had a home). As a young girl, Carvalho lived in the house of her mother's employer in rural Alagoas, Brazil, although she later moved to reside with her brother (10). At the age of fourteen, Carvalho (10) began working for her godfather as a live-in domestic worker in the city of Recife (in the state of Pernambuco, Brazil). She comments on having felt overwhelmed and confused, like many other migrant domestic workers, by the urban infrastructure and technology, including electricity and a piped water supply (10–11). Carvalho (13–14) describes her employers' manipulative strategies to keep her in their service. In particular, she expresses the distress she felt when they concealed a telegram for her that contained news of her sister's ill health, which meant that Carvalho did not visit her sister before her death. Despite the fact that her godfather was a teacher, Carvalho's (14) employers did not encourage her to study, even though one of her motives for coming to Recife was to have access to a school. Following the opening section of her testimonio, details of Carvalho's personal life are generally included only when they can provide an insight into common problems faced by domestic workers and into the causes of those problems. Her priority is to provide a better understanding of "the entire professional category" of domestic workers (Roncador 2014, 175).

Compared to Carvalho's work, *Se necesita muchacha* (Gutiérrez 1983) represents a very different kind of testimonial project: its composition of multiple testimonios enables the book to aspire to polyphony in a more literal way. At the opening of *Se necesita muchacha*, Gutiérrez (94) emphasizes that, although her name is on the front cover, the book is "el resultado de un trabajo colectivo: *su autor es el Sindicato*" (my emphasis; the result of a collective project: *its author is the Union*). When the collection was originally published in Cusco by Bartolomé de las Casas under the title *Basta* (STHC 1982), the author was explicitly recorded as the Sindicato de Trabajadoras del Hogar del Cusco (Cusco Union of Household Workers).

Like "Só a gente que vive é que sabe," *Basta* has also been used as a pedagogical tool. In my January 10, 2019, interview with Alvarez Velarde, I learned that since the late 1990s, while giving evening classes to domestic workers at Cusco's Centro Educativo Básico Alternativo (CEBA), she has encouraged groups of her students to read many of the testimonios together. Some students have had strong emotional reactions to the testimonios because of their ability to identify with the experiences retold in them. This has helped the students to recognize their own problems and to look for solutions. Consequently, Alvarez Velarde believes that the testimonios can be used to raise consciousness among domestic workers about common forms of abuse.

Se necesita muchacha contains twenty-three testimonios that are published under pseudonyms and separated into two parts. The first part of the book includes testimonios that focus on the subjects' entries into domestic service and their experiences of exploitation, while the second section is united by the stories of workers who have been impacted by their involvement in the STHC. The women recorded by Gutiérrez had generally migrated to Cusco from rural areas in Peru to enter domestic service as young girls and were often employed by a distant relative or *madrina* (god-mother). The experiences described in the testimonios display notable similarities to the histories explored in Eugenia Bridikhina's (2007) investigation of child domestic labor in La Paz, Bolivia, throughout the early twentieth century. Bridikhina (5427) argues that child employees found themselves on the lowest rung of the social hierarchy that existed in the servile world of the homes in which they labored. Although they struggled to lodge official complaints against their bosses, the children were able to employ the strategies of resistance to which the weak have recourse: disobedience, transgression, and escape (5440). The testimonios in *Se necesita muchacha* similarly evoke this negotiation between power and resistance and call attention to the testimonial subjects' agency, even in the most difficult circumstances. Furthermore, the testimonios demonstrate that these girls and women frequently face ethnic discrimination because of their indigeneity and suffer because of their unfamiliarity with Spanish.

A comparison of the testimonios examined in this chapter provides insight into the ideological differences between the branches of Catholicism operating in Latin America in the 1970s and 1980s. For example, Carvalho (1982, 15) comments on her struggle with the Church's open disapproval of single mothers before she got involved with the JOC. Unlike the JOC, some of the initial organizations established for domestic workers in Latin America, including the Catholic, anti–liberation theology organization Opus Dei, were conservative and aimed to serve employers' interests by encouraging domestic workers to content themselves with their position (Goldsmith 1989, 230). Other organizations were more welfare-oriented and aimed to support domestic workers, particularly if they became mothers (Blofield 2012, 144). In *La niña, el chocolate, el huevo duro*, for example, Caraballo (1987, 66–75) recounts her experience of being taken in by what was possibly one of the latter type of religious organizations in Montevideo, which initially provided for her during her pregnancy after she had been thrown out of her employer's home.

The third type of domestic workers' organization was linked to liberation theology. These organizations were often ideologically radical and included branches of the JOC. Their influence marks both Carvalho's testimonios and those collected in *Se necesita muchacha*.[26] Indeed, Carvalho's (1982, 20, 77–78) text clearly shows that her consciousness of domestic workers' exploitation, and how to combat it, developed as a consequence of her intense involvement with a burgeoning domestic workers' movement in Recife, which was crucially supported by the JOC and other labor movements. At one point, Carvalho (74) assumed a full-time role at the JOC, though she later returned to paid domestic work. Although the Church was seen as "a relatively safe space for activism" during the Brazilian military dictatorship (Cornwall et al. 2013, 186), Carvalho (1982, 16) mentions that her initial participation in the JOC was threatened by the direct intervention of the authoritarian government. Despite this, Carvalho continued her activism as part of the Associação dos Trabalhadores Domésticos de Recife (Recife Domestic Workers Association), which she helped found in 1979 and which was converted into a labor union in 1988 (Roncador 2004, 170).

Carvalho (1982, 55–57) emphasizes that by linking the struggle to achieve respect for domestic employees and their rights to the Church, it is possible to mobilize the greatest number of workers. This is not only because the Church could provide a physical location for domestic workers to meet, a location that accepted both rich and poor, but also because faith was so important to many workers at the time (56). Carvalho observes that domestic workers' organizations in Brazil that venerate Santa Zita, the patron saint of domestic workers, have proliferated, and that celebrations of her saint's day, April 27, have become more popular than other, secular events explicitly dedicated to domestic workers—probably as a consequence of the continued shame of being identified as a domestic worker (55–57).[27] The celebration of Santa Zita is a trend that also appears to have been led by domestic workers, confirming Suzana Prates's (1989, 287) insight that in order to achieve a degree of group identity, "the domestic employee must be more than the target, the object, of the action; she must be the subject of the action."

In *Se necesita muchacha*, several of the workers interviewed admit that they have been strongly influenced and inspired by the religion teachers that they have encountered while attending evening school. It becomes clear that some of their teachers are adherents of liberation theology and are most probably members of Christian Base Communities, organizations whose ideology combines Marxist theory with Christian principles. My 2019 interviews with Alvarez Velarde and Baufumé revealed that Goutet was one of the religion teachers who gave classes at the evening school attended by various domestic workers in Cusco.[28] Teaching enabled Goutet to converse with the workers and to discover which of them were trapped in particularly difficult circumstances. The individuals would then be encouraged to contact the STHC and, starting in 1992, they could be offered the opportunity to escape their live-in employment by going to stay in the domestic workers' refuge at the Centro Yanapanakusun. Goutet's proximity to different priests enabled her to find a room in Cusco's former seminary for the STHC's initial meetings on Sunday afternoons.[29] The location created the impression that the meetings were religious gatherings rather than Union meetings, which would have been important during the Peruvian military regime and prior to the Union's official recognition by the government.

My 2019 interviews with Alvarez Velarde and Baufumé further revealed that Goutet's Christian beliefs were strongly influenced by liberation theology. Alvarez Velarde describes her as "una laica comprometida" (a socially committed laywoman). For many years, Goutet was a member of the Movimiento de Profesionales Católicos (Movement of Catholic Professionals) and a "militant" in the Unión de Estudiantes Católicos (National Union of Catholic Students or UNEC); according to Baufumé, Goutet received her religious education within UNEC, which allowed her to deliver religion classes at the evening school in Cusco.

Goutet adhered to the branch of liberation theology known as *opción preferencial por el pobre* (OPP), which encouraged its followers to seek out, recognize, and support the poor; Alvarez Velarde suggested that this theology motivated Goutet's desire to become closer to those in need. At a national level, the individual who was most associated with OPP was Father Gustavo Gutiérrez, which perhaps provides a rationale for Goutet's choice of the pseudonym "Ana Gutiérrez" when publishing *Se necesita muchacha*. Father Gutiérrez also cofounded Peru's Instituto Bartolomé de las Casas (Peña 1994, 37, 41), whose publishing house printed *Basta*.

In liberation theology, Marxism is used to provide a class-based analysis of oppression, which is tempered by Christianity's "message of love for and solidarity with the poor" (Yúdice 1991, 26). This characterizes the perspective that can be traced in many of the workers' testimonios in *Se necesita muchacha*, including Jesusa's. She states that her religion classes have revolutionized her understanding of Christianity:

> En la escuela, la profesora de religión nos explicaba muy distinto de las otras profesoras. Yo no entendía, me decía siempre: "¿Cómo es posible? ¿Eso será religión? ¿Ayudar a las demás que están sufriendo? ¿De que hay ricos y pobres y que los ricos explotan a los pobres? No, pues, si religión es: Dios ha creado, y los rezos" [. . .]. Y poco a poco iba entendiendo [. . .]. Después la profesora de religión nos explicó que la señora nos regala ropa vieja, nos explota, y eso entendía porque me pasaba a mí igualito. (Gutiérrez 1983, 347–349)

> At school, the religion teacher explained things to us in a very different way from the other teachers. I didn't understand, I always

said to myself: "How is it possible? Is this really religion? Helping others who are suffering? There are rich and poor people and the rich exploit the poor? No, it can't be, if religion is just: God created all things, and the prayers" [. . .]. Little by little I began to understand [. . .]. Then the religion teacher explained to us that the mistress gives us old clothes as presents, she exploits us, and I understood that because it was exactly what was happening to me.

In another testimonio, Simona similarly observes that "[e]n la clase de religión poco a poco íbamos comprendiendo cómo está la sociedad, quienes son los explotadores, todo" (Gutiérrez 1983, 388; in the religion class little by little we began to understand how society is set up, who the exploiters are, everything). She also comments that her religion teacher (likely Goutet herself) was present at the first Sunday meeting she attended at the Cusco Union's headquarters (Gutiérrez 1983, 387–388).

Liberation theology departs from conventional Marxist thought in its rejection of elitism with regard to knowledge and power (Yúdice 1991, 26). In the testimonios of those who have clearly become deeply involved with the STHC, this level of radicalization can be detected. While a few workers still express elitist aspirations, many no longer desire to ascend in the socioeconomic hierarchy, particularly in terms of employment. Simona explains that she has strongly encouraged her own son to share in the reality faced by poor people in the countryside and by domestic workers. She states that she has done so because "No quiero que mi hijo se vuelva otro explotador" (Gutiérrez 1983, 393; I do not want my son to become another exploiter). Carvalho (1982, 51–52, 69) also expresses this kind of anti-elitism in "Só a gente que vive é que sabe" when she laments other domestic workers' shame at publicly acknowledging their profession and reveals a creeping mistrust of intellectuals. As Yúdice (1991, 8) has commented, testimonios that "emerge from the consciousness-raising experiences of the Christian Base Community movement" tend to be the ones that "undermine rather than reconsolidate patriarchal and paternalistic master narratives," at least to an extent. In this regard, Carvalho's testimonio and *Se necesita muchacha* differ from Caraballo's and da Silva's texts, which, as discussed above, reproduce a distinct Christian narrative of individual suffering and hope for redemption that leads toward a desire for benevolent paternalism.

The religion classes described in *Se necesita muchacha* were some of the few opportunities that members of the Cusco Union had to meet their future possible *compañeras* (comrades). Live-in domestic workers are notoriously difficult to organize on account of their isolation from one another inside their workplaces, which are other people's homes (Chaney and García Castro 1989; Carvalho 1982, 66; Gutiérrez 1983, 92). Furthermore, some employers attempted to scare some domestic workers interviewed in *Se necesita muchacha* by warning them, often using moralistic terminology, of the supposed evils of becoming involved with a labor association (Gutiérrez 1983, 333, 346, 349, 352). In one testimonio, Flora explains that evening classes are the ideal place to speak to other domestic employees about the union because their attendance can be justified for pedagogical reasons; however, certain teachers have either tried to impede her attempts to collaborate or openly criticized what the students are taught by their religion teacher (Gutiérrez 1983, 292–293, 295). Jesusa complains in her testimonio that, aside from her religion teacher, many of the other instructors did not appear to want to educate domestic workers properly "porque quieren que les sirvan gratis" (Gutiérrez 1983, 351; because they want to be served for free).

Creating networks of solidarity with other workers' movements was also a crucial part of the strategy of incipient domestic workers' associations, although Carvalho (1982, 66) admits that, in her own experience, this often presented a challenge because of domestic workers' reticence in sharing their thoughts in meetings when other types of workers were present. Despite this, Carvalho (77–78) acknowledges that "quem me fez eu enxergar (a realidade da situação das empregadas domésticas) não foi doméstica. Foi trabalhador de outras categorias e foi intelectual também. Quer dizer, foi um movimento que tinha padre e tinha leigo trabalhador" (those who made me see [the reality of the situation of domestic workers] were not maids. They were other kinds of workers and intellectuals too. In other words, it was a movement that included priests and secular workers). She emphasizes that abusive employer-employee relationships are never isolated cases because they are a symptom of broader social problems (35). Similarly, Gutiérrez (1983, 92–93) posits that the very existence of domestic workers is a consequence of structural inequalities, "que sólo desaparecerán con esta sociedad" (which will only disappear along with this form of society). This large-scale perspective contributed to Carvalho's (1982, 20) determination to show other domestic workers that "na medida que piora a situação do camponês, do trabalhador, dos operários, a nossa também piora. A luta tem que ser uma só" (if the situation of peasants, workers, and manual laborers worsens, then our situation does too. We must be united in our struggle).

In *Se necesita muchacha*, it becomes clear that the enormous social upheavals experienced in Peru throughout the 1960s and 1970s contributed to some of the domestic employees' feelings of identification with other workers' struggles. The testimonios of Lucía and Jesusa mention the 1962–1965 rural workers' movements in the province of La Convención, which undertook land occupations that were repressed by the Peruvian army under President Fernando Belaúnde Terry (Gutiérrez 1983, 313). Lucía states that her understanding of the campesinos' (rural workers') struggle, which was led by Hugo Blanco, has been renewed by her membership in the STHC, thereby alluding to the emergence of her identity as a worker and her development of a class consciousness (Gutiérrez 1983, 330).[30] Both texts show that relating to other workers' movements supports the difficult, but critical, task of encouraging domestic employees to articulate a class-based worker's identity. However, the tension between the isolated nature of live-in domestic work and the wider collective aims of nascent domestic workers' organizations is also powerfully reflected in the testimonios.

The development of a class identity caused members of these nascent domestic workers' organizations to feel suspicious of broader women's movements, which are usually led by middle-class individuals, as Carvalho (1982, 58) points out. Although Carvalho (58) values the contribution of these movements, in particular their fight for domestic work to be respected, she emphasizes that their members are also those who exploit domestic workers: "são nossas patroas" (they are our bosses). Class interests provide one rationale for the fact that, overall, feminist organizations across Latin America have been slow to take up the issue of domestic workers' rights, although "in some countries individual feminists have adopted the cause" (Blofield 2012, 60). The Mexican author Elena Poniatowska is one example.

In Latin American women's testimonios, "collective womanhood" is occasionally acknowledged by subjects, despite the complexities of women's alliances "across cultures, races, and social class" (Bartow 2008, 508). In her collection of Brazilian women's testimonios, *Brazilian Women Speak*, Daphne Patai (1993, 4) observes that many of the women she interviewed recognized "some sort of bond with other women," including with their potential readers and in spite of their differences. Patai (197–207, 208–212) incorporates the testimonios of both a domestic worker, Conccição, and her boss, Marta, which effectively elucidates the clashing perspectives that domestic workers and their employers have about the nature of their relationship. As Sommer (1988, 107–108) points out, in the testimonio genre, the relationships to others that women describe often underlie their own identities, which thereby indicates the dialogical or collective nature of identity formation. Sommer (108) contrasts the metonymical nature of testimonio, in which "the singular represents the plural not because it replaces

70 PAID TO CARE

or subsumes the group but because the speaker is a distinguishable part of the whole," with the "*metaphor* of autobiography [. . .], which assumes an identity by substituting one (superior) signifier for another (I for we, leader for follower)." Her description of the metonymical relationships, or "lateral identifications" (108), characteristic of testimonial narratives sheds light on the processes at work in Carvalho's text— specifically, how Carvalho endeavors to act as a subject through whom various domestic workers' voices can be filtered.

A similar effect is achieved by the form of *Se necesita muchacha*, which pieces together a collage of the experiences of workers involved with the Cusco Union, many of whom also refer to each other's stories. The testimonio is, therefore, an ideal vehicle through which people can develop and articulate their unionized identities. It is no coincidence that the testimonios composing the second half of *Se necesita muchacha*, whose subjects have already become deeply committed to the union, both reveal a collective consciousness and offer broad theoretical insights into paid domestic work and into the status of domestic workers, much like Gutiérrez's and Carvalho's discourses.[31] Various testimonios in *Se necesita muchacha* acknowledge that the subjects' confidence, class consciousness, and critical thinking have improved as a result of their involvement with the Cusco Union. In the testimonio of Tiburcia, a woman who worked without pay for two years, she states that it is very difficult to come to consciousness on one's own, without the organization's support (Gutiérrez 1983, 265).

It is essential to appreciate the testimonio's potential for the enunciation of a collective self, which can help its subjects to move beyond "the often helpless solitude that has plagued Western women even more than men since the rise of capitalism," as Sommer argues (1988, 110). In a testimonio in *Brazilian Women Speak* (Patai 1993, 198–201), the employer Marta identifies the roots of various conflicts that she has had with domestic workers in her sense that her husband has utterly abandoned her to face all domestic tasks, administration, and childcare on her own. Live-in domestic workers, on the other hand, often suffer isolation in bourgeois homes and alienation from their own class; hence, the *collective* elements of these testimonios' narratives or structures are particularly significant and potentially subversive. Their form also resonates with the impact of the influencer and rapper Preta-Rara's (2016) "Eu empregada doméstica" Facebook page, which has more recently juxtaposed the *relatos* (stories) shared by hundreds of domestic workers and their friends and relatives to create a collective identity and aesthetic via a digital platform (which is discussed in more detail in chapter 4). Indeed, literary testimonios such as *Se necesita muchacha* and "Só a gente que vive é que sabe" appear to have instituted a tradition of artists and scholars in Latin America who have been collaborating with domestic workers in an attempt to ensure that the latter's voices are heard and to contest the stigma they face.

The collective, dialogical elements of *Se necesita muchacha* and "Só a gente que vive é que sabe" are crucial not only in the testimonial subjects' molding of their identities as workers with rights but also in the construction of their respective domestic workers' organizations. This distinguishes these two texts from the testimonios discussed earlier in this chapter and undeniably results from the fact that they were the product of collaborations with intellectuals and academics who had a specific agenda and were shaped by the precepts of liberation theology. A quotation from Egidia Laime, which is included as *Se necesita muchacha*'s epigraph, alludes to the way in which both the union and its related testimonial narratives can be viewed as "a tactic by means of which people engage in the process of self-constitution and survival" (Yúdice 1991, 19). Laime describes the union as having been born out of the tears of domestic workers and states,

> Aún si desaparecen las dirigentes, siempre se levantarán otras compañeras porque el Sindicato no puede desaparecer. [. . .] Para cambiar esta sociedad, para hacer una nueva vida, no es facilito conseguir de la noche a la mañana, *es como un parto que damos para que nazca un nuevo hombre, con sangre, con dolor.* (Gutiérrez 1983, 88 [my emphasis])

> Even if its leaders disappear, other colleagues will always step up because the Union cannot disappear. [. . .] Changing this society, making a new life—these are not things that can be achieved overnight, *they are like the painful and bloody process of giving birth, which we must undergo so that a new man can be born.*

Her comment associates the establishment and consolidation of the union with the birth of a new collective subjectivity, a process that is symbolized via the creation of the testimonial project.

Theorizing Paid Domestic Work

Notwithstanding the important insights they offer, none of the testimonial projects analyzed in this chapter can escape the complex, problematic power dynamics identified by Spivak (1988) in her work on women's subalternity.

She concludes that "the possibility of collectivity is persistently foreclosed through the manipulation of female agency" (283). She also argues that

> belief in the plausibility of global alliance politics is prevalent among women of dominant social groups interested in "international feminism" in the comprador countries. At the other end of the scale, those most separated from any possibility of an alliance [. . .] *are the females of the urban subproletariat.* In their case, the denial and withholding of consumerism and the structure of exploitation is compounded by patriarchal social relations. On the other side of the international division of labor, the subject of exploitation cannot know and speak the text of female exploitation, even if the absurdity of the nonrepresenting intellectual making space for her to speak is achieved. The woman is doubly in shadow. (288 [my emphasis])

Carvalho recounts the problems these kinds of alliances can produce in her own testimonio. She explains that, in her experience of broader women's movements in Recife, the voices of domestic workers tend to be silenced by those of middle-class women: "a classe média é quem domina. As mulheres de classe media é quem fala. Ela fala coisa da gente, mas não dá essa oportunidade da gente *falar*" (Carvalho 1982, 58 [my emphasis]; it is the middle class that dominates. Middle-class women are the ones who speak. They say things about us, but they don't give us this opportunity *to speak*). Despite Spivak's (1988, 308) conclusion that "the subaltern cannot speak" because "representation has not withered away," she insists that "the female intellectual as intellectual has a circumscribed task which she must not disown without a flourish." Spivak (1988, 294) poses the logical question: what, then, "must the elite do to watch out for the continuing construction of the subaltern?"

Having examined the mechanisms by which these testimonios were constructed, the ideologies that shaped them, and the ethical issues they inevitably raise, the remainder of this chapter will draw on the insights they nonetheless provide to elaborate a theory of domestic workers' oppression and exploitation that includes strategies for their emancipation. This section also constitutes an attempt to contribute to the dissemination of these testimonios' insights. Rather than simply using these testimonios as sources for intellectual interpretation, I incorporate the knowledge that they collectively produce into the theoretical framework deployed in this book to analyze cultural representations of paid domestic workers. By doing so, I attempt to unsettle the distinction between intellectual and domestic (or manual) labor that has contributed to the process of marginalizing and othering the latter.

Se necesita muchacha and "Só a gente que vive é que sabe" in particular represent important attempts to generate knowledge and understanding in conjunction with the workers who have recounted and analyzed their own experiences. The element of these domestic workers' testimonios that is most revolutionary, as Beverley (1999, 82) has emphasized in the case of *Me llamo Rigoberta Menchú*, is that they force us to confront the subaltern not simply "as a 'represented' victim of history, but rather as an agent of a transformative historical project that aspires to become hegemonic in its own right." As Roncador (2014, 188) has observed about Carvalho's project, it "goes beyond recovering previous historical conquests such as legal equity for maids' rights as workers in relation to other categories, to denouncing the current situation in which domestic work continues to be devalued."

Despite recognizing the important influence that intellectuals have had on her outlook, Carvalho (1982, 69) struggles with the sense that her words are sometimes taken out of context, or twisted, by them: "Isso eu acho um desrespeito e eu não aceito. E por isso, sem quase eu querer, eu não aceito muitas coisas de intelectual. [. . .] Uma coisa que eu brigo [. . .] é se mudarem o sentido do que eu digo" (I consider this disrespectful and I don't accept it. That is why, almost without wanting to, I don't accept many intellectuals' actions. [. . .] One thing that I fight against [. . .] is if they change the meaning of something I say). In her testimonio, Carvalho emerges as a counterhegemonic organic intellectual: she is not an intellectual by occupation but rather a product of her social group who can diagnose the problems associated with the live-in domestic workers' condition and who can challenge the ideological construction of these employees by the dominant class.[32] She intervenes in "mainstream cultural imaginaries of servants/domestic service" and promotes "'professional consciousness'" among her fellow domestic workers (Roncador 2014, 171).

In *Se necesita muchacha*, similar theoretical observations and ideological critiques emerge from the collective insights produced by the juxtaposition of multiple testimonios. In her introduction, Gutiérrez (1983, 94) explains that "una condición para hacer su grabación era la de no conocer los demás relatos para no dejarse influir. Es así como repeticiones o similitudes resultan ser una muestra de generalidad y diseñan una especie de prototipo de esta trabajadora" (one condition for making your recording was that it would not be possible to hear the other testimonios, in order not to be influenced by them. Consequently, repetitions or similarities are a sign of general truths and create a kind of prototype of these workers).

74 PAID TO CARE

The framework that both Carvalho (1982) and Gutiérrez (1983) develop can be used to analyze the common problems that unite the testimonios discussed in the first part of this chapter as well as the themes that recur throughout the cultural representations of paid domestic workers examined in the remainder of this book. Carvalho is participating not only in a struggle to represent domestic workers but also in a struggle over *how* they are represented. For this reason, she mentions in her testimonio a protest against a police chief who claimed during a radio broadcast that 99 percent of domestic workers were thieves (Carvalho 1982, 33). The radio station would not allow Carvalho and other protesters to challenge his declaration on the air, although one of the station's representatives acknowledged that it was false, and their attempts to publish a statement in the newspapers were largely frustrated (33). As will be discussed in chapter 4, the battle over the denigration of domestic workers, and their public image, has been revived in Brazil by the former domestic worker and current social media influencer Preta-Rara.

All the testimonios analyzed thus far have focused on the subjects' entries into domestic work at a young age, either as children or adolescents. They often lacked a (protective) father figure, or they were sent away by families who were unable or unwilling to care for them. As discussed in the introduction, placing young abandoned or orphaned children, in particular girls, into domestic service was common in various Latin American countries throughout the nineteenth century and the beginning of the twentieth (Allemandi 2015, 33; Bridikhina 2007; Guy 2002, 146–149). Poorer families viewed placement, often mistakenly, as an opportunity for their children whose education they were unable to financially support (Guy 2002, 153–154; Kuznesof 1989, 24). Even though Children's Codes, which attempted to regulate certain forms of child labor, were introduced in Brazil in 1927,[33] in Uruguay in 1934,[34] and in Peru in 1962, the testimonios discussed in this chapter attest to how common it remained for minors to be employed in domestic service throughout the mid-twentieth century and up until the 1980s.[35]

The traumatic experience of being separated from one's biological family at a young age and placed into live-in domestic service has implications for these employees' future relationships with their employers, partners, and even domestic workers' organizations. In fact, many of the problems faced by domestic workers that I discuss can ultimately be traced back to the experience of abandonment and alienation provoked by growing up with a boss who masqueraded as a surrogate parent or godparent and forced the worker to undertake domestic labor that was not properly remunerated.

In *Se necesita muchacha* (Gutiérrez 1983, 232), Fátima emphasizes in her testimonio that she was deeply impressed by the behavior and appearance of older girls who had been to Cusco and returned to her community wearing fashionable urban clothes; this in turn tempted her to enter domestic service so that she could be "elegant" like them.[36] After having lived in the city, however, many women, such as Aurelia and Yolanda, confess that they found it difficult to adapt when they returned to their rural homes (106, 153). The loss of a connection to their own communities coupled with a desire to emulate their employers' often bourgeois lifestyles can have deleterious effects, particularly in terms of individual identity development.[37] The ambivalent mixture of self-criticism and social criticism that is traceable in the discourse of the testimonios analyzed in the first part of this chapter can perhaps be attributed to the alienation engendered by this process of disconnection. Carvalho (1982, 44) suggests that, as a consequence of these issues, a live-in domestic worker has difficulty developing strength of character, and Poniatowska (1983, 52) argues that psychologically, "la sirvienta es un ser inestable, desarraigado, arrimado y criado, es decir, enseñado, amaestrado, moldeado, colado dentro de una forma que la aprisiona" (the servant is an unstable, rootless being, an outsider who is brought up, that is to say, educated, trained, formed, and shaped by a mold that imprisons her). The potential for domestic workers to identify with their employers contributes to the difficulties in organizing and unionizing, as previously discussed.

Poniatowska's (1983) analysis sheds light on the significance of the term *criada* (maid), which has often been used to refer to domestic workers in Latin America. She explains that in Mexico, this name is rooted in the fact that domestic employees have historically been raised (*criadas*) on the master's estate (52). The term *muchacha* carries similar connotations; it has been used to refer to "the maid" but can also simply mean "young girl," thereby alluding to the age and gender of the individual who has traditionally undertaken this role. However, as Roman-Morfin (2015, 80) has observed, these terms continue to be used to refer to domestic workers who are adult women. Consequently, regardless of age or maturity, these women are infantilized as subjects who elude adulthood. A domestic worker is perpetually regarded as a child, adolescent, or criada who is "under another's tutelage and continuously trained to assimilate and comply with codes of conduct enforced by their mistresses" (80). This association provides an insight into debates that were taking place within domestic workers' movements (and that continue today) relating to the contentious issue of the terminology used to refer to domestic workers, as implied by the titles *Se necesita muchacha* and *Muchachas no more* and by Carvalho's (1982, 52) testimonio.

76 PAID TO CARE

The terms used by domestic workers to address their bosses are similarly evocative where the power and emotional relationships established between them are concerned. Surrogate "familial" links, whether biological, historical, or purely symbolic, are a common feature of the testimonios in *Se necesita muchacha*. Many of the subjects reveal that they were told as children that they were being placed with their *madrina* or *padrino* (godfather); even Carvalho (1982, 10) describes her first boss as her *padrinho*. These subjects were led to expect that they were going to live with a substitute parent who would protect them, but this was often not the case, and instead, they were usually treated differently than biological children were. In *Se necesita muchacha* (Gutiérrez 1983, 132), Tomasa, whose mother took her to Puno to enter domestic service at fourteen, reveals that her first employer promised to treat her "como mi hija" (like my daughter). He did not pay her properly; instead, he presented her with clothes and told her their value (132). Various testimonios examined in this chapter attest to the fact that surrogate relationships and the workers' young age are used as an excuse to not provide proper remuneration (de Jesus 2014, 136–137; Gutiérrez 1983, 99–111). Yolanda's testimonio in *Se necesita muchacha* explains that one of her bosses, a nurse who was not her relation, insisted that she address her as *mamá* (Gutiérrez 1983, 152). In the Peruvian context, Gutiérrez explains that landowners and city dwellers, who are often mestizo, expect campesinos to address them as *papá* and *mamá*, which implies the latter's respect, submission, and even fear of the former (152). Tiburcia's testimonio corroborates this information when she states that madrinas tend to think of themselves as mothers (258). It is clear, then, that employer-employee relationships are constructed in such a way as to dominate and exploit young domestic employees to the greatest possible extent. Gutiérrez (90) clarifies that entering service as an *ahijada* (goddaughter) or a poor relative, or being officially or unofficially entrusted to a "guardian," usually means that any rights the domestic worker should be entitled to are ignored entirely.

The desire to be loved and accepted by the surrogate parent-boss leads some of the testimonial subjects to work hard in order to garner approval. In *Se necesita muchacha*, Guadalupe laments,

> La señora me decía: "Hijita, tal cosa," entonces con ganas hacía las cosas, por gusto entregaba mis fuerzas, yo decía tontamente: "Me quiere, por eso voy a hacer las cosas rapidito, más me va a querer," pero en realidad no es pues así, recién me doy cuenta. No me ha puesto al Seguro. (Gutiérrez 1983, 190)

My mistress would say to me: "Daughter, do this," so I did tasks eagerly, I put in lots of effort with pleasure, I stupidly said to myself: "She loves me, that is why I am going to do these things quickly, because she will love me more," but in reality it is not like that, I have been realizing recently. She still hasn't got me social security.

Both she and Flora conclude that it is impossible for an employer-family to truly love their domestic employees (190, 296). Poniatowska characterizes Guadalupe's story as one of *desamor* (1983, 72; a lack of love), and she sums up the situation faced by many of the women when she writes, "la patrona solo las quiere por interés y mientras trabajan para ella" (73; their mistress loves them only out of self-interest and while they work for her). The testimonio of Sara relates that she was given up by her mother when she was just a year old, and she has consequently never experienced the love of a parent or siblings. Narcisa reveals in her testimonio that she was given away by her father in exchange for money when she was just eleven (172–173, 193). The feelings of abandonment by, or distance from, biological families provoked by such situations can often be linked to a desire for love and approval that leaves domestic workers in a vulnerable position.

In some cases, the testimonial subjects' paths toward selfhood (and individuation) have been threatened by their abandonment as children and by having been raised primarily as criadas. Poniatowska (1983, 74–75) emphasizes that the importance of the testimonios collected in *Se necesita muchacha* lies in the fact that they allow this trauma to be expressed and processed. Consequently, all the testimonios examined appear to serve a cathartic function in the sense that they enable the testimonialista to construct a clear sense of self for the reader, which is then imaginarily reflected back toward the testimonialistas themselves: a process of individual subject formation is thus rehearsed. In this regard, it is telling that Conceição, whose testimonio features in *Brazilian Women Speak*, asked for the tape recording of her interview to be played back to her twice so that she could hear her own voice (Patai 1993, 208). However, Carvalho's testimonio and Gutiérrez's collection show how testimonio can permit the construction of a political, as well as an individual, consciousness. In *Se necesita muchacha*, for example, the damage wrought by parental abandonment appears to be remedied to an extent by the support network offered by the Cusco Union, which enables its members to reconstruct their identities as workers and as part of a collective. Aurora, whose testimonio is included in the second part of the collection, even views the union as serving as an alternative family unit. She states,

[N]o conozco cómo será eso de estar al lado de un papá, cómo tratan, todas esas cosas, y por eso lo he tomado al Sindicato como un padre, como una madre, como una familia, esas compañeras son mis tías, ya con eso me basto porque ahora tengo una familia. (Gutiérrez 1983, 375)

I don't know how it would be to be close to a father, how they would treat you, everything like that, and that is why I have taken the Union as a father, as a mother, as a family. These coworkers are my aunts, and that is enough for me because now I have a family.

Carvalho (1982, 48) observes that the lack of a father figure or brother creates problems for many domestic workers in their romantic relationships, in part because they often have not had the opportunity to learn at a young age how to relate to men via their male family members. On another level, she argues that prospective partners frequently assume that the absence of a male relative means that the domestic worker will be unable to protect herself. Consequently, male partners treat her like a prostitute, or make false promises regarding marriage, which represents an escape from the employer's home, in order to coerce her into a sexual relationship, only to disappear if she becomes pregnant (46). As Carvalho would anticipate, both Caraballo's and da Silva's testimonios reveal that their initial partners pressured them into sexual intimacy. Da Silva's (1983, 45) first boyfriend, Leo, purportedly refused to believe that she was sexually inexperienced and used this as his excuse for raping her. Aurelia in *Se necesita muchacha* mentions that she has an eleven-month-old daughter whose father does not support them even though he works in construction (Gutiérrez 1983, 109–110). Like da Silva (1983, 108), Aurelia states that she is resolved not to have a romantic relationship with a man again because they create too much trouble (Gutiérrez 1983, 110).

Some of the testimonios also reveal the frequency with which workers are emotionally manipulated and sexually harassed or abused by male employers (da Silva 1983, 20–21, 34–35, 38). One of the most shocking instances can be found in Petronila's testimonio in *Se necesita muchacha*. She was tricked into working for and supporting a man who pretended to be a campesino named Porfirio, but he was actually a university student, Aníbal, from a landowning family (Gutiérrez 1983, 139–144). Petronila became pregnant with his child, and he promised to marry her, but she later discovered that he and his brothers habitually deceived women, got them pregnant, and then claimed custody of the baby to be raised as a domestic worker (*un empleadito*) (142–143). Petronila refused to give up her son and was forced to go through various court proceedings as a result (146). Petronila reveals that many bosses encourage their sons to get their domestic employees pregnant so that they can use the pregnancy as an excuse to not pay her properly: the bosses realize that if the worker has a baby, she will be less inclined to leave their employ because she does not want to risk separation from her child (148). Carvalho (1982) links the nature of these relationships to live-in domestic workers' isolation and marginalization within their employers' households, which can lead to abuse or to the need to experience some form of love and affection:

> Quando a menina, por exemplo, se perde, na maneira de dizer, com o rico, pelo menos ela sabia que aquele rico não ia casar com ela. É mais um carinho e também—quem é que não entende?—é uma valorização. É negativo, mas quando a menina se enamora com um rapaz rico, ela acha que está sendo valorizada diante das outras colegas, de tudo. (46)

> When a girl, for example, gives herself, as they say, to a wealthy man, at least she is aware that he is not going to marry her. It represents a bit of affection and also a valorization—who doesn't understand that? It is not a good thing, but when a girl falls in love with a rich man, she feels that she is being valued in front of her friends, in front of everyone.

In sum, a lack of love and the absence of protective male role models, who are nonetheless frequently revered in the subjects' memories (Caraballo 1987, 119; da Silva 1983, 13; de Jesus 2014, 124), leave the testimonio subjects in a vulnerable position and encourage them to place great importance on men's approval.

Live-in versus Live-out Domestic Work

The issue of domestic workers' sexual abuse by their bosses (or their bosses' sons) is one of several factors that lead the Cusco Union to advise its members that it is generally preferable to seek live-out (*cama afuera*) rather than live-in (*cama adentro*) employment (Gutiérrez 1983, 111). In a footnote, Gutiérrez (111) suggests that by sharing accommodations with other workers instead, an employee can avoid a situation in which her boss determines her working conditions, exerts an influence over her personal life, and justifies isolating her by invoking moral concerns, thereby ensuring that the employee is always at their disposal. Both Carvalho (1982, 29) and Gutiérrez (1983, 121) emphasize that it is a frequent occurrence for a live-in worker to enter a household on the premise that she will be employed to fill a specific role, for example as a nanny, when she is really expected to *hacer de todo* (take care of everything), including the cleaning, cooking, and laundry. Gutiérrez (121) adds that, for this reason, the union recommends that its members do not accept verbal agreements and instead should request a written contract from their employer that details the responsibilities of their role.

An analysis of these testimonios supports Gutiérrez's (1983, 16) insight that "live-in domestic workers suffer the greatest exploitation and marginalization." Carvalho (1982, 16) defends this view by describing the experience of living in a house "que tem tudo, que você arruma [. . .], mas que você não tem acesso àquela casa. Então, para mim, eu sou marginal naquela casa" (that has everything, that you clean [. . .], but it is not your house. This, for me, means that I am marginalized in that home). If the worker loses her job, then she also becomes homeless; thus, she may be reluctant or unable to leave an abusive situation, which compounds her position of vulnerability. When domestic workers do leave, they often encounter further mistreatment from other families and are forced to relocate again. The testimonios analyzed are united by their subjects' experiences of hypermobility because they move rapidly from one workplace to another. Caraballo (1987, 36) encapsulates this situation when she complains that "a lo último yo parecía uno de esos bultos de encomienda: iba y venía" (in the end I seemed like a parcel being sent here and there). De Jesus (2014, 190) similarly confesses that "eu tinha a impressão de ser uma moeda circulante" (I felt like a piece of currency in circulation).

As Carvalho (1982, 34) suggests, live-in domestic employees are often forced to sacrifice their right to exist as independent individuals with personal lives because their homes are also their workplaces. To illustrate her argument, she notes that many young domestic workers want to wear shorts when it is hot outside, but their bosses are often reluctant to permit it so that the workers do not attract unwanted attention from their husbands (34). Because the domestic workers live where they work, live-in employees may therefore have limited control over the clothes they wear, even when they are not working, which can lead to the feeling that "a gente não é dona da vida da gente" (26; we are not in charge of our own lives).

This position of marginality can lead to the domestic worker's dehumanization by others, even by her employer-family. Carvalho (1982, 21) observes that employers often provide food and shelter, but they do not recognize that the worker "também é uma pessoa, que ela tem necessidade de estudar, de ir a um cinema, de ir numa festa" (is also a person, that she needs to study, to go to the cinema, to go to a party). This is a situation that can compromise live-in domestic workers' abilities to form romantic relationships and families of their own. As Carvalho (26) argues, occupying a position of permanent subservience to employer-families interferes with the worker's freedom to make her own plans and arrangements. She concludes that "enquanto a doméstica for dentro de casa, ela será sempre escrava" (18; while the domestic worker remains within the employer's household, she will always be a slave). By contrast, hourly paid diaristas enjoy greater freedom because they go to their bosses' homes only to work and do not live there (37).

It is the proximity to one's employer that Carvalho identifies as a unique feature of paid domestic labor and, in particular, of live-in domestic work. She repeatedly uses her testimonio to stress the exceptionality of this form of employment vis-à-vis other kinds of jobs:

> O trabalho doméstico, ele é muito diferente dos outros. Porque nesse trabalho caseiro, de casa, o relacionamento com a patroa tanto é mais de choque como também pode ser assim mais na base de amiga. Na fábrica você nunca vai se relacionar com o patrão; você vai com chefe; nunca é com patrão. E a gente é direta com patrão e com patroa. Então se da mais essa afetividade, e se dá também o choque. (Carvalho 1982, 31)

> Domestic work is very different from other kinds of work. Because in this type of work, within the home, the relationship with your mistress is as much one of clashes as it can also be of friendship. At a factory you will never have a close relationship with the boss; you have a manager, you never have a master. And we [domestic workers] are direct with the master and the mistress. So this produces more of an emotional relationship, but it can also create a clash.

The testimonios suggest that the emotional bonds that develop between nannies or domestic workers and their employers' children can be particularly strong, and thus it causes distress when these ties are broken. Da Silva (1983, 34), for instance, struggled to leave a job where she was being harassed by her boss because she was so emotionally attached to his young daughter. De Jesus (2014, 190) vowed to never work as a nanny again after her experience caring for her boss's sick child "porque na convivência aprendemos a amar as crianças" (because we learn to love children when we live with them).

Their testimonios demonstrate the intersectional nature of the prejudice that domestic workers frequently face. The imbrication of gendered and racial violence is made clear by the fact that several of the subjects interviewed in *Se necesita muchacha* had their hair forcibly cut off by their bosses. Two of them stated that their bosses did so because they thought the workers were spending too long combing their hair (Gutiérrez 1983, 205, 220, 345, 367). This constitutes both a physical and symbolic act of violence that targets the tradition among Indigenous women of wearing their hair long or plaited. It also represents a threat to a visible sign of their femininity. Da Silva relates that her hair was also cut off by one of her employers out of jealousy (1983, 22–23), which demonstrates that this is a recurrent form of aggression, which also occurs in the Brazilian context. In a more recent testimonio shared on Preta-Rara's (2016) Facebook page "Eu empregada doméstica," the anonymous author, who recounts her aunt's experience of paid domestic work, relates that the latter was punished for her beauty by having her hair cut off by her employer against her will; she was also forbidden from using accessories and was addressed using masculine pronouns.

The attempt to impose both a gendered and racialized hierarchy of attractiveness is particularly evident in the testimonios shared in *Se necesita muchacha*. Some of the subjects have been treated as though they are dirty, a quality that is associated with their indigeneity; many have been verbally abused with insults such as *cochina* (dirty pig) or *chola* and *india*, which are derogatory terms for an Indigenous person (Gutiérrez 1983, 147, 234, 236, 260, 365). However, it is clear that some of their bosses are also of Indigenous descent and are, consequently, similar in appearance to the domestic worker (204). Racially discriminating against workers appears to be a way for employers to attempt to distinguish themselves from the former.[38] A process of othering and of abjection can be seen as employers both differentiate themselves from the employee and associate her with dirt, disgust, and even bestial or inhuman qualities. In *Diário de Bitita*, de Jesus (2014, 125) describes being taunted as a child by her classmates, who called her *negrinha feia* (ugly little Black girl). She also mentions that one employer-family would not let the priest who wrongly accused her of theft apologize to her because they claimed that "o negro tem a mentalidade de animal. A prova é visível, eles só sabem dançar e beber pinga" (146; Black people have an animal's mentality. The proof is clear: they only know how to dance and drink alcohol).

Across the body of testimonios, there is a prodigious number of references to domestic workers being treated either similarly to or worse than animals; these are provoked both by the poor quality of the food they are offered and by how hard they are expected to work (Gutiérrez 1983, 8, 107–108, 254, 280, 287, 347–349, 385–386, 388; Carvalho 1982, 18, 57). Like some of the workers in *Se necesita muchacha*, Carvalho (1982, 18) observes that many employers appreciate their pet dogs more than domestic employees because, she says, "aquele cachorro é uma coisa de estimação e a gente não é uma coisa de estimação; a gente é trabalho" (the dog is a thing of value and we are not valued; we are labor). Occasionally the testimonial subject's own self-denigrating language sets up a dichotomy between animality and humanity when describing their behavior or status. Da Silva (1983, 25) declares that when she was a child, "eu era um animalzinho sem valor" (I was a worthless little animal), but her subsequent unofficial and transitory adoption by a wealthy family enabled her to become "human." Her declaration parallels one made by Zeli de Oliveira Barbosa (1993) in her testimonio *Ilhota*. Barbosa, who is a live-out domestic worker, contrasts her current neighborhood with the favela where she used to reside, which she describes as a *submundo* (underworld). She concludes that since she has moved, she no longer needs to feel embarrassed about her area, which is "[uma] zona de *pessoas*, na maioria proprietárias" (67 [my emphasis]; [a] neighborhood occupied by decent *people*, most of whom are homeowners).

Part of the explanation for this problematic comparison of the domestic worker's condition to that of an animal is based on the rural origins of most workers. The historical period on which their testimonios reflect, the mid-twentieth century, was characterized by a high level of rural-to-urban migration in Latin America, a fact to which the subjects' experiences attest. Many of them describe arriving in an unknown city where they are, existentially if not practically, disoriented, overwhelmed, and homeless. As they wander through the city, their confusion and displacement are visible. Thus, they become strongly symbolically associated, and associate themselves, with the countryside, wildness, and even barbarity. The following quotation from Egidia Laime inserted in *Se necesita muchacha* prior to Gutiérrez's introduction therefore appears even more astute because she inverts the typical analogy between poor, rural domestic workers and animals by describing rich people thus:

La gente no piensa cómo es la sociedad, vive como un animal, sólo piensa en su barriga. Se crece, se cruza, tiene su cría; cuando la cría es grande, se olvida. Una muerte que viene sin que haya cambiado nada para la sociedad. La muerte del rico es como la muerte del chancho, en sus propias personas pensaron, en llenar su barriga. (Gutiérrez 1983, 87)

People do not think about the state of society, they live like animals, only thinking of their stomachs. They grow up, meet each other, have their children; when their children grow up, they forget them. Their death comes without them having changed anything in society. A rich man's death is like the death of a pig, they have thought only of themselves, of filling their stomachs.

The bestialization of domestic workers and their labor relationships is a trope that recurs throughout the works analyzed in this book. It is a metaphor used to shed light on the dehumanization and devaluation of domestic employees and their labor. The abjection of "women's work" is a consequence of its status as frequently dirty and grotesque from a bourgeois perspective. The cultural representations analyzed in this book reveal the wear and tear enacted upon the female body, which is simultaneously demanded and concealed by late capitalism; they thus foreground the unsettling foundations on which the urban, bourgeois home has been built.

The invisibilization and dehumanization of domestic employees is reinforced by a belief that their work is materially and economically unproductive, as discussed in the introduction. This is a view that Poniatowska parodies when she ironically assumes the voice of a housewife who complains that she has not been able to go to the beauty salon for a manicure because her maid has abandoned her (Gutiérrez 1983, 14). As Roman-Morfin (2015, 82) explains, domestic workers are often seen as a commodity or a luxury item that merely buys housewives leisure time and comfort. This perspective is contested by Gutiérrez (1983, 52, 91) and Carvalho (1982, 43), who both point out the critical roles that domestic workers play in the reproduction of domestic and social life and sometimes in class struggle. Gutiérrez (1983, 91) also observes that domestic workers represent huge savings for the state in terms of public services such as nurseries, laundrettes, and canteens.

Cooking is a domestic occupation that appears to be more highly valued than others throughout the body of testimonios. Various workers appreciate the opportunity to learn how to cook because cooking is viewed as a creative, specialized skill and often attracts better pay than other types of domestic work; cooking enables some workers to develop a greater sense of pride in their employment (Caraballo 1987, 52–53; Carvalho 1982, 19; de Jesus 2014, 199–200; Gutiérrez 1983, 166). The higher valuation may also be a consequence of the fact that cooking creates a more tangible, finished *product* than does cleaning or childcare, which illustrates the impossibility of escaping hegemonic, economic modes of thought, even in the discourse of workers who are radicalized.

Conclusion

The key theme of paid and unpaid domestic work reverberates throughout Latin American women's testimonios, including in the foundational examples of the genre by Domitila Barrios de Chúngara and Rigoberta Menchú. Carvalho's (1982) "Só a gente que vive é que sabe" and Gutiérrez's (1983) *Se necesita muchacha* offer some of the earliest insights provided by domestic workers into their labor associations and processes of unionization.

All the testimonios I have discussed indicate their subjects' growing self-awareness or coming-to-consciousness. However, the testimonios by Caraballo (1987) and da Silva (1983) are marked by a sense of victimhood that leads to a desire for solidarity with others, which is nonetheless ineffectively channeled. Their narratives are shaped by a facet of Catholic ideology that views life as suffering and that focuses on a hope for individual redemption. An analysis of da Silva's relationship to her boss and the editor of her testimonio, Ivna Duvivier, demonstrates how such a connection can culminate in a desire for paternalism that reinforces class-based, postcolonial hierarchies. De Jesus's (2014) *Diário de Bitita* displays commonalities with Caraballo's and da Silva's testimonios, but the author's awareness of the class-, race-, and gender-based discrimination that affects members of the Afro-Brazilian community endows her text, at times, with the capacity to undertake a structural and intersectional critique.

By contrast, the testimonios examined in the second part of this chapter, "Só a gente que vive é que sabe" and *Se necesita muchacha*, attest to the existence of a clear class based identity and political consciousness among domestic workers involved in the association-based, or unionized, struggle for rights in Brazil and Peru in the 1970s and 1980s. Their testimonial forms permit the evocation of collective identities either because testimonio can function metonymically with the testimonialista telling her story with the objective of shedding light on experiences of paid domestic work that are shared by so many others, or because they juxtapose the stories of multiple workers whose histories intersect and resonate with one another's. These texts also evidence the impact of Catholic liberation theology and Marxist thought on nascent domestic workers' associations in Latin America in the 1970s and 1980s, an influence that can also be traced back to the editors or scribes who helped to organize and publish the texts.

Nevertheless, the testimonios examined here, even those analyzed in the second part of the chapter, do not abrogate the ethical concerns that have plagued these kinds of projects. This includes the issue of privileged, European descendant, academic mediators who risk othering or speaking for subaltern subjects. Certain elements of Ana Gutiérrez's *Se necesita muchacha* show that the book presages the move toward the explicit inclusion and recognition of the mediator's outlook and positionality, however, which has become characteristic of contemporary testimonios.

The final section of this chapter draws on the knowledge collectively generated by the testimonios regarding the isolation of live-in domestic workers; the challenges of unionizing employees who identify strongly with their employers or who identify as a surrogate member of their employer-family; the dehumanization of paid domestic workers as a consequence of their commodification by bosses and of the perception that they do not have the right to an independent family or to a social or romantic life; the bestialization of domestic workers, which is in turn a corollary of their dehumanization; and the mistaken belief that domestic work is not economically productive. These testimonial insights constitute a theory of paid domestic work that feeds into the analysis undertaken in chapters 2, 3, and 4. Ultimately, the testimonios represent an underused resource in the study of domestic workers' struggles, unionization, and representation, and they provide a crucial framework for approaching and addressing issues that are specific to paid domestic work, including for reflecting on recent battles over domestic workers' public portrayals.

CHAPTER 2

Labors of Love?

Live-in Domestic Workers in Latin American Fiction Film

IN THIS CHAPTER, I examine the wave of Latin American fiction films released since the turn of the millennium that feature paid domestic workers in key roles.[1] The labor relationships that the films portray serve as microcosms of broader social tensions and for class and gender relations, which can nonetheless be screened by employing a small cast and filming primarily in a single cinematic location: a reconstructed home.[2] I argue that this new direction in Latin American filmmaking is the product of changing attitudes toward the ethics of hiring a live-in domestic worker, particularly among sectors of the Left. In certain cases, these films have constituted clear political interventions at moments of class conflict or have even formed part of campaigns to improve domestic workers' legal rights. Some of the films were inspired by their directors' close relationships to their own paid domestic employees or former nannies, including all those that are the focus of this chapter: *La nana* (Silva, 2009; *The Maid*), *Casa grande* (Barbosa, 2014; The master's house), *Que horas ela volta?* (Muylaert, 2015; *The Second Mother*), and *Roma* (Cuarón, 2018). These films confirm Vázquez Vázquez's (2019, 31–46) view that cinematic portrayals of paid domestic workers in Latin America are still framed by critical upper- or middle-class perspectives rather than by the viewpoints of the domestic employees themselves, which is a consequence of the financial and techno-logical resources and cultural contacts required to produce feature-length films. The vogue for screening the relationship between employers and domestic or childcare workers can also be linked to the emergence of vari-ous Latin American women filmmakers in recent years (Marsh 2011, 258), which is unsurprising given that decisions about hiring domestic help have tended to be made by women.

The films that are the focus of this chapter represent their directors' attempts to address a sense of emotional indebtedness to the domestic workers whose labor, although it was remunerated, is difficult to fully recompense because of the personal sacrifices the employees were often forced to make in their own lives. Consequently, my analysis draws on notions of the gift economy and of affective labor, which both emphasize the difficulty of distinguishing between productive and reproductive and between paid and unpaid forms of work. The filmmakers' own emotional attachments to the paid domestic workers who helped to raise them culminate in the creation of ambivalent films that not only constitute homages to these employees but also risk reinforcing foundational myths according to which the forging of the modern mestizo (mixed-race) nation-state relies on the subjugation of the racial and gender Other (the "live-in maid" or "second mother"). On the one hand, the films deploy bestial imagery to criticize the dehumanization and commodification that the concept of a live-in domestic worker entails, but the films also fall back on a framework of modern Western individualistic feminism, which prevents the productions from resolving or, in some cases, from fully addressing the fact that middle- and upper-class women's independence has been contingent on the emotional and labor exploitation of lower-class, darker-skinned women. Before embarking on this analysis, I will begin by explaining the plots of *Que horas ela volta?*, *Casa grande*, *La nana*, and *Roma* and by briefly examining the films' sociopolitical contexts.

Que horas ela volta?

The Brazilian film *Que horas ela volta?* was released in August of 2015 and has received extensive critical and media attention; it was chosen as the country's nomination for the best foreign-language film category at the 2016 Oscars, but it was not shortlisted. Nonetheless, it had a notable impact abroad, with the well-known Brazilian TV personality Regina Casé (who plays live-in domestic worker Val) and Camila Márdila (who plays Val's daughter Jéssica) sharing the Sundance Film Festival's Best Actress Award. Distribution rights for the production were sold in more than twenty-two countries. In France alone, the film was screened in 122 cinemas, nearly equaling the box-office success of the 2002 Brazilian crime drama *Cidade de Deus* (*City of God*), which was directed by Fernando Meirelles and Kátia Lund (Vázquez Vázquez 2019, 37). However, the director of *Que horas ela volta?*, Anna Muylaert, expressed frustration over her film's relatively limited audience in Brazil by commenting on the irony of the film's difficulty in reaching deprived communities given its narrative that reflects on social inequality and boss-worker relations (Merten and Leal 2015).[3]

The personality of the film's protagonist, Val, was inspired by Muylaert's own childhood nanny, with whom the director was very close (Balloussier and Genestreti 2015). Muylaert has commented on the deep discomfort she experienced as a child when she was asked to draw her family and did not know whether to include her nanny in the image or not (Balloussier and Genestreti 2015).

The film transpires mostly in an upper-class home in the affluent Morumbi district of São Paulo where Val's employers reside. Val has worked for her bosses, Carlos and Bárbara, for the last thirteen years after moving to São Paulo from Pernambuco, in the Brazilian Northeast, where she left her young daughter Jéssica in the care of a woman named Sandra. She sends part of her wage back to Sandra in order to support her daughter. The film opens with an analeptic sequence that shows Val playing with her employers' young son, Fabinho, by the pool in their São Paulo home. Val calls Sandra because she wishes to talk to Jéssica, who is reluctant to come to the phone. The film then flashes forward several years to its own present day, and it quickly becomes clear that Val's propensity for maternal tenderness has been transferred from her own biological daughter to the now adolescent Fabinho. In contrast to her strong connection with Fabinho, her relationship with Jéssica has grown distant because of a conflict with Jéssica's father. Val is therefore surprised when she receives a call from Jéssica, who asks if she can come to São Paulo and stay with her so she can take the Vestibular, the competitive entrance exam that determines the distribution of places at Brazil's public universities. The mother and daughter have not seen each other for ten years. Jéssica's arrival at Carlos and Bárbara's house and her determination to study architecture at the prestigious Universidade de São Paulo (USP) send shockwaves throughout the household. Jéssica does not conceal her disapproval that Val lives with her bosses. Ultimately, Jéssica's inability to accept her mother's and her own lesser status (in the eyes of Val's employers) culminates in Bárbara's demand that Jéssica leave their home. Both Jéssica's candor and her success with the Vestibular, particularly compared to Fabinho's performance, transform Val's resigned attitude to her circumstances. She quits her job and moves in with her daughter, who has rented her own apartment in another neighborhood.

The inspiration behind this narrative of reunion and emotional reconciliation is also personal. Muylaert has revealed that the film is the story of Edna Silva, whom the director employed as a nanny to her own son, Joaquim (Pessoa 2015). This aligns the director's position with that of the employer, which lends weight to the argument that despite the film's attempts to portray Val's viewpoint as a domestic worker, Muylaert's film can be classified as an instance of *cine clasemediero* (Vázquez Vázquez 2019, 40; middle-class cinema). Edna Silva, who is originally from Bahia, met her mother (who was also a domestic worker) only when she was seventeen years old because her father had prohibited their contact. The film's final sequence, which sees Val join Jéssica in her new apartment, was recorded in Edna Silva's home in Campo Limpo, São Paulo (Pessoa 2015). The area presents a visible contrast to Bárbara and Carlos's prosperous Morumbi neighborhood.

Que horas ela volta? has been interpreted by critics as an allegory that explores the divisions in Brazilian society that became evident in the lead-up to and during the 2014 elections, which resulted in the reelection of the PT candidate, Dilma Rousseff, as president. Tensions continued throughout the anti-government protests that took place in the aftermath of the elections and remained until Rousseff's impeachment in August 2016 (Paulino and Janoni 2015). In the film, Jéssica's aspiration to attend USP indicates that she functions as a metonym of the section of the working class that was empowered by the reforms enacted by the PT governments, including during the mandates of President Luiz Inácio Lula da Silva between 2003 and 2010. Under Rousseff's subsequent PT administration, the conflict between those in favor of the social inclusion characteristic of the Lula era and those from an opposing conservative elite reached its zenith, as already discussed in the introduction (Paulino and Janoni 2015). The film channels this social discord through the repeated clashes that take place between Jéssica and Bárbara.

The relationship between employers, domestic workers, and the latter's children has repeatedly been invoked as a symbol for (a lack of) social mobility by those on the Brazilian Left during periods of social tension. At an April 6, 2018, protest against President Lula's controversial imprisonment, which was the result of a corruption conviction that was subsequently annulled, an Afro-Brazilian woman named Nathalia Balbino was photographed holding up a sign stating, "Lula: condenado por colocar a filha da doméstica na faculdade" (Pitasse 2018; Lula: condemned for allowing the maid's daughter to go to university). The image later circulated on social media. In a demonstration on May 15, 2019, against funding cuts to public universities (during President Jair Bolsonaro's administration), the rapper and social media influencer Preta-Rara marched with a sign that said "O governo treme quando o filho da empregada estuda com o filho dele" (The government trembles when the maid's child studies alongside his own). She later shared a photograph of herself holding the placard on her "Eu empregada doméstica" Facebook page, which she started in 2016.

Casa grande

The fraught sociopolitical context to which *Que horas ela volta?* makes veiled reference contributes to the film's similarities to Fellipe Barbosa's *Casa grande*, including in terms of plot development, which certain critics have noted (Souto 2018, 179; Oricchio 2015; Randall 2018b, 11). The film focuses on seventeen-year-old Jean as he (like Fabinho) prepares to take Brazil's competitive university entrance exams and struggles to liberate himself from his controlling upper-class parents, Hugo and Sônia. He lives with them and his sister in an exclusive area of Rio de Janeiro. While Hugo struggles to conceal the fact that he has gambled away the family's fortune, Jean concentrates his efforts on wooing the opposite sex. When his parents are forced to fire their chauffeur, Severino, Jean begins to travel by bus to his renowned private school, São Bento. On the way home, he meets Luiza, a mixed-race eighteen-year-old woman[4] who attends a state school, is also preparing to take the Vestibular, and whose family lives next to Rio de Janeiro's best-known favela, Rocinha. The pair quickly begin a romantic relationship.

Casa grande's exploration of Hugo's financial downfall could support an interpretation of the film as one that sympathizes with a decadent privileged class or as one that yearns nostalgically for a time when the power of this class was more firmly entrenched. The film's principal intertext is Gilberto Freyre's (2003) *Casa grande & senzala* (*The Masters and the Slaves*), which was first published in 1933. The book is a notorious study of the domestic relationships that developed between landowners and enslaved people on Brazil's sugar plantations between the sixteenth and nineteenth centuries. In the film, both the family's surname, Cavalcanti—which belonged to a well-known family of colonial landowners mentioned by Freyre (404–405, 427)[5]—and the mother's strong connection to French culture function as clear symbols of the family's membership in the Brazilian elite. However, various elements of the film's plot, in particular Jean's adolescent troubles, which reflect his father's crisis of upper-class masculinity, enable the movie to enact an explicit sociopolitical critique of the continuation of patriarchal, colonial-style relationships in Brazil today (Randall 2018b, 113–115). Jean's teenage propensity for self-deception and deceit echoes his father's implied involvement in corruption, which is associated with real financial institutions and wealthy individuals named in the film.

Casa grande's temporal setting in 2012 and 2013 is revealed by its explicit references to legal measures and social policies introduced by Brazil's PT government. These references allude both to the film's critique of class and race relations in Brazil and to a concern for the socioeconomic and corruption-related crises that the country faces. Its narrative is framed by two crucial public events. The first is the approval of the Lei de Cotas (Quota Law) by Brazil's Supreme Court in August 2012. The law obliges the country's public universities to reserve a proportion of places for non-White, low-income, and state-school-educated students (people like Luiza in the film) in order to ensure that a greater number of disadvantaged people can access higher education and are able to compete with privately educated students who have often been better prepared to take the Vestibular.[6] Shortly after the film's opening, Jean's teacher initiates a classroom debate to canvass the São Bento students' opinions about the constitutionality of the quota system, which has just been approved. The film concludes almost a year later, in 2013, and a second public event is revealed by a shot of Hugo reading a newspaper article entitled "Ações da OGX, de Eike Batista, vivem pior momento na Bolsa" (Eike Batista's OGX posts record plunge [in share price]). Eike Batista is a well-known Brazilian business magnate; in 2012 he was the richest individual in the country because of his oil and gas company, OGX. By July 2013, his wealth had plunged from $30 billion to $200 million (Spinetto et al. 2013). In the film, Batista's fortunes are tied to those of Jean's father, Hugo, who (it is implied) has invested a large amount of his and his friend's money in Batista's companies.[7] Hugo's ties to Brazil's corrupt financial elite can be inferred not only from his choice to buy shares in Batista's company but also from his links to Daniel Dantas. Dantas, one of Brazil's most prominent bankers, founded the Opportunity financial group. In December 2008, he was convicted of attempting to bribe a police officer in order to avoid other charges and was sentenced to ten years in prison (*The Economist* 2008).[8] In *Casa grande*, while on the phone to a headhunter, Hugo declines to send his résumé to Dantas's company because he worked there before and did not like Daniel, which may imply Hugo's history of involvement in corrupt practices and a strong desire to avoid further association with Dantas's name.

The film's mise-en-scène and production of affect are particularly effective in underscoring the importance of Jean's emotional connections with his family's domestic employees: the driver, Severino; the live-in housekeeper, Rita; and the cook and cleaner, Noêmia. In particular, Severino is a surrogate father figure for Jean after the total breakdown of Jean's relationship with Hugo. Jean is distraught when he discovers that his parents have fired the driver and have lied to him about it by suggesting that Severino had gone on holiday to visit his son. Jean also turns to both Severino and Rita for romantic advice and guidance. He frequently makes clandestine nighttime visits to Rita's apartment, which is located next to the main family home and separated from it by a gate. The position of her dwelling simplistically recalls the spatial relationship, as Freyre describes it in his book, between the master's house and the slave quarters, which were separate from, but on the same plot of land as, the former. The alliances Jean makes with the workers, however, are undermined by the film's sexual politics, which are foregrounded by the spectral repetition of a postcolonial domestic relationship at the film's close.

Casa grande proved a success among national audiences, perhaps because it combines a social conscience that can satisfy bourgeois spectators with a predictably popular coming-of-age narrative formula focusing on adolescent first love and sexual initiation. The film scooped the only prize based on audience votes at the 2014 Rio International Film Festival. Fellipe Barbosa has stated on various occasions that the film is semiautobiographical and has admitted that when he was a teenager, "tinha 'vergonha de ser rico'" (Almeida 2015; he was "ashamed of being rich"). The film represents his attempt to deal with the distress he felt when his own family concealed their financial crisis from him after he had left home (Merten 2015). Prior to that, Fellipe Barbosa, like the character Jean, lived with his parents in a house in Barra da Tijuca, an affluent Rio de Janeiro neighborhood, and studied at São Bento; he was also driven to school by either his father or the family's chauffeur (Almeida 2015). He stated that he wanted *Casa grande* to dramatize the transformation of domestic employer-employee relationships that has taken place in Brazil in recent years (Almeida 2015). One of the dilemmas that Hugo and Sônia face in the film is how to respond to Severino's decision to sue them for unfair dismissal, which Hugo chooses not to appeal because "nenhum patrão ganha processo trabalhista nesse país" (no boss can win a labor lawsuit in this country).

La nana

Sebastián Silva's Chilean film *La nana* also displays notable parallels with *Que horas ela volta?* and *Casa grande*, despite its distinct national context and earlier release in 2009. The film's protagonist, a live-in domestic employee named Raquel, has worked for her employers, Pilar and Mundo, for over twenty years. They reside in an affluent household in Santiago de Chile. Raquel has been intimately involved in the upbringing of Pilar and Mundo's children, and she dotes on their adolescent son, Lucas, but clashes with their older daughter, Camila. As with Val in *Que horas ela volta?*, Raquel's length of time serving her employers appears to have contributed to her estrangement from her own biological family. She has brief, awkward phone calls with her mother, but none of her relatives are ever seen in the film. The film hints that Raquel's total reliance on her employer-family, from a relatively young age, has left her in a state of arrested development.

Raquel's characterization as a working-class woman who appears to have been abandoned by her own biological relatives to enter service for a surrogate family at a young age recalls Gabriel Salazar's (2006) well-known investigation into the prevalence of illegitimate and orphan children in nineteenth-century Chile, a condition that he terms *huachismo*. Salazar (304–314) argues that those children were often left by their impoverished mothers at charitable institutions or given to a favorite *patrón* or *patrona* (boss) to be used as a servant. He discusses the children's sense of neglect by *madres ajenas* (distant mothers) who were often themselves *sirvientas puertas adentro* (live-in maids) and thus "belonged" to a different family (336). While *La nana* intimates that similar circumstances have contributed to Raquel's alienation from her mother, although the viewer is never given enough information to ascertain it for certain, Salazar's description clearly synthesizes Jéssica's feelings about her relationship with Val and Val's proximity to her employer-family in *Que horas ela volta?*, even though this film pertains to a Brazilian rather than a Chilean context. Salazar (2006, 406–415) concludes that *huachismo* "constituyó el origen histórico de la conciencia proletaria en Chile, [. . .] la primera y más firme piedra de la identidad popular" (constituted the historical origin of working-class consciousness in Chile, [. . .] the first and strongest foundation of popular identity). Notably, he adds that many of the mothers who gave birth to illegitimate children in the nineteenth century would have preferred that they die (314). This element of his argument is also pertinent to an analysis of *Roma*'s narrative, as discussed later.

In *La nana*, Raquel's sense of identity loss culminates in her psychological breakdown, which manifests as terrible headaches. To lessen her workload, her boss, Pilar, decides to hire a second live-in domestic worker, an action that Raquel views as a threat to her own role and status in the household. She rebels against the first two prospective recruits by locking them out of the house; however, the third new employee, Lucy, manages to disarm Raquel by empathizing with and befriending her. The friendship prompts Raquel's recovery and transformation into a happier and more independent individual.

Sebastián Silva filmed *La nana* in his childhood home and has stated that the genesis of the screenplay was his experience growing up with domestic workers (Movieweb 2010). He has clarified that Raquel's and Lucy's friendship was inspired by a real relationship that developed between two domestic workers when the director was no longer living at the home (Movieweb 2010). Like Alfonso Cuarón's *Roma*, the film is explicitly dedicated to two of his family's former employees. The relative lack of biographical detail provided about Raquel's character in *La nana*, however, betrays the fact that the film was made from Sebastián Silva's perspective. He has admitted that, while growing up, he was close to his family's *nanas* but knew little of their lives and histories outside of his household (Movieweb 2010). In this sense, the intimacy and distance characteristic of relationships between employers and domestic employees, which Deborah Shaw has noted (2017, 124), can be traced in the directorial perspectives that shape these productions.

Roma

Of all the films discussed in this chapter, Alfonso Cuarón's *Roma* (2018) best illustrates the fact that these four productions are the result of changing cultural attitudes toward paid domestic work and toward live-in domestic workers in particular, which must be understood within the context of the recent campaigns to improve these employees' legal protections. Cuarón's film was released in 2018 and has had an impact in advocating for and improving domestic workers' rights. The director used the film and his celebrity to draw attention to the challenges that domestic workers face, particularly in Mexico, which has been slower than other Latin American nations in implementing measures that would afford these employees rights that are equal to those of other workers (see the introduction). In February 2019, Cuarón praised the Mexican Supreme Court's declaration that it was unconstitutional for domestic workers to not be registered in the country's social security program run by the Instituto Mexicano del Seguro Social (Mexican Social Security Institute, or IMSS), which is an obligatory action for other kinds of employees (Sinembargo 2019). The Supreme Court made the ruling in December 2018, shortly after *Roma* had been released to Mexican audiences, at the end of November. When the IMSS subsequently released the details of a pilot social security program for domestic workers on its Twitter account, it recognized the efforts of the team behind *Roma*, as well as the Centro de Apoyo y Capacitación para las Empleadas del Hogar (Domestic Workers' Training and Support Centre, or CACEH) and the women's organization Fondo Semillas, in achieving progress on the issue (Sinembargo.mx 2019). Endorsement by well-known figures such as Cuarón is crucial in the struggle for domestic workers' rights because once the cause has achieved visibility and support, it becomes very difficult for legislators to publicly oppose equal rights reforms, as Blofield argues (2012, 56). Indeed, *Roma*'s success on the international stage strengthened its potential for impact. Immediately after the film won the prizes for best director, best foreign-language film, and best cinematography at the 2019 Academy Awards, President Andrés Manuel López Obrador announced that his administration was working toward Mexico's ratification of the ILO's Domestic Workers Convention No. 189 (*Excélsior* 2019). More broadly, the film has encouraged domestic workers in the United States to seek greater legal protections, and following *Roma*'s release, the National Domestic Workers Alliance began to push for a law to protect paid domestic employees from poor working practices (*El Universal* 2019). According to this organization's figures, 90 percent of the two million paid domestic workers living in the United States are Black, Hispanic, or Asian (*El Universal* 2019).

Roma's Netflix distribution model, which meant that the film was released with simultaneous and near-simultaneous online streaming and theatrical screenings (D. Shaw 2018b), was also mobilized as part of Cuarón and his team's campaign.[9] Cuarón and the actress Yalitza Aparicio, who plays the film's protagonist, a domestic worker named Cleo, encouraged viewers to organize collective screenings of the film and to use the hashtag #Romatón so that Netflix would make a donation to two organizations that support domestic workers in Mexico. In this regard, *Roma* must be understood as both an activist and a social issue film with a primary goal to influence the world beyond the screen.[10] The film's creators united with digital platforms, charities, and even state organizations to achieve tangible improvements to paid domestic workers' rights in Mexico. Furthermore, *Roma*'s success via Netflix among global audiences demonstrates that the film has international appeal, as did *Que horas ela volta?* Indeed, the personal dilemmas that so many families face in relation to childcare mean that films about paid domestic work can traverse national boundaries yet still dialogue with specific national foundational narratives.

The film *Roma* is set in 1970–1971 in the Roma district of Mexico City, where Cuarón grew up. It was shot in a house in the neighborhood that was set up to look just like the director's childhood home (Tapley 2018). The film's monochrome aesthetic is apt given both its historical setting and the fact that it is informed by the director's own memories. *Roma* nonetheless focuses on documenting the grueling daily routine of its protagonist, Cleo, a live-in domestic worker whose responsibilities range from cleaning and laundering to caring for the four young children of her employers, Sofía and Antonio. Sofía teaches chemistry, and her husband, Antonio, is a doctor who works for the same IMSS that Cuarón and his collaborators targeted in their attempts to ensure that paid domestic workers would receive the same entitlement to social security as other employees. This link is intimated when a pile of papers with the IMSS acronym and logo are shown on Antonio's car seat as he arrives home from work. Over the course of the film, Sofía and Antonio's marriage disintegrates as he shirks his responsibilities to his family and begins an affair with another woman. It is a narrative that parallels the rapid end of Cleo's romantic relationship with her love interest, Fermín, who disappears when she informs him that she is pregnant with his child.

Cleo's experiences are based on those of Cuarón's own former nanny, Liboria Rodríguez, to whom the film is dedicated. Rodríguez was consulted extensively while Cuarón was developing his screenplay and has revealed that when the director offered to pay her for her story, she declined, insisting that she was sharing it out of her love for him (Valdes 2018). In this sense, *Roma* can also be situated specifically within the wave of recent Latin American films that have been inspired by their directors' desires to address an emotional obligation to their families' former domestic employees with whom they enjoyed close personal relationships. Cuarón has even alluded to this obligation by stating in an interview that "tenemos una deuda histórica con las trabajadoras del hogar" (Huffington Post 2018; we have a historical debt to domestic workers).

The relationship depicted between Cleo and her White, European descendant employer-family functions as a microcosm of broader social inequalities and class and racial tensions in Mexico. As Poniatowska (1994) observes, paid domestic work has historically been undertaken by young Indigenous women who have migrated from rural to metropolitan areas, a fact that *Roma* underscores by including Cleo's Mixtec dialogue. The film must be praised for its dogged focus on the grim realities of Cleo's domestic labor combined with epic black-and-white cinematography that exalts her spirit and resilience. Her stoicism in the face of adversity is powerfully portrayed by Aparicio, who trained as a schoolteacher and is from Oaxaca (which is also Rodríguez's native state). Even so, the film's narrative development and its representation of Cleo as an endlessly self-sacrificing Marian figure requires interrogation: the miscarriage of Cleo's child is provoked by a holdup during the Corpus Christi massacre, which took place in Mexico City on June 10, 1971.

Adolescent–Domestic Worker Relationships

The emotional ties that bind young people to their families' domestic employees animate these four films and are ripe for a form of cinematic dramatiza-

98 PAID TO CARE

tion that draws heavily on the production of affect. *Casa grande*, *Que horas ela volta?*, and *La nana* all evoke the tenderness, intimacy, resentment, and even flirtation that characterize the relationships between domestic workers and their employers' adolescent offspring, who function as ciphers for these film directors' younger selves (to greater and lesser extents). Consequently, these films can be fruitfully analyzed by adopting the approach developed by Laura Podalsky (2011) in *The Politics of Affect and Emotion in Contemporary Latin American Cinema*. Podalsky draws on Brian Massumi's (2002, 27–28) distinction between "affect," which is defined as embodied intensities, and "emotion," which is "the socio-linguistic fixing of the quality of an experience" that is, from that point on, "defined as personal." As Deborah Shaw (2017, 128) has pointed out, Podalsky does not focus on films featuring domestic workers, except for Martel's (2001) *La ciénaga*; however, she is interested in the fact that many contemporary Latin American films adopt affectively provocative cinematic techniques as a form of sociopolitical critique, often to express disconnection or alienation (Podalsky 2011, 103–105). Podalsky suggests that these techniques are particularly prominent in films focusing on young people. While contemporary films about youth have been criticized for a lack of political engagement (Bentes 2003, 124–135), Podalsky (2011, 102–103) argues that they often substitute explicit political critique for sensorially laden practices that "attest to the affective charge of everyday life for young adults" by inscribing "contemporary affective disjunction" in terms of "depth perception" and thereby registering "structures of feeling that question (and at times disrupt) dominant discursive formations." The production of cinematic affect is a particularly useful register, not only when examining the shockwaves sent through upper-class households by the arrivals of Jéssica and Luiza in *Que horas ela volta?* and *Casa grande*, but also when interrogating how the bonds that lead domestic workers to be considered (and often to consider themselves) "almost one of the family" simultaneously permit their emotional and labor exploitation. Therefore, I suggest that both fiction and documentary film are particularly apt for undertaking a critique of private privilege and domestic power relations. Film can attest to the affective paradox represented by domestic employer-employee relations and particularly to the intimacy with domestic workers that develops over the course of protagonists' childhoods and adolescence.

The physical and emotional proximity between domestic employees and their employers' children has its roots in the cultural connotations that have become attached to wet nurses and other enslaved people who were common in landowning households during the colonial era in Latin America. The majority of the new wave of Latin American films focusing on domestic workers are set in urban environments, but the few that do use rural settings, for example one section of *Roma* and the whole of *Los dueños* (Toscano and Radusky 2013; The owners), tend to depict hacienda-style ranches, which also signals the colonial origins of the live-in domestic employee-employer relationships. The repeated screening of modern-day domestic employer-employee relationships that are imbued with colonial undertones lends to the argument that these films can be approached as foundational narratives or origin stories, both on a personal level for their directors and on a national, or even regional, level.

This is particularly evident in the case of *Casa grande*, given its direct reference to Freyre's *Casa grande & senzala*, a text that has contributed heavily to the myth of Brazil as a "racial democracy." In his study of the relationship between landowners and enslaved people in the Brazilian Northeast, Freyre (2003, 435) pays particular attention to the intimate relations that he considers crucial to the country's development as a nation, characterized by *mestiçagem* (mixing) on linguistic, religious, cultural, and racial levels. First, it was common for the offspring of a White or European descendant landowner to be tended to by an African or Afro-descendant *ama de leite* or *mãe preta* (wet nurse), with the two often forming extremely close connections (Freyre 2003, 435). Second, Freyre (2003, 367–368, 398–399, 403) argues that the landowners' sons were, from a relatively young age, strongly encouraged to pursue sexual relationships with the families' darker-skinned enslaved women (in particular, with *mulata* women), who were burdened by a popular belief in their promiscuity and potential to corrupt young men. Freyre (2003, 398–399, 459, 403) strongly criticizes this popular belief, arguing that the exploitative power relations that existed under the colonial system and the intimate master-slave relation it enabled from infancy were what provoked "a precoce voluptuosidade, a fome de mulher que aos treze ou quatorze anos faz de todo brasilciro um don-juan" (Freyre 2003, 403; the precocious voluptuousness, that hunger for a woman, which at the age of thirteen or fourteen makes of every Brazilian a Don Juan [Freyre 1963, 329]).

These Freyrian narratives have undoubtedly imbued the modern-day depiction of relations between male teens and female *empregadas* with both maternal and sexual connotations. In *Casa grande*, these traits are condensed in the character of Rita, who is not an Afro-Brazilian woman but is identified with the country's plantation-based history because of her Northeastern accent and relationship to the family's other domestic employees, Severino and Noêmia, who are both darker-skinned people. The contemporary cultural association of the Northeast with the lingering relevance of

Brazil's colonial era exists in various films that depict modern-day female domestic workers, including Kleber Mendonça Filho's 2009 *Recife frio* (*Cold Tropics*) and 2012 *O som ao redor* (*Neighboring Sounds*), which are both set in Recife (Pernambuco); the former makes direct reference to the institution of slavery, while the latter opens with black-and-white images of an old plantation.[11] This cultural link is unsurprising given that the country's sugar plantations were concentrated in the Northeast until the nineteenth century. In *Que horas ela volta?*, Val, who comes from Pernambuco, is also given a regional accent by the actress Regina Casé. However, it is important to acknowledge that in Brazilian fiction films, domestic workers are often played by lighter-skinned (*parda*) women (like Casé) or with a symbolic Northeastern accent, a practice that is suggestive of a racist tendency to "lighten" the reality of paid domestic work for the screen, particularly in more commercial films.[12]

In *Que horas ela volta?*, Val continues to mother the adolescent Fabinho as if he were a small child by cradling his head in her lap, singing to him, and checking that he has properly cleaned his ears. She also acquiesces to his frequent requests for massages and allows him to sleep alongside her in her single bed on one occasion. By contrast, in *Casa grande*, Rita's interactions with Jean are more overtly sexualized. While Rita is still employed by his parents, Jean repeatedly visits her apartment at night and pressures Rita for physical intimacy; she allows him to rub moisturizer on her legs but refuses him sex. The housekeeper also frequently endeavors to "coach" Jean, particularly in his unsuccessful romantic relationships with other women. Consequently, these characters adhere to the same binary stereotypes to which domestic worker characters have broadly been confined in Brazilian cultural representations since the impact of Freyrian thought in the 1930s: the mãe preta and the mulata hipersexualizada (Melo 2016, 1). These tropes are deployed in ambivalent ways that simultaneously critique and risk reinforcing them.

Unsurprisingly, the connotations attached to these stereotypes overlap in Val's, Rita's, and Raquel's portrayals. The reproductive labor traditionally conflated with domestic work and "women's work" encompasses sexual and biological reproduction (including childbearing, surrogacy, and wet-nursing), as well as forms of emotional labor and care work, of which sex work could also be considered a form (Olcott 2011, 3). This conflation gains expression in the awkward synthesis of sexual and maternal connotations that is best encapsulated when, in both *Casa grande* and *La nana*, Rita and Raquel decide to use the fact that they change Jean's and Lucas's semen-stained sheets to embarrass the teens, despite the fact that both women also appear to enjoy the boys' flirtatious attentions.

Domestic Workers' Disempowerment and Limited Fields of Vision

The film *Casa grande* must nonetheless be distinguished from *Que horas ela volta?*, *La nana*, and *Roma* because it frames events primarily from the viewpoint of its teen protagonist, Jean, and focuses on the experiences of his family. Consequently, there are various shots that depict his parents in the foreground, often involved in a professional or public activity, while the domestic workers are relegated to the background, where they are shown cooking or maintaining the garden. A similar kind of mise-en-scène features in *Que horas ela volta?*, when Bárbara is being filmed at home while giving an interview about her work as a trendsetter. Bárbara is initially framed in the foreground on the veranda next to the pool, while Val is shown in the background behind the French windows at the end of the living room and waiting to ask her employer a question. Immediately after, however, the camera cuts to a position just behind Val's head, thereby adopting her view of events and emphasizing the film's frequent alignment and sympathy with her perspective.

In contrast to Fellipe Barbosa's film, *Que horas ela volta?* and *La nana* repeatedly evoke their domestic worker protagonists' limited fields of vision and senses of claustrophobia through their mise-en-scènes. One key strategy employed in *Que horas ela volta?* involves positioning the camera in the small kitchen from which Val serves the family (Souto 2018, 186–187; Vázquez Vázquez 2019, 40). When the camera is situated in Val's kitchen, it often frames the threshold across the hall that leads into the family dining room. Val, who (unlike Jéssica) does not dine with her employers, frequently stands next to the kitchen door, which enables her to eavesdrop on conversation from a concealed position so that she can remain informed of important developments. The film also works to contrast the diminutive size of the home's service quarters, including Val's bedroom, with the spacious modernist design of its family areas. These rooms include a guest bedroom that Jéssica claims for herself and into which Val forces her workmate Edna to spy, by balancing on top of a ladder, so that she can ascertain what Jéssica is doing (studying) in the room during the day.

The portrayal of the domestic workers' spaces and perspectives in *Que horas ela volta?* and *La nana* evokes Val's and Raquel's limited fields of vision, which are symbolically linked to their lack of power and status in the household. In *La nana*, a sense of claustrophobia is created when the camera depicts Raquel's small bedroom; she is shown in this room while her boss, Pilar, is welcoming the new live-in domestic worker and showing her the garden. The camera takes up Raquel's viewpoint, and then a position at

Figure 2.1. Val listens to her employers' conversation from a concealed position in the kitchen, *Que horas ela volta?* (dir. Muylaert, 2015, Gullane, Africa Filmes and Globo Filmes)

her shoulder, as she peers from her window straining to see the new recruit, even though her view is obscured by branches. Raquel clearly resents Pilar's decision to hire extra "help," and this sequence visually reinforces the fact that she has no control over the situation.

In *La nana*, these kinds of framings contribute to the sense that the domestic workers in the film entirely lack their own intimate spaces in the house where they live and labor. As Mariano Véliz (2015, 241) observes, the oscillation between point-of-view shots, which attempt to evoke Raquel's experiences and subjectivity, and more distant, handheld camerawork creates the sense that we are spying on the spy in the film. The total invasion of the workers' privacy in *La nana* is signaled by the inclusion of sequences that show them naked while showering. The lack of respect for live-in domestic workers' spaces within the home and during their free time indicates a denigration of their individuality, as Brites (2007, 103) has suggested. This belittlement is also signaled in *Roma* when Cleo and Adela are forced to exercise by candlelight in their room after work because Teresa (their boss's mother) does not want them to "waste" electricity. In *Casa grande* and *Que horas ela volta?*, this lack of respect arguably contributes to Jean's and Fabinho's sense that they are entitled to disturb Rita and Val in their own accommodations at night, which further reinforces the sense that these workers are constantly at their employers' beck and call.

Bourgeois Homes: The Public and the Private

In all four films, the upper-class homes used as principal filming locations symbolize a bourgeois determination to hold the public and the private realms in a false dichotomy by delineating these domestic spaces from the external world. All the houses are represented as oppressive places that are separated from public space by a mixture of large lawns, thick vegetation, walled perimeters, or metal gates. Consequently, instead of serving as spaces of comfort, the homes often appear to entrap their inhabitants, in particular the live-in domestic workers who are depicted in poorly lit internal spaces, such as the corridors in *Que horas ela volta?*, or behind grated windows. These portrayals reinforce the carceral connotations attached to bourgeois domestic spaces, as Velho (2017, 23–32) has noted in the case of *Que horas ela volta?*. Velho (22–25) argues that the various shots that frame Val and Jéssica by looking down on them from a bird's-eye view contribute to the construction of Bárbara and Carlos's home as a kind of panopticon where the domestic worker and her daughter are always observed by a disciplinary gaze. In *Casa grande*, the sense of being monitored is more literal: the entire house is rigged with cameras and alarms, although the only intruder caught is Jean, both times when he returns from meeting Luiza. His insistence on aligning himself with members of another (lower) class, including Severino, Rita, and Luiza, symbolically casts him as a potential threat to his parents' household.

In *Que horas ela volta?* and *Casa grande*, the security concerns of the wealthy are replicated within the houses themselves, which function as a microcosm of many urban areas in Latin America where affluent families choose to reside in gated communities and high-rise apartment buildings patrolled by private security guards in order to insulate themselves from the lower classes. In *Casa grande*, Hugo and Sônia's paranoia about security verges on the humorous precisely because it is characteristic of the Brazilian middle and upper classes, a trend that has also been powerfully explored on screen in *O som ao redor* and *O clube dos canibais* (Parente 2018; *The Cannibal Club*). Souto (2018, 176) refers to this filmic phenomenon as "a territorialização do lar" (the territorialization of the home), whereby class conflicts are explored within the domestic space through disputes regarding territory and property. One of the most explicit examples of this occurs in the 2013 Argentine film *Los dueños*, in which the laborers on a rural *estancia* (estate) constantly try to take over their employers' home without permission while the latter are away for extended periods.

In *Casa grande*, *Que horas ela volta?*, and *La nana*, a clear example of territorialization includes the fact that the domestic workers are not permitted to make use of the employer-family's leisure spaces, notably the swimming pools, and if they do, this is punished as a transgression. At the beginning of *Que horas ela volta?*, when Fabinho asks Val why she will not join him in the pool, Val replies awkwardly that she does not have a swimming suit.

While she is staying with the family, Jéssica, who does not feel bound by the same social rules as Val, dips her toe into the pool while her mother tends the garden, and Val protests that the space is not destined for Jéssica's enjoyment. Fabinho and his friend then arrive and begin to play fight in the water, eventually pulling Jéssica into the pool with them. Their horrified parents order them out of the water and scold them. This signals the end of polite relations between Jéssica and Bárbara, and Jéssica subsequently attempts to find alternative accommodations. When this fails, she is forced to return to Carlos and Bárbara's. Bárbara is in the process of draining the pool because, she says, she has seen a rat in it; Jéssica immediately understands that the rat is a symbol for herself. Jéssica's alignment with the working class, particularly through her relationship to Val, a domestic worker, converts her into a pollutant, a barbaric threat to upper-class "culture" and security. In these films, the swimming pools that each property boasts function as ciphers, not only of the employer-families' elitism, but also of their desire to subjugate nature (water and animals) to "the artifice of modernity" (Andersson 2014, 78). Axel Andersson (78, 83) argues that the "artificial" in the form of these filmic spaces and other objects, such as cars, are designed to shore up "secluded worlds with their backs turned to society," thus signaling "a highly political interest in private and public worlds."

Later in the film, Bárbara tells Val that Jéssica must remain within the confines of the home's service quarters; in her words, Jéssica must stay "da porta da cozinha para *lá*" (on the *other* side of the kitchen door). Val confirms this order with the response, "Sim, senhora, da porta da cozinha para *cá*, não é?" (Yes, ma'am, on *this* side of the kitchen door, right?).[13] This scene establishes that the kitchen doorframe is one of the most socially charged spaces in the film because it represents the boundary between classes (Vázquez Vázquez 2019, 40). It serves as "a threshold between the worlds of employer and employee" (40).[14] This explanation resonates with Lenira Carvalho's (1982, 16) observation in her testimonio that live-in domestic workers suffer a very specific kind of oppression and discrimination because they reside in and maintain homes to which they do not have full access. In *Roma*, for instance, Cleo is shown trying to watch TV with her employer-family in the evening, but there is no space for her on the sofa and her enjoyment is curtailed by Sofía's request that she bring Antonio a drink. In the films analyzed in this chapter, then, the fear of working-class transgression or invasion is metaphorically represented through the spatial relationships negotiated between employers and employees.

These spatial conflicts reveal employer-families' lack of trust in their employees, in the case of *Que horas ela volta?* and *Casa grande*, even though bosses Bárbara and Sônia refer to live-in domestic workers Val and Rita as practically being parts of their families. The films appear to be channeling concerns about recent changes in the nature of domestic work, which have increased the cost of hiring a live-in domestic worker and have seen increasing numbers of employees working as diaristas who do not reside with their employers (Cornwall et al. 2013, 149). These changes foment suspicion of domestic workers, which, according to Roncador (2007, 128–129), can be traced even further back to the historic moment early in the late nineteenth and early twentieth centuries when former enslaved persons began to move out of their masters' homes and into urban areas in Brazil, namely slums (cortiços). The fact that many employees no longer lived where they labored complicated their status as an extension of the clã familiar (family group) and heightened employer mistrust, which provoked literary portrayals of "a figura do empregado invasor, um estranho no meio familiar" (Roncador 130; the figure of the employee-intruder, a stranger in the family milieu). This dynamic continues to play out in Casa grande and Que horas ela volta?, which show Val and Rita betray the trust of their employers. In Val's case, it is a symbolic betrayal via her connection to Jéssica that upsets established class relations. In Rita's case, it is a literal one: Sônia uses the fact that she finds erotic photographs of Rita posing naked in her and Hugo's bedroom as an excuse to dismiss the housekeeper (and save more money) even though Sônia found the images while snooping through Rita's belongings in Rita's own apartment. The corollary of these two events is that Val chooses to resign her post and move out of Bárbara and Carlos's home, while Rita is fired by Sônia, who laments the betrayal of their fictive kin relationship by invoking the fact that she has treated Rita "como uma filha desde que você chegou aqui" (like a daughter since you arrived here).[15] Interestingly, the same middle- and upper-class paranoia explored in Casa grande is also portrayed in O som ao redor when a domestic worker and a security guard are shown having sex on the bed of an apartment owner who is absent.

Ultimately, the narratives of all the films discussed in this chapter foreground the impossibility of maintaining a clear distinction between the private (domestic) and public spheres. It is a division on which women's social subjugation has been contingent and that the figure of the live-in domestic worker troubles. For the purposes of my analysis, the private sphere refers to the domestic, conjugal, familial domain, and everything that lies beyond it—that is, public regulation and private enterprise (or civil society)—pertains to the public sphere.[16] In "The Fraternal Social Contract," Carole Pateman (189, 36) observes that patriarchalism, "the traditional world order of father-kings," is often represented as having been defeated by the modern "contract theorists," whose ideas paved the way for "capitalist society, liberal representative government and the modern family," because they argued that all people were born free and equal rather than naturally subject to their fathers. Pateman (37) emphasizes, however, that "political theorists can represent the outcome of this theoretical battle as a victory for contract theory because they are silent about the sexual or conjugal aspect of patriarchy," which is portrayed as though it were "non-political or natural and so of no theoretical consequence." The contract theorists could not, like the patriarchalists, subsume men's sexual "right" to women under paternal—that is, political—rule, so instead, the contract theorists concealed its political origins by proclaiming men's conjugal right as natural (39). Pateman (43) concludes, therefore, that "the separation of 'paternal' from political rule, or of the family from the public sphere, is also the separation of women from men through the subjection of women to men." In this way, the "fraternal social contract" instituted a new, "modern patriarchal order" that is divided into public and private spheres, both of which are ruled by men (43).

By dialoguing with Freyre's description of the overtly patriarchal structures established on the colonial sugar plantations, *Casa grande* undermines the division of the public and private realms on which the modern capitalist society depicted in the film also relies. The naturalization of lower-class women's subjection to men is encapsulated by Jean's apparent belief that he is entitled to Rita's body, which he grabs and strokes in spite of her repeated refusals. This representation is clearly meant to recall the colonial relationship between enslaved women and the landowner's sons, who were encouraged to have sex with young, enslaved women because if the slave became pregnant, her offspring would automatically become the landowner's property and increase his prosperity and authority (Freyre 2003, 456). The inextricability of private, domestic relationships and public, professional ones is further emphasized by the film's mise-en-scène. On one occasion, Sônia is shown giving a French class at home in the foreground of the shot, while Severino puts away lawn furniture in the background. This "deep-focus spatial strategy" underscores the family's heavy reliance on their domestic employees (de Luca 2017, 208). On another occasion, while Hugo responds to a headhunter's questions about his professional experience via a video call, Rita serves him coffee, although her body is truncated by the frame.[17]

The framing of employee labor alludes to the ways in which "women's work" has been undervalued and even conceptualized as economically unproductive, including within Marxist theory (Federici 2014). These views have been enabled by the perception that unpaid domestic labor generates not exchange-value but only use-value because the products of the work are not destined for the market but are instead immediately consumed by the family (Coulson et al. 1975, 62). However, this understanding is undermined by the fact that domestic work of all kinds is clearly a necessary condition for the reproduction of labor power (or the workforce), the capitalist's "most indispensable means of production" (Federici 2014, 92). Furthermore, as David Staples (2007, 122) suggests, by conceiving of reproductive labor (housework, childcare, and sexual reproduction) as "nonwork" because it is unwaged and engendered, capital is able to interpret productive labor as work "in the material-ideological sense" and to exploit it as "surplus-value producing labor."

Reproductive and Productive Labor: A False Dichotomy

The films *Casa grande*, *Que horas ela volta?*, and *La nana* all foreground the reliance of prestigious and public forms of employment on the exploitation of paid domestic labor in sequences where these different types of work overlap in the home spaces that they depict (which has already been demonstrated in the case of *Casa grande*). In *Que horas ela volta?*, Bárbara hosts a soiree that clearly plays a role in her work as a trendsetter and that unites many of her fashionable acquaintances, although ostensibly the event is meant to celebrate her birthday. She reminds the journalist who interviews her at home (in a sequence mentioned above) that he should attend the party. Val dons a traditional maid's uniform for the occasion, thereby functioning as a visible symbol of the family's social status. She attempts to serve guests coffee using a plastic black-and-white set that she bought Bárbara as a present, to which Bárbara responds angrily, betraying her belief that the coffee set will strike her friends as gauche. She orders Val to use a different coffee set. In *La nana*, because Pilar's daughter, Camila, will study late into the night with a friend, Camila insists that Raquel must not use the vacuum cleaner outside her room early in the morning; studying is an activity that can be understood as generating added value in that it has the potential to enable Camila to pursue a prestigious career in the future. Consequently, all the domestic workers depicted in these films are consistently undertaking tasks that are essential to their employer-families' successful development in either their professional or academic careers outside of the home. These sequences demonstrate that the oppositions between the private and the public, and between reproductive and productive forms of labor, are ideological ones that have nonetheless had significant social and historical ramifications, particularly in the way that they have mobilized gender. The films show that the ways these domestic spaces operate and the domestic worker's role within them are integral to the functioning of market capitalism in late modernity.

108 PAID TO CARE

Furthermore, in all four films the domestic workers' constant physical activity and productivity can be contrasted with the arguably unproductive tendencies of the families for whom they labor. It is surely no coincidence that the female bosses engage in what can be considered relatively "immaterial" forms of labor, to borrow Hardt and Negri's (2004, 108) term.[18] Pilar in *La nana* is an academic; the trendsetter Bárbara in *Que horas ela volta?* appears to work in the fashion or design industry; Sofía in *Roma* initially teaches chemistry; and Sônia in *Casa grande* gives private French classes, although she later begins selling cosmetics to her friends and acquaintances, which involves gossiping with them during product demonstration sessions. Sônia enters the business to help support her family while Hugo is out of work and in financial difficulties. Prior to that, Hugo worked for a bank and gave classes on financial derivatives, which are another kind of immaterial transaction. A further parallel that can be drawn between the films is the fact that all the employer-husbands are either out of work, shirking their responsibilities to their families, or engaging in nebulous occupations. In *Roma*, Sofía's husband, Antonio, works as a doctor, but he lies to his children about being away on a research trip so that he can travel with his lover and pursue an expensive, newfound passion for diving; he also neglects to send money to sustain his family. In *Que horas ela volta?*, Bárbara's husband, Carlos, is unemployed, sleeps until late in the day, and appears to be depressed, much like Hugo in *Casa grande*. Carlos is an artist who has given up painting, although he reveals to Jéssica that his inheritance is the source of wealth that maintains his family's lifestyle, which further reinforces the family's unproductive and postcolonial associations. In *La nana*, the occupation of Pilar's husband, Mundo, is ambiguous, but when he is not playing golf, he devotes most of his time to building a model ship out of wooden sticks in his study; he refers to this activity as work and is devastated when the model is destroyed during a fight between Raquel and another domestic worker. The somewhat humorous portrayals of Carlos and Mundo as frustrated creative types perhaps function as a self-reflexive and ironic acknowledgment that these films' directors are relatively privileged artists themselves who portray hardworking subaltern figures in what could be considered a potentially fruitless, or immaterial, endeavor.

The Significance of Gift Giving in *Que horas ela volta?* and *La nana*

The labor of bearing, raising, and caring for children has been naturalized within capitalism as "women's work," even though capital lays claim to the future workforce produced by often unpaid social reproductive labor

(Staples 2007, 144). Thus, it is tempting to view such reproductive labor as a debt that needs to be repaid. Indeed, *La nana*, *Que horas ela volta?*, and *Roma* can be interpreted as attempts to account for a debt of care, love, or affection that appears to be difficult to repay, particularly because the films are dedicated (either explicitly or implicitly) to paid domestic workers with whom their directors had close personal relationships. Nonetheless, to shed light on the difficulties of properly accounting for "women's work," it is more helpful to conceptualize domestic work as an element of the gift economy, where goods and services are provided without an explicit condition of reimbursement (Staples 2007, 142). As Staples clarifies, when a woman has a baby, she does not usually expect to be financially compensated: the act is not a traditional economic transaction.

Where waged domestic work is concerned, *La nana* and *Que horas ela volta?* employ gift-related symbolism, even though the domestic employees are paid, to show that it is very difficult to recompense the life and labor that Raquel and Val have dedicated to their employers.[19] Beyond the need to modify any theory of labor that does not recognize domestic work as value-producing work, it is crucial to acknowledge the constant emotional toil that is also required of Raquel and Val, which compels them to make huge personal sacrifices for which they cannot be compensated in any simple sense. These two workers give up almost all their time to serve their employer-families: in Val's case, she cannot escape Fabinho's demands even while sleeping. Time, according to Jacques Derrida (1992, 31), is the only commodity that cannot be owned in any simple sense; consequently, the "incalculable time" of reproductive labor, which "must be expended," cannot be returned (Staples 2007, 144). In *Que horas ela volta?*, Val has lost the opportunity to see her daughter grow up, while in *La nana*, Raquel appears to have sacrificed her youth and the possibility of maturing into an independent woman with an autonomous personal life.

The difficulty of accounting for these kinds of affective or immaterial sacrifices and demands in traditional labor contracts is precisely what permits such heinous exploitation of live-in domestic workers. It is for this reason that physical gifts become such potent symbols in both films. In *Que horas ela volta?*, Bárbara shuns the coffee set that Val buys her for her birthday, which alludes to the fact that Val's labor has also been undervalued. The multiple sacrifices that Val has made in her personal life while caring for Fabinho have not been properly compensated, so when she leaves her post, she makes the symbolic decision of taking the coffee set with her to Jéssica's apartment. In one of the opening sequences of *La nana*, Raquel's employer-family "surprise" her with presents and a cake to celebrate her birthday. They ring a bell to call her into the family dining room, where they have just finished dinner. Raquel, who is eating in the kitchen, pretends not to hear them and initially refuses to accompany the adolescent Lucas when he goes to fetch her. The game that Raquel plays in this sequence revolves around her deep-seated but unspoken sense that both she and her labor—which is synonymous with her life in the film—are undervalued by the family and cannot be recompensed. Raquel later opens the presents, which include a sweater that she dislikes and discards on her bedroom floor.

The Commodification of the Domestic Worker

The fact that Raquel is portrayed as having no life or intimate relationships outside of those with her employer-family in *La nana* (prior to Lucy's arrival) illustrates Carvalho's (1982, 18) argument that while a domestic worker is live-in, her freedom will be compromised: "ela será sempre escrava" (she will always be a slave). The concept of a live-in maid implies the notion that life itself can be commodified, because when a boss pays a worker to spend his or her entire life living with the family and looking after them, it undermines that worker's ability to establish an autonomous life (Ros 2011, 101) or identity. Instead, this employee's life and work are transformed into a commodity, which assumes the form of material support for the bourgeois family in a capitalist market system. The term "commodification" refers to the transformation of relationships that were not previously deemed commercial, but instead personal, into financial transactions. In Karl Marx and Friedrich Engels's 1969 *Manifesto of the Communist Party* (15–16), they attribute the blame for the process of commodification, which has encompassed all areas of life (political, religious, familial), to the bourgeoisie. The commodification of domestic labor, or "women's work," is a clear illustration.

La nana represents the corollary of this attempt to commodify an individual through the film's representation of Raquel's poor mental and physical health. This portrayal nonetheless split critical opinion in Chile, because some argued that the film's frequently comedic portrayal of a neurotic live-in domestic worker was dangerously depoliticized and framed from an upper-class directorial perspective (Pereira 2009; Soto 2011). However, these critiques overlooked the fact that although Raquel's mental and physical illness is personal, it is also inseparable from her labor exploitation (Vázquez 2014, 165) and from the effects of her dehumanization. Her breakdown appears to be provoked by the fact that she identifies very strongly with her employer-family, whose lifestyle she covets, as is indicated when she is shown trying on Pilar's clothes and admiring herself in the mirror. Raquel later goes shopping and purchases an expensive cardigan that is very similar to one of her boss's. These film sequences recall observations made by Carvalho (1982, 44, 45) and various workers in Gutiérrez's (1983, 106, 153, 232) *Se necesita muchacha* who state that by living with their employers, domestic workers often become alienated from their own families and class, preferring instead to emulate their bosses' lifestyles and fashion choices.

Raquel views the other domestic workers that Pilar hires as a threat to her special status in the household and particularly to her intimacy with her employers' children. Consequently, she bullies and humiliates the new employees in a passive-aggressive fashion by locking them out of the house. Once again, conflicts surrounding class affiliation, or alienation in Raquel's case, play out via territorial disputes. Raquel is resentful of Pilar and Mundo's daughter Camila, whose face she has scratched out of her various photographs of the family. Her resentment is perhaps provoked by Camila's looming adulthood, which signifies that she will no longer need Raquel to care for her. On one occasion, Raquel engineers the loss of Camila's kitten, which the family's new Peruvian domestic employee, Mercedes, has agreed to look after. First, Raquel shuts the cat in a drawer, then she encourages it to drown itself in the family pool, and finally she shoves it over the garden wall. Raquel's extreme behavior and inhuman portrayal represent a problematic directorial choice that adheres to the classist stereotype of the vengeful maid and that contrasts with the stereotypes of the self-sacrificing maid with which Val and Cleo can be aligned in *Que horas ela volta?* and *Roma* and of the hypersexualized maid embodied by Rita in *Casa grande*. Regardless, Raquel's characterization also effectively defamiliarizes and foregrounds the consequences of her physical and emotional labor exploitation. The shock provoked by Raquel's conduct alerts the spectator to the consequences of the quiet obedience and constant emotional support that are expected of a live-in domestic worker. Peruvian nanas are sometimes preferred in Chile because they are seen as being more docile (Vázquez 2014, 165–166).[20] This stereotype is acknowledged in *La nana* through the character of Mercedes, who is young, sweet and caring; Raquel, by comparison, is viewed as insolent and difficult.

Raquel's uncanny behavior is reinforced by the fact that she has come to embody the "abject" (Kristeva 1982, 2), or "the jettisoned object," within her employers' household, which she herself appears to intuit. She is associated with the physical waste products of the family's material reproduction when she is shown cleaning up the leftovers of their meals and changing their dirty bedsheets. The sense that her position symbolically aligns her with the abject leads her to become obsessive about cleaning and bleaching the bathroom that she is forced to share with Pilar's new hires, namely, doing so just after they have used it. In fact, her overuse of cleaning products provides a visual explanation for the headaches that she suffers. On an existential level, however, her ailments are provoked by her struggle to cope with her abjection and the fact that she has been reduced to her labor role. In her discussion of the abjection of self, Julia Kristeva (1982, 5) argues that abjection is "at the very peak of its strength when [the] subject, weary of fruitless attempts to identify with something on the outside, finds [. . .] that the impossible constitutes its very *being*, that it *is* none other than abject." Raquel's blackouts (which evoke death and the corpse) suggest her status as abject rather than as a subject who would be able to see outside herself and relate to (and desire) external objects.

Like a child who has not undergone a successful process of individuation and subject formation, Raquel is unable to separate herself from her employer-family and cannot function as an independent adult. In the context of the narrative, this inability is unsurprising because Raquel moved to work with the family at a young age: she is the archetypical criada. Female live-in domestic workers such as Raquel are often conceptualized in the popular imagination as subjects who elude adulthood. These employees remain in a state of dependency for many years because they are expected to comply with "codes of conduct enforced by their mistresses" (Roman-Morfin 2015, 79–80). This compliance makes it difficult for Raquel to develop what Carvalho (1982, 44) terms "uma personalidade decidida" (strength of character) and culminates in problems establishing romantic relationships (48). In *La nana*, Raquel's infantilization is signaled by the soft toys that continue to line the bed in her room and by her inability, despite her romantic interest, to consummate her relationship with Lucy's uncle Eric when the pair go to celebrate Christmas with Lucy's family.

Bestial Imagery in *La nana*, *Que horas ela volta?*, and *Roma*

The alignment of paid domestic workers with the abject is powerfully symbolized in *La nana*, *Que horas ela volta?*, and *Roma* by sequences that employ bestial imagery. One of the most infamous deployments of this kind of device can be traced back to a novel I discussed in the introduction, Lispector's (1964) *A paixão segundo G. H.*, in which the narrator discovers a cockroach in the room of her former domestic worker, Janair, who has just left her employ. Janair is a working-class Afro-descendant woman. Like the cockroach, she is figured as an antagonistic, alien absence-presence who threatens to trouble the established class and racial boundaries that delimit the narrator's world (Giorgi 2014, 88–89). In *Que horas ela volta?*, the boss Bárbara's equation of Val's daughter Jéssica with a rat functions in a similar way; in this case, the metaphor makes explicit Jéssica's status as an unwelcome visitor and as a class interloper in Carlos and Bárbara's home. The film thus draws on the narrative trope of the hidden intruder or parasite, which resonates across a body of works that depict domestic employer-employee relations or that more broadly evoke a bourgeois fear of a working-class invasion both within and outside Latin America. These texts include Julio Cortázar's short story "Casa tomada" (1951; House taken over); Sergio Bizzio's (2004) novel *Rabia* (Rage), which was the inspiration for the eponymous 2009 film by Sebastián Cordero; Kleber Mendonça Filho's (2016) film *Aquarius*; and Bong Joon-ho's (2019) *Parasite*, which in 2020 was the first foreign-language film to win the Academy Award for Best Picture.

In *A paixão segundo G. H.* and *Que horas ela volta?* specifically, the symbols of the cockroach and of the rat reinforce the notion that domestic work and the workers who undertake it are linked to dirt, particularly from a bourgeois perspective. Their association with "disgusting" bodily processes, and thus with the abject, is further foregrounded in *Que horas ela volta?* by Val's frequent proximity to her employer-family's pet dog, Maggie, who uses the external service entrance to the kitchen, as do Val and Jéssica. On one occasion, the pair is shown outside Carlos and Bárbara's home waiting impatiently for Maggie to defecate; Val then cleans up after the dog. Similarly, in *Roma*, Cleo is regularly shown washing the copious amounts of excrement left by her employer-family's pet dog off their driveway. She does this action in the film's opening sequence and repeats it throughout the diegesis, which alludes to the cyclical nature of domestic tasks that are never concluded. The task of washing away excrement aligns Cleo with the abject, a status that is affectively evoked for the audience when on one occasion, her boss Sofía swears angrily at her to clean up the dog mess. Sofía projects onto Cleo the contempt and disgust she feels for herself at a moment when she becomes visibly afraid that her husband is abandoning her. These sequences recall the prodigious number of references made in the domestic workers' testimonios analyzed in chapter 1 to being treated similarly to, or worse than, employers' pet dogs. The implication is that, like these animals, the employees are expected to demonstrate obedience and to become domesticated within the context of their bosses' bourgeois households.

By exploring the ways in which domestic workers are nefariously aligned with animality, these films reveal how their treatment is designed not only to distinguish bosses from employees on the level of race or class but also to differentiate domestic workers in terms of their claims to humanity. Both Cary Wolfe (2013) in *Before the Law* and Gabriel Giorgi (2014) in his analysis of *A paixão segundo G. H.* (Lispector 1964) draw on biopolitical theory to explore the ways in which the animal has been deployed as the limit via which the social order of humanity has been safeguarded. In Lispector's novel, Janair leaves a drawing etched into the wall of her former room, and it depicts three bodies: one feminine, one masculine, and one animal (a dog). Thus, the domestic worker is explicitly figured as an animal (the dog, the cockroach), and the traces of her presence trouble the established domestic hierarchy in the home of the narrator, who tellingly refers to herself as "G. H."—*género humano* (Giorgi 2014, 89–90; humankind). The text thus draws attention to the effort to distinguish between the normalized human body of the narrator and other kinds of bodies, including that of the domestic worker, which are marked by biopolitical signifiers such as race, class, and animality that shore up the boundaries of the "less than human" and "inhuman" (90–92). This distinction constitutes a biopolitical tool that not only animalizes the Other but also inserts different kinds of bodies into a hierarchy in order to distinguish between lives that are valued and those that are considered insignificant (94). The fact that domestic workers are represented as contiguous to animals sheds light on Carvalho's (1982, 18) statement that, for bosses, these employees simply represent "labor"; there is an attempt to reduce them to a body to be exploited—to "bare life" in Agamben's terms (1998, 124). This provides a rationale for the historical and legal discrimination that paid domestic workers have faced in comparison to other kinds of workers. As Wolfe (2013, 6) points out, the gap between humanity and animality, or between *bios* (the qualified life of the citizen) and *zoē* (bare, anonymous life), is a dangerous one because it frames who is recognized and who is not. The animal is not recognized within a humanist framework: it is before the law and outside of its protection. Consequently, those Others who also "fall outside the frame," because they are marked by differences of race, class, gender, nationality, or species, are always threatened with "a non-criminal putting to death" (9).

Clearly, these distinctions are a discursive resource. The body (our animality) unites all humans: it is the condition of our possibility and cannot be repressed (Wolfe 2013, 9–10; Giorgi 2014, 87–88). Lispector's (1964) text emphasizes this fact through the description of the plasma that leaks from the corpse of the cockroach that the narrator finds in the empty domestic worker's quarters (Giorgi 2014, 101). It is in relation to this formless materiality that the text elaborates a new sense of shared potential found in bare life, and this life force is presented as evasive, intangible, and impossible to appropriate (Giorgi 2014, 102–103). This shared potential complicates the

Figure 2.2. Raquel looks at her reflection in the mirror while she is wearing an ape mask, *La nana* (dir. Silva, 2009, Diroriro, Film Tank, and Punto Guión Producciones)

distinction between human and animal, and instead establishes a continuum between the two that challenges traditional social hierarchies and forms of biopolitical control.

In *La nana*, a similar device is deployed: Raquel's dehumanization is most powerfully symbolized and subverted when she puts on an ape mask (which Lucas has previously used to frighten his younger siblings), looks at herself in the mirror, and laughs.[21] However, after removing the mask, Raquel appears troubled, feels unwell, and takes a tablet. The next day she collapses suddenly for the second time and has to be taken to the hospital. The device of the mask foregrounds Raquel's realization that she has become the abject rather than a subject. It is no coincidence that when she puts on the mask, she is framed looking in the mirror, an object associated with self-image that holds importance for the construction of individual identity and subjectivity within psychoanalytic theory. Earlier in the film, she has also been shown looking in the mirror while trying on her boss's clothing, an activity signaling her class alienation and growing sense of identity loss. However, in the scene with the ape mask, the image is particularly uncanny because of the strong similarities between apes and humans (the legal ramifications of which are discussed by Wolfe [2013, 11]). The sequence emphasizes Raquel's symbolic undecidability: it foregrounds her humanity and her simultaneous alignment with the "animal" as a result of her commodification and dehumanization by her employers. Ultimately, her brief figuration as human-animal and her reaction to it work to denaturalize and defamiliarize the hierarchy that enables her subjugation. The mask critiques the fact that she has become the dehumanized personification of the unequal, even violent, power relationships upon which the bourgeois home is constructed, and the dehumanizing aspect of the mask reinforces the notion that her life can be domesticated, owned, or privatized by her employers.

The human-animal binary, and its implications for social hierarchies, has also been subverted in a series of recent Brazilian films that feature paid domestic workers. These films include *Trabalhar cansa* (Rojas and Dutra 2011; *Hard Labor*), *As boas maneiras* (Rojas and Dutra 2017; *Good Manners*), and *O clube dos canibais*. Like *La nana*, all three films combine elements of comedy and horror. In both of Rojas and Dutra's films, the presence of werewolves is linked to the Brazilian elite and their exploitation of the working class, in particular, of live-in domestic workers. It is possible that the title of *As boas maneiras* functions as a reference to "O homem cordial" (The cordial man), a well-known chapter from Holanda's ([1936] 2014) book *Raízes do Brasil* (*Roots of Brazil*). Holanda explains in the chapter that the cordial relations that shape Brazilian society—relations that stem from the prevailing patriarchal, rural culture—constitute not *boas maneiras* (176; good manners) but rather the desire to establish *intimate* relationships with others (178–180). Holanda (241) draws on the etymology of "cordiality" in the word *cordis*, meaning "of the heart," adding that enmity can be just as cordial as friendship in the sense that both relationships develop from the *intimate*, the familial, and the private. The potential brutality and violence of intimate cordial relations is explored in the film *As boas maneiras* through the relationship between Ana, a wealthy White expectant mother, and Clara, a lonely Afro-Brazilian nurse hired by Ana to look after her as yet unborn child. Clara realizes that Ana is being transformed by her pregnancy, which is the product of her relationship to an unknown man who, it is intimated, was a werewolf. Ana dies while giving birth to her son, Joel, who Clara then rears. Together, they struggle to cope with Joel's regular beastly transformations. The film's allegorical dimension reaches its zenith when an infant Joel suckles at Clara's breast, simultaneously drawing blood, in an evocation of violent, intimate class relations. This sequence alludes to the link between contemporary childcare practices in Brazil and the historical use of Afro-Brazilian wet nurses, particularly prior to the abolition of enslavement. In *O clube dos canibais*, a wealthy businessman and his wife repeatedly hire isolated migrants as domestic employees only to seduce, have sex with, murder, and eat them. Consequently, these two films invert the association of cannibalism and werewolves that populate children's horror stories with the influence of Indigenous and African cultures (see Freyre 2003, 411–413); instead, they frame Brazilian middle- and upper-class cordiality as a source of barbarity, which is symbolized by capitalistic, or cannibalistic, vampirism. These films appear to draw on Marx's (2000, 335, 349) descriptions of capital as a "vampire" that "only lives by sucking living labour" and of the capitalist's extension of the working day as akin to "the were-wolf's hunger for surplus-labour." The films also constitute a reaction to the conflicts that split Brazilian society from 2013, which were driven by a sense of fear among the Brazilian elite that was provoked by the enfranchisement of the working class under recent PT governments.

Casa grande and the Repetition of a Freyrian Narrative

While the conclusions of *Que horas ela volta?* and *La nana* attempt to empower their domestic worker protagonists, *Casa grande* is haunted by the repetition of a Freyrian narrative at its close. This may result from the fact that its diegesis is framed primarily from Jean's adolescent perspective. Toward the film's conclusion, when Jean is angry at his father, he runs away from the exam room where he is about to take the Vestibular and tracks down the family's former chauffeur, Severino, whom he finds living in a visibly deprived area. As Jean walks through the neighborhood, the shaky visuals, seemingly shot with a handheld camera, contrast with the static shots that have been used to depict his family's casa grande and those who inhabit it, who are often framed separately from each other or in close-up. The unsteady camera underscores the emotional nature of Jean's reunion with Severino. As they embrace, Jean begins to cry, and their bodies are united in the same frame. It appears that Jean can gain emotional solace only from visiting Severino rather than from his own parents. Like other films depicting domestic workers and their employers, *Casa grande* hints that the path to social change can be found in these kinds of emotional shifts, which are provoked by the creation of "affective alliances" and through the development of a "politics of situated feeling" (Podalsky 2011, 8, 15), as Deborah Shaw (2017, 138) has also observed. At that point in the film, Severino acquires a greater subject status because Jean (and the viewer) discovers that Severino lives with Noêmia and her daughters. Up until this point, the family's former domestic employees have been confined by their labor roles, and our knowledge of their private lives has been limited.

Although Jean appears to reject familial and class-related expectations when he runs away from the Vestibular to reunite with Severino, this symbolic rejection is largely negated when, shortly afterward, Jean sleeps with Rita, whom he meets at a party in Severino's neighborhood, and thereby reenacts a relationship with clear colonial and Freyrian undertones. As the film's director, Anna Muylaert, has stated in response to comparisons between her film *Que horas ela volta?* and *Casa grande*, "achei o final de *Casa grande* machista: comer a empregada não é solução, é repetição" (Balloussier and Genestreti 2015; I thought *Casa grande*'s ending was chauvinistic: sleeping with the maid is not a solution, it is repetition). The film's conclusion, which shows Jean and Rita in bed together in her new apartment after she was fired by Sônia, depicts an experience that Valeria Ribeiro Corossacz (2017, 49–50) has identified both as a rite of passage among White, middle-class men in Brazil and as a form of sexual harassment that has been shaped by Freyrian narratives. Between 2009 and 2012, Corossacz (xii–xiv) interviewed twenty-one affluent White men between the ages of forty-three and sixty who were living in Rio de Janeiro's south zone; some acknowledged the influence of the country's colonial past on their own experiences, and many recounted their adolescent sexual initiation with domestic employees, a relationship that Corossacz argues is central in shoring up the former's dominance on the levels of race, class, and gender.

Tiago de Luca (2017, 212) suggests that *Casa grande*'s ending is not an instance of "power subjugation" because Rita is a character who is "in full and proud control of her sexual agency as a woman." At some moments, the film does appear to invert the power dynamic of this postcolonial sexual relationship via Rita's teasing of Jean, who accuses her of sadism while they watch a horror film on television. However, Rita's strong belief in the need for men to fulfill an aggressively active sexual role demonstrates that she remains confined by the dominant patriarchal system of sexual relations in Brazil (described by Parker 2003, 310–311), which is regurgitated by various characters' comments and which remains a source of humor and largely unproblematized throughout the film. Furthermore, depictions of Sônia's discovery of photographs that show Rita posing naked in her home and of Rita's obsession with recounting her exaggerated sexual escapades to Jean risk converting her into a humorous, sex-crazed stereotype and aligning her with the adolescent male fantasy of the randy maid (Dennison and Shaw 2004, 158–163), a trope that reached its troubling cinematic zenith in the pornochanchadas popular in Brazil during the 1970s, namely in *Como é boa nossa empregada* (Ismar Porto and Victor di Mello 1973; How good our maid is), which features various domestic employees being pursued by sex-crazed young men.

In *Casa grande*'s closing sequence, Jean gets up from Rita's bed, pulls the sheets back to reveal her naked body, which he stares at and kisses, and then climbs up onto her windowsill to smoke a cigarette. De Luca

Figure 2.3. Jean sits on the windowsill and looks down at Rita's body, *Casa grande* (dir. Barbosa, 2014, Migdal Films)

(2017, 212) suggests that placing Rita in the foreground and Jean in the background in this final static scene affirms the way in which "subjectivities dictated through social position may be reinvented as spaces are reappropriated." Given that Jean stares at, and the camera dwells upon, Rita's naked torso, the possible significance of the film's ending does not seem so clearcut; indeed, its brief inversion of sexual power relationships is arguably undone as its mise-en-scène reinstitutes a male gaze.[22] Whether or not Jean has rejected his postcolonial domestic privilege, or has even satisfactorily resolved the film's crisis of hegemonic masculinity by coming of age, is also drawn into doubt given that his relationship to Rita is one that combines sexual and maternal elements. Elisabeth Badinter (1997, 67, 70–71) insists that in order to become a man satisfactorily, it is necessary for the boy to differentiate himself from the feminine, domestic sphere and to define himself against what produced him (the female body). By sleeping with Rita, Jean has not clearly done either. Indeed, earlier on he even asked Rita if he could *treinar* (practice) with her before trying to have sex with Luiza, someone who is not symbolically subsumed within his family.

The film's ending is thus highly ambivalent and could be criticized for indulging in nostalgia for the emotional and sexual exploitation that domestic service can permit. In this sense, *Casa grande* demonstrates further parallels with Freyre's text, which not only condemns the abusive relationships that were enabled by slavery but also fondly reflects on the domestic intimacy between slaves and landowners that, according to Freyre (2003, 367; 1963, 278), led almost all Brazilians to bear

> a marca da influência negra. Da escrava ou sinhama que nos embalou. Que nos deu de mamar. Que nos deu de comer, ela própria amolengando na mão o bolão de comida. Da negra velha que nos contou as primeiras histórias de bicho e de mal-assombrado. Da mulata que nos tirou o primeiro bicho-de-pé de uma coceira tão boa. Da que nos iniciou no amor físico e nos transmitiu, ao ranger da cama-de-vento, a primeira sensação completa de homem.

> the mark of [African] influence. Of the female slave or mammy who rocked us to sleep. Who suckled us. Who fed us, mashing our food with her own hands. The influence of the old woman who told us our first tales of ghost and *bicho*.[23] Of the mulatto girl who relieved us of our first *bicho de pé*,[24] of a pruriency that was so enjoyable. Who initiated us into physical love and, to the creaking of a canvas cot, gave us our first complete sensation of being a man.

As David Lehmann (2008, 209) has pointed out, passages such as this one betray Freyre's subject position: he is aligned with the "us" about whom it is written and to whom it is addressed, an upper-class, educated, White readership. Indeed, Freyre was a member of the Northeastern Brazilian elite, and the way that African influence is represented in his text others and exoticizes it. Jean, *Casa grande*'s focalizer, occupies a similar subject position. It is perhaps for this reason that both the film and Freyre's text are characterized by ambivalence: they function as indictments of the sociopolitical and economic systems that existed in Brazil at different times, but they also yearn for an affective and sexual intimacy that relies on highly unequal power relationships.

Roma: A Modern Mexican Foundational Film

Roma also constitutes a narrative that alludes to collective national myths and functions as a kind of modern Mexican foundational film. It depicts a key historical turning point in Mexico's development into a modern, urban nation following the so-called Mexican miracle, a period of economic growth between 1940 and 1960 (Sánchez Prado 2018). The technological developments that had taken place in the capital in the mid-twentieth century are signaled by film scenes that show the characters attending the cinema, including the Teatro Metropolitan, which opened in 1943, and the now defunct Cine Las Américas, which was built in 1952 (Smith 2018; Martínez 2011). While at the cinema, Cleo is presented with images of modernity, including airplanes and outer space. Carlos Monsiváis (1994) has argued that Mexican cinema played an important role in the formation of the citizenry and national identity in Mexico from the 1930s through the 1950s, particularly for displaced rural peasants struggling to settle in the capital's suburbs. In Geoffrey Kantaris and Rory O'Bryen's (2013, 7–8) terms, cinema in Mexico at that time served the functions of dislodging peasant culture "from its 'organic' rootedness in the rhythms of country-side and agricultural production" while simultaneously conjoining it "both to increasing urbanization (with its attendant industrialization) and to the forms and formats of an incipient transnational visual imaginary dominated largely (but not exclusively) by Hollywood." Although *Roma* is set in the early 1970s, a little later than the period Monsiváis describes, the film intimates that cinema was still fulfilling a similar function at the time, particularly for the characters who have moved to Mexico City for work but maintain ties to Indigenous cultures, languages, and rural areas, including Cleo and Adela, who are both shown attending the cinema in their free time. Nonetheless, the film also attests to the fact that the benefits of the country's modernization and industrialization were unevenly distributed. For instance, Ignacio Sánchez Prado (2018) notes that Cleo's position as a domestic employee is a result of the "devastating effects of the failure of post-Revolutionary agrarian reform, including the mass migration of former peasants to the city." In the film, we learn that Cleo's mother was expelled from her lands by government agents.

Cuarón has also implied that his film can be read as a foundational narrative related not only to his own formative experiences but also to the origins of the nation. He tweeted a passage from Enrique Krauze's (2018) *New York Times* review of the film, which states that the film's most emblematic image is that of Cleo embracing her employers' children at the beach alongside their biological mother, Sofía, thereby forming the "sacramental [. . .] Mexican family tree." Cleo's character recalls the connotations attached to Mexico's "originary" mother: La Chingada (Paz 1950, 86). Octavio Paz equates La Chingada (the repudiated mother) with La Malinche, the lover of and interpreter for the Spanish conquistador Hernán Cortés. The birth of their "illegitimate" son, Martín, has been interpreted as symbolizing the origin of the "modern" mestizo Mexican nation. Paz (87) points out that La Malinche gives herself voluntarily to Cortés, but as soon as she outlives her usefulness to him, he forgets her. Hence, she becomes La Chingada, a

Figure 2.4. Cleo's employer-family embrace her on the beach as the sun sets behind them, *Roma* (dir. Cuarón, 2018, Esperanto Filmoj, Participant, and Pimienta Films)

woman who has been tricked and used and who is thus repudiated. As Paz (88) emphasizes, by rejecting La Malinche, Mexico severs its links with the past and refuses to recognize its Indigenous origins.

In *Roma*, Cleo's own romantic involvement with Fermín echoes La Malinche's narrative; Fermín seduces Cleo and then disappears as soon as she reveals that she is pregnant. When Cleo eventually tracks down Fermín, he insults her and refuses to acknowledge his paternity of her unborn baby. The audience later discovers that Fermín is a member of the government-trained paramilitary organization Los Halcones, the group that attacked and killed student protesters at what became known as the Corpus Christi massacre because it took place on the day of the eponymous Catholic festival. Fermín's culpability in the eventual loss of Cleo's child becomes even more literal in the sequence that depicts the massacre when he enters the shop where Cleo (along with Teresa, her boss's mother) had been planning to purchase a crib; other members of his group threaten customers while Fermín points his own gun directly at Cleo.

Shortly after that scene, *Roma*'s dramatic climax depicts the stillbirth of Cleo's (and Fermín's) daughter, thereby symbolically blocking her potential for futurity and reinforcing the association of Indigenous peoples in Mexico with the colonial past. The planes that soar overhead throughout *Roma*'s diegesis can also be interpreted as allusions to Mexico's rapid modernization and industrialization during the period in which the film is set, but this is a process from which Cleo appears to be excluded. She can only dream of the escape that they represent as she sees them reflected in the pools of water that she slops over the family's driveway.

Cleo's status as surrogate mother to Sofía's children reinforces the way in which these kinds of foundational fictions require the subjugation of the racial Other so that the modern Latin American nation-state can symbolically be forged. Following her miscarriage, Cleo saves the lives of two of Sofía's children who are swept out to sea during a day at the beach after they learn that their father has abandoned them. Cleo does not know how to swim and risks her life by entering the water to rescue them, which signals the literal and symbolic sacrifices that she would make (and has made) for their family. The black-and-white wide-angle shot that tracks Cleo as she runs across the beach's expanse and into the water, along with the amplified sounds of the ocean's waves, creates an epic sequence and reinforces the sense that the film is a Hollywood-inspired homage to Cleo's grace and fortitude. Immediately after rescuing the children, Cleo cries and guiltily admits that she had never wanted her own daughter to be born; her employer-family tells her that they love her, and their emotional embrace is backlit by the setting sun. It is clear that the care and affection that she could have dedicated to her own Indigenous descendant child will continue to be transferred to her employers' White offspring. They form a family symbolically characterized by mestizaje, with the Indigenous woman, Cleo, surrounded by the European descendant woman, Sofía, and her children. It is an image that can be associated with the projection of modern Mexican national identity as fundamentally mestizo, an idea explored in Vasconcelos's (2017) book *La raza cósmica* (first published in 1925), which resonates with Freyre's celebration of mestiçagem in Brazil. Both texts presuppose the subjugation of the Afro-Brazilian or Indigenous elements of this mixing or implicitly associate them with the past. With recourse to *Roma*'s foundational narrative, then, Cleo is both exalted as and relegated to the role of a surrogate member of her employer's family. These kinds of relationships have permitted the emotional and labor exploitation of domestic workers across Latin America, and *Roma*'s ambivalent narrative, at times, risks reinforcing their romanticization.

Empowering Conclusions in *Que horas ela volta?* and *La nana*

In contrast to *Casa grande* and *Roma*, the conclusions of *Que horas ela volta?* and *La nana* endeavor to empower the domestic worker protagonists by endowing them with wider fields of vision, which is achieved through the movement into and out of different domestic spaces. In *Que horas ela volta?*, this process is triggered at the moment when Jéssica is pulled into the forbidden swimming pool by Fabinho and his friend. The pool becomes an affectively charged space that briefly permits the breakdown of the traditional domestic (and social) order, which is probably a result of the pool's cinematic associations with fluidity, transition, and skin contact (Hirsch and Brown 2014). It is the only scene in the film shot in slow motion, as the adolescents throw a football and splash each other in a moment of playful equality. The sequence mobilizes the ball as a symbol of relationality, while the teens' interactions more broadly recall the propensity for games and their related spaces to function as "heterotopias," or enacted utopias, which represent, contest, and invert all the other sites that can be found within a culture (Foucault [1967] 2008, 17), particularly in films about young people (Randall 2015, 219–226). Thus, this sequence could be associated with the potential reconstitution, or even democratization, of class relations in Brazil. It is no coincidence that after Jéssica calls Val to tell her that she has achieved a high score on the Vestibular and has earned a place at USP, Val steps into the pool for the first time and splashes the water in a moment of unprecedented rebellion. The depiction of domestic workers' entries into their employers' swimming pools while the latter are absent is a powerful trope that has been used to symbolize domestic employee insurrections in other Latin American fiction films, including *Los dueños* and Celina Murga's (2007) *Una semana solos* (A week alone).

The perceived liminality and malleability of adolescent desires provide a rationale for their depiction on screen in the fluid space of the swimming pool and for the threat that they pose to established hierarchies (Maguire and Randall 2018, 17). It is the teen characters in *Que horas ela volta?* and *Casa grande*, Jéssica, Fabinho, Jean, and Luiza, who are associated with the potential to create a new, more egalitarian society. This association is a consequence of the various discursive formulations that figure adolescence as a moment of crisis during which teens rebel against the fixed social and class roles that they are expected to play upon their impending entry into adulthood (Frota 2007, 155). I suggest that this understanding of adolescence also forms part of the rationale behind Gabriel Mascaro's (2012) choice to ask various adolescents to film their family's domestic workers and to use the footage as the basis for his documentary *Doméstica*, which is discussed in chapter 3.

Returning to the swimming pool sequence from *Que horas ela volta?*, this moment of rebellion is soon cut short when Bárbara, Carlos, and Val chastise the youngsters and instruct Jéssica to get out of the water. The adults' attempt to impose order on adolescent chaos is visually reinforced by the way the teens are framed from above, namely, from the balcony that leads off Bárbara and Carlos's bedroom and overlooks the pool. A horrified Bárbara is subsequently shown from below as she uses the raised vantage point to watch the scene unfold, a position that emphasizes her domestic authority. It is thus highly symbolic that, toward the film's conclusion, Jéssica rents an apartment with a balcony, which affords a raised view of the surrounding neighborhood and where Val subsequently joins her; prior to this, Val has been confined to dark, claustrophobic spaces within her employers' home and has often been framed from above. Jéssica and Val's balcony is smaller than, but clearly mirrors, Bárbara and Carlos's. It alludes to the fact that Val has achieved some degree of "domestic sovereignty," which, as Carvalho (Carvalho and Parisius 1999, 112) points out, has constituted a fundamental stage in the domestic worker's process of acquiring and demanding not only a "worker's identity" but also a "person's identity." The extended field of vision and brighter lighting associated with the balcony, and with Val's taxi ride through the city to the new apartment during which she gazes out of the window (Velho 2017, 62), are linked to the greater degree of influence and control that she now has over her own life after leaving her live-in employment. Also, while on the apartment's balcony, Val and Jéssica are finally able to address Val's absence from Jéssica's childhood and to begin to mend their relationship.

La nana also concludes with a sequence that symbolically extends Raquel's field of vision and gestures toward her growing independence. Inspired by her friend and coworker Lucy, Raquel takes up jogging, thereby moving outside of and away from the employer-family's home that had previously entrapped her. By the end of the film, Lucy has resigned her post and departed Pilar and Mundo's household; however, she has had a profound impact on Raquel's psychological and emotional state. Lucy provoked in Raquel a nascent self-awareness of the impact of her emotionally and physically exploitative labor. Earlier in the film, on the only other occasion that Raquel leaves the house alone, she goes to an upscale area of the city where she appears disoriented and confused and is forced to ask a stranger for directions. Her inability to interpret the urban space recalls Carvalho's (1982, 35) warning that live-in domestic workers are prone to isolation because they are confined to the home, making them overly reliant on others, and often do not know how to travel around the city independently. However, when Raquel goes out jogging in the final sequence of *La nana*, she does not need to ask anyone for directions. Jogging is an activity that finally provides her with some privacy: the camera frames her on her own in a medium shot as she runs with her headphones on and outside her employers' domain. Both Val's and Raquel's movement into new spaces, and the broadening of their perspectives, can be read optimistically as a product of these two films' desires to reflect on evolving domestic employer-employee relationships; they can also be interpreted as a sign that sociocultural attitudes toward paid domestic work, in particular toward live-in employees, are in a process of transition in Latin America, especially among privileged, left-leaning sectors of society.

Absent Fathers, Dominant Mothers, and "Future Girls": Modern Western Individualistic Feminism

The fact that these films depict weak male characters while they endeavor to empower female characters is significant. In *Casa grande* and *Que horas ela volta?*, the parallels between Jean's and Fabinho's portrayals are notable. Despite their privileged upbringings, both young men are unprepared to take the Vestibular: Jean flees the exam room, and Fabinho is distraught when he does not score highly enough to get into a good university, instead opting to take a gap year in Australia. Jean is uncertain about his future career path, and Fabinho spends much of his time smoking marijuana, a fact that distresses his parents. The young men's insecurities in romantic relationships are also symbolized when they both ask women of a similar age (Luiza and Jéssica) whether they are virgins, a question that betrays their own inexperience. They also frequently lie to those around them, Fabinho about his drug habits and Jean about his ability to dance *forró* (to impress Luiza). Their portrayal is suggestive of a crisis of elite masculinity, which is further reinforced by their relationships with their fathers, who are unemployed and struggle to assert themselves in their relationships with their wives. In *Casa grande*, Jean's inability to shed his virginity appears to present a particular problem: the possession of a woman's body is figured as the crucial threshold that must be crossed in order for him to enter manhood. Indeed, Pateman (1989, 38) suggests that the genesis of political power lies in man's conjugal or sex right, rather than in his fatherhood, because in order to have sons, men must have sexual access to a woman's body. It is thus highly symbolic that both Jean and his father, Hugo, are denied sex by their respective partners. On one occasion, the film cuts from a sequence that depicts Luiza refusing to have sex with Jean to Hugo and Sônia in bed with Sônia responding to Hugo's advances by saying, "Tô rezando" (I am praying).

The depiction of strong female characters and weak or absent father figures is a feature of all four films discussed in this chapter. The domestic workers' female bosses (Bárbara, Sônia, Pilar, and Sofía) are ultimately presented both as dominating at home (in the private domain) and as succeeding at work (in the public domain). The reversal of reason and emotion, which respectively are traditionally coded as masculine and feminine, is intimated by Pilar's and Jéssica's portrayals as intellectually and academically successful individuals in *La nana* and *Que horas ela volta?*[25] In many senses, these films' portrayals of female empowerment constitute a simple inversion of the association of territory and of the gaze with masculine power, while leaving other social paradoxes unsolved. The fact that the films remain haunted by traditional, masculine modes of viewing is best illustrated in *Que horas ela volta?* by Carlos's numerous inappropriate attempts to pursue a romantic relationship with Jéssica. During a discussion about Carlos's paintings, Jéssica states that she has "fallen in love" with one of his works; the camera then frames Carlos's gaze, which lingers on her as he responds, "É? Apaixonou?" (Really? You fell in love?). The growth of their friendship culminates in Carlos's awkward marriage proposal to Jéssica, which he later pretends was a joke.

The fixation on Jéssica that is intimated in *Que horas ela volta?* (via Carlos's gaze) lends to an interpretation of the film suggesting that she functions as an overdetermined symbol of Lulismo, the "new Brazil" that was emerging prior to Rousseff's impeachment in 2016 (Sá 2018, 324). In contrast to Fabinho and Jean, Jéssica and Luiza appear better prepared for their impending adulthood. Indeed, toward the film's conclusion, the audience discovers together with Val that Jéssica has already become a parent, which signals that she has left her childhood firmly behind. Both are state-school-educated young women who provoke upset in the households that they enter by questioning naturalized elite privilege. Despite not having had the same opportunities as Fabinho and Jean, Jéssica and Luiza both know they want to study engineering and architecture, respectively, in college, and they are thus symbolically associated with constructing a more egalitarian Brazil in the future. Jéssica wishes to study architecture because she believes it is "um instrumento de mudança social" (a tool for social change). She is given a tour of USP's School of Architecture and Oscar Niemeyer's Copan building, which are two of São Paulo's best-known modernist landmarks; both buildings were designed by Communists (Sá 2018, 317). The portrayals of the two young women can be viewed as a development on slightly earlier Latin American films that tend to figure pre-adolescent boys as synonymous with the rebuilding of their nations' futures, particularly following periods of dictatorship or economic crisis; these films include Walter Salles's (1998) *Central do Brasil* (*Central Station*), Andrés Wood's (2004) *Machuca*, and Cao Hamburger's (2006) *O ano em que meus pais saíram de férias* (*The Year My Parents Went on Vacation*).[26] (Appropriately, Michel Joelsas, the child actor who plays Mauro in Hamburger's film and embodies the hope for Brazil's post-dictatorship future, portrays Fabinho in Muylaert's *Que horas ela volta?*)

Although girlhood has been figured within modern theories of subjectivity as queer because it has no clear endpoint (other than those defined in relation to the masculine subject, i.e., by becoming a wife or mother) (Driscoll 2002, 54, 57), Jéssica and Luiza appear self-possessed and in control of their professional destinies. They could be characterized as what Anita Harris (2004, 6) terms "future girls," who, she argues, are frequently figured in late-capitalist discourse as having the flexible subjectivities that are necessary to compete in a precarious market-driven society. Jéssica's and Luiza's extremely positive depictions and abilities to overcome significant obstacles in order to achieve their goals hint at both films' ultimate reliance on neoliberal ideology, in spite of their simultaneous critique of it. In *La nana*, Lucy fulfills a similar, though less overtly allegorical, role. Like Jéssica and Luiza, Lucy is a modernizing influence; her arrival in the employers' household transforms the existing interpersonal dynamics. She is an aspirational young woman who is unable to reconcile herself to a life of live-in domestic servitude.

The mothers and "future girl" figures in *Casa grande*, *Que horas ela volta?*, and *La nana* demonstrate great resilience and sometimes enjoy professional and academic successes, but these films' representations of autonomous feminist empowerment (and related inversions of traditional, gendered power relationships) cannot resolve the question of who will care for these women's children and maintain their households while they are away undertaking more "prestigious" forms of labor. This conundrum is powerfully intimated by the title of Muylaert's film, which draws on a phrase uttered by both Fabinho and Jéssica: "Que horas ela (a mãe) volta?" (What time is she [Mom] coming home?). In this film, after Val has quit her job and moved in with Jéssica, she tells her daughter to send for her grandson, Jorge (whom Jéssica has left in the Northeast), so that Val can look after him while Jéssica is studying. Although the film represents a moment of class transcendence in the form of Jéssica's success, Val is still destined to undertake unremunerated emotional labor (of a different form). Drawing on the film's English-language title, Val stops being a surrogate to Fabinho, who has just left home, to take up a role as a "second mother" to Jorge. It is a narrative that raises the question whether a domestic worker is ever able to retire, a problem also highlighted in the testimonios analyzed in chapter 1 (Carvalho 1982, 32) and by Jocelyn Olcott (2011, 27), who argues that historically, both paid and unpaid reproductive laborers in Latin America have often found themselves without access to a pension and in a position where they were compelled to "take up the slack" in tending the young, elderly, and infirm. Furthermore, although Val has left paid domestic work, she expresses interest in becoming a massage therapist because Fabinho has told her that she is "a melhor massagista do mundo" (the best masseuse in the world). Her ambition reinforces Staples's (2007, 144) argument that even when reproductive labor is refused, it often "flows into other reaches of the general economy, including commodification."

Roma is similarly unable to eschew the dilemma that the other three films discussed in this chapter also confront: Sofía ultimately relies on Cleo to maintain her home and care for her children while she pursues a full-time career in publishing, which she takes up toward the end of the film in order to support her family following her separation from her husband. Prior to this, and upon her abandonment by her husband, Sofía warns Cleo, "siempre estamos solas" (we women are always alone). While *Roma* displays some elements of an intersectional critique, all the films espouse modern, Western feminist individualism, meaning they leave unresolved the issue that middle- and upper-class women's professional independence has frequently been won off the back of the subjugation of lower-class, darker-skinned women (Spivak 1985). Furthermore, the films are prone to ambivalently romanticizing the close emotional relationships established between the employers' children and the domestic worker protagonists (to differing degrees), in part because the films are the product of their directors' well-meaning desires to address an emotional debt to their families' own former domestic workers.

Conclusion

I began this chapter by examining the filmic techniques used to evoke live-in paid domestic workers' limited fields of vision and marginalization within their employers' houses. The territorialization of the home in these films expresses middle- and upper-class fears surrounding the entry of the working class into spaces considered "reserved" for employers. These anxieties are linked to a bourgeois desire to maintain a clear separation between the "private" (domestic and familial) and the "public" realms, but the figure of the live-in domestic worker undermines this distinction, namely, in the way that their reproductive labor permits the employer-family's participation in more prestigious or "productive" forms of work outside the home. In the cases of *Casa grande*, *Que horas ela volta?*, and *La nana*, the way that productive and reproductive labor overlap is explored via the films' mise-en-scènes within the homes that serve as their settings.

Ultimately, all the productions discussed in this chapter constitute odes to their directors' childhood domestic workers; they betray a desire to atone for an affective debt to these employees that is nonetheless difficult (if not impossible) to recompense. Both *Que horas ela volta?* and *La nana* explore this desire through their deployment of gift-related symbolism. In addition, *Roma*, *La nana*, and *Que horas ela volta?* critique the ways in which the practice of employing live-in domestic labor results in attempts to commodify or dehumanize the workers, whose rights to privacy and to an independent family life are dramatically compromised by their employment. The films do so through their deployment of bestial imagery, which underscores these employees' alignment with the abject (e.g., dirt) from a bourgeois perspective and threatens their status as subjects.

Overall, the productions oscillate ambivalently between constructing affective alliances with and adopting the perspectives of their domestic worker protagonists and deploying well-known stereotypes regarding these employees. Although *Casa grande* constitutes an indictment of Brazil's corrupt socioeconomic system and its perpetuation of inequality, the sexual politics in the film risk reinforcing a postcolonial (Freyrian) power relationship at the story's close. Similarly, *Roma*'s climax also reproduces a foundational narrative that celebrates mestizaje but symbolically relegates the country's Indigenous population to the past. While the endings of *Que horas ela volta?* and *La nana* endeavor to empower their domestic worker protagonists by endowing them with broader fields of vision and greater freedom, all four films rely (to greater and lesser degrees) on a modern, Western individualistic feminist framework, the contradictions of which the films are unable to resolve or reflect upon fully. This framework emerges as the films invert traditional male-female power hierarchies through their characterizations of resilient or successful mother or "future girl" figures and through the ways that they intimate crises of elite masculinity. Despite the potentially intersectional elements of *Roma*'s critique and the empowering aspects of *Que horas ela volta?* and *La nana*'s endings, the resolutions achieved at these films' conclusions are contingent on their domestic worker protagonists remaining in situations where they appear resigned to, or even happy with, their position providing more remunerated or unremunerated care so that their employers, or in Val's case, her daughter, can go out to do more "prestigious" forms of work. Despite their narrative limitations, these films have provoked public debate on the exploitative nature of live-in domestic work and on structural inequality in Latin America more broadly; they have even, in the case of *Roma*, had a tangible impact in advocating for and improving paid domestic workers' rights.

CHAPTER 3

Immaterial Labors

Spectral Domestic Workers in Brazilian and Argentine Documentary

IN THIS CHAPTER, I analyze contemporary Latin American documentaries that are the products of artists' or employers' collaborations with current or former domestic workers, which often shed as much light on the subjectivity of the employer as they do on the employee's. The works I assess in this chapter form part of a plethora of recent documentaries made in the region that feature paid domestic or care workers as protagonists.[1] I suggest that all the documentaries analyzed in this chapter are characterized by the depiction of spectral (or ghostly) domestic employees because paid domestic work has not been properly accounted for by traditional capitalistic economic models. By redirecting the audience's attention to paid domestic work and to the individuals who undertake it, the documentaries constitute a political intervention.

Following brief overviews of the contexts and plots of the documentaries, the analysis is divided into two parts. The first part focuses on Lucrecia Martel's (1999) *Las dependencias* (The outbuildings) but also references João Moreira Salles's (2007) *Santiago* and Rodrigo Moreno's (2014) Argentine fiction film *Réimon*. *Las dependencias* explores how the domestic employees of Argentine authors Silvina Ocampo and Adolfo Bioy Casares not only materially supported the famous couple but also provided creative inspiration for Ocampo's writing. The documentary serves as a starting point for showing how the films analyzed in the first half of the chapter blur the distinction between "artist" and "servant." All three films probe anxieties about what counts as work by exploring different forms of immaterial labor. As discussed previously, immaterial labor encompasses forms of work whose principal products are affects, social and emotional relationships, or forms of communication, although this kind of labor almost always involves material tasks as well (Hardt and Negri 2004, 108–109).

131

Artistic, creative, domestic, and care work are all forms of immaterial labor, and the films raise thorny questions about the ways in which these forms of employment are both undervalued and valued differently in economic, social, and cultural terms.

In the second part of the chapter, I return to an analysis of *Santiago* but compare it with two other Brazilian documentaries, Consuelo Lins's (2010) *Babás* (Nannies) and Gabriel Mascaro's (2012) *Doméstica* (Housemaid). All three documentaries are dedicated to domestic workers who were filmed by the children of their current or former employers, and the films can thus be fruitfully approached as domestic or experimental ethnographies and forms of autofiction. I discuss how elements of these documentaries betray a nostalgic yearning for the intimate relationships that have been permitted by forms of live-in domestic service that are becoming less common in Brazil.[2] Nonetheless, the films simultaneously undertake a critical exploration of the ways in which contemporary domestic labor relationships are haunted by the legacy of colonial hierarchies of power, including those founded on forms of race- and gender-based oppression. Ultimately, I show how these Brazilian documentaries examine the spectral nature of contemporary domestic labor relations by reflecting on their own filmic forms. They employ different cinematic technologies to explore how modes of filmmaking and image production have changed (or not) over time and how these modes are implicated with power hierarchies themselves. These documentaries meditate on celluloid film's and photography's frustrated relationships to the "index" (the physical trace of a person or object now gone) in order to explore not only a childish desire for lost intimacy with paid domestic employees and the way in which these emotional relationships haunt late capitalism in Brazil but also how the filmmakers are haunted by Brazil's enslaver past.

It is likely that colonial history resonates more strongly throughout the Brazilian documentaries than in the Argentine *Las dependencias* because Brazil was the last country in the Western world to abolish enslavement, doing so in 1888, and because the Afro-Brazilian majority population remains politically marginalized today. However, *Las dependencias* is united with *Santiago* and *Babás* in that all three of the documentaries feature White (former) domestic employees, the majority of whom are either European migrants or the descendants of such migrants.[3] In this sense, all four documentaries are concerned with the history of domestic service in Latin America in the nineteenth century and the first half of the twentieth, which was shaped both by slavery and by the migration of large numbers of White, working-class Europeans.

The Documentaries and Their Methods: *Las dependencias*, *Santiago*, *Babás*, and *Doméstica*

The made-for-television documentary *Las dependencias*[4] provides insight into the life of the Argentine author Silvina Ocampo (1903–1993) by focusing on two of her domestic employees who appear to have served as a creative stimulus for her writing: Elena Ivulich and Jovita Iglesias. Both Ivulich and Iglesias were employed by Ocampo and her husband, the Argentine writer Adolfo Bioy Casares (1914–1999), over lengthy periods. Ivulich began working as Ocampo's secretary when she was around twenty years old, and Iglesias was first informally employed by Ocampo when she was twenty-four years old in 1949, having recently arrived in Argentina from Spain (Iglesias and Arias 2003, 17–21). Iglesias worked as a seamstress for both Ocampo and Bioy Casares while also taking on responsibility for a variety of other domestic tasks.[5]

Many of Ocampo's poems and short stories feature domestic servant characters,[6] and together with the Argentine writer José (Pepe) Bianco, Ocampo also translated Jean Genet's renowned French play *Les bonnes* ([1947] 2001; The maids) into Spanish under the title *Las criadas*. The translation was published in 1948 in the Argentine literary magazine *Sur*, edited by Silvina Ocampo's sister Victoria Ocampo (Mancini 2018, 104). The Ocampo sisters had a notoriously antagonistic relationship and are known to have disputed the services of their favorite domestic employee, Fani: the event marked Silvina's later literary work (Mancini 2018, 102, 109–111).[7] Indeed, the jealousy provoked by the services of "good" domestic workers is powerfully and humorously explored in Silvina's short story "Las esclavas de las criadas" (The slaves of the servants) in her collection *Los días de la noche* (1970; The days of the night). María Julia Rossi (2020, 142) argues that in Ocampo's later literary works, the individual identities and subjectivities of her servant characters become better defined, and a critique is developed of the ways that the relationship between employer and servant is supposed to function as the central axis that structures the servant's identity. Consequently, *Las dependencias* aptly brings Ocampo's domestic employees center stage so that they can take the lead in painting an intimate portrait of their former employer, while also commenting on their own biographies and interests.

In the documentary, Ivulich's and Iglesias's accounts are given greater precedence than that of Ocampo's husband, which could be viewed as an irreverent artistic choice by the screenplay authors, Graciela Speranza and Adriana Mancini, and by the director. However, it is not altogether surprising, because domestic employees and their roles in bourgeois home spaces are a concern that unites Martel's fiction filmmaking, from her Salta Trilogy (2001–2008) to *Zama* (2017).[8] The parallels between the fictional literary and cinematic universes that Ocampo and Martel create are striking and appear to have been shaped by the women's upbringings in large, upper-middle-class Argentine families (Mullaly, n.d., 3). Their works are imbued with a deep interest in intimate relations of class, power, and otherness, an interest that is frequently channeled either through the adoption of the perspective of child protagonists or via the depiction of domestic workers (Kratje 2017, 12; Page 2009, 186; Mullaly, n.d., 3).[9]

The other three documentaries I examine in the second part of this chapter are Brazilian works, and all stage real, affective encounters between domestic employees and employers that encourage the audience to reflect on the ways in which sociopolitical and historical processes have shaped the personal, familial realm. The films do so by drawing on various techniques that have come to characterize contemporary Brazilian documentary production, including the incorporation of home video and archive footage, experimentation with forms of self-representation, and the use of interviews (Xavier 2009; Lins and Mesquita 2008). The importance of interviews and even confrontational encounters between filmmaker and subjects in *Santiago*, *Babás*, and *Doméstica* attest to the influence of the renowned Brazilian documentary maker Eduardo Coutinho on all three directors discussed in this section (Xavier 2009, 211).

Salles's *Santiago* has been hailed as one of the best Latin American films of recent years by the critics Edgardo Dieleke and Gabriela Nouzeilles (2008, 139) and Artur Xexeó (2013), while Luiz Carlos Merten (2012) has called it "talvez o maior documentário da história do cinema brasileiro" (perhaps the greatest Brazilian documentary of all time). Its watershed status accounts for the clear marks of its influence on Lins's and Mascaro's documentaries, in terms of both theme and performative, self-reflexive form. While all the documentaries discussed in the second part of this chapter offer a valuable and uncomfortable interrogation of socioeconomic and cultural privilege, *Santiago* arguably institutes a thematic genre in the canon of Brazilian documentary that had previously been defined by middle- and upper-class directors filming those who are vulnerable and impoverished in productions about "street children," urban violence, or the rural Northeast (Dieleke and Nouzeilles 2008, 148). The lives of the upper class had hitherto been a "silent terrain" (Allen 2013, 183), and Salles has argued that *Santiago* differs in the way that it provides insight into "the dominant class," or even into "the relations that are established between the dominant class and those it dominates" (Dieleke and Nouzeilles 2008, 148).

The documentary *Santiago* focuses on the conflictive and collaborative encounter between a domestic employee and the child of his employers. It is Salles's homage to his family's former butler, Santiago Badariotti Merlo, an eccentric figure whom the director had known since he was born and of whom he was clearly fond. Santiago's status as a retired White male butler who had been employed by one of the most privileged families in Brazil certainly distinguishes his experiences from those of the primarily Afro-descendant domestic workers depicted in the other Brazilian documentaries examined in this chapter.

The film consists of the footage that Salles and his crew recorded of Santiago at the latter's apartment in the affluent Leblon neighborhood of Rio de Janeiro over the course of five days in 1992. Santiago was eighty years old at the time. He had worked for the Moreira Salles family for thirty years, from 1956 until 1986, while they resided in a modernist mansion in the Gávea neighborhood of Rio de Janeiro (Merten 2007; Furtado 2019, 152). The director's father, Walter Moreira Salles, was a wealthy businessman and founder of Brazil's largest banking institution; he also served as ambassador to the United States in the 1950s (Furtado 2019, 152). Consequently, Santiago was employed by the family at a moment when they enjoyed great privilege and influence in Brazil's political, cultural, and social circles. In the documentary, Santiago recalls hosting the Rockefellers, the president of Mexico, and the former Brazilian presidents Juscelino Kubitschek and João Goulart at the Gávea home, where he was part of a team of twenty-two servants.

Initially, Salles had planned to make Santiago the protagonist of a documentary that would revolve around the themes of life, death, memory, and oblivion. The Gávea mansion and the former butler would have served as a historical allegory for Brazil's golden age in the mid-twentieth century, marked by the construction of the new capital, Brasília, and the popularity of bossa nova, followed by the country's decline in the 1990s, when the footage was recorded, the house was abandoned, and the country was blighted by high levels of inflation (Dieleke and Nouzeilles 2008, 144–145). However, the director became frustrated with the project and did not return to edit the footage he had amassed until after Santiago's death in 1994; he finally released the documentary in 2007. Salles has admitted that during the editing process, he realized that he, too, was a character in the film and that he could not make the documentary without acknowledging it (Dieleke and Nouzeilles 2008, 148; Anjos and Doppenschmitt 2008; Oricchio 2009). Consequently, he incorporates a self-reflexive, first-person voiceover[10] that comments on the raw footage and culminates in a painful admission of personal privilege, because he recognizes the self-serving spirit in which he filmed a documentary that was meant to be about the former butler but was just as much about himself. In this regard, the relationship of care and the hierarchy of power that would have existed when Santiago was the Salles's employee is replicated at the level of the documentary.

Lins's 2010 documentary short, *Babás*, constitutes an elegy to nannies across Brazil and appears to be a product of the director's desire to atone for their treatment in what could be considered an attempt, at least in part, to extirpate feelings of middle-class guilt.[11] This impression is reinforced by the film's first-person nondiegetic voiceover,[12] which at times enables Lins, a filmmaker and academic from Rio de Janeiro, to interrogate her own privilege by recognizing the female employees who played a crucial role in raising her, her siblings, and her own children.

Babás is a good example of what Catherine Russell (1999, 238) terms "found-footage filmmaking," because Lins addresses the legacy of enslavement that weighs on modern-day relationships between nannies and employers in Brazil by retrieving and examining her own home videos, family footage recorded by others, and archival photographs. She also pieces together paintings and job advertisements, produced from the late nineteenth century to the present day, in such a way as to sketch out a genealogy of Brazil's *babás*. Like so many Latin American shorts, Lins's film has depended on free online distribution in order to circulate; it is available on YouTube, Vimeo, and PortaCurtas and can thus be considered part of what Debra Castillo (2007) has termed the "New New Latin American cinema": short films produced by filmmakers with limited resources who are often interested in experimenting with form.

Mascaro's (2012) *Doméstica* also did not have a wide commercial distribution,[13] despite its director's growing renown as a visual artist. Mascaro, who is based in Recife (Pernambuco), belongs to the "novíssimo cinema brasileiro" (newest Brazilian cinema) generation, which is characterized by the creation of filmmaking collectives outside Rio de Janeiro and São Paulo that often do not draw on state funding mechanisms (Ikeda 2012). Many of these filmmakers operate on limited budgets and use digital equipment to produce works that are formally and aesthetically innovative (*Revista E* 2013, 20; Ikeda 2012). Much of Mascaro's art is concerned with class-based conflict, and he has admitted that he was inspired to make *Doméstica* when his non-Brazilian wife said that she did not want to hire a nanny to help with their childcare needs; she expressed concerns about "progressive" friends who employed such workers and expected the workers to sleep overnight in their homes without paying them overtime (Salem 2013). Her comment made Mascaro reflect on the ways that the current system of domestic work in Brazil presents continuities with the country's colonial past, an insight that features explicitly in the English-language blurb on the documentary's DVD case (though not in the Portuguese-language version) and implicitly in the film's diegesis.[14]

Mascaro, unlike Lins, does not appear in his documentary, but the experimental method he adopted to make it culminates in various direct encounters between domestic employees and their employer-families. The director placed advertisements in several Brazilian schools inviting teenagers to participate in making a documentary about their domestic workers (Furtado 2019, 161). Over a hundred volunteers were interviewed by Mascaro's assistants, and thirteen adolescent and domestic worker pairs were selected, although only seven pairs appear in the final film.[15] The employees featured had been working for their employer-families for fifteen or sixteen years, approximately the adolescents' entire lives. The participants were provided with a camera, a tripod, and a microphone and were asked to film their domestic workers for one week. They were also given guidelines to follow while filming, ones that encouraged them to include themselves in the footage, to focus on gaining the employee's consent to be recorded, and to leave the camera out whenever it appeared that conflict was imminent (161–162).[16] After filming, the adolescents surrendered the raw footage to Mascaro, who edited over 120 hours of material to produce a seventy-five-minute documentary composed of seven segments (Merten 2013), each of which focuses on the experiences of a different domestic worker.[17]

Las dependencias: Domestic and Artistic Labors

Of all the documentaries analyzed in this chapter, *Las dependencias* most openly addresses the creative inspiration that domestic workers have provided for their artist-employer. A discussion of this film thus leads into an exploration of the ways in which paid domestic labor haunts artists and intellectuals in late capitalism. Through the work's focus on Ocampo's secretary, Ivulich, and the seamstress, Iglesias, *Las dependencias* implies that the writer's domestic employees not only supported her work materially but also served as muses for her fiction. Ivulich states that she enjoyed her work, which involved typing up multiple versions of Ocampo's texts, which the author originally drafted by hand. Iglesias, who has subsequently published a book based on her experiences working for Ocampo and Bioy Casares,[18] explains that Ocampo liked to watch others working and showed an interest in her life. Iglesias claims that "en todos los libros hay algo de lo que yo le decía pero, claro, transformado a otros nombres y a otras cosas" (in all her books there are elements of things I told her but, of course, transformed into other things and under different names). In the documentary, an interview with Ocampo's friends Ernesto Schoo and Juan José Hernández reinforces the sense that her close relationship with Iglesias had an influence on Ocampo's narratives when they observe that seamstresses are staple figures in the author's oeuvre. Laurence Mullaly (n.d., 4) argues that Ocampo endeavored to return the creative inspiration, care, and loyalty that her employees provided by endowing her servant characters with agency, particularly in her later narratives.

Similarly, *Las dependencias* centers Ivulich's and Iglesias's testimonies and endeavors to allow their perspectives, voices, and interests to shine through rather than simply using their accounts to invoke the presence of their deceased employer. At one point, Ivulich reveals that she, like Ocampo, also writes poetry, and she is invited to recite one of her compositions, the comical and cautionary "Filomena y Filemón." Later on, Ivulich performs a second composition about nurses, which she had dedicated to her employer when she was ill. The secretary modestly insists that her poems are simple and infantile, but by including her renditions alongside an analysis of Ocampo's own works, the documentary gestures toward the possibility of eroding the distinction between "low" and "high" culture.

The sequence featuring Ivulich's recitation of "Filomena y Filemón" is directly preceded by a discussion of Ocampo's short stories, which both Schoo and Hernández conclude are "como fábulas" (like fables). Schoo and Hernández focus on "Las vestiduras peligrosas" (The dangerous garments) (Ocampo 1970), whose first-person narrator is a seamstress and former *pantalonera* (trouser maker) called Piluca. The story portrays Piluca's relationship with her employer, Artemia, who instructs Piluca to make her a series of revealing, provocative outfits, of which the seamstress does not approve. Artemia becomes distraught when she reads in the newspaper about women in other countries who go out wearing clothes that are seemingly identical to hers and who all become victims of rape. The seamstress advises Artemia to wear dark trousers and a man's shirt, which she makes for her. The story's conclusion serves as a feminist critique of gendered expectations and the male gaze: when Artemia goes out dressed like a man, she is attacked by a group of youths who rape and stab her because they think she is *uma tramposa* (deceitful). This ending is read aloud by Iglesias in *Las dependencias*. Prior to this, the documentary cuts between Schoo's and Hernández's discussion of the text and Iglesias's descriptions of the kinds of clothes that Ocampo liked wearing and that she would make for her, including trousers.

While speaking, Iglesias is shown seated, with a thread in her hands and fabric in her lap, visually evoking not only her former employment but also the metaphorical equation often made between sewing (or weaving) and (women's) writing—or fabulizing. Consequently, the documentary unsettles the distinction between creative or artistic work and domestic labor as well as domesticity more broadly. The film's portrayal of Ivulich and Iglesias enables it to allude to the constructed nature of supposedly distinct categories, such as author and servant.

The form and thematic focus of *Las dependencias* thereby indicate that the classical distinction between labor (*poiesis*), intellectual or artistic activity, and political action (*praxis*) has dissolved in today's society, an idea that is explored by Paolo Virno (2004, 49–50). Drawing on Hardt and Negri's thought (2004), Virno (2004, 61) argues that in late capitalism, "activity without an end product, previously a special and problematic case [. . . ,] becomes the prototype of all wage labor." Hardt and Negri's discussions of the qualitative hegemony of immaterial labor provide a rationale for the intense interest sparked by different forms of paid domestic and care work in recent years. Gutiérrez-Rodríguez (2010, 100–101) crucially points out that while immaterial labor may have become qualitatively hegemonic, not all forms of it are treated equally. Features of "women's work" have become "general characteristics of the subjectivities demanded by the new modes of production," but paid domestic work is particularly denigrated because of its colonial baggage, feminization, and racialization, a fact that Hardt and Negri's framework fails to recognize.

Santiago: Virtuosic Labor

Paid domestic workers feature as spectral or ghostly figures in contemporary works by many Latin American artists precisely because the creation of immaterial products is a defining element of both domestic and artistic labors. Although the latter attracts a cultural capital (and status) that domestic work does not, and some artists enjoy financial success, many artists are also precariously employed and not properly remunerated.[19] This fact, together with a previously unacknowledged reliance on relationships with domestic employees that have been shaped by colonial legacies, means that the figure of the domestic worker appears to haunt the artist, cultural critic, or intellectual.

Salles's *Santiago* evocatively foregrounds the shared immaterial status of domestic service, artistic performance, intellectual activity, and cultural criticism through its focus on the butler, a figure who, Virno (2004, 53–54) suggests, presents a problem for Marx's distinction between productive and unproductive labor. Virno explains that Marx differentiated between two principal types of intellectual labor. First, there is immaterial or mental activity that results in commodities that exist separately from the individual who produces them, for example books or paintings; second, there are similar activities that do not result in an end product that is separate from the act of producing it (Virno 2004, 53). The latter constitutes activities that find their principal fulfillment (and purpose) in themselves without "being objectivized into an end product that can surpass them" (53). This second type of labor includes all forms of employment that culminate chiefly in a virtuoso performance that requires the presence of others, for example: "[concert] pianists, *butlers*, dancers, teachers, orators etc." (54 [my emphasis]).[20] This type of labor causes problems for Marx's theory because productive labor (the first type) "is precisely and only that kind of labor which produces surplus-value" (54). Marx's ideas are disrupted by "the strong resemblance" between the activities of performing artists and "servile duties," which, though "thankless and frustrating," do not produce "surplus value" in his view and thus "return to the realm of non-productive labor" (54). According to Marx, who failed to recognize the importance of reproductive labor because he accepted the capitalist criteria for what constitutes work (Federici 2014, 88), "servile labor" does not produce "surplus value" because no *capital* is invested in it, even though "a wage is paid (example: the personal services of a butler)" (Virno 2004, 54).[21]

Virno's and Marx's discussion of virtuosic labor sheds light on the reasons why being a butler is viewed as a particularly performative role. After all, a butler is employed to be *seen* by guests and to signal the refined status of their employers. In this respect, butlers constitute a type of domestic employee very different from the predominantly female cleaners, nannies, and cooks, who are often expected to go unnoticed, yet the products of "butlering" are even more immaterial and difficult to pin down. Indeed, Santiago appears to have made such an excellent butler because of his dedication to and love of performance. Salles recalls parties held by his parents when he was a boy at which he would play at serving drinks to guests; it was Santiago, the director says, who taught him how to carry the tray properly to ensure that the glasses would not spill over. Significantly, however, Santiago complemented this physical labor with an aristocratic and "cultured" demeanor, an air that he also displays through his devotion to religion, literature, and classical music.

Toward the beginning of the documentary, Salles recollects an incident involving Santiago that created a strong impression on him when he was a child. Late one night, he awoke to the sound of music and discovered Santiago playing the piano in a different part of the house. Salles was taken aback that Santiago, who had finished work, was still wearing a tailcoat; when Salles asked why, Santiago responded, "porque é Beethoven, meu filho" (because this is Beethoven, my dear). The film's nondiegetic voiceover subsequently comments, "Não sei se eu contaria a história de Beethoven no filme de 1992. Talvez sim, mas somente por achar que ela dizia respeito apenas a Santiago. Hoje sei que ela também é sobre mim. Sobre uma certa noção de respeito que era dele e que talvez ele quisesse me ensinar." (I don't know if I would have told the Beethoven story in the film I was making in 1992. Perhaps I would have, but only because of what it said about Santiago. Today I know that this story is also about me. It's about a certain notion of respect that he had and that perhaps he wanted to teach me.) The importance of valuing great art and live performance seems to be a meaningful lesson to pass on to Salles, who became an artist himself.

The butler's enthusiasm and respect for live performance is emphasized both in this sequence and in several others when his love of theater, music, and dance is discussed. For instance, Santiago recalls going to see Wagner's Ring cycle as well as an occasion when he took the son of his former employer in Buenos Aires to the Teatro Colón to watch *The Barber of Seville*, which featured "la gran Lily Pons" (the great Lily Pons), a famous French American soprano. At these moments, the documentary appears to imply that the butler was an artistic performer and cultural critic who could have earned his living through either of these professions or as an intellectual. Salles alludes to this, in my view, in the documentary's closing postscript through the description of a sequence from the end of the film *Tokyo Story*, produced in 1953 by the Japanese director Yasujiro Ozu, which inspired Salles at the time he was shooting *Santiago*. The voiceover makes the following comments about the scene:

> A filha caçula pergunta: "A vida não é uma decepção?" Sua cunhada responde com um sorriso franco e generoso: "Sim, ela é." Acho que é uma resposta que Santiago compreenderia. [. . .] Foi salvo por coisas tão gratuitas quanto a dança no parque de que gostava tanto.[22] Com elas, quem sabe?, pôde suportar a melancolia de quem suspeita que as coisas não fazem mesmo muito sentido. (Salles 2007)

142 PAID TO CARE

> The youngest daughter asks: "Isn't life a disappointment?" Her sister-in-law replies with a frank and generous smile: "Yes, it is." I think this is a response that Santiago would understand. [. . .] He was saved by priceless things, like the dance in the park that he liked so much. Because of them—who knows?—perhaps he was able to cope with the melancholy that must be experienced by someone who suspects that things really don't make much sense.

Through the framework of performance and virtuosity, then, it is possible to tease out the ways in which *Santiago* implicitly encourages us to question the wildly differing values that are attributed to different kinds of labor and, by extension, to the individuals who carry them out. As Elena Poniatowska (1983, 54 [discussed in chapter 1]) suggests in her prologue to *Se necesita muchacha*, the division between academic and manual labors, between "el cerebro y las manos" (the brain and the hands), is a famous one, but can the boss's alternative "destiny" to that of the domestic employee really be justified? The butler Santiago displays the passion and dedication of an artist, critic, and intellectual, but he is a migrant who is descended from servants, albeit those at the top of the domestic service hierarchy. Santiago proudly states that his grandmother was a lady-in-waiting to an Italian noblewoman, a fact that undoubtedly circumscribed his life opportunities in various respects. The butler's heritage attests to the persistence of historical divisions between masters and servants and employers and employees (Souto 2019, 102). However, by dwelling on the butler, his paid employment, *and* his artistic and intellectual pursuits, the documentary questions why one kind of immaterial labor (creative production) should be valued so much more highly—at least in cultural if not always in economic terms— than another (domestic work).

Réimon: Slow Cinema and Aesthetic Value

Moreno's fiction film *Réimon* makes the question of value even more explicit through its use of slow cinema techniques and its employment of a nonprofessional actor as its domestic worker protagonist. Even though the film's narrative is fictional, it bears so many similarities to the narratives of the documentaries analyzed in this chapter that it demands attention here.[23] The film's protagonist, Ramona, is a domestic employee who travels substantial distances each day from her home in the deprived outskirts of Buenos Aires to the more affluent city center, where she cleans upscale houses and apartments. The film's narrative and cinematic strategies encourage the viewer to reflect on the wildly disparate values attached to different kinds of work, as well as on the difficulty of accounting for certain forms of immaterial labor (e.g., domestic and artistic work), which culminates in their invisibilization and economic undervaluation.

The use of slow cinema techniques lies at the heart of *Réimon*'s critique. In their exploration of slow-cinema films, Tiago de Luca and Nuno Barradas Jorge (2016, 2) observe that these often feature extremely long takes, decentered and understated modes of storytelling, and a pronounced emphasis on quietude and the everyday, including a focus on quotidian chores that are often "recorded in minute detail and real time." These techniques are also characteristics of Mascaro's *Doméstica* and of Cuarón's fiction film *Roma*: they both include lengthy sequences that dwell on their domestic worker subjects while they are cooking, cleaning, and even scooping up dog excrement. De Luca and Jorge (2016, 13) note that "marginal labour is at the core of many slow films," and Karl Schoonover (2016, 157) observes that slow films' depictions of work are enhanced by the use of nonprofessional actors. According to Schoonover (157), natural actors are chosen for characteristics that "index their personal histories"; consequently, they are able to perform labor "without performing," and often at a slower pace than that of a professional actor. He argues that the slow film's attempt "to make empty or non-productive time visible," for instance, through a focus on "unproductive" laborers, "reverberates with a late twentieth-century anxiety about how to quantify human labor and the more general concern about the value of human life in late modernity." He concludes that the question of labor haunts the contemplation of these films (157–158).

In *Réimon*, the character of Ramona is interpreted by a nonprofessional actor, Marcela Días, whose real family and house appear in Moreno's film. As Ramona is shown cleaning, the camera dwells on her movements in lengthy sequences that are characterized by close-ups of her hands, arms, and other parts of her body. Furthermore, Ramona is often depicted gracefully placing her employers' belongings back in their rightful places or arranging their trinkets in aesthetically pleasing formations, which constitutes a kind of unseen performance. In one of the apartments that she cleans, Ramona's employers are always absent, which reinforces her portrayal as a ghostly presence who imbues the dwelling with vitality in spite of its emptiness. Her depiction resonates with Gutiérrez-Rodríguez's (2010, 140–141) argument that it is the affective quality of domestic labor that gives it so much value but that continues to be underappreciated in traditional economic models.

In its slow evocation of her domestic labors, the film thus reconfigures "well-established notions of aesthetic and cultural worthiness," to borrow

144 PAID TO CARE

de Luca and Jorge's (2016, 14) terms. Slow cinema techniques endeavor not only to make paid domestic work more visible but also to inscribe it with aesthetic value and thereby both challenge the bourgeois assumption that domestic labor is unworthy of our time or attention and simultaneously blur the boundary between domestic and artistic work. This kind of slow approach also characterizes passages of the other documentaries analyzed in this chapter, which lends to my argument that the question of domestic labor haunts these films, their forms, and their directors. By dwelling on paid domestic work and tasks, on labor that is often unseen or even *invisibilized*, these documentaries constitute a political act. They choose to highlight a form of labor that is undervalued in all senses: culturally, politically, and economically.

Ramona's characterization enables the film to disrupt the distinction between high and low culture, as do *Las dependencias* and *Santiago*. In the latter, the butler's eclectic cultural tastes are foregrounded in the film's voiceover, which points out that he loved Beethoven, Fred Astaire, the French aristocracy, and Hollywood nobility. Similarly, Ramona lives in a working-class neighborhood and is briefly shown watching what sounds like a popular telenovela at home, but her musical tastes provide a clear parallel with Santiago's. She expresses a preference for Schubert and Debussy; the latter's "Prelude to the Afternoon of a Faun" becomes the musical motif associated with her. Ramona plays it twice on a sound system belonging to an absent employer while taking a break from cleaning. These films thus refute the stereotypical association of domestic workers with low or popular, rather than high, culture. Instead they stage, as Julia Kratje (2018, 168) argues in the case of *Réimon*, "un arte de igualdad" (an aesthetics of equality), which also functions as an "ethics." Kratje further observes that Ramona's snatched moments of musical respite enable the film to reflect on who has the privilege of leisure time.

This critique is also enacted through the film's portrayal of two of Ramona's employers, who give her the nickname "Réimon"[24] and read out passages from (or inspired by) Marx's *Das Kapital*, a book that reflects on the ways in which capital (allied with employers and landowners) vampiristically extracts maximum value from employees' labor while simultaneously sucking energy from their persons.[25] One of the passages read out loud, which is taken from an article by Angel Ferrero and Iván Gordillo (2008), indirectly meditates on Ramona's situation when it criticizes the fact that, because of the poor design of many urban areas, workers must undertake long journeys to reach their employment, hours that are nonetheless not factored into their total working hours or remuneration. This leaves workers with barely enough time to recuperate (to eat and to sleep), let alone to pursue alternative, unpaid, or leisure activities.

Ramona cleans and cooks for her Marxist intellectual bosses and their friends while they study, smoke, and listen to music. On one occasion, she is forced to interrupt her work to dance with her male boss to a popular Argentine song in the folk style.[26] The film's ironic depiction of these employers recalls Poniatowska's (1983, 54) scathing comment that domestic workers do not appreciate "a los intelectuales de izquierda que dejan 'un tiraderote de colillas y de botellas de toda la noche que se están platicando [. . .], y allí se están y no hay modo de hacer limpieza ni de abrir la ventana para sacar toda la humareda que no sé cómo no se ahogan'" (leftist intellectuals who leave "a messy trail of cigarette butts and bottles after a whole night of chatting [. . .], and they stay there and there's no way of cleaning or even of opening the window to get rid of all the smoke—so much of it that I don't know how they don't choke"). The fact that the employers are shown reading academic tracts to one another out loud while still in their pajamas, a form of performative oratory that requires an audience and creates no end product, heightens the film's critical reflection on popular perceptions of the relative immateriality and productivity of intellectual labor versus domestic work. Indeed, these sequences could be interpreted as attempts to encourage the film's target audience to participate in some self-reflection.

Finally, *Réimon* also serves as a meditation on the ways that artistic labor is *sometimes* invisibilized and devalued much as domestic work is, which is unsurprising given that elements of both these forms of employment have been categorized alternately as unproductive and immaterial. *Réimon*'s use of opening intertitles signals that its own creation was contingent on an often unacknowledged system of film production, which involved lengthy and laborious processes of preproduction, shooting, and postproduction, as well as the collaborative contributions of various individuals, some of whom were not properly paid, including the lead producer, the director of photography, and the director himself.

Las dependencias: Haunted Houses

While in *Réimon* the opening intertitles draw attention to the potential spectrality of immaterial labor, *Las dependencias* deploys haunting, slow sequences to evoke how Ocampo was inspired by, and depended on, her domestic employees in ways that are difficult to account for economically. The fact that Ocampo's real employees appear to have served as an invisible source of inspiration for her writing uncannily parallels the immaterial status of the care and support they provided for the author, which the film implies were just as important as the material products of their domestic labor. Laurence Mullaly (n.d., 3) suggests that even Ocampo's use of Spanish was influenced by her interactions with her employees,[27] and in the documentary, both Schoo and Hernández point out her aptitude for reproducing the voices of individuals from different social strata in her writing, including "el habla de la calle" (the language of the streets). The benefits that Ocampo reaped from her relationships to domestic employees, including by re-creating their forms of expression in her literature as in the case of her short story "Las vestiduras peligrosas," could be termed "positive externalities," a term that refers to social wealth "created outside the direct productive process, the value of which can be captured only in part by capital" (Hardt and Negri 2004, 147). The social knowledge and forms of communication that Ocampo could draw on because of her close relationships with her employees arguably fit into this category and are thus difficult or even impossible to account for in traditional economic terms. Consequently, the immaterial products of such labor relationships, including their social, emotional, and communicative elements, could be said to haunt capitalistic economic models.

Las dependencias subtly explores the ways in which real relationships with domestic workers haunt Ocampo and her fiction through the use of repeated black-and-white sequences that are filmed with a shaky camera and depict different spaces in her apartment. These sequences, which certainly draw on a slow aesthetic, recur throughout the documentary and are often accompanied by unsettling, mournful music on the film's nondiegetic soundtrack. Additionally, the sequences contrast markedly with the accounts provided by Ivulich, Iglesias, Hernández, Schoo, and Bioy Casares, which are usually filmed in color using a still camera. The second time a black-and-white sequence is included, it shows a typed copy of a poem entitled "La casa autobiográfica" (Autobiographical house), which is covered with handwritten corrections. Ocampo would later publish the poem under a different title, "La casa natal" (Ocampo 1962; Childhood home). A recording of a section of the poem being read by someone who sounds like Ocampo is played as the film cuts to show a marginal domestic space: a corridor through which the camera slowly floats in a ghostly manner, as Kratje (2017, 16) also points out.[28] The poem explores Ocampo's love of the servants' quarters.

> Yo huía de las salas, de la gran escalera,
> Del comedor severo con oro en la dulcera,

Del mueble, de los cuadros, de orgullosas presencias,
Porque a mí me gustaban sólo las dependencias,
Que estaban destinadas para la servidumbre.

I would flee from the living rooms, from the large stairway,
From the severe dining room with a golden sweet jar,
From the furnishings, from the paintings, from proud guests,
Because I only liked the service quarters,
Which were destined for the domestic staff.

The poem is recited a second time, and at greater length, at the end of film as black-and-white footage of Ocampo's apartment is intercut with the closing credits sequence.

On one level, these spectral sequences could be interpreted as an attempt to invoke the ghost of the deceased Ocampo: the uncanny music is repeated when old black-and-white photographs and videos of the author are shown, and the documentary intimates that her former domestic employees are haunted by their employer's memory. Iglesias states that she was in awe of Ocampo, who was "imponente" (imposing). On another level, however, the black-and-white sequences and the repeated readings of "La casa natal" are designed to indicate the ways in which real domestic workers supported, inspired, and consequently haunted Ocampo and her literary production.[29] As Deborah Martin (2016, 10) suggests, sound in Martel's filmmaking is not merely used to support the visual image but also has "thematic and narrative importance" and is used to "suggest further layers to reality, something beyond the frame, beyond the visible or tangible." For instance, Martel's (2004) film *La niña santa*, which is set in a decadent hotel in Salta, Argentina, deploys the repeated trope of an employee loudly spraying a can of air freshener in ways that catch the spectator's attention. In *Zama* (2017), which is set in a colonial outpost in eighteenth-century Paraguay, Black enslaved people and workers are often shown in the background, but the director finds ways to foreground their presence, including one sequence where a domestic servant pulls a noisy, creaky fan back and forth while the White protagonists hold a conversation. In both these sequences, Martel deploys the symbols of the air freshener or fan not only to allude to the sense that there is literally a bad odor or overwhelming humidity in the locations that they depict but also to metaphorically intimate that the unpleasant elements of these spaces are associated with a rotten ruling class. The scenes also use amplified diegetic sounds to denaturalize the power dynamics that characterize employer-employee relations. The appeal of her

148 PAID TO CARE

films to "extra-visual epistemologies," through the use of sounds and the evocation of other senses, "undermines cinematic and visual regimes that uphold the mind-body separation and which are associated with a Cartesian, a Western [. . .] way of seeing" (Martin 2016, 21). In this sense, *Las dependencias* and Martel's other films echo the blurring of intellectual and domestic (or material) life that Ocampo's literature represents, particularly through their interest in servant characters.

On a broader level, these sequences can also be interpreted as an allusion to the fact that paid domestic workers constitute a spectral presence within the bourgeois home because they and their work have historically been present but marginalized and suppressed. Indeed, many of the homes portrayed in recent Latin American films and documentaries that portray relationships between domestic employees and employers function as allegorical locations that either display postcolonial characteristics or are temporally out-of-sync with their productions' settings. Barbosa's (2014) *Casa grande*, which I analyzed in chapter 2, is a clear illustration: although it is set between 2012 and 2013, its title serves as a reference to Freyre's book *Casa grande & senzala*, which was first published in 1933 and was a study of the domestic relationships that developed between landowners and enslaved people on Brazilian sugar plantations between the sixteenth and nineteenth centuries. Marco Dutra and Caetano Gotardo's (2020) fiction film *Todos os mortos* (*All the Dead Ones*) is set in the aftermath of the abolition of enslavement in Brazil; the story revolves around a decadent coffee-producing family's relationships to the Afro-Brazilians whom they had previously enslaved and, later, to different potential domestic employees. As the plot develops, however, the intrusion into its setting of various symbols of modernity (electrical tools, high-rise apartment buildings, and graffiti) signals that the film's characters are actually ghosts haunting a modern-day São Paulo.

Other powerful examples include the filmography of the Brazilian director Kleber Mendonça Filho, whose 2012 film *O som ao redor* opens with shots of an old plantation before focusing on the unsettling dynamics of employer-employee relationships in a contemporary apartment complex. His 2019 film *Bacurau* is set in its own present day but transpires partly in an old plantation house where guests are briefly served by a domestic worker. *Aquarius* (2016) focuses on Clara, a retired music critic whose work resulted in a decidedly immaterial product: cultural appreciation. She refuses to vacate her fabulous but decadent art deco apartment complex that is earmarked for demolition by a large construction company. Clara is frequently accompanied by her domestic employee, Ladjane, and is also haunted by the memory of her family's previous domestic worker, whom she is reminded of when leafing through an old family album in which the worker is shown either in the background of or partly cut out of various photographs. Clara had believed the former employee to be a thief and is revisited by her in a nightmare. Finally, in Mendonça Filho's humorous, dystopian 2009 short film *Recife frio*, an Argentine news correspondent reports on the effects a dramatic climate event has had on Recife, the capital of Pernambuco state, in Northeast Brazil, where the city's formerly tropical temperatures have permanently plummeted to between forty-one and fifty-seven degrees Fahrenheit. The reporter visits an affluent family living in a beachside penthouse apartment, which is poorly insulated. One of the adolescent sons has compelled the family's live-in domestic worker to swap rooms with him. She is shown shivering in a large, airy suite, as he warms himself with a hairdryer while watching porn in a small, windowless room: the *quarto da empregada* (the maid's room). The film informs viewers that "the maid's room" is an architectural phenomenon that dates to living arrangements established during the colonial period; it is the only instance in the short when an archival image is used. I suggest, therefore, that the pervasive trace left by minor servant characters in earlier cultural productions has been transformed in these contemporary films into the portrayal of spectral domestic worker figures who are deployed to provide the audience with an insight into the endurance of a colonial past whose effects linger in the present day.

Nonetheless, in these evocations of the colonial era, it is sometimes also possible to detect a certain degree of nostalgia for paternalistic servile relationships. In the documentary *Las dependencias*, Ocampo's yearning for the servants' quarters is explored through the nostalgic evocation of her childhood home in "La casa natal." In the film, Bioy Casares states that domestic servants were so prevalent in her writing because of "la nostalgia de su infancia, de chica, la más chica de la familia, un poco relegada al piso de los cocineros y de los mucamos, y eso era como un vivo recuerdo de infancia" (her nostalgia for her childhood, when she was a girl, the youngest in the family, somewhat relegated to the area used by the cooks and the servants, which was like a living memory of her childhood). In the documentaries I explore in the second part of this chapter, intimate relationships with domestic workers are also strongly associated with infancy and childhood homes or the memories of them.

The nostalgia that *Babás*, *Doméstica*, and *Santiago* at times betray is due in part to the fact that live-in domestic work is slowly becoming less common, a development that transforms the nature of employer-employee relations. In *Babás* and *Santiago*, this painful loss of childhood (and

150 PAID TO CARE

colonial) intimacy with domestic servants, from the employer-director's perspective, is ultimately evoked through these films' explorations of the frustrated relationship of documentary and photography to the index (the trace of a person, object, or relationship now gone). Their self-reflexivity and *Doméstica*'s performativity mean that all three documentaries are able to meditate to differing degrees on the ethics of portraying domestic workers in a way that the fiction films analyzed in the previous chapter do not.

Experimental Domestic Ethnographies: *Babás, Doméstica, and Santiago*

All three documentaries were either made or filmed by members of their domestic worker subjects' (former) employer-families, which means that the films can be fruitfully analyzed through the lenses of "experimental" and "domestic ethnography" (Russell 1999; Renov 1999). These two frameworks shed light on the films' anthropological aspirations but without eliding the colonial gaze and practices in which ethnographic modes of documentary filmmaking are inevitably mired. The films document intimate domestic employer-employee relations while also evoking the struggles and perspectives of the latter by adopting a variety of experimental documentary techniques.

Traditionally, ethnographic film has been used to document the culture of a group and to provide "empirical evidence" on which to base statements about a particular culture (Russell 1999, 10): it has historically been used by researchers from the Global North to document Indigenous peoples or communities in the Global South and often assumes a level of veracity or objectivity. However, this ethnographic relationship has been criticized as constructing "the global north as 'the source of theoretical knowledge,'" while "the so-called 'less developed' world" appears relegated to the production of culture or, at best, "local knowledge" (Schiwy 2009, 3). Hence, the power dynamics on which ethnographic filmmaking depend risk reproducing the "hierarchies of race, ethnicity, and mastery implicit in colonial culture" (Russell 1999, 10).

By contrast, Russell (1999, xvii [my emphases]) defines "*experimental* ethnography" as the attempt to dismantle "the universalist impulse of realist aesthetics into a *clash* of voices, cultures, bodies, and languages." She suggests that ethnography, which is "grounded in an identification with the cultural other," demonstrates a parallel with, and can be productively complicated by, experimental film- and video-making practices, which are drawn "not only to the marginalia of media culture, but also to marginal cultures" (19). She argues that "'the human condition' needs to be rethought as one of on-going cultural encounter, translation, and transition," and that it is "avant-garde" video-making practices that "provide the tools for this operation" (xvii).

Russell's argument is an apt framework for an analysis of *Babás*, *Doméstica*, and *Santiago* because their directors clearly wrestle with the question of how to represent domestic workers' experiences ethically and effectively given that their subjects can be considered as Others on the level of either class, race, gender, or (in the case of Santiago) sexuality. Consequently, the directors collate different kinds of images and footage and endeavor to incorporate a polyphony of voices and distinct perspectives on paid domestic work by using interviews and voiceovers. When discussing the perception of *Santiago* as an unfinished film, Salles has admitted that he ascribes to an approach that approximates "experimental ethnography" (Dieleke and Nouzeilles 2008, 142 [my emphasis]), and he has emphasized his belief that documentary should "not have to maintain the *imperialist pretension* of a total occupation of the territory. Santiago is an enigma, he continues to be an enigma, and that doesn't bother me." In the cases of both *Santiago* and *Doméstica*, which feature artistic disagreements and clashes between the domestic workers and those who film them, their experimental forms at times appear to threaten the traditional filming hierarchy because they foreground the contested power dynamics that shape the relationships they depict. During their best moments, all three films acknowledge the propensity of those behind the camera to misunderstand or ignore domestic workers' personal histories and experiences, which suggests that while these documentaries may spring from feelings of class guilt, their experimental approaches are also designed to signal an implicit sympathy with the workers they depict. The documentaries appear to aim to challenge audiences to reconsider popular cultural assumptions surrounding the roles that domestic employees have been designated for so long.

In the context of an analysis of these films, the concept of experimental ethnography can be usefully combined with the framework of domestic ethnography, which Michael Renov (1999, 141) defines as work that "engages in the documentation of family members" or people "with whom the maker has maintained long-standing everyday relations and has thus achieved a level of casual intimacy."[30] The documentaries discussed here, which focus on long-standing relationships between employer-families and (often live-in) paid domestic workers, can be categorized as forms of domestic ethnography. Nonetheless, the relationships they examine are more complex and hierarchical than those depicted in traditional domestic ethnographies, which take a parent, sibling, or child as their object (Renov 1999, 141–142), because they are structured by postcolonial hierarchies of race and class and are on occasion shaped by narratives of fictive kinship.

Domestic ethnographies tend to implicate the filmmaker (or the "self") because the lives of the artist and the subject are interwoven by their intimate ties (Renov 1999, 141; Furtado 2019, 145). Consequently, experimental ethnographies demand critical self-reflection on the documentarian's position of (post)colonial dominion, and domestic ethnographies make this interrogation unavoidable because they explore the experiences of a subject with whom the filmmaker is implicated by a close connection. It is for this reason that *Doméstica* and *Santiago* have also been described as "autoethnographies" and "autofictions" (Andrade 2017, 37; Oricchio 2009). As Renov (1999, 141) explains, "domestic ethnography is a kind of supplementary autobiographical practice; it functions as a vehicle of self-examination, a means through which to construct self-knowledge," namely, by interrogating the ways in which the self is constructed in relation to an intimate or familial other. As a result, those involved in filming these documentaries also become characters in them.

In both *Santiago* and *Babás*, the self-reflexive first-person voiceovers are a key device used to acknowledge the filmmakers' direct and personal implications in the narratives that they weave. The voiceovers provide an insight into the directors' intimate relationships with the domestic workers depicted, while also serving as outlets for confessions of personal guilt. Nonetheless, neither Salles nor Lins voice these commentaries themselves. In the case of *Santiago*, the voiceover was recorded by the director's brother Fernando Moreira Salles, while in *Babás* it was recorded by Lins's friend Flávia Castro. The choice to use the voice of a family member or friend for the films' first-person voiceovers introduces a layer of "fiction" into the two documentaries, to borrow Salles's own term (Oricchio 2009). It is a device that upholds the principles of experimental or domestic ethnography because the element of fiction alludes to the fact that these films do not aspire to serve as objective truths. Instead, the films make it explicit that they are constructed from their directors' perspectives, which are compromised by their personal involvement in the relationships depicted.

This striking, formal resemblance between *Santiago* and *Babás*—which, in my view, can be attributed to the inspiration that Salles's film provided for Lins's film—is reinforced by their openings. *Santiago*'s voiceover comments, "Há treze anos, quando fiz essas imagens, pensava que o filme começaria assim" (Thirteen years ago, when I recorded these images, I thought that the film would start like this). The narration then discusses Salles's original plan to open the documentary by focusing on three photographs of his childhood home in Gávea, which like the rest of the film are recorded in black and white. *Babás* also opens with a black-and-white photograph, one that features an Afro-Brazilian wet nurse and her young charge. The narrator comments, "Quando vi essa foto pela primeira vez, pensei que se um dia fizesse um filme sobre babás, começaria com essa imagem" (When I saw this photograph for the first time, I thought that if one day I were to make a film about nannies, it would start with this image). These opening statements are tentative. Salles and Lins appear to want to signal that they began these projects with a particular concept or thesis in mind that they later modified. In other words, they purport to chart an evolution in their directors' thinking about the implications of their privilege, the nature and history of power relationships between employers and domestic employees, and the ethics of documentary filmmaking more broadly.

All three films discussed in this chapter are united in that they constitute somewhat distanced reflections on raw film footage, which aligns them once again with experimental ethnographic practices. This is made explicit in *Santiago*'s subtitle *Uma reflexão sobre o material bruto* (A reflection on raw footage). The creative inspiration that Salles's film provided for *Doméstica* is signaled on the latter's DVD case, which states that the seven adolescents recruited to film their families' domestic employees were asked to "entregar *o material bruto* para o director realizar um filme" (*Doméstica* 2012 [my emphasis]; hand over *the raw footage* so that the director could make a film). Consequently, in *Doméstica*, the distance between the director and the raw footage is both spatial and affective, because Mascaro never had direct contact with the adolescents who recorded their domestic workers and whose footage he edited; he has also stated that the documentary is about "a terceirização do olhar" (Mascaro 2021; subcontracting the gaze). By contrast, in *Santiago* and *Babás*, the distance is temporal because the directors look back on the footage of employees with whom they were intimate that they recorded several years prior. In Salles's case, it is the footage for a film that he had previously abandoned, while in Lins's case, it includes her own home videos, though she also incorporates archival found footage that was recorded by others.

In all three films, the decision to reflect, at a certain remove, on raw footage is "political," because doing so produces conflicts, clashes, and "dissensus" (Rancière 2003, 226).[31] This choice makes elements of the raw footage that otherwise might have been overlooked, ignored, or cut visible and audible, including takes that emphasize (former) domestic employees' propensities for resistance. In all these documentaries, then, those involved in making the films surrendered certain elements of power traditionally associated with directing a production. Salles and Lins relinquish traditional directorial anonymity because they acknowledge the ways in which they are compromised by the footage, both via their films' first-person voiceovers and by appearing or being heard on screen. Mascaro had limited influence over the footage and shots from which he constructed *Doméstica*, and the adolescent camerapeople who filmed the employees had no control over the director's final cut of the footage, which resulted in a depiction that many of the teens had likely not intended.

Despite this, Lins, Salles, and Mascaro ultimately retained editorial and thus authorial control over the material collected. While Mascaro, unlike Lins and Salles, does not appear in *Doméstica* in such a way as to self-reflexively foreground his ultimate control over the documentary's narrative, he has not attempted to conceal his control in interviews, stating that his subjective response to and reading of the footage given to him by the adolescents emerged at the moment he began to organize and edit the material (Andrade 2017, 40; *Revista E* 2013, 20). Consequently, the director's ideological project remains plain. His editorial choices result in a politically motivated documentary that explores the unequal power dynamics that characterize all the working relationships depicted. As Russell (1999, 19) argues, experimental ethnographic filmmakers "remain implicated in paradigms of modernism and colonialism, even as they seek ways of revising the production of otherness in representation." This is an insurmountable conundrum, as Salles (2009, 225) has suggested in his own theorization of the documentary form. He argues that "naïve" and "canonical definitions of documentary," which emphasize "objectivity" and an "uncontaminated access to reality," should be left aside, because they do not account for "the painstaking process of choosing lenses, defining framing and especially selecting, discarding and splicing hours and hours of raw footage." In these documentaries, experimental ethnographic approaches that foreground thorny issues of control and coloniality encourage the viewer to meditate on the ways in which filmmaking itself remains implicated in the same hierarchies of power and modes of exploitation that shape the domestic labor relationships they depict.

The performative nature of both documentary and home video is also strongly foregrounded in *Doméstica*, *Babás*, and *Santiago*, which all include sequences that feature their subjects dancing or singing for the benefit of the camera. These films can thus be categorized, to greater and lesser degrees, as performative and self-reflexive documentaries, modes that originally emerged in the late 1980s and 1990s (Bruzzi 2006, 3). The films either include the apparatus of filmmaking in their own mise-en-scènes or emphasize their subjects' interactions with the camera and crew, thereby foregrounding the effects of the latter's presence on the subjects' performance. Although this appears to represent a move away from a conception of documentary as an objective form that truthfully conveys facts, these films, like their predecessors, are still concerned with representing reality, yet they are "more aware of the inevitable falsification or subjectification such representation entails" and of the inevitable "distance between image and event" (Bruzzi 2006, 187, 217). Mascaro (2021) has stated that *Doméstica* revolves around the issue of representation and interrogates the fictionalization that documentary-making entails.

In other words, the relationships of those behind the camera to the domestic workers they film become the focus of productions that are also interrogating the nature of the documentary form and its troubled relationship to veracity. In her analysis of *Santiago*, Kratje (2017, 31) observes that although these two aims may appear antagonistic, they are ultimately complementary. This is the case, in my view, because all three documentaries dwell on the prior reluctance of Lins, Salles, and the adolescent camerapeople in *Doméstica* to confront the *uncomfortable truth* about their relationships with paid domestic employees. Their anxieties about what Kratje (31) calls "the fundamental problem" of how to represent "the Other" are channeled through their implicit and explicit meditations on documentary's frustrated relationship to the "index."

The Index

A "genuine index" serves as evidence of the existence of an object (the referent) at the moment during which the representation (or sign) of it was produced (Rosen 2001, 19). Examples of a genuine index include celluloid photographs and films, footprints, and weather vanes because they all "testify to the fact that the referent was present and left its legible trace directly in representation" (Doane 2002, 70). Celluloid photographs, for instance, are produced when light rays strike the chemical emulsion on photographic paper after the rays have been reflected from "the concrete objects in the actual spatial field" that is being pictured (Rosen 2001, 18). Consequently, a photograph is both "iconic" and "indexical" because it closely resembles the objects it represents and was forged by its physical connection to that object (Doane 2002, 92–93).[32] By contrast, a painting does not have the same degree of "credibility" because it cannot serve as "evidence" of the presence of the object (or referent) at a moment during which the sign (the painting) was produced (Rosen 2001, 19). The significance of the index is therefore heightened by virtue of its "existential bond" to the referent, which distinguishes it from a symbol, which is "sustained by a conventional, or habitual, or lawlike relation between itself and its object (for example language)" (Doane 2002, 92). The adoption of digital photography and filmmaking in the 1990s severed the material, or "indexical," connection between object and image that had previously defined photography and cinema (Mulvey 2006, 19). The digital, as an "abstract information system" predicated on a series of zeros and ones, precipitated a "crisis of the photographic sign" and undermined its hitherto "privileged relation to reality" (Mulvey 2006, 19).

In their works about the index and its relationship to cinema and time, both Philip Rosen (2001) and Mary Ann Doane (2002) draw on the work of the American philosopher Charles Sanders Peirce. When Peirce was writing in the nineteenth century, there was an upsurge in interest about different forms of archive, including museums and zoos, as well as about new archival technologies, such as photography and film. The impulse to archive was intensified by the desire to document anthropological "discoveries" and colonial hoards. In the case of the three documentaries I have discussed, their interrogation of the significance of the index and their experimentation with ethnographic filmmaking are used to critique the postcolonial dynamics inherent to traditional forms of archiving and of documentary-making.

The index can be viewed as spectral, or ghostly, because it is a form of physical *trace*. A sense of an object's earlier presence lingers through the index because the index was produced by the object's imprint, for example, on celluloid film. However, the object represented may no longer actually be present (it could have vanished or died), and the index provides nothing more than physical evidence of the relationship between the object and its sign. As Doane (2002, 94 [my emphasis]) argues, "the index, more insistently than any other type of sign, is *haunted* by its object" because "the index is 'actually modified' by its object" and thus "puts its addressee into a 'real connection' with its object." Rosen (2001, 21–22) suggests that the index tends to be fetishized by viewers because of our human obsession with defeating death and preserving the self; this explains the spectator's investment in cinematic images that can in some sense preserve or archive the past by attesting to its *physical presence* in a bygone moment. In sum, theories of the index, the archive, and the afterimage are all linked to the problem of how to represent time and circulate around the (in)accessibility of the present in representation.

The troubled relationship to the index emerges as a concern in *Santiago*, *Babás*, and briefly in *Doméstica* when these films meditate on the significance of old photographs and celluloid film footage that feature (former) domestic workers. The problem of how to represent diminished affective ties to domestic workers becomes entangled with the frustrated relationship of the index to the notion of "presence" on film. In my view, *Santiago* and *Babás* use this device to express a feeling of nostalgia for the loss of childhood intimacy that characterized past relationships to domestic employees.[33] The intense emotions that old photographs and archival footage of deceased family members can provoke by simulating a sense of the latter's presence reinforces the impression that these films use old footage to work through the loss of childhood attachments to paid domestic workers.[34] It is no coincidence that *Santiago* is filmed entirely in black and white, while *Babás* (like *Las dependencias*) features monochrome sequences. Just as in the fiction film *Roma*, this aesthetic signals that these films express a certain degree of nostalgia for *anachronistic* relationships to individuals who were viewed not unproblematically as surrogate-parent figures and as servants rather than as workers.

Babás: Delayed Cinema and Found-Footage Filmmaking

In *Babás*, Lins interrogates the significance of indexical images and found footage from the late nineteenth and early twentieth centuries by drawing on the potential of digital tools. She does so to shed a painful light on the nature of her own relationships with paid domestic workers in the documentary's more recent past. The voiceover in the film reveals that Lins trawled through archival films and family photographs and found that, despite many middle- and upper-class households' dependence on them to function, "é raro encontrar imagens de babás e empregadas domésticas nos arquivos públicos ou familiares no Brasil. Quando aparecem, é quase sempre por acaso, em meio a cenas com crianças em filmes de família" (it is unusual to find images of nannies and domestic employees in Brazil's public or family archives. When they appear, it is almost always by chance, in the midst of scenes featuring children in home video footage). After this, a rare example is shown: a piece of film from 1913 entitled "Baptisado do Paulo" (Paulo's baptism). The camera scans across a family group in a medium shot and suddenly pauses when it reaches an Afro-Brazilian woman who looks up and lingers just behind the other subjects, cradling a baby in her arms in a gesture that suggests she is the infant Paulo's nanny.

Prior to the advent of digital film, it would have been necessary to play celluloid footage such as this from start to finish at the pace of twenty-four frames per second to create the "illusion of movement" (Mulvey 2006,

Figure 3.1. A domestic worker who appears in archival footage entitled "Paulo's Baptism" (1913), *Babás* (dir. Lins, 2010, Consuelo Lins)

21–22). However, the digitization of archival film means that it can now be paused, rewound, fast-forwarded, and edited together in ways that were not previously possible, thereby allowing "old films" to be seen with "new eyes" (Mulvey 2006, 26). Laura Mulvey (8) terms this process "delayed cinema," which refers to the "delay in time during which some detail has lain dormant [. . .] waiting to be noticed" (2006, 8). It describes the technique that Lins adopts in *Babás* when the film of Paulo's baptism is shown. She exploits the capacity of digitization to freeze the archive footage and draw attention to the nanny as she suddenly looks up and returns the camera's gaze.

This detail can also be understood as the image's *punctum*, an element of the film that probably went unnoticed by the videographer but that captivated Lins's (and later the viewer's) attention. The punctum is "poignant" because its presence is a result of the camera's inability to distinguish between its intended subject and the subject's surroundings (Barthes 1993, 27).[35] In the style of an experimental, domestic ethnography, Lins uses the techniques of delayed cinema to interrogate archival family footage and its significance. Instead of simply reproducing family films that endeavor to conceal or marginalize the labor that sustains domestic bliss, the documentary harnesses the potential of digital tools to reread these indexical images. She juxtaposes and reexamines them so that the audience notices their punctum: in this case, the Afro-Brazilian nanny working to comfort baby Paulo so that the idealized image of an important family celebration can be recorded. When the footage of the nanny is paused, a bell rings out on the documentary's extradiegetic soundtrack as if to signal the surprising discovery of the image's punctum.

The force of the punctum is also a key technique employed in Daniela Ortiz's (2010) online photobook *97 empleadas domésticas* (97 domestic workers), which is designed to foreground the subtle presence of domestic workers at the margins of family photographs uploaded to Facebook (as I will discuss in chapter 4). In both Lins's and Ortiz's works, the artists employ experimental visual techniques that are designed to interrogate and to complicate the happy, harmonious, and totalizing image of the family that has been prevalent in home videos and family albums since the development of amateur film in the early twentieth century (Expósito n.d., 50).

In *Babás*, these techniques are employed to draw asynchronous connections between childcare practices in different eras. Following the footage of the baptismal party in 1913, the documentary links the Afro-Brazilian nanny's smart dress to the attire in which nineteenth-century wet nurses are often depicted by showing a series of their photographic portraits (which include their young charges). *Babás* thus implies that the legacy of enslavement continued to haunt the experiences of paid domestic workers in Brazil throughout the twentieth century and that there has not been a simplistic or teleological historical progression toward less exploitative labor practices. Like *Santiago*, *Babás* takes footage collected in the past and uses it as a site of *distanced* contemplation and contestation rather than as a raw material that simplistically documents history.

The film's narrative implies that juxtaposing archival footage with her own home videos lets the director perceive hitherto unnoticed details in the videos, as well as uncanny similarities between the two sources. After introducing five domestic workers who have been employed by Lins or other members of her family, the documentary focuses on the story of Denise Tavares da Silva, who has worked for the director for twelve years, including as a nanny to Lins's son Joaquim. Lins then includes two of her own home videos where Denise is visible, which, the voiceover observes, is a rare occurrence—just as it is unusual to find images of domestic employees in archival family footage. One of Lins's home videos is a humorous piece of holiday footage that she filmed in 1998 and that shows a young Joaquim being playfully encouraged to try out *a dança da bundinha* (the butt dance) by Denise and three other women. It is a dance that, the voiceover suggests, "talvez eu não ensinasse" (perhaps I wouldn't have taught him). Following the holiday video in *Babás*, an eerily similar sequence from home video footage recorded in the 1920s is played. It was filmed by Júlio de Mattos, a doctor from São Paulo state (Blank 2012). The video shows Mattos's young daughter Marieta

160 PAID TO CARE

being encouraged to dance the Charleston by her Afro-Brazilian nanny, who lingers at the edge of the frame, just as Denise does in Lins's footage. The popular association in Brazil of both dances with African heritage means that the juxtaposition of these family videos creates an implied link between childcare practices in the country throughout the twentieth century and their origins in the cultural legacy of African enslavement.

Babás thus strongly emphasizes the social, cultural, and affective products of domestic labor, similarly to *Santiago* and *Las dependencias*. These products are in some sense priceless, because it is very difficult to place a financial value on the love, care, and affection provided by a nanny with whom a family is intimate (Zelizer 2009, 179–181). Indeed, all the documentaries analyzed in this chapter play on the ways in which emotional ties between domestic employees and employer-families complicate any notion of domestic work as a purely economic transaction or commodity by foregrounding the slippage between labor and affect. In *Babás*, the homage that Lins pays the women whose "help" she can never fully articulate or quantify (in the voiceover's terms) appears to express her hope that the personal and emotional attachments that have developed between her family and these workers mean that these labor relationships resist total commodification.

However, labor relationships are commercial transactions, and the attempt to commodify affective labor can be experienced as alienating because it results in an attempt to place an economic value on an individual's capacity to care, communicate, and relate to others. The notion of a live-in domestic worker further clarifies this because the concept is predicated on the assumption that an individual's life can be almost entirely commodified. By paying a worker to live permanently in a home and to care for a family that is not their own, the employee may be prevented from establishing an autonomous personal or family life, as the testimonios of paid domestic workers examined in chapter 1 have shown.

Babás's experimental documentary practice thus sheds light on the way that the commodification of Afro-Brazilian women's domestic labor has its origins in enslavement and on the way in which this legacy implicates its director's own contemporary employment practices. The documentary directly confronts the ethics of employing a live-in domestic worker when another piece of Lins's home video footage featuring Denise is played. It shows Denise ironing as the voiceover comments that she used to live in Lins's home from Monday to Saturday while Joaquim was a toddler. This meant that Denise could see her own four-year-old daughter only on Sundays, something that, the narrator admits, Lins preferred not to think about at the time.

IMMATERIAL LABORS   161

Figure 3.2. An archival photograph of Artur Gomes Leal and his wet nurse, Mônica (taken by F. Villela 1860), *Babás* (dir. Lins, 2010, Consuelo Lins)

Lins's documentary opens and closes by meditating on the same black-and-white image. It depicts the young Artur Gomes Leal, who leans his head on the shoulder of his Afro-Brazilian wet nurse, Mônica. This well-known photograph was taken in 1860 in Recife, prior to the abolition of enslavement in Brazil. At the film's opening, the narrator confirms the cultural significance of the relationship between the pair by citing the historian Luiz Felipe Alencastro (1997, 440), who wrote that "quase todo o Brasil cabe nessa foto" (almost the whole of Brazil fits into this photo). The film subsequently cuts to show several modern-day *babás* looking after children next to a beach in Rio de Janeiro's south zone. The amplified sound of the ocean lapping at the shore on the film's diegetic soundtrack alludes to the history of transatlantic enslavement that has shaped the nature of these modern-day relationships. The voiceover adds that the impact of the physical and emotional affection that all these women have provided for the children for whom they care has been "amolengar, adocicar, amaciar a cultura portuguesa" (to sweeten and soften [Brazil's] Portuguese culture). This theme, which runs throughout the documentary, enables Lins to demonstrate the difficulty of condensing domestic labor relationships into purely commercial transactions. The theme also functions as an allusion both to these women's affective exploitation and to their centrality to the maintenance of "comfortable" domestic spaces for many families.

However, the narrator's comments also uncannily echo those of modernist writers such as Gilberto Freyre, Carlos Drummond de Andrade, and José Lins do Rego, in whose texts the trope of the loving and caring mammy, which carried connotations of cultural mixing related to the notion of milk kinship, arguably reached its zenith (Roncador 2014, 72, 87, 115). Freyre (2003, 435), in particular, emphasizes the importance of the relationships between the enslaved mães-pretas and the landowner's children to the formation of Brazilian culture and language during the colonial era. Lins employs the same vocabulary that Freyre uses to describe the softening effects that African or Afro-descendant wet nurses had in their physical and emotional relationships with their young charges. He repeatedly uses the word "amolengar" (Freyre 2003, 367, 419), which is often translated as "to mash" with reference to a child's food, and "amaciar" (391, 414), which is used when referring to the influence that he suggests these women's language had on the "softening" of European Portuguese (414–415). Afro-Brazilian women's bodies play a key role in a Freyrian schema of racial miscegenation, which has taken on a quasi-mythical status in popular understandings of Brazilian national identity. His texts have been used to perpetuate a vision of Brazil as a racial democracy, which masks the reality that Black and mixed-race Brazilians are much more likely to be poor and to suffer as a consequence of the racism still present in the country (de Luca 2017, 210).

The opening of *Babás* thus risks regurgitating and reinforcing a romanticized conception of Afro-Brazilian women's physical availability and role as "natural caregivers." The indexical nature of Mônica and Artur's portrait explains why it is imbued with so much significance in *Babás*. The photograph attests not only to the physical presence of these individuals in the past but also to the emotional bond between them in the narrative that the documentary constructs. While indexical photographs tend to connote historicity through their representation of "isolated present moments" that are experienced by the viewer as "already past" (Doane 2002, 103), this image is reanimated in the context of the documentary's "movement" when it is placed alongside recent film footage of nannies walking and playing with children in Rio de Janeiro. The opening not only suggests the still photograph's symbolic relationship of conjunction to the documentary's present day but also cultivates the sense of nostalgia that Mulvey (2006, 31) associates with indexical photographs, which contain a physical relationship to a now-lost desired object or individual. The representation of the body of the wet nurse or nanny risks becoming overdetermined within the historical and cultural narrative that *Babás* constructs. Indeed, the film's focus on the sociocultural legacy of nannies (or surrogate mothers) alludes to the way in which the familial or domestic realm often appears to threaten or subsume the public or national sphere in Brazil.

The documentary's recourse to indexical documents, and in particular to the photograph of Arthur Gomes Leal and Mônica, verges perhaps unconsciously on an attempt to incorporate the figure of the babá into a national foundational fiction, a problematic gesture given that, as Doris Sommer (1991) has demonstrated, such narratives obscure the role of the subaltern Other in the "birth" and reproduction of modern Latin American nation-states. Similar to the Tabajara princess Iracema, the Indigenous mother from José de Alencar's (1865) eponymous novel who must be sacrificed so that Brazil's new Lusotropical nation can survive and progress (Sommer 1991, 169–171), the "black mammy" presented in *Babás* is the Other of the White mother. The nanny or wet nurse is thought of as a second mother; she is the *specter* of the biological mother and acquires the negative maternal connotations relating to the provocation of childhood desire and sexuality. However, both figural women are equated with the space of the nation and are expected to protect (in differing ways) its future political subject (symbolized as a middle- or upper-class boy) in order to safeguard the national future. It is no coincidence that at one point, the voiceover in *Babás* meditates on a painting that is said to depict Dom Pedro II in the arms of his Afro-Brazilian wet nurse. Pedro II was the second and last monarch of the Empire of Brazil before its proclamation as a republic in 1889.

The sense of nostalgia for a kin-like intimacy with live-in domestic employees is reinforced at the film's close when the narrator directly links the relationship between Mônica and Artur Gomes Leal portrayed in the photograph from 1860 to Lins's own familial experiences. The camera pans out from the portrait to depict it as one piece of a collage composed of many other color photographs of domestic workers and their employers' children. To the director's credit, the voiceover modifies the statement made by Alencastro that was originally deployed at the film's opening. The narrator states, "Não sei se todo o Brasil cabe nessa imagem. Mas da história da minha família, e de tantas outras famílias brasileiras, essa fotografia certamente faz parte" (I don't know if the whole of Brazil fits into this image. But this photo certainly constitutes part of my own family's history, as well as that of so many other Brazilian families). Although the film mobilizes this image and its connotations as part of a collective national myth, the film's conclusion somewhat undermines this narrative by acknowledging that the image does not serve as a founding fiction for the whole of Brazil and that the image's framing and content are classist and more pertinent to the history of bourgeois families. Ultimately, then, as well as having organized and edited all the images and recordings used, Lins's elegy to babás is thoroughly interpolated by the director's own experiences: in attempting to tell the story of the Other, the documentary ends up meditating in large part on her own memories and subjectivity.

While the expression and exploration of emotional attachment in *Babás* somewhat obfuscates an interrogation of domestic labor relationships that are highly unequal, these relationships are addressed to an extent through the interviews with former nannies that are incorporated toward the documentary's conclusion. The interviews constitute the element of Lins's film that most strongly resonates with the interview-based practice found in *Doméstica* and *Santiago*. However, given their brevity, the interviews in *Babás* only scratch the surface of the gender- and race-based discrimination the employees have faced.

These interviews do enable the documentary to begin to reflect on the significance that independent accommodations can hold for domestic workers. Lins meets with several domestic workers who are employed by her friends or acquaintances in what appear to be the employees' own homes.[36] One woman recalls her refusal of an employer's offer to buy her an apartment. The proposal formed part of her boss's attempt to persuade her to not get married or have a family and house of her own. These concerns reflect those that are identified in chapter 1 in the testimonios produced by unionized domestic employees. As Lenira Carvalho (Carvalho and Parisius 1999, 112) has argued, achieving domestic (and familial) sovereignty has represented a fundamental stage in the domestic worker's process of acquiring and demanding both a person's identity and a worker's identity.

It is for this reason, in my view, that Lins's documentary concludes with the director's visit to her own former nanny, Iraci Campigotto, who shows off her home for the camera.[37] She reveals that while she worked for Lins's family, she was able to return home only once a month. During the reunion with Iraci, Lins briefly appears on screen at the edge of the frame, a gesture that serves to foreground her personal implication in the narrative she has constructed. The voiceover muses that Lins is unsure about what she inherited from Iraci, that it was "*talvez* uma certa disciplina para o trabalho e uma organização que não identifico nos meus pais" (*perhaps* a certain work ethic and sense of organization that I don't see in my own parents). The comment suggests, once again, that *Babás* has been strongly inspired by *Santiago* because it recalls the phraseology and tone of the narration in the latter when Salles reflects on the sense of "respect" for virtuoso performance that the butler "*perhaps* wanted to teach him."

However, in *Santiago*, the voiceover makes the uncomfortable admission that Salles's original documentary was a narcissistic endeavor that revolved around the director himself. In *Babás*, the narration never goes so far. It reveals that Lins did not feel at liberty to interview her own domestic employees at the time of filming because she thought that "essas conversas podiam ser comprometidas pela situação patroa-empregada" (these conversations could be compromised by the boss-employee relationship). She also generally chooses to erase her interventions from the interviews included in the documentary, omissions that signal the documentary's tendency to elide the personal implication that a more radical, experimental domestic ethnography demands. The interpersonal clashes and conflicts that make both *Santiago* and *Doméstica* so uncomfortable to view are thus circumvented in *Babás*.

Doméstica: Performativity, Selfie Culture, and the Index

The methodology that Mascaro adopted for *Doméstica* can be aligned with the *confrontational* interview-based practice for which the renowned Brazilian documentarist Eduardo Coutinho is known and that has become a hallmark of Brazilian documentary.[38] By giving cameras to the adolescents rather than to the domestic workers themselves, Mascaro (2021) has suggested that *Doméstica* avoids pretending that it is possible to give the employees a voice via the documentary in any simple sense; instead, this technique foregrounds the disputes that surround the right to speak and the power that comes with that right. Using the adolescents is a gesture that epitomizes Mascaro's commitment to an avant-garde practice, namely, by attempting to obfuscate a singular ethics of this documentary's gaze. As the filmmaker has explained, he was interested in dramatizing "the negotiation of the image between the teenagers and their maids" (Oliveira 2020, 151). To achieve this, he needed to make "explicit" the power dynamics between them, "without tilting the balance of these relationships" (151). Consequently, in five of *Doméstica*'s seven segments, White adolescents film Afro-Brazilian employees, thereby foregrounding and attesting to the legacy of enslavement that continues to haunt contemporary domestic labor relationships. Although this technique may appear counterintuitive, it is why the teenagers were asked to film the domestic workers' daily realities, rather than asking the latter to do so themselves.

Furthermore, the teenagers' control of the camera permits a triangulation of the domestic space, which allows the audience to see the interactions between the employees and other members of the family that they serve, including their (adult) bosses. The fact that a family member is doing the filming enables those on camera to act in a more spontaneous manner, without being disturbed by an alien film crew.[39] Both the workers and the employers are also frequently willing to concede interviews to the teenagers about the history of their intimate professional and personal relationships. Lúcia Nagib (2009, 206–207) observes that these kinds of collaborative documentary-making projects have the potential to result in "the crumbling of the usual filming hierarchy (the subject above the object, the director above the crew and the cast) through the productive clashing of active subjectivities behind and before the camera. It is a process of general empowerment and emancipation that frontally opposes the 'romance of victimization.'" This crumbling of the traditional filming hierarchy is compounded in *Doméstica* because the employees usually have a maternal or paternal relationship to the young people behind the camera and because childhood itself is frequently figured as the Other of adulthood. The adolescents occupy a liminal space in their households: some of their actions betray the fact that they have begun to identify with their parents' class values and positions of authority—which culminates in gestures that other the domestic workers—yet the adolescents also maintain a childlike intimacy with the employees. Therefore, the power relationship between them is diluted when compared to the adult employer-employee relationship. As a consequence of this and of the complicity that often exists between the domestic workers and the teens, the former are sometimes able to exert control over their visual portrayals.

Many of the interpersonal clashes and misunderstandings portrayed in *Doméstica* arise from its subjects' propensity to perform for the camera. On one level, this is undoubtedly a product of our contemporary selfie culture, which is pervaded by celebrity, reality television, and social media, all of which rely on a willingness to exhibit elements of our private lives. On another level, the performative behavior of the subjects is encouraged by the equipment that the teens were given to film their families' employees. They were supplied with tripods along with digital cameras. This meant that they could set up the camera, see what was framed in the shot on the preview screen (or "viewfinder"), and walk into and out of the frame freely: no one needed to hold the camera while it was recording. In the past, when using Super 8 or video cameras, it would not have been possible to see the image until it was later revealed or screened on a VHS player, as Souto (2019, 142) has pointed out. As my discussion of *Doméstica* will show, the documentary's performativity works to underscore the links between domestic labor, virtuosity, and affect that have been explored in the other films examined in this chapter.

Vanuza and Claudomiro: Performance and Catharsis

The first of *Doméstica*'s segments features the adolescent Claudomiro Carvalho Neto,[40] who films his family's domestic worker Vanuza Santos de Oliveira. It is typical of many other segments in the documentary because it frequently features the presence of the principal cameraman, who seems to enjoy filming himself. Despite this, Claudomiro often appears to relinquish control of the camera to Vanuza, thus allowing her to choose how to portray herself, which results in footage that shows Vanuza listening or singing along to melancholic or romantic songs while she works. Her enjoyment of performance serves as a striking parallel with that of other domestic workers depicted in *Doméstica* and also with that of Santiago.

At one point, when Vanuza is driving Claudomiro to English class, he asks her if she really never had any ambitions other than to become a domestic worker. Vanuza appears to be uncomfortable. She eventually explains that she has worked from a young age out of socioeconomic necessity and that she has since faced a variety of problems in her family life. The interview underscores that, although the pair are close, Claudomiro is unable to empathize fully with her past experiences. After Claudomiro has left the car and abandoned the camera, Vanuza places it on the dashboard so that it is filming her while she drives. She begins singing along to a popular song on the radio, "O mal pela raiz" (Cut out evil at its roots) by Reginaldo Rossi, which features melodramatic lyrics.[41] When the song is concluding, she bursts into tears and states, "é muito difícil você gostar, amar e não ser [bem] tratada, respeitada, valorizada" (it is very difficult to like, to love, and not to be [well] treated, respected, or valued). It is clearly a statement that reflects on her own personal and professional life, as well as the lives of many of the other employees represented in the film.

It is clear that Vanuza is performing a particular role, which appears to be liberating and cathartic for her. In the sequences where she takes control of the camera, the effect can be likened to that identified in the testimonios of paid domestic workers analyzed in chapter 1. As Yúdice (1991, 19) has pointed out, in testimonial writing, a subaltern subject is able to "engage in a process of self-constitution and survival." Being the focus of the camera's attention frequently leads to a dramatic outpouring of emotion and grief from many of the domestic employees who appear to have been confined within a particular role and limited space within their employers' households. Furthermore, the sequences illustrate how *Doméstica* works as an instance of experimental domestic ethnography. Claudomiro's intimate relationship to Vanuza appears to permit moments in which Vanuza exerts some control over her portrayal. This "sharing of textual authority" nonetheless

168 PAID TO CARE

results in moments of "authorial crisis" (Renov 1999, 146) when a segment draws attention to Claudomiro's and Vanuza's clashing viewpoints and contrasting visions of the overarching shape that their narrative is likely to take.

Flávia and Bia: Performance and Conflict

In a comparably performative segment, the domestic worker Flávia Santos Silva is shown bickering with the adolescent Ana Beatriz de Oliveira, also known as Bia, because Flávia keeps dancing and singing in front of the camera. Flávia reminds the child that *she* is the employee, and the film is meant to focus on *her*. Flávia and Bia's segment thus "eschews any idea of a harmonious conviviality" that may be associated with a "collaborative" documentary project, "resembling much rather a battle of egos on a filming arena" (Nagib 2009, 205). The documentary draws on their personal confrontations in order to defamiliarize an unequal power relationship that is made theatrical as a result of the presence of the camera.

We learn that Flávia's boss, Bia's mother, is also a domestic employee who works in someone else's home. She employs Flávia to look after her house and her children, in particular her disabled son, while she is away. Her household is visibly less affluent than several of the others in the documentary. Consequently, Flávia's story foregrounds the levels of violence and discrimination that *different* domestic workers in the documentary face. She tells Bia about the extremely brutal experiences of gender and domestic violence that resulted in the loss of her own unborn children and how the events led her to her current role. Her segment illustrates why, "within the arena of ethnographic film, 'handing the camera over' to a native filmmaker often simply perpetuates the realist aesthetics that the film's experimental form attempts to dislodge. The 'authentic identity' of the filmmaker is not [. . .] a sufficient revision of ethnographic practice because differences exist *within* cultures and communities just as surely as they do between cultural identities" (Russell 1999, 11 [my emphasis]).

Gracinha and Alana: Processes of Othering and Haunting Affects

The performativity that Mascaro's experimental documentary technique provokes often allows the domestic employees to project elements of their *personal* histories or preferences.[42] This represents a clear contrast to *Babás*, which presents its subjects primarily in terms of their *professional* identity as nannies (Souto 2019, 98). Just like Vanuza's and Flávia's segments, the segment featuring Maria das Graças Almeida, known as Gracinha, also allows the viewer to learn a little about her cultural tastes and individual interests, including the football team she supports, Esporte Clube Bahia. The segment opens as Gracinha sings and dances along to a song in front of the camera while she is in the kitchen. The adolescent who has been assigned the task of filming her, Alana Santos Fahel, appears at the doorway telling the employee that the music is very loud, which implies that this is another piece of footage over which the employee has exercised some control.

In a subsequent sequence, Alana films Gracinha in poor lighting and grainy close-up. The teenager describes Gracinha's unusual, nocturnal working habits almost as if she were an animal. Alana later zooms the camera in on Gracinha, who is sleeping on the sofa, where she has paused to nap while cleaning the living room at night. By choosing to include this kind of footage, Mascaro refuses to dismiss the effects of othering; instead, his documentary adopts an experimental, performative ethnographic methodology in order to acknowledge that otherness is a "discursive construction" that is "reified in colonial culture," which remains "a structural component" of both historical and psychological desire (Russell 1999, 24). The sequence exemplifies how the documentary is able to *defamiliarize* domestic relationships of power and affect by making the workers the objects of the adolescents' cameras.

Later on, Gracinha proudly shows off her bed and the orthopedic mattress that her employer bought her because she struggles with back pain. The way the sequence alludes to her physical discomfort via close-ups and bodily gestures could be deemed haptic in that they institute, to borrow Laura Marks's (2000, 172) terms, an embodied relationship to the image through camera movements that achieve sensuous effects. The tactile visuality that is evident in the adolescent's images of Gracinha is nonetheless mournful, as Marks's (192) description of the haptic predicts. These sequences point painfully to the limits of the filmmaker's and audience's sensory knowledge and emotional understanding of Gracinha as she comments on the recent death of her only son, whom she had not been able to see because she lives with her employers and returns home only once every two weeks, sometimes even less frequently. When her son was murdered, Gracinha was caring for Alana's grandmother following surgery and had not gone home for three months. Even though her relationship with her son had been compromised by her job and marginalized from her daily life, her grief hauntingly saturates the domestic space in which she is filmed.

Helena and Juana: Kin Ties and Postcolonial Relationships

Gracinha's segment concludes shortly after she has spoken about the death of her son and as she is shown washing dishes at the kitchen sink. The film cuts to focus on the domestic employee Helena Araújo, who is also at a sink but doing laundry; she has her back turned to her baby daughter, Maria Fernanda, who stares curiously at the camera from her stroller. The film thus forms an implicit link between Helena's daughter and Gracinha's loss of her own son. The link alludes to the presence and absence of these women's biological children, who may face neglect as a consequence of the nature of their mothers' work regardless of their proximity. The segment that focuses on Helena is made more troubling by the fact that her boss, Lúcia, is frequently shown holding and caring for Maria Fernanda while Helena does the housework. Although Lúcia's support appears to be well-intentioned, her confession that when Maria Fernanda was born, she felt as though she was having another child alludes to a postcolonial nostalgia for paternalistic servile relationships. At times the footage suggests that Lúcia is attempting to usurp Helena's status as the baby's mother.

The teen who films Helena, Juana Souza de Castro, insists that Helena "é da família" (is part of the family) and that she views Helena as if she were an older sister. Nonetheless, Juana admits that Helena's accommodations are behind the main family home in a separate building; her facial expression betrays the discomfort this dissonance produces. While filming Helena's room, Juana draws attention to a collage of photos that Lúcia made that depict a newborn Maria Fernanda being held by various members of Lúcia's family. Nonetheless, the separate location of Helena's accommodations has the uncanny potential to evoke the well-known relationship of colonial plantation buildings that Freyre (2003) describes, with senzalas positioned away from the casa grande. This evocation is reinforced by the generational ties between Helena and her boss's family. Lúcia explains that Helena's parents worked on her family's ranch and that she chose to bring Helena, instead of a different employee, with her when she moved to Salvador because she trusted Helena's family; she later adds that Helena did also want to come.

Despite Juana's and Lúcia's eagerness to present a positive picture of their intimacy with Helena, this segment problematizes the common claim made by employers that their domestic worker constitutes another member of their family. Mascaro's documentary underscores the employer strategies that attempt to refashion household service as a labor of love rather than as contractual labor and that often seek to manage class disparities, racial tensions, and feelings of discomfort or guilt. Another earlier segment that is edited to complicate an appeal to kin ties features the domestic worker Dilma dos Santos Souza and the adolescent Perla Sachs Kindi. Perla chooses to film the momentous day on which Dilma is invited for the first time to join her family at their traditional Jewish Shabat meal, seemingly an attempt to portray their relationship in a pleasing light. However, this choice ironically foregrounds the fact that the non-Jewish Dilma has never been invited to eat with the family at this occasion before, even though she has been baking the bread served at it for many years.

Helena's segment demonstrates that while affective ties between employers and employees prevent these relationships from being categorized purely as commercial transactions, the situation of live-in domestic workers facilitates emotional domination and subjective repression that harks back to the colonial era. Helena barely speaks during her segment, and at one point even asks to not be recorded despite the fact that the film is meant to focus on her. In the earlier segment, Gracinha also asks Alana to stop filming her on one occasion. However, while Alana appears to encourage Gracinha to talk by engaging her with direct questions, Juana and Lúcia tend to usurp Helena's "poder de fala" (Andrade 2017, 44; power of speech). Helena appears to have been given little opportunity to represent herself and, in Souto's (2019, 148 [my emphasis]) terms, "cruza o espaço da cena fugazmente *como um fantasma*" (crosses the scene fleetingly *like a specter*). Helena's depiction resonates with that of Sérgio de Jesus, a figure who appears both haunting and haunted and who is the only male domestic worker featured in *Doméstica*. In his segment, he remains silent as the adolescent Jenifer Rodrigues Régis and her mother provide lengthy testimonies in which they suggest that Sérgio's wife left him because he could no longer support her or his children, and consequently, he came to work for them. Sérgio seems dejected and even emasculated by the process of being filmed. The segment thus draws attention to intersectionality in unexpected ways by exploring the impact that boss-worker relations can have on traditionally gendered power dynamics.

Lucimar and Luiz Felipe: Ethics and the Index

In the documentary's final segment, the adolescent Luiz Felipe Godinho asks his domestic worker Lucimar Roza to sign a consent form, which implies that all the teens obtained the workers' permission to record them for the project. By including sequences such as this one, and others that encourage the audience to question the employees' enthusiasm about being filmed, *Doméstica* explicitly addresses the ethical concerns that arise when producing visual representations of the Other in a way that the fiction films analyzed in chapter 2 do not. However, like *Santiago*, *Doméstica* does not endeavor to resolve these ethical dilemmas. Indeed, Helena's and Sérgio's

Figure 3.3. A photograph of Lucimar and Luiz Felipe's mother as children, *Doméstica* (dir. Mascaro, 2012, Desvia)

reluctance to speak in front of the camera, and Helena's and Gracinha's requests to not be recorded, raise the issue that many of the employees may have felt compelled to agree when their employers' children asked to film them and viewed the activity as just another unremunerated affective transaction.

Luiz Felipe interviews his mother, who reveals that she has known Lucimar since she was born because Lucimar is the daughter of her own great-grandmother's housekeeper. She recalls wistfully that she used to love playing with Lucimar as a child; they are just a few years apart in terms of age. She admits that she never imagined Lucimar would work for her as an adult, stating ominously that at the beginning, it was difficult because "eu tinha que me impor como patroa e ela era Lucimar, minha amiga de sempre" (I had to impose myself as a boss and she was Lucimar, my old friend). Shortly after her statement, Luiz Felipe films a collection of musical memorabilia, including tickets to see Paul McCartney and a black-and-white photograph of John Lennon. A recording of Bob Dylan's 1963 "Blowin' in the Wind" can be heard in the background. The camera scans slowly down to reveal a wristwatch laying on a counter, a symbol of the passage of time, before continuing to show an open, worn album of family photographs. It lingers on a photograph taken in 1969, which appears to show Lucimar and his mother as small children. Two more images are shown of the pair when they were slightly older; in the second photograph, they each clutch one hand of the same doll. The lyrics of Dylan's song can be heard asking, "How many years can some people exist / Before they're allowed to be free?" in what is undoubtedly a veiled reference to the fact that the descendants of enslaved people are those who are most likely to work as live-in domestic employees today. The film then cuts to show Luiz Felipe himself as he continues singing and playing the song on his own guitar.

Luiz Felipe seems to have sensed a certain melancholic nostalgia for the playful, childish relationship that his mother and Lucimar have lost. This sense is reinforced by the indexical nature of the old still photographs that are shown, which bring "a resonance of 'then' to the surface" (Mulvey 2006, 13), particularly because they are combined with the use of songs and musical memorabilia that also evoke a similar bygone era and the passing of time. The scene implies that the pair's formerly close childhood connection now haunts their much more hierarchical relationship. The segment closes by framing Lucimar with the photo album on her lap as she is interviewed by Luiz Felipe in what appears to be her small maid's room. The difficulties that the transformation of a childhood friendship into a boss-worker relationship may have produced are only intimated. Lucimar pauses before answering Luiz Felipe's probing questions about the relationship and about whether she is happy. Eventually she says that it is "agradável" (agreeable) to work for a family with whom she has ties, concluding tentatively, "eu considero que eu tenho liberdade" (I think that I have freedom).

Santiago: Performativity and Conflict

Elements of *Santiago*'s and *Doméstica*'s critiques of oppressive labor relationships are effective because of their dramatization of discomfort and the clashes between those behind the camera and the domestic workers they film. This strategy forms part of their bids to avoid collapsing into an unproblematized objectification of the Other. The role that performance plays in documentaries such as these becomes a crucial way of signaling their attempts at honesty. In *Santiago*, the former butler is shown offering to perform what could be called different set pieces, including anecdotes, prayers in Latin, songs on the castanets, and a "hand dance." However, while he is acting these out, the audience often sees or hears Santiago being interrupted by the director, or another member of his crew, asking him to modify and repeat his performance. It is very likely that these instructions would have been edited out of the film were Salles to have made the documentary that he originally planned but then abandoned. Santiago's repeated silencing recalls the uncomfortable sequences in *Doméstica* when certain employees are given little opportunity to speak for themselves.

On one level, Salles's self-reflexive inclusion of the instructions draws attention to the way in which Santiago's performances were staged to achieve a particular effect, as well as signaling the lack of freedom Santiago had while giving them. On another level, these sequences imply that the affective and corporeal labor that the former butler used to carry out for Salles's family has been transformed into an alternative form of immaterial, artistic performance. The fact that all the (former) employees in the documentaries examined in this chapter may have felt compelled to participate in filming complicates their legacy and draws attention to the ways in which paid domestic labor relations haunt these films' processes of production.

The performative and affective demands that Salles makes of Santiago are a sign of the cordial nature of their relationship. Cordiality has been identified as a Brazilian national trait and describes the importance of establishing *intimate* relationships with others, even when these relationships belong to the commercial or political realms (Holanda 2014, 178–180). The concept is associated with the Brazilian sociologist Sérgio Buarque de Holanda, who argued that cordiality could be traced back to the colonial era, when it was the norm for political power and influence to be concentrated in the hands of a few landowners in the context of the country's prevailing patriarchal, rural culture (2014, 85–86).[43] Salles has reflected on the cordiality of his ties to Santiago:

> In Brazil, you know, we have a great deal of difficulty in distinguishing impersonal, formal relationships, from those that are personal. At the same time as I gave [Santiago] orders, each one contained a sincere affection. And vice versa, he was a servant and he liked me very much, in a very personal way. In the film, arrogance and affection exist in an incomplete mixture, where you cannot distinguish which is one and which the other. (Dieleke and Nouzeilles 2008, 145)

The film's mise-en-scène betrays a desire to shore up the hierarchical distinction between an employer's adult son and a former employee that exists alongside their intimacy. When Santiago is being interviewed, he is always positioned at a distance from the camera. His body is often framed by doorways or other objects. The documentary's voiceover enables Salles to reflect on the ambivalent nature of his relationship to Santiago, which he claims to have lacked a conscious awareness of at the time of filming. This represents a parallel with the distanced meditation on Lins's relationship to Denise in *Babás*. The following voiceover extract from *Santiago* includes what must have been one of the most difficult admissions for Salles to make, because the narrator acknowledges the director's implication in the material recorded and thus confirms the documentary's status as an experimental domestic ethnography (emphasis is my own):

> Não existem planos fechados nesse filme, nenhum close de rosto. [Santiago] está sempre distante. Penso que a distância não aconteceu por acaso. Ao longo da edição, entendi o que agora parece evidente. A maneira como conduzi as entrevistas me afastou dele. Desde o início, havia uma ambiguidade insuperável entre nós que explica o desconforto de Santiago. É que ele não era apenas meu personagem; eu, não era apenas un documentarista. Durante os cinco dias de filmagem, *eu nunca deixei de ser o filho do dono da casa, ele nunca deixou de ser o nosso mordomo.*

> There are no close-range shots in this film, no facial close-ups. [Santiago] is always distant. I don't think that distance was a coincidence. As I was editing the film, I understood what seems so obvious now. The way that I directed the interviews distanced me from him. From the start, there was an insurmountable ambiguity between us that explains Santiago's discomfort. It's that he wasn't just my character, and I wasn't just a documentary-maker. During the five days of filming, *I never stopped being the boss's son and he never stopped being our butler.*

The distance between the pair is the central problem that the whole documentary revolves around and that its experimental form is designed to address.

The distanced intimacy that Salles's privilege permits culminates in the documentary's most painful interaction. Toward the end of filming, when the crew was recording sound but the camera was not rolling, Santiago tried to confess an intimate detail about his private life. The sound of Santiago's voice juxtaposed with a blank screen heightens the sense that this is a particularly personal admission. Santiago addresses the director affectionately as "Joãozinho" and begins to explain that he belongs to a group of "seres malditos" (wicked beings). The director quickly cuts him off, with a response that intimates both privilege and prejudice, "Não, isso não precisa [. . .]. Esse lado a gente não vai" (No, that's not necessary [. . .]. We don't need to go there). The voiceover had previously lamented of this interaction that "quando Santiago tentou me falar do que lhe era mais íntimo, eu não

176 PAID TO CARE

liguei a câmera" (when Santiago tried to talk to me about what was most personal to him, I did not even switch on the camera).

Although Santiago's sexuality is never openly discussed, it is alluded to earlier in the documentary when he describes his fascination with the physiques of male boxers whom he compares to Roman gladiators. Salles himself has also suggested that Santiago's discouraged disclosure was likely related to his sexuality (Dieleke and Nouzeilles 2008, 144). The director has admitted that he is not sure whether he responded in the right way: "I could not tell whether he realized that he was speaking not only to me, but also to the public at large [. . .]. I felt that it was something he might later regret. Today I have my doubts [. . .]. He wanted to talk about it. Maybe it was important for him to talk" (Dieleke and Nouzeilles 2008, 143–144).

A focus on the orders that shape Santiago's (not so) spontaneous performances eventually opens into a broader interrogation of the "truth claims" made by traditional, observational documentaries. In a statement that is suggestive of the profound influence that the move toward self-reflexive and performative documentary has had on him, Salles has explained, "*Santiago* is a film in which I basically consider the form [. . .]. Discussing the form I can say to you: 'Consider how the documentary is made, consider how you should position yourselves before that which you see, [. . .] consider if you should believe what I tell you'" (Dieleke and Nouzeilles 2008, 148). This influence is made clearest around halfway through the documentary when the nondiegetic voiceover meditates on the adjustments that were made to Salles's former Gávea home, which was vacant at the time of filming. The narrator ponders the extent to which he and his crew dressed the seemingly abandoned scenery to create the perfect impression. The narrator comments specifically on several similar shots that were taken of the swimming pool.[44] In the third shot, a leaf falls into the frame; it appears to have been a coincidence, except that in the following take another leaf falls into the water and then another in exactly the same place. The narrator questions, "Quais são as chances[? . . .] Neste dia ventava realmente? Ou a água da piscina foi agitada por uma mão fora de quadro?" (What are the chances[? . . .] Was it really windy that day? Or was the water in the swimming pool disturbed by a hand just outside the frame?). The narrator concludes, "Tudo deve ser visto com uma certa desconfiança" (You should treat everything you see with a certain distrust). Just as in two films I discussed in chapter 2, *Que horas ela volta?* (Muylaert 2015) and *Casa grande* (Barbosa 2014), the swimming pool returns here as a highly symbolic site of (contested) social privilege. The water also alludes to forms of veiling or screening, and thus raises questions about truthfulness: what does it reveal or conceal under its surface?

Santiago: Indexicality and Haunting

The swimming pool at the Gávea home also appears in the documentary just over ten minutes earlier.[45] First, the same black-and-white establishing shot of the pool mentioned previously is shown. Then, the screen goes black, and the film cuts to an old piece of home video, the only one that features in the film. It is a scene distinguished by its use of color. There is no comment from the narrator while this footage is played, but it also forms part of the film's distanced meditation on the limits of its own veracity where its representation of the house and of the butler are concerned. Indeed, it is no coincidence that a piece of music by the composer Zbigniew Preisner entitled "Tu ne mentiras pas" (You must not lie) has been played on the film's soundtrack just prior to, and at the beginning of, this sequence.

The footage shows three young boys and two adults playing in the pool together. Gustavo Procopio Furtado (2019, 143, 152) suggests that the people are the Salles children together with their parents and that the footage was shot with Super 8 film in the mid-1960s. Salles would have been a very small boy, because he was born in 1962. The youngest of the children, who is probably the director himself,[46] is crying and is eventually handed to a woman with a towel who appears to have been his nanny. The camera briefly cuts away from the pool to show her carrying off the boy. She is accompanied by another woman, seemingly also an employee, who is maneuvering a stroller. These women inhabit the margins of the frame. Initially, one of their hands is shown resting on the railing that demarcates the swimming pool and separates them from it while the camera's focus remains on the family in the water. Furtado (144) describes the hand as the image's punctum, an accidental element that nonetheless ends up being "the source of the image's thrust." It punctures this scene of domestic bliss by drawing attention to the labor that made it possible. This footage confirms that domestic workers are often marginalized or erased from home videos, which serve as the archives of family memory. Having been filmed on Super 8, the punctum's privileged indexical connection to the reality it represents heightens its significance.

The questions that *Santiago* raises about the documentary form and about *how* a particular narrative is told through the process of editing, cutting, and splicing can be related to the process of archiving. Like literary *testimonios* and documentaries, archives are simultaneously inscriptions, appropriations, and confiscations of memory: none of these collections are innocent, as Jacques Derrida has argued (Baecque et al. 2015, 39). The ways that paid domestic workers tend to haunt these curated bourgeois collages of family unity are reinforced by my analysis of Daniela Ortiz's *97 empleadas domésticas* in chapter 4 and by my earlier, brief analysis of Mendonça Filho's *Aquarius*.

Santiago is insistent on maintaining the visibility of these traces of paid domestic labor, which forms part of the documentary's attempt to achieve a greater degree of honesty, along with its self-reflexive and performative form. In fact, by making the former butler the focus, the documentary foregrounds domestic work as a central theme. While Furtado (2019, 152) argues that "the film's most important center of gravity is not the butler, but the memory of the familial home, which is mediated by the butler," the director himself has recognized that the most compelling element of the footage is "a natureza áspera da relação que se establecera entre mim e Santiago durante aqueles cinco dias em que o entrevistei nos anos 90. Áspera e impura, por mesclar curiosidade e prepotência, carinho e arrogância" (Anjos and Doppenschmitt 2008; the harsh nature of the relationship that had been established between myself and Santiago over the course of those five days when I interviewed him in the 90s. It is harsh and impure because the relationship mixes curiosity, cockiness, affection and arrogance). Although the film was originally meant to be about the Gávea home, with Santiago serving as the keeper of its memories and without featuring the director as a character, this concept was abandoned. It did not work, because the footage revolved principally around Salles's relationship to Santiago. The film is dedicated to Salles's family, but its title belongs to the butler.

The home video of the pool may be the only footage in the documentary that contains an indexical connection to the reality it represents. However, in 1992, Salles recorded Santiago at his apartment not long before his death in 1994, which means that this footage is also imbued with great emotional significance. Furthermore, it forms part of the film's broader archival project, which involves the juxtaposition of different audiovisual materials that were produced at distinct moments and that are recycled in such a way as to foreground the senses of nostalgia and loss that drive the documentary. Salles has also betrayed his desire to preserve Santiago's presence (along with his memories of his childhood home) when calling the butler "the referent" (Dieleke and Nouzeilles 2008, 145), the term that Doane (2002, 70) uses to describe the desired object that leaves an indexical trace.

The sense that Santiago is both a haunting and a haunted character is emphasized in one of the film's most performative sequences, which features his "hand dance." It involves Santiago interpreting a piece of somber baroque music through the use of expressive hand movements. Santiago claimed to do this every day as a form of exercise, although it is also possible

IMMATERIAL LABORS 179

Figure 3.4. Santiago performing his hand-dance, *Santiago* (dir. Salles, 2007, VideoFilmes)

that the focus on his hands here, like the presence of the hand of the family's nanny in the home video, functions as an affective nod to the manual labor that he undertook in supporting the Salles family and in the running of their household. The hand dance is one of the documentary's longest and slowest scenes, having been filmed in two long takes, according to the voiceover, and lasting just over three minutes. On one level, the inclusion of these lengthy takes could be interpreted as signaling a respect for this moment in the film's profilmic reality. Where a "classical" cinematic approach might have involved cutting and editing the film to create a faster, more engaging pace (Rosen 2001, 4), Salles chooses a slower pace in what appears to be an attempt to be faithful to Santiago's performance. On another level, it evokes the documentary's desire to preserve Santiago's living presence or to reanimate him even after his death. The sequence is notable for its focus on the *movement* of the subject's hands and for constituting one of the few close-ups of Santiago's body; usually, he is shown seated and stationary or at a distance. The focus contributes to the impression that there is a mournful desire for a lost proximity to the former employee on the part of the filmmaker. Furthermore, it reinforces the sense that these documentaries are haunted both by the unrepresentable (the past) and by the Other (in these cases, paid domestic workers).

The voiceover reveals that Santiago asked the film crew to record his hand dance, which illustrates his propensity for rebelliousness. Indeed, it is not the only instance when he attempts to exercise control over the filming

180   PAID TO CARE

process; the raw footage shows that he would sometimes resist the instructions he received and would make his own suggestions instead. His tendency to push back aligns him with the "transgressive" approach that Jacques Rancière (2003, 223) argues the working class must adopt in order to appropriate "an intellectual equality whose privilege others [have] reserved for themselves." The aging former butler appears to intuit Salles's desire to record and preserve him before the director does himself. He even jokes that the documentary is an attempt to embalm him by saying, "Me van a embalsamar, están preparando todas las cosas" (They're going to embalm me, they're preparing everything for it), thereby signaling his understanding that "film makes history out of the present" (Doane 2002, 104). Santiago recognizes that "the origin of art, of the making of a likeness," including via the cinematic image, is driven by the (frustrated) human desire to overcome death and "embalm time against corruption," an argument made by André Bazin, one of the earliest and most influential film theorists (Mulvey 2006, 64). Santiago's comprehension of the importance of archiving is illustrated by the fact that he devoted much of his free time to producing taxonomies of aristocratic European families and collecting up to thirty thousand pages of this material, which he tied up with ribbons and stored.[47] The voiceover adds that he likened himself to monks in the Middle Ages who used to transcribe important texts. In the documentary, Santiago explains that he produces the archives in order to salvage the histories from oblivion and that the characters they feature save him from loneliness. The depiction of his character and of his passions erodes the distinction between domestic work and intellectual or artistic labor toward which *Las dependencias* and *Réimon* were shown to gesture, as discussed in the first part of this chapter.

Conclusion

All the documentaries discussed in this chapter are characterized by the depiction of spectral or ghostly domestic employees. The reasons for this are twofold. On one level, paid domestic work has not been properly accounted for by traditional, capitalist economic models. Instead, it has been categorized as a form of reproductive (rather than productive) labor because its products are consumed immediately and have not been viewed as producing surplus value (Staples 2007, 122). This view results in portrayals of paid domestic workers as haunting figures whose presence resurges despite attempts to minimize or conceal their contributions. The first part of the chapter examines three films that interrogate the ways in which middle- and upper-class artists and intellectuals are haunted by paid domestic workers, precisely because the creation of *immaterial products* is a defining element of both artistic or intellectual creation and domestic labor. *Las dependencias*, *Santiago*, and *Réimon* use a variety of cinematic techniques, including soundtrack, slow sequences, and an emphasis on performance, to question the wildly differing economic values and cultural capital that are nonetheless attributed to these forms of work. For example, *Las dependencias* focuses on the testimonies of Silvina Ocampo's former employees and uses spectral black-and-white sequences to gesture toward the ways in which real domestic workers supported, inspired, and consequently haunted her literary output. Also, all three films deconstruct rigid distinctions between the categories of artist and servant. In *Santiago* this distinction is achieved via a focus on the retired butler's (love of) virtuosic performances, while in *Réimon*, an evocation of the protagonist's high-brow cultural tastes creates a similar impact.

On another (related) level, the Brazilian documentaries examined in the second part of this chapter evoke a sense of spectrality via their explorations of contemporary domestic labor relations in Brazil that are haunted by colonial hierarchies of power, including the legacy of Afro-Brazilian enslavement. *Babás*, *Doméstica*, and *Santiago* are experimental domestic ethnographies that constitute distanced meditations on footage of domestic workers filmed by their directors some years previously or recorded by others. The gazes that the films interrogate or construct are, nonetheless, simultaneously compromised by the intimate relationships of those behind the camera with the (former) domestic employees represented. The similarities between these films' forms and the techniques that they employ attest to the undeniable inspiration that Salles's *Santiago* provided for Lins's *Babás* and Mascaro's *Doméstica*. Ultimately, the three documentaries examine the spectral nature of contemporary domestic labor relations by reflecting on their own filmic forms. Their explorations of the thorny relationship of documentary to the index (meaning the trace of a person, object, or relationship now gone) enables the films to meditate on the loss of childhood intimacy with domestic workers from the employer's or director's perspective. Nonetheless, the use of indexical images in *Babás* verges on an attempt to incorporate the figure of the nanny into a Brazilian foundational fiction, which risks romanticizing the subjugation of the subaltern Other in a narrative that represents the birth and reproduction of the modern mestizo Latin American nation-state. By contrast, the performative modes adopted in *Santiago* and *Doméstica* produce conflicts, clashes, and dissensus in their attempts to avoid collapsing into an unproblematized objectification of the Other. All three documentaries' self-reflexivity, and *Santiago*'s and *Doméstica*'s performativity, nonetheless means that they are able to address (to differing degrees) the ethical concerns that arise when producing visual representations of paid domestic workers in a way that the fiction films analyzed in chapter 2 do not.

By using their experimental approaches to foreground the issues of control and coloniality associated with traditional ethnography and to undermine the notion that documentary offers an objective perspective, these three films encourage audiences to consider the ways in which filmmaking itself remains implicated in the same hierarchies of power and modes of exploitation that shape the paid domestic labor relationships they portray. In sum, these documentaries demonstrate that the affective, immaterial qualities of paid domestic labor relationships mean that they cannot be boiled down to purely commercial transactions, but the films also interrogate the ways in which affective ties permit unseen labor exploitation. The (former) employees depicted may have felt compelled to participate in works being made by their (former) bosses or members of their employer-family, which draws attention to the ways in which these paid domestic labor relations also haunt the films' own processes of production.

CHAPTER 4

Domestic Workers in the Digital Domain

BOTH PROJECTS THAT ARE THE FOCUS of this chapter draw on digital tools and creative techniques to make sociocultural interventions in collaboration with, or on behalf of, paid domestic workers. The texts constitute forms of artivism that address not only these workers' mistreatment but also the issue of *how* they are represented in media and culture.[1] In this respect, the projects' objectives are aligned with those identified in the collective testimonios of paid domestic workers that were published in the 1980s, which I analyzed in chapter 1. These more recent works have nonetheless benefited from the increased potential for circulation that social media sites and digital technologies can provide. The Peruvian artist Daniela Ortiz's 2010 physical and virtual exhibition *97 empleadas domésticas* (97 domestic workers) appropriates photographs posted by upper-class, Lima-based families on their personal Facebook pages; each image features at least one domestic employee either in the background or at the edges of the frame. The Afro-Brazilian rapper and influencer Preta-Rara also utilized Facebook, but as a platform rather than a resource, to create a page in 2016 entitled "Eu empregada doméstica" (I domestic worker) that she has used to share the stories of current and former domestic workers and their families; in 2019 she published a collection of these digital testimonios as a print book with Letramento Press under the same title as her Facebook page. While *97 empleadas domésticas* responds to attempts to invisibilize paid domestic work (on cultural, social, and economic levels), *Eu, empregada doméstica* contests the prejudices and negative stereotypes about paid domestic workers that are perpetuated in mainstream media and in popular culture.

Enacting these critiques online or via social media is a powerful gesture because the digital arena has become a key battleground in the struggles surrounding identity politics, in particular relating to the question of oppressed groups' lack of and rights to representation. Indeed, these digital texts are

183

cultural representations that examine how paid domestic workers are represented socially. Consequently, they come up against the thorny ethical issues inevitably raised when attempting to enable the voices of a subaltern group to be heard and to advocate on their behalf. Furthermore, the projects' creative forms of activism rely on a social media platform—Facebook—that has upended privacy norms in the service of "surveillance capitalism" (Zuboff 2019). Facebook's business model is predicated on an imperative to share personal details (Dijck 2013, 45–67), which has created a culture where users often post information and images not only of themselves but also of others—often without the latter's consent and sometimes publicly, so that anyone with an internet connection and Facebook login can see them. The personal data generated by users' interactions with the site is then harvested by third parties who benefit from it financially. The creative digital methodologies that Ortiz and Preta-Rara adopted for *97 empleadas domésticas* and *Eu, empregada doméstica* are thus beleaguered by the same ethical issues surrounding privacy, consent, and digital literacy that Facebook bears, though this does not invalidate the activist interventions made by these works.

The projects I analyze in this chapter form part of a recent flurry of digital and visual artivism focused on the issue of domestic and cleaning workers' rights and treatment in Latin America.[2] While my analysis will focus on *97 empleadas domésticas* and *Eu, empregada doméstica*, I will also trace the connections between them and other recent digital productions, including a series of works about the challenges that domestic employees have faced during the Covid-19 pandemic as well as the well-known Argentine artist Lola Arias's 2010–2012 portable transmedia exhibition *Mucamas* (Hotel maids), which focuses on hotel cleaners rather than paid domestic workers. Although the dynamics of paid domestic work are distinct from those of hotel cleaning, in some important respects, both types of employment constitute forms of care work that are heavily involved in the creation of specific affects. While domestic workers are often required to build intimate relationships with members of their employer-family (in particular with the children), the work of hotel cleaners should remain unseen yet contributes to the creation of a specific environment and experience that guests expect during their stay. By including elements of *Mucamas*, my analysis can explore the similar techniques and aesthetics employed by both Arias and Ortiz in works that critically examine attempts to repress or conceal domestic, cleaning, and care work. Like the film *Roma* (Cuarón 2018), which was streamed by Netflix and used as a vehicle for social and political activism, all the works discussed in this chapter confirm Hilda

DOMESTIC WORKERS IN THE DIGITAL DOMAIN   185

Chacón's (2018, 1–2) assertion that "art, technology, and advocacy are intimately intertwined in the culture of online production and consumption in Latin America."[3]

97 empleadas domésticas

Ortiz's exhibition *97 empleadas domésticas* was designed to critique hegemonic modes of self-representation on social media and the continuing coloniality of paid domestic labor relations in Latin America. Ortiz is a Peruvian artist who was born in Cusco in 1985 and lived in Barcelona, Spain, for several years. She relocated to Spain when she was twenty-one (Aulestia Benítez 2019, 162), but in 2020, she returned to Peru after becoming the target of online attacks and receiving threats of physical violence following an appearance on Spanish television during which she argued that Barcelona's Columbus Monument should be taken down because it is a colonial symbol that serves to reinforce institutional racism (Mas de Xaxàs 2020). Ortiz is a conceptual artist whose works constitute visual experiments (including the appropriation of images) and draw on performative techniques (including the occupation of public spaces) in the service of sociopolitical activism and critique. Her art generates spaces of conflict and discomfort through which conceptions of race, class, gender, and nationality can be interrogated in order to illustrate the ways in which society is founded on different forms of inclusion and exclusion (àngels barcelona, n.d., "Daniela Ortiz"). The methods and objectives that characterize her interventions resonate with works produced by other young Latin American artists, including Preta-Rara and Lola Arias, particularly in their explorations of the intersection between the personal and the political.

Art, labor, and political activism are linked in ways that unify much of Ortiz's oeuvre, an observation that has also been made by Marcelo Expósito (2010, 52) and Ana Elizabeth Aulestia Benítez (2019, 162). Because of this linkage, her works can be productively compared with the documentaries I analyzed in chapter 3, which also constitute political interventions and playfully blur the boundaries between different forms of immaterial labor, namely, domestic and artistic work. For example, while she was living in Barcelona, Ortiz used her artistic practice to reflect on her employment in a boutique chocolate shop by creating *P1-P2* (Ortiz 2010b), an exhibition that illustrates the way in which her works have aimed to denaturalize and denounce the exploitative demands of different forms of paid labor. For the *P1-P2* exhibition, Ortiz developed precise architectural plans of the chocolate shop to demonstrate how much space is provided for shoppers to

186 PAID TO CARE

browse products and how little space is allocated for the shop assistants to carry out their duties (Ortiz 2010b). Following the exhibition of *P1-P2*, Ortiz's employers were alerted to the sensitive nature of the information that she had shared, including security details such as the location of the boutique's alarm and safe. Ortiz was subsequently fired, and the event affected the approach she took in her next exhibition, *97 empleadas domésticas*, which she was preparing at the same time (Expósito 2010, 53).

The exhibition of *97 empleadas domésticas* was displayed in Zaragoza, Spain, at the Casa de la Mujer and in Eindhoven, the Netherlands, at the Van Abbemuseum. The images used in the installation were also collected in a PDF file that functions as a photobook, which was uploaded to the artist's web page.[4] Ortiz has suggested that *97 empleadas domésticas* was inspired by her rereading of *El primer nueva corónica y buen gobierno* (The first new chronicle and good government), which was first published in 1615 by Felipe Guamán Poma de Ayala Ortiz and recorded events in Peru during the colonial period.[5] Guamán Poma, who was a Quechua *cronista* (chronicler), produced the text so that it could be sent to the king of Spain, Felipe III, to persuade him to bring an end to the colonial destruction being wrought in the region. After Daniela Ortiz moved to Barcelona, she began searching online for images that were thematically related to the illustrations in Guamán Poma's chronicle "para ver si en Perú las relaciones entre blancos e indígenas se mantenían igual hasta ahora" (Ortiz 2012, 96; to see if in Peru the relationship between White people and Indigenous people has remained the same until the present day). Ortiz has said that the first photograph that she found reminded her of image number 152 from Guamán Poma's chronicle.[6] It depicts Rumi Ñaui, an emissary of the last Inca emperor, Atahualpa, who is attempting to bribe the Spanish colonizers Francisco Pizarro and Diego de Almagro. In an effort to persuade them to return to Europe, Rumi Ñaui presents them with two young Indigenous women who are shown kneeling in the center of the illustration while the men figure at its edges. The composition of this image reminded Ortiz (2012, 96) of one that she had found on Facebook that features a uniformed female domestic worker in the middle of the photograph staring back at the camera and who is surrounded by White employers (or guests) at the sides and in the background of the image.[7]

The way in which the domestic worker returns the gaze of the photographer, as well as the viewer, recalls other images that have resonated across my book and that have fascinated different artists, such as the found-footage film of a 1913 baptism in *Babás* (Lins 2010) that is paused to draw attention to the presence of an Afro-Brazilian nanny who looks up at the camera from the background (see chapter 3) and the clip from a 1936 short film *Rio City of Splendour* in which a young domestic worker repeatedly looks back at the camera while a White child in a bathing suit lounges on her lap (FitzPatrick 2016; see my introduction). The fundamental inscrutability of the workers' expressions in these images, which nonetheless betray hints of curiosity, suspicion, or defiance, is suggestive not only of our inability to fully understand the subjects' lived experiences but also of their refusal to serve as passive objects of the filmmaker's or photographer's gaze.

Ultimately, Ortiz (2012, 96) chose not to include the original picture that she found on Facebook in the final exhibition because it was not representative of the more than four hundred photographs featuring domestic workers that she had collected from the site. She found that instead of appearing in the center or foreground of the photographs, domestic employees tended to feature in the background or to be almost entirely cropped out of the frame. Consequently, the original photograph inverts the visual hierarchy common to the images eventually included in the exhibition (Expósito 2010, 54).

By drawing attention to Guamán Poma's chronicle as the original source of inspiration for *97 empleadas domésticas* (Ortiz 2012, 96; Expósito 2010, 54), Ortiz is making it clear that the exhibition aims to foreground how modern-day relationships to domestic workers have been shaped by Peru's colonial history, which involved the subjugation of Indigenous people by Europeans. The photographs included in the exhibition reflect that paid domestic workers in Peru are predominantly of Andean Indigenous origin and the vast majority (95 percent) are women (Pérez and Llanos 2017). Ortiz created *97 empleadas domésticas* in 2010, after the approval of partial rights reform for domestic workers in Peru in 2003 but prior to the 2020 introduction of Law 31047, which aims to guarantee equal rights for the sector in line with the ILO Convention No. 189. Pérez and Gandolfi (2020, 82) nonetheless criticize the state's negligence in ensuring the law's successful implementation, particularly during the Covid-19 pandemic.[8]

The photographs that consitute Ortiz's exhibition generally depict family holidays or celebrations, either at home or in locations such as parks, beaches, swimming pools, and even a maternity ward. Their intended purpose was to commemorate important moments that radiate family unity, happiness, and success. Nonetheless, the subtle presence of paid domestic workers, either in the background or at the margins of these photographs, emphasizes the fact that their employer-families' leisure and joyful moments of togetherness are contingent on the employees' labor. The workers are alternately shown cooking, serving guests at gatherings, or facilitating the play of their employers' children. The photographs thus

188 PAID TO CARE

raise the question of who is permitted the right to leisure and family time. While the employers have it in abundance, it is likely that the employees do not because of the demands of their work. Carvalho (1982) identifies this as a key issue in her theorization of the live-in domestic worker's condition (see chapter 1), and it is a concern that also recurs throughout the films I analyzed in chapters 2 and 3.

Swimming pool and beach locations abound in the photographs (Ortiz 2010a, 13, 18, 26, 30, 37).[9] Pools are a feature of bourgeois family life in Latin America and function as a class marker, just as they are also used as tropes in certain films discussed in chapters 2 and 3.[10] In both the photographs and the films, these watery spaces are reserved for the enjoyment of employer-families and, in particular, their children. The paid domestic workers are always shown outside the water and at the edge of the pool, often distinguished by their white uniforms. Their restricted access to these spaces is symbolic both of broader social inequalities and of middle- and upper-class fears of the working class, given the association of water with the potential for contact and "contamination."

The centrality of these locations in Ortiz's series was probably inspired by a job that she took when she was still living in Peru, one that involved filming wealthy families who frequent a beach south of Lima called Playa de Asia (Expósito 2010, 49). The job was recommended to her as a way of saving enough money to be able to move to Spain. Ortiz has stated that the families she was filming told her to ensure that their domestic employees did not appear in the images that she was recording of their children playing (49). At around the same time that Ortiz was working at Playa de Asia, in early 2007, the questions of whether domestic workers should be expected to wear their uniforms at the beach and whether they should be allowed to swim in the sea sparked a public discussion in Lima. The polemic centered on Playa de Asia, which was subsequently the site of a protest by human-rights activists who denounced attempts to allow domestic workers to bathe only after dusk or to prevent them from meeting up at the beach altogether (*El Universo* 2007). In ways that are suggestive of the influence that these events had on her exhibition, the images that Ortiz chose to use in 97 *empleadas domésticas* foreground the issue of domestic workers' relegation from spaces reserved for their employers.

This analysis of 97 *empleadas domésticas*, and the prior discussion of her earlier work, *P1-P2*, has made it clear that her critiques of the power dynamics constitutive of highly unequal or exploitative labor relations are repeatedly articulated and contested through the lens of (public and private) space. They address the questions of who has access to different spaces and how they are divided up. It is likely that Ortiz's interest in these issues also influenced a second project related to paid domestic work that the artist completed in 2011: *Habitaciones de servicio* (Maids' rooms). This work constitutes an architectural analysis of sixteen homes belonging to upper-class, Lima-based families that criticizes the diminutive sizes of the rooms allocated to live-in domestic workers. The exhibition included images of the façades of the houses, which were all built between 1930 and 2012; architectural plans, including the dimensions of the "service quarters"; and the résumés of the architects who designed the homes. A brochure that said "habitaciones de servicio. No hay excusa para su ubicación y dimensiones" (maids rooms: there is no excuse for their location and dimensions) was designed for visitors of the exhibition to take with them; it was also distributed in architecture schools in Lima (Ortiz 2011). Lola Arias's (2010) portable installation *Mucamas* similarly explores the relationship between diminutive spaces and the denigration of cleaning and care work. The artist collaborated with staff at different branches of the Ibis hotel chain in various countries to co-create the exhibition, which staged elements of the employees' biographies in mock-ups of the same hotel rooms that they cleaned. After a visitor to the exhibition passed through the hotel rooms, they were met by one of the cleaners, who showed them the behind-the-scenes "service" areas of the hotel, which contrasted markedly with the guest areas in terms of comfort and dimensions.[11]

The attempt to minimize or conceal paid domestic labor, including by containing workers within small spaces or limited areas, is also addressed in *97 empleadas domésticas* by Ortiz's selection of photographs in which domestic workers either can be glimpsed only at the very margins of the frame, are almost invisible in the background of the image, or are on the other side of a threshold, for example, of the kitchen or a preparation area (Ortiz 2010a, 10, 12, 22, 23, 27, 29, 38, 39). In several photographs, the bodies of domestic employees are truncated or almost entirely cut out of the image by the photographer. It is common for only their disembodied hands to be visible in compositions, which alludes to the ways in which their employment threatens to reduce them to laboring bodies. In many of the images used in *97 empleadas domésticas*, the workers are holding on to a child (4, 12, 15, 16, 19, 21, 30), or they feature as a physical support for the baby or toddler who is having their photograph taken (17, 20, 29, 32, 38, 40). In one particularly striking picture, a domestic worker holds up a young child wearing a giraffe suit in front of her in what seems to be a purposeful attempt to cover her entire face and most of her torso (40). These images recall a comment made in Consuelo Lins's (2010) documentary short *Babás* (discussed in chapter 3), which addresses a photographic portrait of a young boy and his wet nurse from 1860; the voiceover questions whether the wet nurse was included simply because she was the only one who could make the child keep still.

The attempt to repress or conceal these families' dependence on paid domestic workers, which is evident in the photographs, produces uncanny images that attest to the ways in which these employees' labor returns to haunt the upper classes. This theme and technique also resonate with Lola Arias's *Mucamas* and throughout the documentaries analyzed in chapter 3. In *97 empleadas domésticas*, domestic workers often emerge from the shadows, and in one image, an employee's legs are visible only because they are reflected in a mirror that appears in the photograph (Ortiz 2020, 3). The composition of this particular image recalls a similarly spectral technique used in *Mucamas*, which also serves to denaturalize the invisibilization of cleaning and care work by drawing attention to the fact that hotel cleaners are treated as anonymous *fantasmas* (ghosts).[12] In a video of the exhibition that was staged in the Ibis Hotel in Zurich, Switzerland, a male visitor is shown entering the ensuite bathroom of one of the hotel bedrooms where an installation is staged.[13] He hears Alexandre, a Brazilian cleaner, stating, "Look at yourself in the mirror: do you see me?" Both the viewer of the video and the guest suddenly see in the mirror the reflection of a photograph of Alexandre that is posted inside the shower. The video focuses on the mirror, holding the guest and Alexandre's images alongside each other in the same frame. The sequence foregrounds *Mucamas*'s attempt to redress the cleaners' spectral status. It reminds us our lives depend on each other in ways that we cannot control (Sosa 2019, 199) or that we would prefer simply not to acknowledge openly.

A comparable technique was employed in *97 empleadas domésticas* when the exhibition was originally installed in a gallery space. Visitors were exposed to the series of photographs first; the title of the project was displayed only at the end of the exhibition (Sacco and Panella 2018, 146). In their analysis, Victoria Sacco and Verónica Panella (154) argue that because the exhibition was set out this way, many visitors would not have realized that it was about domestic workers until the end, when they saw the title; they suggest that viewers were then likely to return and look through the photographs in a new light. It is a concept that "interpela al receptor violentamente, lo oblige a indentificarse con el autor de la imagen, porque pone en evidencia su ceguera" (Sacco and Panella 2018, 154; violently interpellates the viewer and forces them to identify themselves with the photographers of these images, because it reveals their blindness). The exhibition's photobook replicates this effect by opening with a blank page that is followed by the series of images, two more blank pages, and then the title. The domestic workers' labor is invisibilized, in part, because it is naturalized as the responsibility of women and racial Others; indeed, the use of the feminine noun for "employee" in Spanish, *empleada,* in the exhibition's title foregrounds the gendered nature of paid domestic work in Peru, while the photographs themselves attest to its racialization (Sacco and Panella 2018, 154, 156). However, the organization of both the exhibition and the photobook are designed precisely to denaturalize the demands of this labor and make it visible: the domestic workers in the shadows and at the margins of the images jump out at the spectator as soon as they become aware of the project's thematic focus.

In this sense, the exhibition relies on the force of these photographs' punctums, a notion outlined by Roland Barthes (1993) in *Camera Lucida* that encapsulates the surprise or shock experienced by viewers when they notice the domestic workers in Ortiz's exhibition. Barthes (1993, 26–28) contrasts the punctum with what he terms "the studium," which is the general field or scene that a photograph represents. Laura Mulvey (2006, 62) explains that the studium pertains to the "social, cultural or other meanings that have been consciously invested in the image" by the photographer. Conversely, the punctum is a detail that is "poignant precisely because its presence is a mark of the camera's indifference, its inability to discriminate between its [intended] subject and the subject's surrounding" (Mulvey 2006, 61). Indeed, an image's punctum may even have been unnoticed by the photographer, but it suddenly captivates the attention or emotion of the viewer (61). Barthes (1993, 27) suggests that the punctum rises from the scene depicted in the photograph, shoots out, and pierces the viewer; he states that "a photograph's punctum is that accident which pricks me." Hence, Mulvey (2006, 62) argues that the punctum belongs to the viewer, while the studium belongs to the photographer.

In the case of *97 empleadas domésticas,* the punctum also belongs to Ortiz, who appropriated these photographs and reread them to produce a meaning and a sociopolitical critique that were not intended by the original photographers. She has written openly about the fact that there were images that she found and chose not to include because they were "demasiado bonitas" (Ortiz 2012, 97; too pretty). In some of the photographs that she did select, the presence of the domestic worker is so subtle that it is remarkable that Ortiz identified them. The exhibition relies on her skill as a reader and curator of images, which is illustrated by her suggestive juxtaposition of photographs, including two close-up portraits of children with blond hair and blue eyes who stare into the camera, while at the right-hand sides of both frames, Indigenous or Indigenous descendant domestic

192 PAID TO CARE

workers are shown in profile supporting them; in one case, only the tips of the employee's forehead, nose, and lips are visible (Ortiz 2010a, 32). The two photos' compositions are eerily similar. The punctum is a concept that also helps to shed light on the impact of the indexical home video and found footage, discussed in chapter 3, that are reused and appropriated in *Babás* and *Santiago* and that revolve around the presence of domestic employees at the margins of or in the background of the frame. In addition, the punctum is pertinent to an understanding of Mendonça Filho's (2016) fiction film *Aquarius*, also briefly addressed in chapter 3, which—like the documentaries mentioned—depicts a spectral (former) domestic employee who haunts the film's upper-middle-class protagonist, Clara, in a nightmare. Before her dream, Clara has been shown leafing through an old family photo album in which she comes across an old picture of the domestic worker whose name she cannot immediately remember but whom she believed to be a thief. In the photo, the domestic worker's body is rather uncannily truncated by the image's frame. Once again, then, these films, like *97 empleadas domésticas*, signal the force and importance of the punctum as an element of their critiques, which attempt to make visible how much bourgeois families rely on the labor of paid domestic workers.

97 empleadas domésticas has nonetheless raised ethical questions, because its creation involved the appropriation of photographs that were taken by others and posted on their personal Facebook pages; the photos were reused by Ortiz without the page owners' consent. Ortiz has reproduced excerpts of the threats that she received electronically from the parents and relatives of children who are featured in the photographs, including threats to destroy her career and to sue her on the grounds that it is illegal to use images of minors without their parents' authorization (Ortiz 2012, 98). The fact that the exhibition subverts these photographs' studiums, their intended meanings and functions as warm and jovial upper-class family portraits, contributed to this backlash. The images were not taken to reflect on class- and race-based inequalities, and yet, through Ortiz's juxtaposition of their punctums, they do. One of the relatives who wrote to Ortiz to complain appealed to the artist on these grounds, asking her to recognize that they are family photos and that it is unethical to reproduce them without having sought permission (98). The artist responded to these complaints in an open letter that was published in 2013 in which she states that many of those who appear in the photographs are socialites who frequently feature on the Facebook pages of national magazines where their names and those of their children are often posted without their explicit permission (Ortiz 2013). Ortiz adds that these families waived their right to privacy when they introduced a labor relation into their homes, which converts them into a place of work, where the state and civil society must ensure that the relevant labor rights are being upheld. Ortiz's open letter, her documentation of the complaints provoked by the exhibition (Ortiz 2012), and her public insistence on the influence of Guamán Poma's colonial chronicle and of her former job at Playa de Asia (Expósito 2010; Ortiz 2012) demonstrate that the polemical discourses that surround her interventions are as important as the works themselves. In the case of *97 empleadas domésticas*, these narratives play a role in achieving one of the exhibition's aims: producing discomfort that draws attention to the treatment of paid domestic workers in Peru.

The photographs that Ortiz used had already been uploaded to Facebook and made public, which weakens the complaints subsequently made by their creators (or their relatives) that the images of children cannot legally be reproduced without parental permission. When a Facebook user publishes content on their profile or page as "public" (rather than limiting content to those whom they have designated on the website as "friends" or "family"), then that content becomes universally accessible to anyone on the network, including those who are not the owner's direct contacts. Facebook's controls are not capable of limiting how those who receive information on the platform may use it, particularly outside Facebook itself, which is stated in the site's terms of service (Dijck 2013, 60).[14] This is what Ortiz (2013) cites in her letter, and what is acknowledged by one of the complainants who mentions that the photographs the artist appropriated belong to his daughter and granddaughters, whereas his own are protected because he is a professional photographer who knows how to safeguard his rights (Ortiz 2012, 98). Ortiz thus exploits Facebook's poor privacy controls to create her artwork.

Consequently, the controversy raises questions both about digital literacy and about how we conceptualize social media. Despite the fact that social networking sites are set up precisely to encourage users to *publicly* share details of their personal or private lives, not only with contacts, but also with third parties and companies connecting to the site (Dijck 2013, 45–67), the way that we use platforms like Facebook is (or has been) similar to the way that people use family photo albums or home videos, which are made to be shown to select individuals (i.e., friends or family). These images therefore exhibit "an *expectation* of privacy in their subject matter and/or in their perceived address" (Baron 2021, 26). Consequently, Jaimie Baron (27) argues that the reuse of these kinds of images is always also "a misuse" whose ethics must be interrogated. Baron (9) distinguishes these cultural issues from the copyright legalities surrounding appropriation. In her exploration of the ethics of audiovisual appropriation in the digital era, Baron focuses on film, though her insights are also applicable to photography. She argues that every reuse of a preexisting recording, in particular recordings that pertain to "reality" rather than fiction, is in some sense a misuse because its "new use was not intended, or at least not anticipated, by its original producer" (8). However, not all misuses are necessarily unethical; the ethics of an appropriation depends on multiple factors, including context, consent, the intention of the misuse, the identity of the appropriationist, and the individual values of the viewer (5, 15).

In fact, the critiques developed in several of the works analyzed in this book depend on the appropriation of preexisting "actuality" recordings of paid domestic workers, which were then deployed for purposes that often differ from those for which they were created.[15] Just as the forms of experimental domestic ethnography developed in *Babás* and *Doméstica* (analyzed in chapter 3) deconstruct the warmth and conviviality projected by appropriated home video footage and found bourgeois family films from the late nineteenth century to the present day, *97 empleadas domésticas* adopts a similar methodology to interrogate these kinds of images online in the social media era. The difference between Ortiz's project and the two documentaries is that for the latter, it is either implied or made explicit that the (former) domestic workers gave their consent to be filmed, where possible. For Mascaro's (2021) project *Doméstica*, one of the adolescents who was chosen to film his family's domestic worker is shown asking her to sign a consent form; however, the extent to which it is possible to establish true willingness to participate even in these documentary projects is limited given the unequal nature of the current or past domestic labor relationships that they explore.[16]

In the case of *97 empleadas domésticas*, Ortiz did not ask those who appear in the photographs, including the paid domestic workers, for permission to reproduce them. In addition, it is possible that the workers who had their photos taken and shared on Facebook by their employers had not given their consent in the first place, which Ortiz (2013) acknowledges in her letter, particularly because in many cases the workers appear to have been included in the frame by accident. In this sense, the exhibition risks being contingent on a double disregard for these domestic workers' rights to exert control over their own images and representation. This leads Sacco and Panella (2018, 163) to describe Ortiz's methodology as a critique made on behalf of, rather than in collaboration with, these domestic workers. The exhibition thus raises important ethical questions that should not be disregarded about whether the domestic workers pictured would have wished to have been used as symbols for structural inequalities in a way that masks their individuality and risks compounding perceptions of their subalternity.

Ortiz's objectives for the exhibition do not compensate for the serious ethical concerns raised, but these objectives do help us to understand the methodology the artist adopted. *97 empleadas domésticas*'s appropriation is characterized by what Baron (2021, 17, citing Vivian Sobchack) terms the "humane gaze," which "visibly and significantly encodes in the image its own subjective responsiveness to what it sees." With reference to audiovisual materials, Baron (18) explains that whereas "the filmmaker's 'gaze' is encoded in the cinematography," in the case of appropriation, "the appropriationist's 'gaze' is constituted primarily through [their] selection and editing of the found recording." Consequently, the act of appropriation may signal that the gaze of the original producer requires interrogation. This framework can deepen our understanding of the processes at work in Mascaro's (2012) *Doméstica*, in which the director edited footage of paid domestic workers that had been recorded by the adolescent children of their employers, none of whom had any contact with the director. Mascaro subsequently confessed that the film is the product of his "encontro afetivo e político" (affective and political response) to the raw material given to him (*Revista E* 2013, 20).[17] Baron's (2021, 20, 54) insights also shed light on the nature of Ortiz's photographic appropriations: by attending closely to and juxtaposing the images she found, the artist reveals details, or punctums, that have been suppressed and that are likely to have been overlooked or ignored by the original photographers. By adopting this kind of technique, Ortiz's appropriation can shed light on a *public* issue and appeal to a sense of "shared humanity"; her rereading of the intimate images is undeniably a misuse, but her aim is not merely to gratify viewers' curiosity or to target the individual employer-families who are featured in the photographs.

Ortiz's exhibition constitutes a social critique of a postcolonial labor relation that develops largely within the domestic sphere but that is (or should be) governed by the state. The exhibition's methodology and layout are designed to prompt viewers to question their own unconscious biases. Ortiz has stated that after the project had been published, viewers sent her related visual references, including black-and-white photographic portraits taken in a studio in Lima in the early twentieth century that show nannies (or wet nurses) with their faces either obscured or even entirely concealed by headscarves as they hold their infant charges up for the camera (Ortiz 2012, 97).[18] These photos strongly recall the images of wet nurses that Lins included in her documentary *Babás*. The fact that Ortiz's project has drawn attention to historical continuities suggests that the exhibition has achieved its desired aims. Although her methodology is not collaborative, which distinguishes her exhibition from Preta-Rara's collective testimonial project *Eu, empregada doméstica* and from Arias's cocreation of hotel installations for *Mucamas,* and despite the significant ethical concerns Ortiz's methodology raises, *97 empleadas domésticas* foregrounds the persistent coloniality of contemporary domestic labor relations in Peru. The exhibition emphasizes the invisibilization of paid domestic labor within hegemonic visual regimes and utilizes this erasure to critique domestic worker subjugation.

"Eu empregada doméstica"

The continuing coloniality of modern-day paid domestic labor relations is also central to the Facebook page "Eu empregada doméstica." Its creator, Preta-Rara (also known as Joyce Fernandes),[19] who was born in Santos, São Paulo, was a domestic worker for seven years, following in the footsteps of both her mother, Maria Helena da Silva, and her grandmother, Noêmia Caetano Fernandes. In the 2019 edited book *Eu, empregada doméstica: A senzala moderna é o quartinho da empregada* (I, domestic worker: The maid's room is the modern slave quarters), selected testimonios from the original Facebook page are prefaced by the stories of Preta-Rara's mother and grandmother as well Preta-Rara's own (Preta-Rara 2019, 15–29). Her family's testimonios are printed on black pages in white ink, which visually alludes to the legacy of African and Afro-Brazilian slavery that has culminated in generations of the same family all entering paid domestic employment in Brazil. They precede the Facebook testimonios, which are printed on white pages in black ink. In her own story, Preta-Rara (22–24) recalls her experiences as a child when she accompanied her mother to work in other people's homes. After leaving school, she tried to get a secretarial job, but was racially discriminated against and was compelled to work as a domestic employee until she got into college to study history and later became a teacher. She now devotes herself primarily to her career as a rap musician and to her activism and online presence.

Preta-Rara set up the Facebook page "Eu empregada doméstica" in 2016 after she received an overwhelming response to a post in which she had written about her own past experiences as a domestic worker; in less than twenty-four hours, the post had ten thousand "likes" and had been shared over five thousand times (Preta-Rara 2019, 7–8, 26). She has explained that this inspired her to expose "não só a minha história, mas dividir isso com os meus seguidores aqui no Facebook e incentivar as pessoas contarem os seus relatos ou relatos das mulheres de suas famílias que já foram ou são empregada doméstica. Recebi muitos relatos e resolvi criar

[a] página para divulgar" (Preta-Rara 2016; not only my story, but also to share this with my followers here on Facebook and to encourage people to tell their own stories, or the stories of women in their families who have been, or still are, domestic workers. I received many testimonios and I decided to create [the] page to share them).[20] Individuals were invited to send their stories to Preta-Rara by email. Before sharing them on the page, Preta-Rara would generally anonymize them so that only the author's initials, and occasionally their location, appeared. She would also add the project's hashtag, #EuEmpregadaDoméstica, as well as her own hashtag #PretaRara. These hashtags also feature heavily in the edited collection, appearing next to each of the page numbers, and in large and bold print on the outer edge of the back cover, as well as on the back matter (Preta-Rara 2019). Their prominence attests to the project's use of what Guobin Yang (2016, 15) terms "hashtag activism," which encourages "audience participation" as others read, share, comment, and publish posts using the same hashtag. Yang (14, 16) notes that this type of digital activism has been particularly salient among marginalized groups in response to struggles surrounding gender equality or racial justice because it permits a degree of "narrative agency" in cases where social conditions have constrained the capacity for other forms of agency.

Preta-Rara's use of hashtag activism, together with the popularity of Facebook in Brazil,[21] meant that her initiative quickly garnered international media attention. She became the focus of features on BBC Brasil (Barrucho 2016a) and the BBC News website (Barrucho 2016b). In Brazil, she was interviewed on TV Globo, the country's largest cable network, and she was invited to speak at TEDx São Paulo in January 2017 (Preta-Rara 2019, 27–28).[22] Media interest helped to catapult the "Eu empregada doméstica" page, and by 2019, Preta-Rara had been sent over four thousand stories about paid domestic work (29). As of February 2023, the page has over 163,000 followers. Her use of the page exemplifies how forms of digital activism have the potential to garner both national and international attention. In spite of the page's focus on the experiences of Brazilian domestic workers, the concerns explored on the page have resonated with global audiences. Many of the testimonios shared on the page have received hundreds of reactions and comments, which frequently offer solidarity and include replies that detail similar experiences.[23] Lisa Blankenship (2019, 63) argues that the page's effectiveness stems from the fact that it brings together individuals' stories, thus fostering the reader's identification with the Other while underscoring that the Other's suffering is both personal and structural in a way that abstract statistics cannot. She terms this device "rhetorical empathy" and suggests that the use of personal narratives is "a defining characteristic of feminist rhetoric" that has "long been used by women for social change" (64), for example, as part of the #MeToo movement or through the Everyday Feminism website. In this regard, the "Eu empregada doméstica" page and its impact is an example of what Sara Ahmed (2017) has called a "feminist snap," a collective outburst of anger at hitherto normalized injustice and abuse.

Preta-Rara's Facebook page and edited collection can also be situated within the established tradition of literary testimonio that has flourished in Latin America since the mid-1960s because the stories shared originate in individuals' lived experiences, which have often been characterized by a marginalization that has also been experienced by others. Consequently, the page serves as a vehicle for resistance to subjugation through its articulation of collective solidarity. The role that Preta-Rara has played in collating, publishing, and promoting the testimonios mirrors the position occupied by the editors or scribes of earlier testimonial publications.[24] Furthermore, the aims of the Facebook page and edited collection broadly dovetail with those identified in the collective literary testimonios of domestic work published in the 1980s that I analyzed in chapter 1, notwithstanding small adjustments to suit the altered legal context in which paid domestic workers now find themselves in Brazil. These earlier testimonios of paid domestic work include *Se necesita muchacha* (Gutiérrez 1983) and "Só a gente que vive é que sabe" (Carvalho 1982), which both aimed to establish and elaborate paid domestic workers' unionized identities, contest their exploitation, and garner support for future rights reform.

While *Se necesita muchacha* united multiple domestic workers' testimonios in one volume to create a collective textuality and aesthetic that emphasizes their shared struggles, Preta-Rara's "Eu empregada doméstica" Facebook page adopts a similar technique by mobilizing a digital platform. This allows the page to feature thousands of individual stories and responses in a way that has dramatically augmented the potential for testimonios to circulate and to articulate collective solidarity while also denouncing the exploitation of paid domestic workers and the cultural stigma they often face. Indeed, the online description of the Facebook page states that one of its objectives is to "mudar a situação dessas mulheres que a patroa dizem que são como se fossem da família, porém não são tratadas como seus entes queridos" (Preta-Rara 2016; change the circumstances of these women whose bosses say that they are practically a part of the family, but who are not treated in the same way as their loved ones). The page endeavors to challenge the various forms of race-, class-, and gender-based discrimi-

DOMESTIC WORKERS IN THE DIGITAL DOMAIN   199

nation that paid domestic workers suffer. Preta-Rara has also used the page and the platform created by it to raise awareness of and increase respect for domestic workers' legal rights, which were brought in line with those guaranteed to other kinds of workers following the landmark constitutional amendment on paid domestic work approved in Brazil in 2013.[25] For example, in 2016, she collaborated with the launch and promotion of the *Guia de direitos das trabalhadoras domésticas* (Preta-Rara 2019, 27; Guide to domestic workers' rights). In addition, she has used the Facebook page to share screenshots of abusive job advertisements, which she then denounces.

In this sense, Preta-Rara's project can be viewed as both a contribution to and a continuation of the kinds of work that paid domestic workers' unions have traditionally done. However, unlike the collective testimonios of domestic work analyzed in chapter 1, Preta-Rara's project is not explicitly linked to a particular union. In spite of this, the edited collection, more so than the Facebook page, inserts itself into the history of the unionized struggle for domestic workers' rights in Brazil. The front inner cover features praise for the book from Benedita da Silva, a PT politician and former domestic worker (Preta-Rara 2019), and she states that Preta-Rara's collection demonstrates that the work of Laudelina de Campos Melo (1904–1991), a foundational figure in the struggle for domestic workers' rights in Brazil, is being continued. Campos Melo was an Afro-Brazilian activist and organizer who worked as a domestic employee. She created the first association to defend the rights of paid domestic workers in Brazil in Santos in 1936. In 1961, she founded the Association of Domestic Workers in Campinas (São Paulo), which later became an official union in 1988 and played a crucial part in the struggle for domestic workers' rights. Her biography is outlined in the book's preface (12).

In addition, the book's opening materials consistently use the term *trabalhadora doméstica* (domestic worker) instead of *empregada doméstica* (domestic employee or maid), including in Preta-Rara's own dedication and introduction. This contrasts with the use of the term *empregada* in the original hashtag that sparked the creation of the Facebook page. The use of *trabalhadora* in Portuguese is clearly designed to reinforce the collection's message that domestic employees are workers with rights, a statement that has been at the heart of union campaigns. The book's preface, authored by the researcher Taina Aparecida Silva Santos, argues that its testimonios serve as evidence of the need for and impact of equal rights reform and includes a hyperlink to the original proposal for a constitutional amendment on domestic workers' rights, called the PEC 66/2012 (Preta-Rara 2019, 13). Despite this, in the book the issues of the PEC and domestic workers' legal rights are mentioned explicitly on only three occasions in the testimonios themselves (51, 82, 144), which contrasts with the way that the topic is foregrounded in the book's front matter. Preta-Rara (29) concludes her own testimonio by stating, "Peço para que [as trabalhadoras domésticas] continuem existindo e resistindo e, principalmente, cobrando nossos direitos" (I implore [domestic workers] to continue existing and resisting and, most of all, demanding our rights be respected). It is a phrase that underscores her desire for the collection to inspire social activism.

Nonetheless, the Facebook page's similarity to earlier testimonial texts means that it also raises comparable ethical conundrums, which are compounded by its digital platform. The page's explicit activist objectives coexist with more implicit ones, which include promoting Preta-Rara herself, in particular, her professional, artistic, and political activities, and amplifying her influence on social media. Although Preta-Rara was a domestic worker in the past, she is now among the "highest profile Black Brazilians" (Londoño 2021). The effectiveness of the Facebook page relies on Preta-Rara's heightened visibility, which is a consequence of her acquired cultural capital. In turn, the success of the page has helped give her the platform to pursue other endeavors. It enabled her in 2017 to launch her YouTube miniseries "Nossa voz ecoa" (Our voices echo), which addresses topics including racism, machismo, fatphobia, and hip-hop; more recently, she has taken up a role presenting a talk show for Globo TV (Londoño 2021). These dynamics also operate at the level of the edited print collection, which was published under Preta-Rara's stage name, a gesture criticized in earlier literary testimonios when a scribe's name was recorded as that of the author rather than using the name of the testimonial subject themselves or the name of their collective (see chapter 1). The book's cover art also constitutes a pictorial representation of the artist wearing a turban and large hoop earrings; her face is drawn against a purple background in a nod to her trademark hair color. The image was inspired by the photograph used on the cover of Preta-Rara's 2015 debut rap album, *Audácia* (Audacity), in which she is similarly shown in profile and uses the same accessories and makeup. Also, the book's back inner cover flap features her Instagram handle.

In other words, the project's potential for impact enjoys a symbiotic relationship to Preta-Rara's success as a social media influencer, a strand of her career that the project has helped consolidate. At the time of writing, Preta-Rara had 186,000 followers on Instagram and was following 1,212 accounts. Tama Leaver, Tim Highfield, and Crystal Abidin's (2000, n.p.) discussion of Instagram culture suggests that influencers can usually be identified through "a high-follower to low-following ratio." They add that influencers adopt "techniques of relatability" by purporting to make "extensive disclosures" about their everyday or personal lives as well as by engaging with "positive self-branding strategies" in order to "groom followers to consume their content aspirationally" (Leaver et al. 2020, n.p.); influencers are then able to monetize their audience by participating in paid partnerships or promotions. This description perfectly synthesizes Preta-Rara's social media activities, which involve posting paid advertisements targeted at Brazilian audiences, including for Johnnie Walker whiskey and the perfume shop O Boticário. The monetization of her following, and the various forms of self-promotion identified earlier, sit uncomfortably alongside the activist agenda that characterizes "Eu empregada doméstica." The page serves as a reminder that although the digital arena can be a powerful site for political protest, it also converts activism into another form of labor in the social media attention economy. Pages like "Eu empregada doméstica" involve the creation of an online community that tempts users to interact with others by responding to or liking posts and thereby sharing even more personal data that can be harvested for profit to financially benefit social media companies as well as the third parties with which the companies encourage users to connect.

The strong impulse toward both financial profit and image control that are characteristic of social media sites such as Instagram and Facebook are key drivers behind the ethical issues raised here and constitute an inherent part of the ecosystems currently created by social media platforms. Emiliano Treré (2018, 143–147) cautions against the tendency to romanticize the horizontality afforded by digital platforms and methods of communication when these are used by protest organizations. Their purported "horizontality" is often complicated by the ways in which these movements use hybrid forms of digital activism by blending the use of old and new media, corporate and alternative platforms, and internal and external forms of communication (146). This is all pertinent in the case of the "Eu empregada doméstica" Facebook page. Only the owner of the Facebook page, Preta-Rara herself, can create posts on it. This means that although other Facebook users can like, share, and comment freely on the posts, in many other respects, the page functions vertically, with Preta-Rara operating as a gatekeeper, which complicates the idea that the page gives a "voice to the voiceless," to borrow the artist's own terms (Barrucho 2016b). For instance, anyone who wants to share a story has to email it to her first so that the relevant hashtags can be added to it. The potential that the page provides for individuals to exert "narrative agency" is thus circumscribed. This appears to have led to complaints from individuals whose testimonios had not been shared for a while after they had originally submitted them by email, which provoked Preta-Rara to post an apology on the page. The use of a corporate platform such as Facebook also brings limitations: although Preta-Rara controls the content that is posted on the page, she cannot modify various aspects of it herself, including its format (in contrast to a self-built website). For example, on the left-hand side of the "Eu empregada doméstica page," there is an advertisement inviting users to "Add your business to Facebook. Showcase your work, create ads and connect with customers or supporters"; immediately beneath this ad, there is a button the user can click to begin creating a page.[26] It is a default feature that underlines how the labor that users invest in the production of their own Facebook content serves the social media platform's own interests.

Despite all the work that Preta-Rara has done to advocate for domestic workers and Afro-Brazilian women, the curatorial control she exercises over the page has also culminated in other expressions of discontent among members of the virtual community. Debates have been staged in the page's comments with regard to the rapper's posts about her political activities and political party affiliations, with some followers complaining that the page should not serve as a forum for those. These kinds of comments have been provoked by Preta-Rara's choice to share a photograph of herself with President Luiz Inácio Lula da Silva, a member of the PT, just before he was imprisoned on April 7, 2018, on corruption charges, which have since been annulled. On May 15, 2019, she also shared an image of herself at an antigovernment demonstration and protesting against the funding cuts to public universities that were implemented by President Jair Bolsonaro's administration. In response to criticism, Preta-Rara posted the following statement on the page on April 24, 2020 (which had received over 1,300 likes by June 18, 2021):

> Eu acho estranho algumas pessoas que seguem aqui não perceber ou fingir que não vê o posicionamento político/social/ artístico da página. Hoje estive numa live com a Dilma Roussef responsável pela efetivação da lei da Pec das Doméstica, Benedita da Silva—deputada federal responsável pela implementação da Pec das Doméstica e Luiza Batista presidente da Federação das Trabalhadoras Domésticas. Ou seja, mulheres que foram importantes da luta para assegurar os direitos dessas trabalhadoras. Quem não concorda com as postagens e fala que vai deixar de seguir, é só deixar, não precisa avisar ou ficar xingando mulheres que tiveram mega importância na luta. É isso, pq aqui não se cria não e eu

deixo todo os comentários mas, apagarei o xingamento gratuito de alguns que nem aqui deveriam estar.

I think it's strange that some people who follow this page don't understand or pretend not to notice the political/social/creative position taken by this page. Today I did a Facebook Live with Dilma Rousseff, who was responsible for the approval of the Constitutional Amendment [PEC] on Domestic Work, Benedita da Silva—an MP who was responsible for the implementation of the PEC, and Luiza Batista, who is president of the Domestic Workers' Federation. These women were important in the fight to secure domestic workers' labor rights. Whoever doesn't agree with these posts and says that they will stop following, should just stop following, there's no need to let me know or to insult women who've played a super important role in our struggle. That's all, there's no space for this kind of thing here, and I leave all the comments but, I will delete the unnecessary insults from some people who shouldn't even be here.

These tensions serve as a reminder that those who interact with the page do not constitute a monolithic Other that can be easily represented as a singular entity. Instead, its contributors occupy multiple distinct (political) positions and have had diverse experiences. Nonetheless, the 2019 print collection acknowledges this effectively by permanently juxtaposing testimonios written from different perspectives. Alongside many testimonios by (former) domestic workers and their relatives that document abusive domestic employer-employee relationships, Preta-Rara (2019) has also chosen to include a few contributions written by the relatives or acquaintances of those who employ domestic workers (95, 96, 163, 151, 166–167) and several by domestic workers who have enjoyed positive relationships with employers (46, 70, 98, 105, 126, 129, 138, 139, 147, 148, 156, 179, 194, 197, 204).

Preta-Rara (2019, 7) has stated that the testimonios included in the book are unedited (*inéditos*): "O editorial da Letramento e eu optamos por deixá-los na íntegra, assim como eu os recebi, sem edição e/ou cortes, para darmos voz aquelas que sempre foram silenciadas" (The publisher Letramento Press and I decided to leave them as they are, in their entirety, just as I received them. We haven't edited or cut them, in order to give a voice to those who have always been silenced). This claim constitutes an invocation of the testimonios' authenticity, which is the source of their power because they purport to allow subjugated individuals to voice their truth in their own words. It has the same objective as similar claims made by the editors of the testimonios of domestic work published in the 1980s. These statements are included, at least in part, in an attempt to appeal to readers. However, just as in the earlier texts, Preta-Rara's statement is a claim that can be complicated, because various hashtags are generally added to the testimonios posted on the Facebook page and because changes have often been made to the testimonios to ensure the authors' anonymity, usually for their own protection or at the contributor's specific request (115). In the printed volume, in most cases, the testimonios have also been anonymized, although identifying material has occasionally not been removed. In one instance, this appears to have been an editorial slip: the same testimonio is included twice in the volume, but on the second occasion, the final sentence, in which the subject names her abusive employer, has not been removed (99, 111). In this instance and on a couple of other occasions, the inclusion of names and other specific details raises ethical concerns because the lack of anonymity could allow the domestic worker to be identified and put in a difficult position by their employer, which is particularly troubling when it is not the domestic worker themselves who shared the testimonio and when the story relates to a current labor relation (74–75). Indeed, one individual writes that her aunt, who was a domestic worker, almost lost her job after she published "[um] pequeno desabafo" (a small outburst) on Facebook, which illustrates the risks of sharing testimonios like these publicly online (88–89).

Consequently, Preta-Rara's project, like Ortiz's, raises ethical questions relating to consent and the (in)visibility of marginalized subjects. With regard to visibility, the project arguably confronts an impossible conundrum: while the page provides a platform to raise awareness about the experiences of domestic workers and the prejudice they face, as individuals these workers continue to remain invisible. However, when a testimonio could reveal the domestic worker's identity, doing so risks compounding their vulnerability. Ultimately, the organization of the Facebook page and the presentation of the print collection contribute most effectively to Preta-Rara's renown.

The Facebook page thus illustrates a Spivakian bind (1988): first, it is very difficult to make space for the subaltern to speak without speaking for them, and second, once the subaltern has become someone who is listened to, it is likely that they are no longer subaltern. The fact that the majority of the testimonios in *Eu, empregada doméstica* (2019) were originally shared by individuals *other than the domestic workers themselves* or by *former* domestic workers also disrupts the claim that the project is giving a voice to the voiceless. In many cases, the testimonios were provided by the *children* of domestic workers, most often by a younger female relative, such as a granddaughter or niece, who wanted to tell of their relative's struggle or by a daughter who wanted to recount her mother's battle to provide her with better opportunities in an attempt to ensure that she would not end up doing the same kind of work (Preta-Rara 2019, 42–43, 56, 64–65, 72, 76, 82–84, 86–87, 88, 94, 97, 100–101, 106–107, 111, 115, 116, 121, 125–126, 136, 137, 144, 148–150, 150–151). In some cases, the daughters who have shared the stories lived with their mothers at their places of employment or accompanied them on cleaning jobs; occasionally, they have been employed as domestic workers for a short period themselves, but in many cases, they have not. These kinds of testimonios account for more than forty of the stories in the volume, though this may well be an underestimate because in some cases, the author reveals that their story is about their mother, but they do not betray their gender identity. This is also a trend that reflects the fact that (paid) domestic labor and its effects continue to be feminized concerns.

In total, over half the testimonios included in the print collection have been provided by individuals who identify themselves either as the friend or relative of the domestic worker who is the focus of the story or as a relative or acquaintance of the employee's boss. It is unlikely that in all these cases the subject of the story was informed that the contributor planned to write about their experience and that the subject of the story consented to it being published on a Facebook page where posts are made public so that they can be viewed and shared by anyone with access to the internet and a Facebook login. Consequently, the use of Facebook as a platform provokes ethical concerns about consent, digital literacy, and appropriation in the era of social media. Though the project is less self-reflexive than *97 empleadas domésticas*, an analysis of it sheds a similar light on the potentially negative consequences of the "imperative of sharing" that is integral to Facebook's business model (Dijck 2013, 45–67).

The page's online format has probably constrained its capacity to allow the voices of current domestic workers to be heard. Brazil continues to have a digital divide that leaves many of the poorest Brazilians, including domestic workers, with either little or no internet access or few to none of the devices required to use it. Although the share of Brazilian households with internet access has risen significantly in recent years, in 2018 nearly a quarter of Brazilian adults had never used the internet, and data shows that internet use is closely linked to levels of education, income, and age

(OECD 2020). In particular, live-in domestic workers may not have access to a device that they can use privately to contribute a story to the page. Both literacy skills and digital competency could also be issues that prevent paid domestic employees from being able to share their testimonios. It is thus unsurprising that so many of the testimonios have been shared by the children of domestic workers because young people in Brazil are more likely to use social media platforms than older generations are.[27] In one of the testimonios included in the print volume, a former domestic worker explicitly states that her fifteen-year-old daughter made her aware of the page's existence (Preta-Rara 2019, 120–121).

Despite these limitations, the *Eu, empregada doméstica* project and Preta-Rara's social media content more broadly have fulfilled a very valuable role within the Brazilian media landscape. Alida Louisa Perrine (2019) has analyzed the way in which Preta-Rara has mobilized an aesthetics of *audácia* (audacity), using the artist's own term, to create aspirational online content for young Black women in particular. Preta-Rara uses her music, her body, and her social media presence as sites of "cultural resistance" that affirm her and the Black women and girls who listen to her music and follow her, thereby challenging "racist and sexist imagery of black women" and contesting the idea, deeply ingrained in the Brazilian social imaginary, that Black women's bodies are destined for servitude (Perrine 2019, 22, 25). In this regard, Preta-Rara's strategies can be aligned with those of other Afro-Brazilian media producers who have created representations that problematize stereotypical representations of domestic workers and that "focus on Afro-Brazilian women as subjects with inner lives in ways that deviate from the mainstream media" (Gillam 2016, 1044), including the Afro-Brazilian media outlets analyzed by Reighan Gillam.[28] Gillam (1043) argues that the work of these media producers is essential because the struggle to improve the treatment of domestic workers in Brazil "involves not only legislation but also a redefinition of the image of domestic work" and "a social and cultural shift in how domestic workers are viewed."

The testimonios shared on the "Eu empregada doméstica" Facebook page and collected in the 2019 *Eu, empregada doméstica* book constitute a valuable resource in this regard. A comparative analysis of this body of texts provides plural insights into the paid domestic worker's condition, how it is perceived, and how it has evolved over recent decades. There are striking thematic similarities between them and the testimonios of domestic work published in the 1980s. This is a result, in part, of the fact that many of the testimonios in Preta-Rara's collection relate to *past* experiences of paid domestic work, including ones from the 1970s, 1980s, 1990s, and early in the first decade of the twenty-first century, all prior to the implementation of equal rights reform. However, the similarities are also a consequence of the fact that sociocultural changes in attitudes toward domestic employees, including a willingness to respect their improved legal protections, have been slow. The granddaughter of a woman who worked as a domestic employee for over thirty-five years writes that her grandmother was told by one boss that the new rights were valid only for younger domestic workers starting out now (Preta-Rara 2019, 82). In contrast to the testimonios of the 1980s, the problems faced by live-in domestic workers feature strongly in *Eu, empregada doméstica*, but they are not its principal focus. This reflects a shift away from live-in domestic work in Brazil in recent times, which constitutes a generational and cultural trend that has also been observed in statistical studies.[29]

The collection underscores the fact that paid domestic work is undertaken predominantly by young, working-class Afro-Brazilian women. The intersection of these characteristics makes these workers vulnerable both to physical abuse and sexual assault, particularly when employees live in their employers' homes (Preta-Rara 2019, 95). In some cases, the testimonios link the sexualization and perceived vulnerability of Afro-descendant women in Brazil to employers' sexual harassment of them (75, 77, 177). Like the workers who wrote testimonios in the 1980s, many of the domestic workers whose stories are included in the collection began working from a young age. At least fifty (out of 286) explicitly mention starting work while under the age of eighteen, either because their family could not support them or because their employer indicated that they would provide them with opportunities that never materialized (133, 175). These experiences are connected to deep-seated personal traumas. One former domestic employee who began working when she was eleven years old explains that she had suicidal thoughts and, after being raped at work, suffered from depression (123). These individuals' vulnerabilities are frequently compounded by the fact that they are rural-to-urban migrants who are isolated from their families or support networks (47, 49, 70, 77, 118, 168, 179).

While the employment of a minor is associated with the invocation of fictive kin relations that contribute to workers' exploitation (Preta-Rara 2019, 175),[30] several of the testimonios in the collection also document negative experiences related to being employed by actual family members (44, 71, 88, 93, 109, 116, 128, 141, 150, 158). One individual writes that she was compelled to accept a job as a domestic employee for her brother's boss by her own grandmother because she was "a unica negra da familia" (67; the only black woman in the family). The "intimate" nature of family relationships intensifies the potential for mistreatment and humiliation (44, 128). The informality that characterizes working arrangements culminates in job and wage insecurity in posts where employees are not given a legal contract (67, 130, 150, 159). This in turn results in situations where specific responsibilities have not been clearly defined and domestic workers are expected to "faz de tudo" (do everything) or, in other words, to take care of all household tasks (35, 54, 70, 107, 109, 117, 118, 128, 132, 136, 140, 144, 152, 179, 188, 190, 191, 192, 199, 202). Like the testimonios discussed in chapter 1, many of the stories shared in the collection describe doing work that was never properly remunerated or where the workers were given food, board, clothes, or other kinds of "gifts" instead of a monetary salary (41, 82, 88, 102, 113, 155, 170, 173, 187). The experiences recounted in other testimonios provide insight into issues surrounding payment: they draw attention to the fact that paid domestic labor is denigrated because of its association with the burden of *unpaid* care work, which has been borne disproportionately by women (127). One woman explains that her mother, who worked for the same couple for twenty years, began to care for them in old age after she had officially retired; before their deaths, the couple promised that their children would reimburse her for this labor but ultimately, they refused to do so (149).

The extreme socioeconomic inequality that characterizes many domestic labor relationships is often explored in the testimonios through the symbol of food. It is the theme that reverberates most strongly throughout the collection and is mentioned on at least eighty occasions. Common experiences include having to wait for long periods before being allowed to eat (for example, until after employers' have finished their meals) or not being offered food at all (33, 44, 70, 103, 104, 107, 137, 141, 146, 155, 164, 168, 171, 174, 186, 193, 198, 201, 205), being given leftovers or offered food that had either spoiled or was of poor quality (32, 35, 37, 41, 51, 54, 56, 66, 71, 103, 117, 133, 120, 122, 129, 131–132, 133, 134, 142, 153, 160, 161, 178, 187, 190), and being asked to eat different food in a separate area (including outside the main house) or to eat off plates and use cutlery that are different from those used by the employers (72, 78, 80, 92, 96, 106, 114, 169, 171, 175, 176, 178, 191). Some of the texts also mention being expected to eat either the same or worse quality of food than that given by employers to their pets (126, 138, 174, 208); this expectation constitutes a strong parallel with the bestial imagery used to explore workers' inhumane treatment that is employed in both the testimonios discussed in chapter 1 and the fiction films analyzed in chapter 2.

In cultural terms, food and eating are endowed with very strong social and symbolic connotations in Brazil: what you eat and where you eat constitute clear class markers. Indeed, the association of poverty and hunger has marked Brazilian cultural production since at least the development and deployment of an "estética da fome" (aesthetics of hunger) in the politically engaged films of the Cinema Novo movement (Rocha 1995), such as Nelson Pereira dos Santos's 1963 film *Vidas secas (Barren Lives)* in which a migrant family in the country's arid Northeast is compelled to eat both their pet parrot and their dog, Baléia, to avoid starvation. Food recurs as a symbol in Clarice Lispector's seminal 1977 novella *A hora da estrela* (2002; The hour of the star), which explores power dynamics shaped by gender and class through a focus on the masochistic relationship between a wealthy male narrator and his poverty-stricken Northeastern protagonist, Macabéa, who cannot manage to digest "rich" foods.

In *Eu, empregada doméstica*, issues surrounding food can be related to other forms of spatial separation that employers impose to cement the divisions between themselves and their employees, who are often viewed as a source of symbolic pollution within their households (L. Barbosa 2008). One testimonio recounts a boss's disgust at the idea that a domestic worker would use the same bathroom as herself (Preta-Rara 2019, 167), while another mentions an employer's insistence that her employee use the service elevator and not the one reserved for residents (124). The daughter of one former live-in domestic worker recalls the time when they both resided at the home of her mother's employers; she states that "a noite, quando todos estavam em casa, ficava apenas da cozinha para o quarto, que era ao lado. Não me aceitavam convivendo na casa" (115; in the evenings, when all of them were at home, I was confined to the kitchen and our bedroom, which was right next to it. They didn't accept me living together with them in the house). Her experience resonates strongly with the fictional confrontation depicted in the Brazilian film *Que horas ela volta?* (Muylaert 2015) in which the daughter of the live-in domestic worker Val is banned from entering the "family areas" of Val's employers' home while she is staying with them. The underlying territorialization of the home is exposed both by this prohibition and by the use of cinematography that foregrounds the way in which the threshold to the kitchen represents a dividing line (see chapter 2 for further discussion). Just as in *Que horas ela volta?* and *97 empleadas domésticas*, the symbolic site of the swimming pool also appears in *Eu, empregada doméstica* as a contested domestic space with strong class connotations. Three testimonios identify the swimming pools used by their employers as areas to which domestic employees were not permitted access (Preta-Rara 2019, 100, 113, 132).

The same class-based fears that motivate employers' attempts to impose spatial divisions also underlie the distrust that shapes boss-worker relations, an issue identified in so many of the testimonios in the collection (Preta-Rara 2019, 48, 62, 137, 143, 178, 187, 188, 190). Several domestic workers describe having been "tested" by their employers, who left money around the house to see whether they would take it (31, 38, 112, 168, 199–200), while many others recount that they were either suspected or wrongly accused of stealing (34, 39, 57, 60, 83, 95, 97, 124, 128–129, 132, 135, 145, 152, 156, 165, 166, 177, 182, 196, 206). Another theme that unifies various accounts is the sense of surveillance that many workers experience while laboring in others' homes (168). The child of a former domestic worker mentions that her mother's employers would hide in their home when they had said they would be out so that they could spy on her to catch her doing something wrong (133).

The experiences described thus far relating to abuse, sexual assault, food associations, spatial divisions, and theft accusations culminate in strong feelings of shame and anger among paid domestic workers and their families (Preta-Rara 2019, 83–84, 112, 126, 128, 131–132, 152, 166, 182, 199–200). In fact, humiliation is the affect that reverberates most strongly throughout the collection and is mentioned explicitly on at least forty-four occasions. One worker describes an occasion when she was symbolically humiliated by her employer, who obliged her to wear a plain white uniform while attending a family birthday party in order to make it clear that she was an employee and not a guest (43).

These kinds of occurrences are the result of paid domestic workers' dehumanization by their bosses, some of whom are reported to behave as if employees were their property (Preta-Rara 2019, 75, 80). Several of the testimonial subjects either imply or explicitly state that the legacy of Afro-Brazilian enslavement is at the root of certain employers' apparent disdain for domestic workers' humanity and individuality (84, 125, 145, 150, 183, 185, 190, 193, 199). The testimonios also include references to the Freyrian casa grande, which invokes the country's lingering coloniality (80, 154, 186, 200). One individual tells of a friend who described a domestic worker who was "gifted" to her by her parents as one of the "best wedding presents" she had received, for example (43). A domestic worker's daughter relates that when her mother was pregnant, her employer tried to trick her into taking abortion medication against her will. She explains that this was the action "de quem achava ter soberania sobre o corpo e a vontade [da minha mãe]" (94; of someone who believed they had sovereignty over [my mother's] body and her wishes). This sense of ownership can also be linked to some domestic workers' traumatic experiences of having been imprisoned by employers (33, 47, 70, 92, 114, 131, 141, 143). Occurrences such as these are indicative of the ways in which paid domestic work can jeopardize employees' freedom to establish autonomous personal lives and emotional relationships, a theme that also resonates throughout the testimonios published in the 1980s. One former domestic worker recalls an abusive employer who tried to intervene in her plans to get married (129), while another writes that "o pior de tudo e que os patrões de doméstico acham que a gente não tem direito de ter vida social e família" (149; worst of all is the fact that employers think that we don't have a right to a social or family life).

In their testimonios, some domestic workers express hopes for improved employer-employee relationships based on appeals to a shared sense of humanity (Preta-Rara 2019, 108, 144, 176, 187); however, other former domestic employees denigrate paid domestic work as a form of employment altogether (44, 149). One individual even states, "se um dia tudo der errado, e eu tiver que virar doméstica de novo, EU ME MATO!! Por favor, não me julguem" (177; if one day everything goes wrong, and I have to become a maid again, I WILL KILL MYSELF!! Please, don't judge me). Consequently, multiple testimonios conclude with a celebration of no longer being a paid domestic worker. Those who have left the profession are often eager to emphasize that they are now doing something "better." There are around forty testimonios that constitute clear narratives of personal or familial success (66, 69–70, 71, 78, 81, 88, 92, 101, 103, 105, 107, 110, 116, 125, 126, 127, 132–133). This trend coincides with one identified by Juliano Spyer (2017, 3) in his ethnographic investigation of the use of social media among low-income Brazilians; he found that individuals knowingly shared (what he considered to be) very personal or intimate details about themselves publicly on their Facebook timelines with the intention of displaying their "achievements" and "moral values." In some cases, these narratives of personal or familial achievement risk reproducing the paid domestic worker as a subaltern figure, although there are a few testimonios in which individuals express genuine pride in the job that either they or their mothers undertook and, in the latter case, gratitude for the opportunities that their mothers worked hard to provide for them (105, 203, 204, 215).

Many of the testimonios of familial success have been written by the children of former domestic workers, and while they highlight personal triumphs, some also identify the importance that structural changes have had for their opportunities. These include the increased access to higher education facilitated by the introduction of quotas for Afro-Brazilian and state-educated students by Brazil's PT governments. Indeed, one testimonio (Preta-Rara 2019, 86–87) closely echoes the narrative depicted in the fiction film *Que horas ela volta?*, discussed in chapter 2. The testimonios were often written by the children of paid domestic workers who celebrate the fact that they got into public or private universities (48, 82, 86–87, 100–101, 133–134, 136–137, 199–200). One of them concludes by directly addressing the Brazilian upper middle class and elite: "Vai ter preto e pobre nas 'suas' universidades, nos 'seus' espaços e onde mais a gente quiser" (200; You are going to have Black people and poor people in "your" universities, in "your" spaces and wherever else we like).

It is clear, then, that *Eu, empregada doméstica* intervenes in emotive disputes that revolve around the ways in which paid domestic workers, and Afro-Brazilian working-class women more broadly, are represented in the Brazilian social and cultural imaginary. The testimonios' overall impact is to condemn or contest paid domestic workers' subalternization. One individual, for instance, describes not getting invited for a job interview because she was registered as a domestic employee on her work permit (Preta-Rara 2019, 197). This kind of prejudice and structural discrimination culminates in feelings of shame surrounding the profession that, in her testimonio so many years earlier, Carvalho (1982, 51–52, 55–57) identifies as a key problem that needs to be addressed; the repetition suggests that in cultural terms, not much has changed when compared to the advancements achieved in the area of rights reform. Some *Eu, empregada doméstica* contributors believe that the project has offered a crucial opportunity for dialogue to tackle cultural prejudice (Preta-Rara 2019, 130). For instance, in the few testimonios shared by the relatives of employers, there is evidence that the Facebook page has raised consciousness among individuals who had not previously reflected on the nature of paid domestic work. The adult son of one employer writes about his parents' domestic worker, who had always looked after him but whose dedication he had never fully appreciated until he started reading the posts on the "Eu empregada doméstica" page. He admits, "Nada possa retribuir o quanto ela se deu para mim" (72; There is no way of repaying her for everything she gave to me). It is a comment that draws attention to the affective, emotional, or care-based elements of domestic labor that do not seem to have been satisfactorily compensated by the monetary reward provided, an idea discussed in depth in chapter 2.

Despite its limitations and the ethical concerns discussed above, the Facebook page has helped to weave a collective digital identity for domestic workers in Brazil through the various testimonios shared by many current and former workers, as well as by their relatives and friends. More broadly, the project, including the physical edited collection, has also served as a platform to promote domestic workers' activism and rights. It articulates Hardt and Negri's (2004) conception of "the multitude" by exploring the hegemonic forms of oppression that unite the experiences of so many domestic employees. Although the mosaic of voices the project constructs is "certainly fragmented" and "itinerant," to borrow Hilda Chacón's (2018, 7) terms when describing collective forms of online activism in Latin America, "its presence and impact are undeniable."

Domestic Workers and Digital Artivism during the Covid-19 Pandemic

The spate of digital works on domestic workers' rights and treatment in Latin America has only intensified in the wake of the Covid-19 pandemic, during which these employees were used as a powerful symbol in public discourse for the ways that the virus exacerbated existing inequalities in the region in terms of mobility, income security, healthcare, and housing.[31] In Brazil, the artist Cristiano Suarez (2020a, 2020b) published on his social media profiles a pair of illustrations, *Pandemia romântica n.1: covid-se* (Romantic pandemic no. 1: Covid yourself) and *Pandemia romântica n.2: live-se* (Romantic pandemic no. 2: live yourself), that explore these dynamics. The illustrations re-create and parody the aesthetics of Instagram posts made by young White influencers in upmarket apartments who remind their followers to prioritize their well-being during quarantine while their domestic employees can be glimpsed in the background maintaining their glamorous lifestyles. In a similar vein, Leandro Assis and Triscila Oliveira have created *Confinada*, an online graphic novel series published on Assis's Instagram account (@leandro_assis_ilustra), which began in April 2020 and followed the development of the pandemic in Brazil. It charts the relationship between the wealthy White influencer Fran and her Afro-Brazilian domestic employee, Ju, who goes into quarantine with her employer and is consequently unable to return home to see her own daughter.[32] Fran contracts Covid-19, which she implies is the fault of the domestic worker. Shortly afterward, Fran is canceled and loses her lucrative advertising contracts when it emerges that she caught (and spread) the virus by hosting a party at her apartment during lockdown (Assis and Oliveira no. 52). Ju subsequently takes over Fran's Instagram account while her boss is away and posts a series of videos criticizing both Fran and her followers. Ju's posts go viral, and she is invited to create paid online content as part of a network of Afro-Brazilian and LGBTQ+ influencers (no. 66). These characters' respective story arcs dramatize struggles related to the representation of oppressed or marginalized groups that have played out in Brazil, particularly online. Recent examples of this include degrading social media content shared by employers to "celebrate" their employees' return to work after Covid-19 lockdowns, such as one widely criticized video posted on Instagram by two White employers who made their Afro-Brazilian employee perform a dance routine with them, which is directly referenced in the *Confinada* series (no. 13).[33] Both Suarez's and Assis and Oliveira's works are thus highly self-reflexive in that they use social media as a platform while also critiquing Instagram culture. Indeed, Ju's narrative in *Confinada* is undoubtedly influenced by that of Preta-Rara, who is featured as the first guest on Ju's new online series (no. 68). Ju is depicted wearing a colorful headscarf and hoop earrings beneath the caption "Oi, eu sou a Ju: reflexões de uma ex-empregada doméstica" (Hi, I'm Ju: reflections of an ex-domestic worker). The illustration strongly recalls the cover image used for Preta-Rara's book of collected testimonios, *Eu, empregada doméstica*, which features the author (as discussed earlier). *Confinada*'s narrative development attests to the impact that Preta-Rara's Facebook page and book have had on subsequent digital interventions related not only to the issue of Afro-Brazilian women's representation but also to domestic workers' rights in the region.

In Mexico, another testimonial project that utilizes a format similar to that of *Eu, empregada doméstica* has recently emerged in direct response to the pandemic. *Nuestras voces cuentan* (Santiago Páramo 2020; Our voices count) is a book featuring domestic workers' testimonios collected via the Facebook page of a network of domestic employees entitled "Mi Trabajo Cuenta" (My Work Counts). The collection, which is available to read online or to download as a PDF file, addresses the additional pressures placed on paid domestic workers by the global pandemic. It was sponsored by several organizations in Mexico that support domestic workers, including Mi Trabajo Cuenta, the pro-democracy collective Nosotrxs, the National Domestic Workers' Union (Sindicato Nacional de Trabajadores y Trabajadoras del Hogar—SINACTRAHO), and the Support and Training Center for Domestic Workers (Centro de Apoyo y Capacitación para Empleadas del Hogar—CACEH).[34] The title of the project of which the testimonial publication formed a part is "Yo, empleada del hogar por un trabajo digno" (I, domestic worker for a dignified job), a phrase that resonates with the hashtag that Preta-Rara used for her own Facebook page, "Eu empregada doméstica" (I domestic worker). Like the book *Eu, empregada doméstica*, *Nuestras voces cuentan* is also the product of a network or (online) community that endeavors to contribute to the work that domestic employees' labor unions have traditionally done. As the physical and PDF

DOMESTIC WORKERS IN THE DIGITAL DOMAIN 215

editions of these digital collections show, there continues to be an impulse to produce downloadable or printed versions of these texts, which is arguably a response to anxieties surrounding the ephemerality and ownership of online content.

Nuestras voces cuentan also serves as a tool of social activism that inspires its readers to take action. It opens and closes with texts that mention recent legal changes that have improved domestic workers' rights in Mexico. These are authored by key players in SINACTRAHO, including the union's founder, Marcelina Bautista Bautista, who implores employers to fulfill their obligations to their employees during and after the pandemic (Santiago Páramo 2020, 44); she tells bosses and readers, "¡Haz lo correcto! No seas indiferente y pon el ejemplo" (Do the right thing! Don't be indifferent and set a good example). This recalls the conclusion of Preta-Rara's (2019, 8) introduction in *Eu, empregada doméstica*, in which she challenges her readers by asking, "E você está fazendo o quê para alterar essa condição das trabalhadora doméstica?" (And what are *you* doing to change the circumstances of paid domestic workers?).

In *Nuestras voces cuentan*, the testimonios of the domestic employees are divided into four thematic sections that focus on live-in domestic workers, those who were fired or laid off during the pandemic, those who continued to work, and those who maintained their salary. This structure serves to emphasize the similar and different challenges faced by domestic workers employed in distinct contexts, while also reinforcing Bautista's concluding message. The concerns that this collection raises include the implications of domestic workers' mobility (or lack thereof) during the pandemic (Santiago Páramo 2020, 13); their increased precarity and inability to access basic goods, including as a result of a lack of government support (23, 25–26, 28); the health risks that their work entails (27); and the lack of value attributed to paid domestic work (26, 38, 43)—an issue that resonates across all the texts analyzed in this book. The themes identified in *Nuestras voces cuentan* also recur in other works that depict the experiences of domestic workers in Latin America during the Covid-19 pandemic, which constitute a crucial avenue for future research.

Conclusion

This chapter has traced the connections between several works of digital or visual artivism that not only address the mistreatment of Latin American domestic and cleaning workers but also constitute critical meditations on the ways in which these employees have traditionally been represented in media and culture. While *97 empleadas domésticas* is a visual and digital intervention made on behalf of paid domestic workers in Peru and in response to their invisibilization within hegemonic modes of self-representation on social media, *Eu, empregada doméstica* constitutes a more collective attempt to contest the prejudices that paid domestic workers have historically faced in Brazil. As Preta-Rara's initiative developed, it was repackaged to form part of a broader struggle for domestic workers' rights, and it can be situated within the tradition of testimonial literature in Latin America. Both Ortiz's and Preta-Rara's works enact powerful critiques of the continuing coloniality of paid domestic labor relations in the region; however, neither of them can solve the ethical dilemmas inevitably provoked when attempting to make visible the struggles of a subaltern group. Although their uses of digital platforms have enabled them to attract greater public attention, the ethical issues that they raise are in fact compounded by their reliance on social media ecosystems, namely, Facebook. This is because the site's business model is predicated on the imperative to share personal details, which has created a culture where individuals post information about, or images of, not only themselves but also others—often without their consent. Usually, posting is done with the objective of self-promotion, but in the case of social media influencers, posting also monetizes their following, which means that the site and third parties can then profit from users' data as a corollary. Nonetheless, these works simultaneously constitute a crucial part of a wave of artivism related to domestic workers' representation and treatment in Latin America, which has continued in the wake of the Covid-19 pandemic. They are an important element in the cultural struggle to change historical public attitudes toward domestic workers that have culminated in workers' exploitation, discrimination, and a continuing lack of respect for their legal rights.

Conclusion

I HAVE EXAMINED a wave of Latin American cultural texts, produced since the 1980s, that are the product either of direct collaborations with or of intimate relationships with paid domestic workers. These texts both dialogue with and rework complex and contradictory foundational narratives that seized on domestic employees and enslaved persons (in particular wet nurses) as figures who could symbolize the reimagination of various Latin American countries as modern, mixed-race nations from the early twentieth century onward. These narratives have frequently naturalized the subjugation of Afro- and Indigenous descendant domestic employees or obfuscated their mistreatment. The cultural representations I have analyzed critique these myths while also sometimes betraying an ambivalent nostalgia for intimate relationships with live-in paid domestic workers, for instance, in the case of some of the films discussed. These works illustrate the profound impact that domestic labor relations have had on the development of Latin American society and culture, not only because these relations are integral to the organization of so many middle- and upper-class homes in the region, but also because they transcend the domestic sphere by shaping and reflecting wider socioeconomic and political relationships as well.

The figure of the paid domestic worker, who is engaged in a labor relation that is regulated by state laws but that transpires within the space of the home, has sparked intense interest in recent years. This is because this figure complicates the deep-seated ideological divisions between the public and private realms (and incidentally, the personal and the political realms too) that structure contemporary liberal societies. Paid domestic workers have recently been used as potent symbols of race, class, gender, and regional inequalities within public debates at a time when all the countries that are the focus of this study have taken steps to improve these workers' legal rights. These changes have unsurprisingly provoked both positive and negative reactions, for example, regarding the increase in cost of hiring a live-in domestic employee. Discussions such as these that revolve around the perception that there is a "crisis of servitude" or "servant problem" have recurred at moments of social transformation, for example, in the period following the abolition of enslavement (Roncador 2014, 3) and in the mid-twentieth century, when women began entering the paid workforce outside the home in greater numbers (Pite 2011, 106–109). My analysis has shown how the cultural representations that I have discussed, such as Anna Muylaert's *Que horas ela volta?* (2015), have tapped into the often contentious dynamics of national debates that adopt both domestic workers and their children as symbols of either stagnant or improved social mobility. This is because paid domestic work is a profession that generations of female members from the same family have often entered into, as foregrounded in both the format and content of Preta-Rara's *Eu, empregada doméstica* (2019), a print collection of the digital testimonios originally published on the eponymous Facebook page.

In many cases, then, the texts I have explored begin to upset traditional distinctions between cultural production and activism, while also self-reflexively intervening in debates about who is represented and how. While the literary testimonios that were published in the 1980s in collaboration with or on behalf of burgeoning domestic workers' organizations formed part of campaigns to raise awareness about these employees' exploitation and to garner support for rights reform (see chapter 1), the stories shared much more recently on Preta-Rara's (2016) Facebook page have been repackaged as part of an attempt to clamor for paid domestic workers' newly improved legal rights to be respected (see chapter 4). Alfonso Cuarón's film *Roma* (2018) is the most powerful example of a cultural production centered on the story of a paid domestic worker that has been deployed to galvanize the campaign for these employees' rights. As I discussed in chapter 2, the team behind *Roma* collaborated with domestic workers' organizations, mobilized Cuarón's celebrity, and drew on forms of online and offline activism to pressure the Mexican government into launching a pilot program to include domestic workers in the social security system and into ratifying the International Labour Organization's Domestic Workers' Convention. Clearly, collaborative campaigns such as *Roma* are necessary not only to achieve reform but also to encourage a change in sociocultural attitudes toward paid domestic workers so that their labor rights are respected. All the works I analyzed in this book are designed to contribute to processes of consciousness-raising and self-reflection among audiences by deploying techniques that have the potential to denaturalize racialized, gendered, and classist assumptions about who should be doing domestic work and how domestic workers can be treated.

In my analysis, I found that cultural representations are a particularly privileged medium for an interrogation of paid domestic labor relations because of their capacity to evoke the affective ties that bind employer-families and live-in domestic workers and to account for the enormous toll that these relations can take for the latter, including in their personal, romantic, and familial lives. I demonstrated that a common device employed in recent fiction and documentary films to explore these affective dynamics is the dramatization of the relationship between domestic employees and their employers' children, as shown in my discussions of *Roma*, *La nana* (Silva 2009), *Que horas ela volta?*, *Casa grande* (Barbosa 2014), *Doméstica* (Mascaro 2012), *Babás* (Lins 2010), and *Santiago* (Salles 2007).

The difficulty of accounting for the affective (or immaterial) products of paid domestic work by using traditional economic models culminates in the portrayal of haunting or haunted domestic employees and servants in films such as *Santiago*, *Babás*, and *Doméstica*. This is also the case in the films of Lucrecia Martel, *Las dependencias* (1999) and *Zama* (2017), and in those of Kleber Mendonça Filho, including *Aquarius* (2016). The use of ghostly presences or of devices from the horror genre, such as in the Brazilian films *As boas maneiras* (Rojas and Dutra 2017) and *Todos os mortos* (Gotardo and Dutra 2020), also draws attention to the ways in which paid domestic labor relationships in Latin America continue to be shaped by the legacy of colonialism.

The wave of recent Latin American films that have been inspired by intimate relationships with domestic workers constitutes a cultural phenomenon, which I discussed in chapters 2 and 3. These films either are designed as odes to (former) domestic workers or adopt domestic workers as protagonists in an attempt to empower them and endow them with a greater level of agency. The latter is achieved in films such as *Que horas ela volta?* and *La nana* by granting their domestic worker characters expanded fields of vision or access to spaces outside their bosses' households at the conclusions of their narratives. All the cinematic works I discussed represent a contrast to the formulaic telenovela narratives featuring domestic workers that became popular in Latin America during the second half of the twentieth century and that draw on gender-, class-, and race-related stereotypes that they do not problematize. Nonetheless, the films I analyzed in this book are still ultimately framed by middle- or upper-class directorial perspectives that have drawn criticism and that result in these films' ambivalent oscillations between adopting the perspectives of their domestic worker protagonists and risking their objectification, romanticization, silencing, or at times reduction to humorous stereotypes.

The digital and literary works I addressed in chapters 1 and 4, such as "Só a gente que vive é que sabe" (Carvalho 1982), *Se necesita muchacha* (Gutiérrez 1983), *Diário de Bitita* (de Jesus 1986), and *Eu, empregada doméstica*, demonstrate that both paid and unpaid domestic work are key themes that reverberate throughout the genre of Latin American women's testimonio, including foundational testimonial texts by Domitila Barrios de Chúngara and Rigoberta Menchú. While the testimonios of paid domestic workers endeavor to serve as platforms for the employees' own voices to be heard, they are also mediated on the levels of ideology, content, and promotion by various gatekeepers, including scribes, academics, publishers, social media influencers, and even employers of domestic workers. The interplay between artist and subject, both in these works and in the films I analyzed in chapters 2 and 3, means that they all evoke or interrogate the power relationships between employers and domestic employees at a formal level.

In chapter 1, I showed that Latin American literary testimonios by paid domestic workers published in the 1980s provide valuable early insights into these employees' nascent labor associations and processes of unionization, although they have been the focus of little scholarly attention. My analysis draws on the knowledge these testimonios collectively produce as part of my theoretical framework, which pays particular attention to the issues of domestic work undertaken by (female) minors, the isolation of live-in employees, the challenges of unionizing workers who identify strongly with their employers (including as surrogate members of the family), and the dehumanization and bestialization of paid domestic workers as a consequence of their commodification by bosses. While all the testimonios contain evidence of their subjects' growing self-awareness, this group of texts can be divided broadly into two types: those that focus on domestic workers' individual struggles and those that take up collective concerns. Ramona Caraballo's (1987) and Francisca Souza da Silva's (1983) testimonios exemplify the first type and are shaped by a facet of Catholic ideology that views life as suffering and that invokes hope for individual redemption. Carolina Maria de Jesus's *Diário de Bitita* displays commonalities with Caraballo's and da Silva's texts, but the author's awareness of the class-, race-, and gender-based discrimination faced by the Afro-Brazilian community enables her testimonio to undertake a structural and intersectional critique in certain places. The second collective type of testimonio is engaged in domestic workers' attempts to organize and unionize across Latin America in the 1970s and 1980s, as my close textual analysis and interviews have demonstrated. While Lenira Carvalho's "Só a gente que vive é que sabe" functions metonymically by deploying elements of her biography and experiences to theorize about the broader challenges that confront paid domestic workers, Ana Gutiérrez's *Se necesita muchacha* juxtaposes the testimonios of multiple employees, many of whom had become involved in Cusco's Domestic Workers' Union (STHC). Both testimonios were deeply influenced by a distinct branch of Catholicism—that of liberation theology, which combines Marxist critique with a Christian compassion for the impoverished. Neither of the testimonios resolve the ethical concerns that such projects inevitably engender because they frequently rely on the interventions of middle-class or academic scribes whose ideologies and religious beliefs mark the testimonio's form and content. My analysis reveals, for example, that Ana Gutiérrez, a pseudonym used by the academic Cristina Goutet when publishing *Se necesita muchacha*, was an adherent of a branch of liberation theology known as "opción preferencial por el pobre," or OPP. In Peru, where *Se necesita muchacha* was first published under the title *Basta* (STHC 1982), the individual most associated with OPP was Father Gustavo Gutiérrez, which provides a rationale for Goutet's choice of pseudonym. Father Gutiérrez founded Peru's Instituto Bartolomé de las Casas, whose publishing house printed *Basta*.

In chapter 2, I analyzed four contemporary fiction films that focus on live-in domestic workers and that are all intensely personal: *Que horas ela volta?*, *La nana*, *Casa grande*, and *Roma*. They are either inspired by the experience of growing up alongside domestic employees or explicitly dedicated to the employees who helped to raise these films' directors. My analysis shows how this culminates in the creation of films characterized by a desire to atone for an affective (or emotional) debt to these employees that appears difficult to recompense. Both *Que horas ela volta?* and *La nana*, for example, explore this desire through their use of gift-related symbolism. All the films analyzed in chapter 2 exploit the capacity of cinema to reconstruct bourgeois domestic spaces in order to play on the continuing significance of the maid's room across Latin America, to the extent that this has become an identifiable cinematic trope. Employer-employee relations enable these works to dramatize the broader class- and race-based inequalities that afflict their societies, but all within the space of a reconstructed home, which is expedient when making a film on a budget. In many cases, by depicting the territorialization of the household, the films evoke middle- and upper-class fears surrounding the entry of the working-class into spaces that the former consider "reserved" for themselves (Souto 2018, 176). The figure of the live-in domestic worker is also used to undermine both the distinction between public and private in these films and the notion that the reproductive labor of these employees is economically unproductive. Their mise-en-scènes frequently dramatize the ways in which the labor of domestic workers permits the employer-family's participation in what are traditionally perceived as more prestigious or productive forms of work (or education). In addition, *Roma, La nana,* and *Que horas ela volta?* critique the ways in which live-in domestic labor culminates in attempts either to commodify or dehumanize domestic workers, whose rights to privacy and to an autonomous family life are radically compromised by their employment. The films do so through their use of bestial imagery, which underscores the alignment of these workers with the abject (or with dirt) from a bourgeois perspective and which threatens their status as subjects. Ultimately, I show that all four films' narrative resolutions rely (to greater and lesser extents) on a modern Western individualistic and feminist framework, the contradictions of which they are unable to reflect upon fully. These frameworks emerge as the films simply invert traditional male-female power hierarchies. Despite the potentially intersectional elements of *Roma*'s critique and the empowering aspects of *Que horas ela volta?* and *La nana*'s endings, the ambivalent resolutions achieved at these films' conclusions are contingent on their domestic-worker protagonists remaining in situations where they appear resigned to or even happy with their positions, providing more (remunerated or unremunerated) care so that others can leave the home to undertake more "prestigious" forms of work. Despite their narrative limitations, all the fiction films I analyzed have provoked public debate on the nature of live-in domestic work; they have even, in the case of *Roma,* had an impact in improving these employees' legal rights.

In chapter 3, I examined the Argentine and Brazilian documentaries *Las dependencias, Santiago, Babás,* and *Doméstica* and found that all four films are characterized by the portrayal either of spectral domestic employees or of haunting relationships. The reasons for this are twofold. First, domestic work has not been properly accounted for by traditional, capitalist economic models, which results in the depiction of domestic workers as spectral figures whose presence resurges despite attempts to minimize or conceal their contributions. Second, domestic labor relations continue to be haunted by colonial legacies of power. In the first part of the chapter, I examined films that interrogate the ways in which middle- and upper-class artists and intellectuals are haunted by paid domestic employees because the creation of immaterial products is a defining element of both artistic and domestic labor, yet these forms of work have wildly differing levels of cultural capital. *Las dependencias,* for instance, attempts to deconstruct rigid distinctions

CONCLUSION 223

between the categories of "artist" and "servant." The defamiliarizing use of sound in this documentary alludes to the ways in which real domestic workers supported, inspired, and consequently haunted the Argentine author Silvina Ocampo's literary production.

In the second part of the chapter, I analyzed the films *Santiago*, *Babás*, and *Doméstica*, which all explore the ways in which contemporary domestic labor relationships in Brazil are haunted by the legacy of colonialism and slavery. All three films are experimental domestic ethnographies that constitute distanced meditations on footage of domestic workers that has been recorded by their former employer or by their (former) employers' children. My analysis showed that the similarities between these films' themes, forms, and techniques are a consequence of the inspiration that Salles's watershed film *Santiago* provided for Lins's and Mascaro's later documentaries. Their explorations of the complex relationship of documentary to the index (the trace of a person, object, or relationship now gone) enables them to evoke the loss of childhood intimacy with domestic workers—from the employer's or director's perspective. However, these films also adopt experimental techniques that enable them to reflect, often painfully, on the intimate power relationships between those behind the camera and the (former) domestic employees being filmed, as well as on the ethics of using the latter as documentary subjects. The directors' uses of performative and self-reflexive techniques, as well as delayed cinema, foreground the issues of control and coloniality associated with traditional ethnography, thereby encouraging audiences to consider the ways in which filmmaking itself remains implicated in the same hierarchies of power and modes of exploitation that shape the paid domestic labor relationships the films portray.

In chapter 4, I traced the connections between works of digital and visual artivism that address the treatment of paid domestic and cleaning workers. I focused principally on Daniela Ortiz's (2010) *97 empleadas domésticas* and Preta-Rara's (2019) *Eu, empregada doméstica*. Both these works are critical meditations on dominant representations of domestic employees in media and culture. While Ortiz appropriated images from employers' Facebook profiles that featured traces of domestic workers so that she could critique attempts to marginalize them and to conceal their presence, Preta-Rara's "Eu empregada doméstica" Facebook page constitutes a more collective attempt to contest the prejudices that domestic workers face. My analysis showed that as Preta-Rara's initiative developed and resulted in the publication of a print collection of selected testimonios shared on the original Facebook page, it was refashioned to form an explicit part of the historical struggle for domestic workers' rights in Brazil that has been undertaken in particular by labor unions. Although these two projects' distinct uses of Facebook enabled them to attract public attention, the ethical issues they raise regarding mediation and appropriation are compounded by their reliance on the site. Facebook's business model is contingent on users' willingness to share personal details, which has created an online culture where individuals post information about (or images of) not only themselves but also others, and not necessarily with the latter's consent. This benefits the site, which enables third parties to monetize users' data, a fact that sits uncomfortably alongside the activist agendas that characterize these initiatives. Despite this, both works also constitute a crucial part of the wave of artivism related to domestic workers' representation and treatment in Latin America, which has continued in the wake of the Covid-19 pandemic, as shown by my discussion of the *Confinada* online graphic novel series (Assis and Oliveira 2020) and another collection of digital testimonios from Mexico, *Nuestras voces cuentan* (Santiago Páramo 2020). Both this text and Preta-Rara's initiative are understood as a continuation of the tradition of testimonial literature in the region; they show how the genre has adapted to the digital age and continues to be used to advocate for subaltern groups.

I have identified a number of avenues for future research on related topics. First and foremost, as Sarah Ann Wells (2016, 101) has argued, the ubiquity of work has made it into a blind spot in studies of cinema that can nonetheless be approached from a variety of different angles. Further research on this topic would shed light not only on the representation of different forms of work as objects (or themes) in Latin American cinema but also on the labor of filmmaking itself, including the ethical questions raised by harnessing the labor of nonprofessional actors that I briefly touched on in chapter 3. While labor emerged as a concern in the politically engaged Cinema Novo films produced in Brazil in the 1960s, its centrality as a theme was confirmed by films recorded at the end of the 1970s that depicted the metalworkers' strike of 1979, which strengthened these workers and resulted in the creation of the Worker's Party (Wells 2016, 102–104).[1] A number of films from across Latin America have also focused on the experience of non-domestic cleaning workers, care workers, and sex workers, such as *Iracema* (Bodanzky and Senna 1975), *Anjos do sol* (Lagemann 2006; Angels of the sun), *Patrícia* (Carlomagno 2014), *Alanis* (Berneri 2017), *La camarista* (Avilés 2018; *The Chambermaid*), and *By the Name of Tania* (Liénard and Jiménez 2019). Despite their consistent denigration as types of "non-work" (Hoerder et al. 2015, 4), these forms of labor are united by the creation of affective or immaterial products, and a study comparing these workers' representations could help to shed light on the links between them, including common challenges and forms of abuse or marginalization. Furthermore, in many cases, these workers' experiences are intersected by the impacts of internal and external migration. While cultural representations of migrant Latin American and Latina domestic workers in the United States have already been examined (Mata 2014), little research has focused on the growing number of depictions of migrant domestic workers' experiences in Europe, such as the portrayals in the documentaries *En otra casa* (Rousselot 2015; *Far from Home*) and *¡Cuidado, resbala!* (Camacho Gómez 2013; Careful, it's slippery!), as well as in a testimonio titled *Morte às vassouras* (Canto 2016; Death to brooms). Finally, the impact of the Covid-19 pandemic on casualized or precarious workers, in particular (migrant) domestic, care, and sex workers, and how this has been represented in cultural production or forms of artivism also require further examination, as I suggested in chapter 4.

APPENDIX 1

Latin American Testimonios Exploring (Paid) Domestic Work and Published in the Late Twentieth and Early Twenty-First Centuries

Barbosa, Zeli de Oliveira. 1993. *Ilhota: Testemunho de uma vida* [Ilhota: Testimony of a life]. Porto Alegre, Brazil: UE da Secretaria Municipal da Cultura.

Basseti, Rosalina Ferreira. 1987. *Testemunha de uma vida* [Witness of a life]. Vitória, Brazil: Conselho Estadual de Cultura.

Burgos, Elizabeth. 1998. *Me llamo Rigoberta Menchú y así me nació la conciencia* [I, Rigoberta Menchú]. 15th ed. Coyoacán, Mexico: Siglo Veintiuno Editores. First published in 1983.

Caraballo, Ramona. 1987. *La niña, el chocolate, el huevo duro* [The girl, the chocolate, the boiled egg]. [Montevideo?]: Monte Sexto.

Carvalho, Lenira. 1982. "Só a gente que vive é que sabe: Depoimento de uma doméstica" [Only those who live it can understand: Testimony of a domestic worker]. In *Cadernos de educação popular 4*, edited by Vozes and Nova, 9–78. Petrópolis, Brazil: Vozes.

Carvalho, Lenira, and Cornélia Parisius. 1999. *A luta que me fez crescer* [The struggle that made me grow]. Recife, Brazil: DAD Bagaço.

da Silva, Francisca Souza. 1983. *Ai de vós! Diário de uma doméstica* [Woe unto you! Diary of a domestic worker]. Rio de Janeiro: Civilização Brasileira.

de Jesus, Carolina Maria. 2014. *Diário de Bitita* [Bitita's Diary]. São Paulo: SESI-SP Editora. First published in 1986.

Gutiérrez, Ana. 1983. *Se necesita muchacha* [Maid wanted]. Mexico, DF: Fondo de Cultura Económica.

Iglesias, Jovita, and Silvia Renée Arias. 2003. *Los Bioy* [The Bioys]. Barcelona: Fabula Tusquets Editores.

Núñez, Mary. 2018. *¿Domésticas o esclavas?* [Domestic workers or slaves?]. Montevideo: Doble Clic Editoras.

Oliveira, Dora de. 1970. *Confissões de uma doméstica* [Confessions of a domestic worker]. Rio de Janeiro: Editora Leitura.

Patai, Daphne. 1993. *Brazilian Women Speak: Contemporary Life Stories.*

New Brunswick, NJ: Rutgers University Press. First published in 1988.

Poniatowska, Elena. 2016. *Hasta no verte Jesús mío* [*Here's to You, Jesusa!*]. Madrid: Alianza Editorial. First published in 1969.

Preta-Rara. 2019. *Eu, empregada doméstica* [*I, domestic worker*]. Belo Horizonte, Brazil: Letramento.

Santiago Páramo, Andrea, ed. 2020. *Nuestras voces cuentan: Historias de trabajadoras del hogar durante la pandemia de Covid-19* [*Our voices count: stories of domestic workers during the Covid-19 pandemic*]. Ciudad de Mexico: Nosotr@s por la Democracia.

Sindicato de Trabajadoras del Hogar del Cusco. 1982. *Basta: Testimonios* [Enough: Testimonies]. Cusco, Peru: Bartolomé de las Casas.

Valderrama Fernández, Ricardo, and Carmen Escalante Gutiérrez. 2014. *Gregorio Condori Mamani & Asunta Quispe Huamán*. Cusco, Peru: Ceques Editores. First published in 1977.

Viezzer, Moema. 2013. *"Si me permiten hablar . . ." : Testimonio de Domitila una mujer de las minas de Bolivia* [*"Let Me Speak . . .": Testimony of Domitila, a Woman of the Bolivian Mines*] Mexico, DF: Siglo Veintiuno Editores. First published in 1977.

APPENDIX 2

Filmography: Latin American Fiction Films Released since 2000 That Feature Paid Domestic Workers in Key Roles

Atán, Cecilia, and Valeria Pivato, dirs. 2017. *La novia del desierto* [The desert bride]. Coproduced by Haddock Films (Buenos Aires) and Ceibita Films (Valparaíso, Chile).

Barbosa, Fellipe, dir. 2014. *Casa grande* [The master's house]. Rio de Janeiro: Migdal Films.

Benaim, Abner, dir. 2010. *Chance*. Coproduced by Apertura Films (Panama City, Panama) and Rio Negro (Mexico City).

Bustamante, Jayro, dir. 2019. *La llorona* [The weeping woman]. Coproduced by La Casa de Production (Guatemala City) and Les Films du Volcan (Paris).

Carnevale, Marcos, dir. 2011. *Viudas* [Widows]. Coproduced by Aleph Media (Buenos Aires), Corbelli Producciones (Buenos Aires), Patagonik (Buenos Aires) and Tronera (Buenos Aires).

Caro Cruz, César, dir. 2017. *Mayordomo* [Butler]. Coproduced by Filamento Films S.A. (San José, Costa Rica) and Películas Plot S.A. (Santiago de Chile).

Carri, Albertina, dir. 2002. *Barbie también puede estar triste* [Barbie can be sad too]. Buenos Aires: NQVAC.

Clariond, Andrés, dir. 2014. *Hilda*. Coproduced by Cinematográfica CR (San José, Costa Rica), Equipment & Film Design (Mexico City) and Pimienta Films (Mexico City).

Cordero, Sebastián, dir. 2009. *Rabia* [Rage]. Coproduced by WAG (Paris), Dynamo (Bogotá, Colombia) and Euskal Irrati Telebista (Bilbao, Spain).

Cuarón, Alfonso, dir. 2018. *Roma*. Coproduced by Esperanto Filmoj (Los Angeles), Participant (Culver City, US) and Pimienta Films (Mexico City).

Dutra, Marco, and Caetano Gotardo, dirs. 2020. *Todos os mortos* [*All the Dead Ones*]. Coproduced by Bord Cadre Films (Geneva, Switzerland), Dezenove Som e Imagens (São Paulo), Filmes do Caixote (São Paulo) and Good Fortune Films (Paris).

Filho, Kleber Mendonça, dir. 2009. *Recife frio* [*Cold Tropics*]. Recife, Brazil: CinemaScópio.

230 APPENDIX 2

Filho, Kleber Mendonça, dir. 2012. *O som ao redor* [*Neighboring Sounds*]. Coproduced by Hubert Bals Fund (Rotterdam, Netherlands) and CinemaScópio (Recife, Brazil).

Filho, Kleber Mendonça, dir. 2016. *Aquarius*. Coproduced by CinemaScópio (Recife, Brazil), SBS Productions (Paris), Globo Filmes (Rio de Janeiro), VideoFilmes (Rio de Janeiro) and Quanta (São Paulo).

Franco, Michel, dir. 2020. *Nuevo orden* [*New Order*]. Coproduced by Les Films d'Ici (Paris) and Teorema Films (Vitoria-Gasteiz, Spain).

Gaggero, Jorge, dir. 2004. *Cama adentro* [*Live-in Maid*]. Coproduced by Aquafilms (Cologne, Germany), Filmanova (A Coruña, Spain), Libido Cine (Buenos Aires) and San Luis Cine (San Luis, Argentina).

García, Mariano, Javier Sintiolo, and Christian D'Annunzio, dirs. 2015. *Me doy cuenta* [I realize]. Buenos Aires: Mariano García.

González, María Paz, dir. 2019. *Lina de Lima* [Lina from Lima]. Coproduced by Quijote Films (Santiago de Chile), Gema Films (Buenos Aires) and Carapulkra Films (Lima, Peru).

Katz, Ana, dir. 2015. *Mi amiga del parque* [My friend from the park]. Coproduced by Campo Cine (Buenos Aires), Mutante Cine (Montevideo) and Río Rojo Contenidos (Buenos Aires).

Kogut, Sandra, dir. 2019. *Três verões* [Three summers]. Coproduced by Gloria Films Production (Paris) and República Pureza Films (Rio de Janeiro).

Lerman, Diego, dir. 2006. *Mientras tanto* [Meanwhile]. Coproduced by BD Cine (Buenos Aires), Campo Cine (Buenos Aires) and Pyramide Productions (Paris).

Llosa, Claudia, dir. 2009. *La teta asustada* [*The Milk of Sorrow*]. Coproduced by Oberón Cinematográfica (Barcelona), Televisió de Catalunya (Barcelona), Televisión Española (Madrid), Vela Producciones (Guatemala City) and Wanda Visión S.A. (Madrid).

López Fernández, Mauricio, dir. 2010. *La visita* [The guest]. Coproduced by Le Tiro Cine (Buenos Aires) and Pinda Producciones (Santiago de Chile).

Lordello, Marcelo, dir. 2012. *Eles voltam* [They will return]. Coproduced by Trincheira Filmes (Recife, Brazil), D7 Filmes (São Paulo) and Plano 9 Produções Audiovisuais (Recife, Brazil).

Loza, Santiago, dir. 2013. *La paz* [Peace]. Coproduced by Frutacine (Buenos Aires) and Centro Cultural Yaneramai (La Paz, Bolivia).

Márquez, Francisco, dir. 2020. *Un crimen común* [A common crime]. Coproduced by Bord Cadre Films (Geneva, Switzerland), Multiverso Produções (São Paulo), Pensar con las Manos (Buenos Aires) and Sovereign Films (London).

Martel, Lucrecia, dir. 2001. *La ciénaga* [The swamp]. Coproduced by 4k Films (São Paulo), Wanda Visión S.A. (Spain), Cuatro Cabezas (Buenos Aires) and TS Productions (Paris).

Martel, Lucrecia, dir. 2008. *La mujer sin cabeza* [*The Headless Woman*].

Coproduced by Aquafilms (Cologne, Germany), El Deseo (Madrid), R&C Produzioni (Rome), Slot Machine (Paris) and Teodora Films (Rome).

Martel, Lucrecia, dir. 2017. *Zama*. Coproduced by Bananeira Filmes (Rio de Janeiro), Canana Films (Mexico City), El Deseo (Madrid), KNM (Polk City, US), Lemming Film (Amsterdam), Louverture Films (New York), MPM Film (Paris), O Som e a Fúria (Lisbon), Patagonik (Buenos Aires), Perdomo Productions (Sosua, Dominican Republic), Picnic Producciones (Buenos Aires), Rei Cine (Buenos Aires) and Schortcut Films (Beirut, Lebanon).

Martinessi, Marcelo, dir. 2018. *Las herederas* [The heiresses]. Coproduced by Pandora Filmproduktion (Cologne, Germany), Mutante Cine (Montevideo), Esquina Filmes (Rio de Janeiro) and Norsk Filmproduksjon (Oslo, Norway).

Meirelles, Fernando, and Nando Olival, dirs. 2001. *Domésticas—O filme* [Maids: The film]. São Paulo: O2 Filmes.

Moreno, Rodrigo, dir. 2014. *Réimon*. Coproduced by Compañía Amateur (Buenos Aires), Rohfilm (Berlin), and Universidad del Cine (Buenos Aires).

Murga, Celina, dir. 2007. *Una semana solos* [A week alone]. Buenos Aires: Tresmilmundos Cine.

Muylaert, Anna, dir. 2015. *Que horas ela volta?* [*The Second Mother*]. Coproduced by Gullane (São Paulo), Africa Filmes (São Paulo) and Globo Filmes (Rio de Janeiro).

Parente, Guto, dir. 2018. *O clube dos canibais* [*The Cannibal Club*]. Fortaleza, Brazil: Tardo Filmes.

Porra, Ulises, and Silvina Schnicer, dirs. 2021. *Carajita*. Coproduced by Wooden Boat Productions (Santo Domingo, Dominican Republic), Pucará Cine (Buenos Aires) and Red Management (London).

Puenzo, Lucía, dir. 2009. *El niño pez* [*The Fish Child*]. Coproduced by Historias Cinematográficas (Buenos Aires), MK2 Films (Paris), Televisión Española (Madrid) and Wanda Visión S.A. (Madrid).

Rojas, Juliana, and Marco Dutra, dirs. 2011. *Trabalhar cansa* [*Hard Labor*]. Coproduced by Dezenove Som e Imagens (São Paulo), Africa Filmes (São Paulo), Filmes do Caixote (São Paulo), Agência Nacional do Cinema (Rio de Janeiro) and Lupo (São Paulo).

Rojas, Juliana, and Marco Dutra, dirs. 2017. *As boas maneiras* [*Good Manners*]. Coproduced by Good Fortune Films (Paris), Urban Factory (Paris), Dezenove Som e Imagens (São Paulo) and Globo Filmes (Rio de Janeiro).

Salles, Walter, and Daniela Thomas, dirs. 2006. *Loin du 16e* [Far from the 16th]. In *Paris je t'aime* [*Paris, I love you*]. Coproduced by Canal+ (Paris) and Victoires International (Paris).

Salles, Walter, and Daniela Thomas, dirs. 2008. *Linha de passe* [*Offside*]. Coproduced by Media Rights Capital (Beverly Hills, US), Pathé Pictures

International (Paris) and VideoFilmes (Rio de Janeiro).

Scherson, Alicia, dir. 2005. *Play*. Coproduced by Parox (Santiago de Chile), Morocha Films (Buenos Aires), La Ventura (Madrid), Paraiso Productions (Arrecife, Spain) and Providencia (Asunción, Paraguay).

Silva, Sebastián, dir. 2009. *La nana* [*The Maid*]. Coproduced by Diroriro (Santiago de Chile), Film Tank (Highbridge, UK) and Punto Guión Producciones (Monterrey, Mexico).

Szifron, Damián, dir. 2014. *Relatos salvajes* [*Wild Tales*]. Coproduced by K&S Films (Buenos Aires), El Deseo (Madrid), Telefe (Buenos Aires), Canal+ (Paris) and Film Factory Entertainment (Barcelona).

Toscano, Agustín, and Ezequiel Radusky, dirs. 2013. *Los dueños* [The owners]. Buenos Aires: Rizoma Films.

Valdivia, Juan Carlos, dir. 2009. *Zona sur* [Southern district]. La Paz, Bolivia: Cinenómada.

Valenta Rinner, Lukas, dir. 2016. *Los decentes* [*A Decent Woman*]. Coproduced by Filmgarten (Vienna, Austria), Jeonju Cinema Project (Jeonju, South Korea) and Nabis Filmgroup (Buenos Aires).

APPENDIX 3

Filmography: Contemporary Latin American Documentaries
That Focus on Paid Domestic or Care Workers

Adriazola, Carolina, and José Luiz Sepúlveda, dirs. 2009. *Mitómana*. Santiago de Chile: Mitómana Producciones.

Benaim, Abner, dir. 2010. *Empleadas y patrones* [*Maids and Bosses*]. Coproduced by Apertura Films (Panama City) and Barakacine Producciones (Buenos Aires).

Cabral, Natalia, and Oriol Estrada, dirs. 2014. *Tú y yo* [You and me]. Santo Domingo, Dominican Republic: Faula Films.

Coutinho, Eduardo, dir. 2007. *Jogo de cena* [*Playing*]. Coproduced by Matizar (Rio de Janeiro) and VideoFilmes (Rio de Janeiro).

Diniz, Felipe, dir. 2016. *Domésticas* [Maids]. Porto Alegre, Brazil: Casa de Cinema de Porto Alegre.

Fernández Geara, Tatiana, dir. 2015. *Nana* [Nanny]. Santo Domingo, Dominican Republic: Cine Carmelita.

Franca, Belisário, dir. 2016. *Menino 23* [*Boy 23*]. Coproduced by Giros Filmes (Rio de Janeiro), Globo Filmes (Rio de Janeiro), Globo News (Rio de Janeiro) and Canal Brasil (Rio de Janeiro).

García del Pino, Virginia, dir. 2012. *Sí, señora* [Yes, ma'am]. Mexico, DF: Garage Films.

Herrera Córdoba, Matías, dir. 2009. *Criada* [Maid]. Coproduced by El Calefón Cine (Córdoba, Argentina) and Habitación 1520 Producciones (Buenos Aires).

Kind, Luciana, and Ana Carolina Abreu Cavalcanti, dirs. 2022. *Serviço* [Service]. Minas Gerais, Brazil: Luciana Kind.

Lins, Consuelo, dir. 2010. *Babás* [Nannies]. Rio de Janeiro: Consuelo Lins.

Lordello, Marcelo, dir. 2010. *Vigias* [Watchmen]. Recife, Brazil: Trincheira Filmes.

Martel, Lucrecia, dir. 1999. *Las dependencias* [The outbuildings]. Coproduced by Bin Cine y Video (Buenos Aires) and Secretaria de Cultura (Buenos Aires).

Mascaro, Gabriel, dir. 2012. *Doméstica* [Housemaid]. Recife, Brazil: Desvia.

Salles, João Moreira, dir. 2007. *Santiago: Uma reflexão sobre o material bruto* [Santiago: A reflection on raw footage]. Rio de Janeiro: VideoFilmes.

APPENDIX 4

Filmography: Other Films and Television Shows Mentioned in Text

Avilés, Lila, dir. 2018. *La camarista* [*The Chambermaid*]. Coproduced by Amplitud (Guadalajara, Mexico), Bambú Audiovisual (Madrid) and La Panda (Los Angeles).

Bahrani, Ramin, dir. 2021. *The White Tiger*. Coproduced by Lava Media (Singapore), Array (Los Angeles), Noruz Films (New York) and Purple Pebble Pictures (Mumbai, India).

Barrios Porras, Carlos, and Carlos Gassols, dirs. 1969–1971. *Simplemente María* [Simply María]. Lima, Peru: Empresa Editora Panamericana.

Berneri, Anahi, dir. 2017. *Alanis*. Coproduced by Laura Cine (Berlin), Rosaura Films (Buenos Aires) and Varsovia (Buenos Aires).

Bodanzky, Jorge, and Orlando Senna. 1975. *Iracema: Uma transa amazônica* [Iracema: An Amazonian transaction]. Coproduced by Stop Film (São Paulo) and Zweites Deutsches Fernsehen (Mainz, Germany).

Bong Joon-ho, dir. 2019. *Parasite*. Coproduced by CJ Entertainment (Seoul, South Korea) and Barunson E&A (Seoul, South Korea).

Camacho Gómez, María, dir. 2013. *¡Cuidado resbala!* [Careful, it's slippery!]. Málaga, Spain: La Mirada Invertida.

Carlomagno, Alexandre, dir. 2014. *Patrícia—o filme* [Patricia: the film]. Ribeirão Preto, Brazil: Kasa Produtora Cultural.

Columbus, Chris, dir. 1993. *Mrs. Doubtfire*. Coproduced by Twentieth Century Fox (Los Angeles) and Blue Wolf Productions (Paris).

Cuarón, Alfonso, dir. 2013. *Gravity*. Coproduced by Warner Bros. (Burbank, US), Esperanto Filmoj (Los Angeles) and Heyday Films (Borehamwood, UK).

D'Amato, Cris, dir. 2015. *Linda de morrer* [*Drop Dead Gorgeous*]. Coproduced by Globo Filmes (Rio de Janeiro) and Migdal Filmes (Rio de Janeiro).

di Mello, Victor, and Ismar Porto, dirs. 1973. *Como é boa nossa empregada* [How good our maid is]. Coproduced by Atlântida (Rio de Janeiro), Kiko Filmes (Rio de Janeiro) and Vidya P.C. (Rio de Janeiro).

Farrelly, Peter, dir. 2018. *Green Book*. Coproduced by Participant (Los

Angeles), Dreamworks Pictures (Universal City, US), Innisfree Pictures (Los Angeles), Louisiana Entertainment (Baton Rouge, US) and Wessler Entertainment (Los Angeles).

Fellowes, Julian, dir. 2010–2015. *Downton Abbey*. Coproduced by Carnival Films (London) and WGBH-TV (Boston, US).

Filho, Kleber Mendonça, dir. 2019. *Bacurau*. Coproduced by CinemaScópio (Recife, Brazil), SBS Productions (Paris), Globo Filmes (Rio de Janeiro), Símio Filmes (Recife, Brazil), Arte France Cinéma (Strasbourg, France), Telecine Productions (Mumbai, India) and Canal Brasil (Rio de Janeiro).

FitzPatrick, James A., dir. 2016. *Rio de Janeiro: City of Splendour*. Beverly Hills, US: Metro-Goldwyn-Mayer. First released in 1936 by Metro-Goldwyn-Mayer. Released in 2016 in *Traveltalks Shorts, Vol. 1* by Warner Home Video.

Hamburger, Cao, dir. 2006. *O ano em que meus pais saíram de férias* [*The Year My Parents Went on Vacation*]. Coproduced by Gullane (São Paulo), Caos Produções Cinematográficas (São Paulo), Miravista (Burbank, US) and Globo Filmes (Rio de Janeiro).

Lagemann, Rudi, dir. 2006. *Anjos do sol* [Angels of the sun]. Coproduced by Apema Filmes (Delhi, India), CaradeCão Filmes (Rio de Janeiro) and Globo Filmes (Rio de Janeiro).

Liénard, Bénédicte, and Mary Jimenez, dirs. 2019. *By the Name of Tania*. Coproduced by Clin d'oeil Films (Leuven, Belgium), Dérives Productions (La Rochelle, France), BALDR Film (Amsterdam) and CBA (Bristol, UK).

Martel, Lurecia. 2004. *La niña santa* [*The Holy Girl*]. La Pasionaria S.R.L. (Buenos Aires), R&C Produzioni (Rome), Teodora Films (Rome), El Deseo (Madrid) and Lita Stantic Producciones (Buenos Aires).

Ozu, Yasujirô, dir. 1953. *Tokyo Story*. Tokyo, Shochiku.

Rousselot, Vanessa, dir. 2015. *En otra casa* [*Far from Home*]. Paris, La Huit.

Salles, Walter, dir. 1998. *Central do Brasil* [*Central Station*]. Coproduced by MACT Productions, RioFilme (Rio de Janeiro) and VideoFilmes (Rio de Janeiro).

Santos, Nelson Pereira dos, dir. 1963. *Vidas secas* [*Barren Lives*]. Coproduced by L. C. Barreto Produções Cinematográficas (Rio de Janeiro) and Regina Filmes (Rio de Janeiro).

Stevenson, Robert, dir. 1964. *Mary Poppins*. Burbank, US, Walt Disney Productions.

Taylor, Tate, dir. 2011. *The Help*. Coproduced by DreamWorks Pictures (Universal City, US), Reliance Entertainment (Mumbai, India), Participant Media (Los Angeles), 1492 Pictures (Alameda, US) and Harbinger Pictures (Austin, US).

Wise, Robert, dir. 1965. *The Sound of Music*. Coproduced by Robert Wise Productions (Westwood, US) and Argyle Enterprises (Westwood, US)

Wood, Andrés, dir. 2004. *Machuca*. Coproduced by Wood Producciones (Santiago de Chile) and Tornasol Films (Madrid).

Notes

Introduction

1. FitzPatrick became known as "the voice of the globe" due to his narration of his *Traveltalks* shorts and is listed on the IMDb website (n.d.) as the (uncredited) narrator.
2. Testimonios constitute a literary genre that proliferated in Latin America from the mid-1960s. These texts originate in firsthand experiences of social or political injustice, and their narratives are marked by an oral quality. Often, the subjects of the testimonios recount their experiences to scribes (such as writers, scholars, or journalists), who then transcribe, edit, and publish their stories. The word "testimonio" is used when describing these texts throughout this book, even when discussing testimonios from Brazil, because it is the term most strongly associated with this specific literary genre (rather than the terms "testimony" in English or *testemunho* in Portuguese). For further discussion of the testimonio genre, see chapter 1.
3. Unless otherwise stated, all translations throughout the book are my own.
4. These authors include Carlos Drummond de Andrade, José Lins do Rego, and Jorge Amado (via his protagonist Gabriela) (Melo 2016, 5).
5. The term *criada* came into use as early as the mid-sixteenth century when many unmarried Spanish women immigrating to Spanish America were listed on passenger rolls as criadas, or servants (Kuznesof 1989, 21).
6. The clearest equivalent to *del hogar* (of the home) that exists in Portuguese is *do lar*, but the term *trabalhadora do lar* is a synonym for "housewife" (*dona de casa*), which could account in part for continued use, even by activitsts, of the term *doméstica* (domestic) when referring to paid domestic workers in Brazil.
7. Live-out or hourly paid domestic work may also be referred to as *trabajo de entrada por salida*, particularly in Mexico.
8. For further information about the mobilization and organization of Brazilian domestic workers, see Louisa Acciari's PhD dissertation (Acciari 2018b).

238 NOTES TO PAGES 14–37

9. The following Latin American and Caribbean countries had ratified ILO Convention No. 189 as of January 2023: Antigua and Barbuda, Argentina, Bolivia, Brazil, Chile, Colombia, Costa Rica, Dominican Republic, Ecuador, Grenada, Guyana, Jamaica, Mexico, Nicaragua, Panama, Paraguay, Peru, and Uruguay.

10. To view the photograph, see https://www.correiobraziliense.com.br/app/noticia/politica/2016/03/14/interna_politica,522052/memes-claudio-pracownik.shtml.

11. Maria Angélica Lima was tracked down by the *Folha de São Paulo* newspaper; she made it clear that she sympathized with the antigovernment protests but also that she went on the march with her employers because she was working and was obliged to do so (L. Franco 2016).

12. Many of these have already been cited, e.g., Staab and Maher 2006; Goldstein 2013; Brites 2014; de Casanova 2015; Pinho 2015; Acciari 2018a, 2018b; Fernández 2018; Goldsmith 1989, 2013; Pereyra 2019; Pérez and Gandolfi 2020; and Canevaro 2020, among others.

13. See the "Theorizing Paid Domestic Work" section of chapter 1.

14. See also Sueli Carneiro 2011 and Djamila Ribeiro 2017.

15. The plot is reminiscent of the narrative arc of the *fotonovelas rosa* (captioned photographs telling a love story) that were produced in the 1960s and 1970s in Latin America and were targeted at a working-class female readership, including paid domestic workers. When a domestic worker featured as a heroine in a fotonovela, it was generally because her sweet nature had led the hero to realize that she was his true love (rather than his previous, cruel, upper-class female partner), thereby demonstrating that social class is not important where romance is concerned (Flora 1989, 144).

16. The title functions as a pun by playing on the word *boa*, which can mean either "nice" or "sexy" when used to describe a woman, often depending on the word's placement within a phrase.

17. See, for instance, María Paz González's (2019) musical *Lina de Lima* (Lina from Lima).

Chapter 1: Paid Domestic Workers' Testimonios in Latin America

1. See appendix 1 for a list of testimonios published by women in Latin America who have either been directly involved in, or are concerned with, (paid) domestic work.

2. Notwithstanding the important contribution made by Roncador's analysis of Brazilian testimonios of domestic service, in particular of texts by Lenira Carvalho (Roncador 2004; 2014, 153–188). In her PhD thesis, Lucía Campanella (2016, 287–310) also examines the theme of domestic service in the 1983 testimonio of Rigoberta Menchú and in Carolina

NOTES TO PAGES 38–47   239

Maria de Jesus's *Quarto de despejo* ([1960] 2021) by analyzing them alongside comparable texts published in France.

3. Caraballo (1987, 7) was first sent to an adoptive employer-family in 1946 when she was four years old. Da Silva (1983, 22) began undertaking domestic tasks for an abusive boss around 1946 when she was six. De Jesus (2014, 143–161) entered domestic service in the 1930s as a teenager.

4. The Peruvian military junta concluded in 1980, and both the Brazilian and Uruguayan military regimes came to an end in 1985.

5. It should be noted that certain testimonios (including Menchú's) gained attention and visibility by being championed by US academics, who then added testimonios to their syllabi. Roncador (2004, 167) suggests that this is a key reason for the greater critical attention paid to Spanish American testimonios, as compared to Brazilian testemunhos, with the exception of de Jesus's *Quarto de despejo* ([1960] 2021; The garbage room).

6. A concern to ensure the reader's belief in the truth and authenticity of Ramona Caraballo's (1987) testimonio, for example, is betrayed in the subtitle chosen for the text: *Historia verídica y real para personas formadas* (13; A true and real story for educated individuals).

7. Chúngara states that she is proud to have "sangre india" (Viezzer 1999, 17; Indigenous blood). Her father was an Indigenous man, but she does not know if he was Aymaran or Quechuan because he spoke both languages (49).

8. Unless otherwise stated, brackets surrounding ellipsis indicate that I have omitted intervening material.

9. *Diário de Bitita* was first published in French. All the testimonios that compose *Brazilian Women Speak* were translated into English and published in the United States by Rutgers University Press.

10. Happily, the testimonio was at least published under da Silva's own name, in contrast to the better-known testimonios of Rigoberta Menchú and Domitila Barrios de Chúngara, whose interlocutors are identified as these texts' authors (Elizabeth Burgos and Moema Viezzer, respectively).

11. The term "romanticizing victimization" must be distinguished from the Portuguese *vitimismo*, which has acquired specific, negative connotations in the Brazilian context because it has been used to disqualify the struggles and demands of racial and sexual minorities.

12. For more information regarding Costa's motivations, see Roncador 2014, 163.

13. This was revealed in a journalistic article published by Rocío Silva Santisteban in 2007 and has been confirmed by interviews that I have conducted subsequently with Cristina Goutet's friends and colleagues Isabel Baufumé (2019) and Angelica Alvarez Velarde (2019). Sadly, Goutet died in 2009, so it was not possible to ask her how she went about collecting the testimonios.

240 NOTES TO PAGES 47–54

14. Laime's photograph is featured on page 6 of *Se necesita muchacha* (1983).

15. The 1971 date was corroborated by Baufumé (2019).

16. It was a great success for the Cusco Union to receive state recognition in 1972. Shortly afterward, in 1973, the Peruvian Ministry of Labour refused to recognize the Sindicato Nacional de Trabajadores/as del Hogar del Perú (Peruvian National Domestic Workers Union, or SINTRAHOGARP). Domestic worker organizations that were independent of the Catholic Church often met with hostility from the state at that time (Blofield 2012, 22).

17. The STHC continues to exist but is no longer particularly active, having struggled to recruit new members in recent years (Alvarez Velarde 2019). Since 1992, the Centro Yanapanakusun, which is a domestic workers' refuge and training center, has been supporting young women and children who arrive in Cusco and face exploitation, isolation, and mistreatment at their place of work (CAITH, n.d.).

18. Gutiérrez (1983, 94) states that the contributors' names have been changed because the political situation in many Latin American countries "no permite que se indentifique a ningún luchador" (does not allow for those involved in resistance to be identified).

19. In the more recent *Brazilian Women Speak* (1993), for instance, Daphne Patai includes a lengthy self-reflexive introduction in which the author-academic discusses her aims and objectives in collecting a variety of Brazilian women's testimonios, including the testimonios of a domestic worker and her employer.

20. The French edition of the text features an afterword by the French sociologist and journalist Alain Labrousse, whose research addresses Indigenous peoples' identity and political mobilization in Bolivia and Peru (among other topics).

21. It is possible that Gutiérrez made these changes to avoid breaching her copyright agreement with Bartolomé de las Casas, *Basta*'s publishing house.

22. Poniatowska united various civil rights activists' testimonios in *Fuerte es el silencio* (1980; Silence is strong), and compiled those of earthquake survivors in *Nada, nadie* (1988; *Nothing, Nobody*). In 1971 she published *La noche de Tlatelolco* (1998; *Massacre in Mexico*), which creates a collage of eyewitness testimonies of the Tlatelolco massacre.

23. The Popul Vuh is a pre-Columbian creation narrative that recounts the history and mythology of the K'iche' people, who inhabit modern-day Guatemala.

24. There is debate about whether *Hasta no verte Jesús mío* should be considered a novel, a testimonio, an autobiography, or a hybrid of all three (D. Shaw 1996, 1).

25. It seems probable that there was only one (first edition) print run of the

text. After a lengthy search, I acquired a copy from Librería El Antigal in Buenos Aires, Argentina.

26. Domestic workers' movements in Brazil were also undoubtedly influenced by the activism of Afro-Brazilian feminists and scholars whose ideas are discussed in the introduction.

27. Similarly, Hutchinson (2010, 70) reveals that the Federación de Empleadas de Casa Particular (Federation of Household Workers), which was mobilized by the JOC in Chile in the mid-twentieth century, had a much larger membership than did the secular union SINTRACAP, which had been active in Santiago since the 1920s. She argues that this fact demonstrates that "radical Christianity—with the church's institutional and normative support—nurtured *empleadas*' sociability and trade militancy in ways that its secular union counterpart did not. [. . .] Only the Federation provided the [. . .] religious framework that would incite broader *empleada* participation" (70). The Chilean Federation of Household Workers also venerated Santa Zita.

28. Domestic workers who came to Cusco and had previously received little or no formal education attended Cusco's Centro Educativo Básico Alternativo (CEBA) night school for two principal reasons: because they could work during the day and because students of any age could enroll to study at any educational level (Alvarez Velarde 2019, interview).

29. The seminary is now Cusco's Hotel Monasterio.

30. Blanco's movement presaged sweeping land reforms introduced by Peru's military government in 1968. The redistribution of land affected the lives of many Indigenous workers living in rural areas who labored on the *hacendado*'s (landowner's) property and whose wives and children would often have been employed in that household. The colonial dynamics of this situation were amplified in places like Cusco, which has a large rural Indigenous (Quechua) population.

31. See for instance Fátima's and Lucía's testimonios (Gutiérrez 1983, 213–236, 313–339).

32. Here, I am drawing on Antonio Gramsci's ([1971] 2003) discussion of the "organic intellectual," a figure that he contrasts with the category of the "traditional intellectual," which is used to describe professional intellectuals, i.e., academics. Organic intellectuals can emerge from any social class and constitute the element of it that theorizes and organizes. They may hold any job characteristic of their class, but they are distinguished by the way that they direct the ideas and aspirations of the class to which they organically belong (Gramsci 2003, 3). Organic intellectuals may or may not identify with the dominant (capitalist) class.

33. It was only in 2008 that the Brazilian government explicitly prohibited adolescents and children under eighteen years old from doing domestic work (Cornwall et al. 2013, 150).

34. The Uruguayan Código del Niño of 1934 explicitly discriminated against children employed in domestic service by excluding them from the protection that prevented minors under the age of eighteen from doing nocturnal labor (Sala de sesiones 1934).

35. For further information on the migration patterns of young girls and adolescents who arrived in Lima from rural areas in the 1980s and who often found employment as live-in domestic workers, see Bunster and Chaney 1985, 17–22.

36. The envy of fashionable, expensive items associated both with their employers and with the city also permeates de Jesus's (2014, 103, 202) and Caraballo's (1987, 47) testimonios.

37. An extreme example of this can be found in a video published on the Centro Yanapanakusun page in which one woman recounts the traumatic experience of literally being renamed by her employers. When she arrived in Cusco she spoke Quechua (not Spanish) and her bosses decided to call her Raquel (CAITH).

38. In contrast to the Brazilian and Peruvian testimonios discussed, the issue of race does not appear to be as relevant in Ramona Caraballo's experience of paid domestic work in Uruguay. Nonetheless, she does refer to herself on one occasion as "bastante morocha" (Caraballo 1987, 60; quite dark-skinned).

Chapter 2: Labors of Love?

1. See appendix 2 for a full list.

2. This practice is expedient for Latin American filmmakers producing art house or independent productions with limited financial resources. For example, on October 17, 2018, during a Q and A session after the screening of O clube dos canibais (Parente 2018; The Cannibal Club) at the BFI London Film Festival, the film's producer, Ticiana Augusto Lima, revealed that the team behind the production had to conceive of a project that they could execute on a restricted budget. Filming almost entirely at one location inside a mansion responded to this need, while the portrayal of the homeowners' cannibalistic attitude toward their hired help allowed social satire and class tensions to remain the film's focus.

3. During two weeks at the Brazilian box office, Que horas ela volta? sold 66,100 tickets, while another Brazilian production, the 2015 comedy Linda de morrer (Drop Dead Gorgeous) directed by Cris D'Amato, had an audience of 734,700 over the course of three weeks (Merten and Leal 2015).

4. In the movie, Luiza identifies as parda (brown-skinned); she states that her mother is mulata and her father, Japanese.

5. An idiom in Brazil that plays on the power and privilege of the Cavalcanti family is "quem viver em Pernambuco não há de estar enganado: Que, ou

há de ser Cavalcanti, ou há de ser cavalgado" (If you live in Pernambuco, do not be fooled: either you are a Cavalcanti, or you get crushed). "Cavalcanti" is also the surname of the actor who plays Jean: Thales Cavalcanti.

6. The law is called Lei de Cotas para o Ensino Superior (Presidência da república 2012).

7. Batista was convicted of corruption after the film was made (*BBC News* 2018).

8. Dantas was later acquitted on a technicality (*Folha de São Paulo* 2016).

9. For a discussion of the controversy generated by Cuarón's choice of a Netflix distribution model, see Paul Julian Smith's (2019) book. Smith (196–197) notes that the film's online distribution raised questions about its accessibility to working-class audiences in Mexico who primarily use free-to-air TV, while more affluent individuals have Netflix subscriptions.

10. In her analysis of the social issue documentary *Who Is Dayani Cristal?* (directed by Marc Silver and produced by Pulse Films in London, 2013), Deborah Shaw (2018a, 262) argues that these kinds of films bring together filmmakers, actors, social media, and social impact staff employed on the production and on related projects "to serve the bigger story of the social issue."

11. For a more detailed reading of boss-worker relationships in Kleber Mendonça Filho's films, in particular the 2016 film *Aquarius*, see Dennison 2018.

12. According to the National Household Survey 2009, the majority of domestic workers in Brazil (59.3 percent) are Black (Cornwall et al. 2013, 149; PNAD 2010).

13. See the introduction for a more in-depth discussion of the architectural design of Latin American homes with service quarters.

14. The film's original title was *The Kitchen Door* (Vázquez Vázquez 2019, 40).

15. The notion of fictive kin relationships to paid domestic workers is also explored in a blog post about Alfonso Cuarón's *Roma* by Simca Simpson Lapp (2019).

16. Carole Pateman (1989, 34) notes that this was the distinction through which our modern notion of society was constituted by the contract theorists. However, in many discussions of civil society, "public regulation" is contrasted with "private enterprise," thereby presupposing that "the politically relevant separation between public and private is drawn *within* 'civil society.'"

17. This technique recalls those used by Martel (2008) in *La mujer sin cabeza*, which is shot from a similar subject's perspective—that of the bourgeois female protagonist. Deborah Shaw (2017, 136) observes that, as a result of the framing, the employees are often registered by the camera as they "spoil" the composition by passing in front of it, featuring at the edge of the frame, or appearing out of focus.

244 NOTES TO PAGES 108–133

18. "Immaterial labor" can be defined as work that creates immaterial products, including ideas, information, relationships, or emotional responses (Hardt and Negri 2004, 108). Consequently, immaterial labor includes forms of affective and intellectual work (108). Affective labor is work that produces "affects," which can be bodily and psychological. Intellectual labor encompasses analytical tasks and the production of ideas, symbols, texts, and images (108).

19. Jorge Gaggero's *Cama adentro* (2005; *Live-in Maid*) is another film that deploys copious gift-related symbolism. Domestic worker Dora has worked for her employer Beba for 28 years and struggles to leave Beba's employ even when Beba is no longer able to pay her salary. The women's exchange of gifts is used in the film to signal the personal sacrifices that Dora has made as a result of living and laboring in Beba's home and the sense that the emotional bond between the women transcends their labor relationship.

20. A 2002 study found that middle-class employers of Peruvian domestic workers in Santiago de Chile praised them as being superior employees who are more "devoted, caring and submissive" than Chilean workers, while the employers simultaneously denigrated Peruvian women as dirty, criminal, uneducated, or uncivilized (Staab and Maher 2006, 87–88). The employers' praise "served to discipline the Chilean working class," who were perceived by the middle-class employers as no longer knowing "their place" (87).

21. The significance of this image is confirmed by its use as the backdrop to the film's DVD menu.

22. This image was used in the film's publicity campaign and on at least one version of its DVD cover.

23. In this context *bicho* could be translated as "monster" but it can be used to refer to any nondescript animal.

24. Samuel Putnam, who translated Freyre's 1963 edition into English, explains on page 278 that a *bicho de pé* is a type of flea that burrows beneath the skin of the foot and lays its eggs there.

25. As Karina Vázquez (2014, 172) has also noted in the case of Pilar.

26. For a more detailed analysis of *Machuca* and *O ano em que meus pais saíram de férias*, see Randall 2017, 35–66; for an interpretation of *Central do Brasil*, see Deborah Shaw 2003.

Chapter 3: Immaterial Labors

1. See appendix 3 for a full list.

2. See the introduction for further discussion, as well as the report by the Institute for Applied Economic Research (2016).

3. In *Las dependencias*, Jovita Iglesias reveals that she emigrated from Galicia, Spain, to Argentina. In *Babás*, the director, Consuelo Lins, interviews Iraci, the domestic worker who was employed by Lins's family when she

NOTES TO PAGES 133–136 245

was a child, and Iraci explains that her family came to Brazil from Italy in the nineteenth century. Santiago Badariotti Merlo, the subject of Salles's *Santiago*, was also of Italian heritage.

4. *Las dependencias* closed Canal 7's "Seis mujeres" programming cycle, which was broadcast in 1999.

5. According to the account Iglesias (2003) provides in her (auto)biography *Los Bioy*, she was introduced to Ocampo by her aunt on December 23, 1949. Ocampo asked Iglesias (and her aunt and uncle) to live in her suite of apartments, watch over her domestic employees, and take care of her home while she and Bioy Casares were away in Europe. It was at this time that Iglesias began sewing things for Ocampo (Iglesias and Arias 2003, 19–22). After Iglesias's marriage to José (Pepe) Montes Blanco, her husband did tasks for the Bioy Casares family as well. The details of Iglesias's labor contract are never clarified in *Los Bioy*, a text that dwells instead on the intimate nature of her relationship with her famous employers.

6. These include the collections *Viaje olvidado* (1937), *La furia y otros cuentos* (1959), and *Las invitadas* (1961). For a detailed analysis of servant characters in Ocampo's writing, see Rossi 2020. I have chosen to refer to these characters as "servants" because it is the term often used for domestic workers in Ocampo's works.

7. Fani, whose full name was Estefanía, migrated from Spain to Argentina. She originally worked for the Ocampos' aunt, who dubbed her "Fani" because it was an easier name to shout (Mancini 2018, 106–107). Fani was later employed by Silvina and Victoria's family and served as Silvina's nanny. Silvina spoke of her unhappiness as a child when Fani left to work for Victoria at her new home following the latter's marriage (Mancini 2018, 108–109).

8. For further analysis of servant characters in Martel's cinematography, see Deborah Shaw 2017 and Martin 2016, 9. Shaw's chapter undertakes detailed analysis of the films *La ciénaga* (2001), *La niña santa* (2004), and *La mujer sin cabeza* (2008).

9. Martel's signature winged glasses may also function as an homage to Ocampo, who was famously photographed wearing a similar style (Pérez Zabala 2019).

10. The voiceover is narrated by Fernando Moreira Salles, one of João Moreira Salles's brothers. This choice may respond, in part, to the director's desire to make the film for his family as a way of memorializing their former home and relationship to Santiago. The narrator of the international version of the film is Fernando Alves Pinto.

11. In her analysis of Brazilian documentaries that explore relationships of power and class within the home, Mariana Souto (2019, 94) has also observed that *Babás* appears to be driven by "um desejo de indenização de uma dívida histórica" (a desire to compensate a historical debt).

12. The voiceover narration is read by Flávia Castro (rather than by Lins

246 NOTES TO PAGES 137–141

herself). *Babás* is available on YouTube with English subtitles at https://www.youtube.com/watch?v=JTIfgGr_Y3Q&ab_channel=Filmesquevoam, accessed February 5, 2023.

13. *Doméstica* (like *Babás*) is available on YouTube, but without subtitles in English, at https://www.youtube.com/watch?v=Se5QUGucJMA&ab_channel=Direito2015.2, accessed August 5, 2021.

14. *Doméstica*'s English-language blurb reads: "Seven adolescents take on the mission of filming, for one week, their family's housemaids and hand over the footage to the director to make a film. The images that confront us uncover the complex relationship that exists between housemaids and their employers, a relationship that confuses intimacy and power in the workplace and provides us with an insight into the echoes of a colonial past that linger in contemporary Brazil."

15. Mascaro told me in an email that thirteen pairs were selected, but the author I cited, Gustavo Procopio Furtado (2019, 161), who has also been in contact with the director, states that ten were originally chosen.

16. Mascaro shared a copy of these guidelines with Furtado (2019, 161–162), who discusses them in his analysis of *Doméstica*.

17. Mascaro's *Doméstica* has previously been compared to an earlier Brazilian fiction film with a very similar title: *Domésticas—O Filme*, directed by Fernando Meirelles and Nando Olival in 2001. Like *Doméstica*, *Domésticas—O Filme* threads together several storylines that focus on different domestic workers and that "coalesce" in the creation of a "social tapestry" (Oliveira 2020, 145). However, *Domésticas—O Filme*'s comical depiction of stereotypical domestic worker characters strongly differentiates it from Mascaro's later documentary.

18. *Los Bioy* (Iglesias and Arias 2003) takes a form similar to that of many of the testimonios analyzed in chapter 1. Iglesias recounted her memories of working for Ocampo and Bioy Casares to Silvia Renée Arias, a writer and journalist, but Iglesias and Arias are identified as coauthors of the work.

19. A similar observation has been made by Campanella (2018, 199–204) in her analysis of Millena Lízia's performances in *Empregada para um cubo branco* (2014; Working for a white cube) and *Faço faxina* (2016–2017; I clean). In *Empregada para um cubo branco*, which Lízia performed on December 4, 2014, at Juiz de Fora Federal University (Brazil), Lízia enacted the role of a cleaner during the inauguration of an exhibition at a gallery; attendees slowly became aware of her performance as she began using products with a strong smell and making exaggerated gestures. In *Faço faxina*, Lízia offered her services as a domestic cleaner in various private homes in Rio de Janeiro.

20. Virno (2004, 54) acknowledges that even virtuoso performances can in principle produce surplus value if organized in a capitalistic fashion so that they are a source of profit (presumably that could be reinvested).

NOTES TO PAGES 142–158   247

21. For a discussion of the ways in which domestic work undoubtedly is productive of "surplus value," see pp. 24–25 of this book.
22. This is a reference to a sequence from Vincente Minnelli's 1953 film *The Band Wagon*, which was produced by Metro-Goldwyn-Mayer in the United States. It shows Fred Astaire and Cyd Charisse breaking into dance in Central Park; Salles includes the sequence in *Santiago* because it was the butler's favorite film. Astaire was also his favorite dancer.
23. Furthermore, all the films addressed in this chapter trouble the distinction between fiction and documentary film, in particular *Réimon* and *Santiago*. *Réimon*'s director, Moreno, has even directly questioned this distinction in an interview about the film (García Calvo 2015).
24. Paul Merchant (2022, 163) has noted that the nickname is a phonetic rendering of the English name "Raymond," which is traditionally used by men, and constitutes either "the exercise of control over Ramona's gender identity, or a disavowal of the fact that this supposedly Marxist couple is using the labor of a female and racially distinct other as the background to their own domestic life."
25. Bibliographic details of these passages are provided in *Réimon*'s closing credits sequence.
26. "Espuela y facón" (The spur and the knife) by Walter Yonsky (1995).
27. Mullaly states that much of the Ocampo sisters' education would have been conducted in French and English rather than in Spanish; Ocampo also wrote her first texts in the two languages (n.d., 3).
28. Various recordings of Ocampo, Bioy Casares, Jorge Luis Borges, and Manuel Peyrou chatting or reading their works are played on the film's soundtrack. They are listed as "Las voces" in the film's closing credits.
29. Catherine Grant and Deborah Martin (2021) have produced the video essay *Rites of THE PASSAGE*, which explores the ways in which ghostly presences haunt Martel's oeuvre and evoke the specters of colonialism.
30. Furtado (2019, 143–172) also employs Renov's framework in his comparative analysis of *Babás*, *Doméstica*, and *Santiago*.
31. Jacques Rancière (2003, 226) argues that the essence of politics is "dissensus" and that dissensus itself is the production, within a determined sensible world, of a given that is heterogeneous to it. He concludes, "Politics is aesthetic in that it makes visible what had been excluded from a perceptual field, and in that it makes audible what used to be inaudible."
32. Not all indexes are iconic. For example, smoke does not closely resemble fire, and a weather vane does not resemble wind (Doane 2002, 93).
33. It is important to acknowledge here that in *Doméstica*, the affective intimacy that characterizes some relationships with domestic workers is also explored via the distinct technique of asking *adolescents* to film their families' employees.
34. In *Las dependencias*, this relationship is reversed. Martel's documentary

incorporates old photographs and recordings of Silvina Ocampo, the protagonists' deceased former employer, who becomes the film's desired "object" instead of the domestic workers themselves.

35. Roland Barthes (1993, 26–28) coined the term "punctum" in *Camera Lucida* to describe an effect of still photography rather than of film. He describes it as an "accident which pricks" the viewer and contrasts it with a photograph's *studium*: the general field or scene that the photographer consciously intended to represent and that is invested with a specific social or cultural meaning.

36. These women are not introduced using their names, but the names of the nannies who appear in the film are listed in the closing credits.

37. It is important to note that the documentary's focus on the importance of home ownership (or domestic sovereignty) can also be indicative of an underlying feminist individualist perspective and can serve as a reminder that access to this idealized form of domesticity is often reserved for the middle or upper classes.

38. See Ismail Xavier's (2009, 211–217) discussion of Coutinho's "documentary of the encounter" for a description.

39. In her analysis, Souto (2019, 119) terms these kinds of productions "filmes-dispositivo" (device films), in which characters film other characters. They use a "dispositivo de infiltração" (an infiltration device) to gain entry into an intimate environment that would not be possible otherwise or that would be altered too dramatically by the presence of an outsider, such as an unfamiliar director (124–125).

40. There are some discrepancies regarding the spelling of Claudomiro's name, which is given as "Claudomiro Carvalho Neto" on the film's DVD case but is recorded as "Valdomiro Canaleo Neto" in the documentary's credits. Since he appears to say that his name is Claudomiro toward the documentary's opening, I am using "Claudomiro" here.

41. Furtado (2020, 161) notes that the song belongs to the musical genre known in Brazil as *brega*, which is characterized by "romantic themes and popular appeal" but which has historically been deemed by cultural elites to be of "poor taste."

42. Oliveira (2020, 161) has also made this observation, stating that "the audience has no choice but to gaze at Mascaro's subjects as fellow human beings."

43. The significance of cordiality and intimacy in recent depictions of boss-worker relationships in Brazilian film and television has been explored in a series of articles. See Dennison 2018; Perdigão 2018; Sá 2018; and Randall 2018a.

44. I am referring here to the shots of the swimming pool included in the film at 40:17.

45. Here I am referring to the shots of the swimming pool included in the film at 27:46.

NOTES TO PAGES 183–190   249

46. João Moreira Salles is the youngest of Walter Moreira Salles's four sons (K. Carneiro 2021).
47. He left his manuscripts to João Moreira Salles.

Chapter 4: Domestic Workers in the Digital Domain

1. "Artivism" refers to artistic and creative practices that are combined with forms of activism or protest in the service of political aims.
2. In addition to the works that are the focus of this chapter, these include *La otra* (Natalia Iguiñiz, Peru, 2001; *The Other*), *Lugar común* (Ruby Rumié and Justine Graham, Colombia, 2008; Common ground), *Mucamas* (Arias 2010; Hotel maids), *Habitaciones de servicio* (Ortiz 2011; Servants' quarters), *Fronteras* (Raúl Charlín, Chile, 2012; Borders), *Faço faxina* (Millena Lízia, Brazil, 2016–2017; I clean), *Invisible Commutes* (Montoya Robledo et al. 2020), the *Confinada* series (Assis and Oliveira 2020; Confined), and *Nuestras voces cuentan* (Santiago Páramo 2020; Our voices count).
3. Chacón's observation dovetails with Paolo Virno's (2004, 49–50) argument that the classical distinction between labor, intellectual or artistic activity, and political action has dissolved in contemporary society, a framework used in the analysis of the documentaries examined in chapter 3.
4. At the time of writing, Ortiz's website was temporarily unavailable, but the photobook is available online via Internet Archive, see: https://ia600505.us.archive.org/21/items/97EmpleadasDomesticasOrtizPublicacion/97_empleadas_dome%CC%81sticas_ortiz_publicacio%CC%81n.pdf. Accessed February 9, 2023.
5. Felipe Guamán Poma de Ayala Ortiz (1615), *El primer nueva corónica y buen gobierno* (Copenhagen, Denmark: Det Kongelige Bibliotek). http://www5.kb.dk/permalink/2006/poma/titlepage/en/image/?open=idm2. Accessed February 9, 2023.
6. This image number pertains to the version of the chronicle cited above. It is possible to view the image via this link: http://www5.kb.dk/permalink/2006/poma/381/en/image/?open=idm476. Accessed February 9, 2023.
7. To view this image alongside the illustration from the chronicle, see Ortiz 2012, 96 or Expósito 2010, 53.
8. For a more detailed overview of the recent history of paid domestic work in Peru, including changes to domestic workers' legal rights, see the introduction.
9. The page numbers used here and from here on refer to the photobook version of the exhibition; see Ortiz 2010a.
10. See the analysis of *Que horas ela volta?* in chapter 2 and of *Santiago* in chapter 3.
11. Elements of the installations are also available to view online; see Arias's website at https://lolaarias.com/es/maids (accessed April 22, 2021) and the

Ciudades Paralelas website at http://ciudadesparalelas.org/hotelesp.html (accessed April 22, 2021).

12. This term is used in the exhibition's blurb, which can be seen at https://lolaarias.com/es/maids/. Accessed June 24, 2021.

13. The video of the Hotel Zurich exhibition is available on YouTube at https://www.youtube.com/watch?v=p4kQKMYM0Pc&ab_channel=ExpanderFilm. Accessed June 24, 2021.

14. Research has nonetheless shown that it is rare for users to consult the terms of service of social media platforms in any depth (Obar and Oeldorf-Hirsch 2020, 128); this is probably because terms of service are often lengthy texts that use complex language (LePan 2020).

15. "Actuality recording" is the term used by Baron (2021, 8) to refer to films that seek to represent "reality."

16. See chapter 3 for further discussion of these issues.

17. See chapter 3 for further discussion of the director's process.

18. These photographs are either very similar to or the same as the images featuring Indigenous or Afro-descendant nannies and wet nurses with their employers' children that were taken between 1879 and 1913 and can now be found at the Courret photography archive in Lima.

19. "Preta-Rara" is Fernandes's stage name; it translates into English as "unique Black woman."

20. I have reproduced quotations from both the "Eu empregada doméstica" Facebook page and the edited collection as they appear and have not amended these to account for errors or typos.

21. In 2015, the year before Preta-Rara launched the page, Facebook and Messenger had over sixty-three million users in Brazil (Statista 2020); in 2020 Facebook continued to be the country's most popular social networking site, attracting more than half of all social media site visits (Statista 2020).

22. Her TEDx talk, "Me, the maid," is available to view on YouTube at https://www.youtube.com/watch?v=_d_n-z3s8Lo&ab_channel=TEDxTalks. Accessed April 22, 2021.

23. Lisa Blankenship (2019, 76, 81) points out that Facebook's algorithms combined with the page follower numbers mean that the stories could potentially have been seen by tens of thousands of individuals, although it is likely that many users would have scrolled through or past the texts without fully engaging with them.

24. The role of the scribe or editor is discussed at greater length in chapter 1.

25. For a more detailed overview of the history of paid domestic work and domestic workers' rights in Brazil, see the introduction.

26. This advertisement was visible on the page while I was writing this chapter and was still present as of August 2022.

27. In 2020, 92 percent of people in Brazil between sixteen and twenty-four

years old and 86 percent of people between twenty-five and thirty-four years old were using social media, but usage dropped to 67 percent among those between forty-five and fifty-nine years old and to 50 percent among those over sixty years old (Statista 2020).

28. Gillam's analysis focuses on representations of domestic workers in *Revista raça* (Race magazine) and the *Dandaras* radio program.

29. See the report by the Institute for Applied Economic Research (2016, 24).

30. On rare occasions, fictive kin relations are invoked when describing a positive relationship to an employer; see, for example, Preta-Rara 2019, 126.

31. For further discussion of this in the Brazilian context, see Randall 2020. See also the recorded webinar "Domestic Workers' Resistance in Brazil," co-organized by Patricia Pinho, Cleide Pinto and Valeria Ribeiro-Corossacz at Dolores Huerta Center for the Americas, UC Santa Cruz, January 5, 2021.The webinar addresses the "Cuide de quem te cuida" (Look after the person who cares for you) campaign by the national union (Fenatrad) to raise awareness among employers about the challenges faced by domestic workers in Brazil during the Covid-19 pandemic. See https://www.youtube.com/watch?v=5xBsvgBE1RI&t=9s&ab_channel=ResearchCenterfortheAmericasUCSantaCruz. Accessed August 9, 2022.

32. Assis and Triscila have set up separate mock Instagram profiles for the main characters: @soujuh_95 and @franclementeoficial. Accessed February 11, 2023.

33. Further instances of this kind of degrading content were spotlighted in an episode of the satirical current affairs program *GregNews*, which was dedicated to the topic of paid domestic workers (produced by HBO Brasil, filmed in Rio de Janeiro, directed by Alessandra Orofino, and broadcast on June 5, 2020). See https://www.youtube.com/watch?v=v7V4tIUYLP8. Accessed April 8, 2021.

34. CACEH is one of the domestic workers' organizations that collaborated with Alfonso Cuarón and the team behind *Roma* to raise the profile of domestic workers' struggles in Mexico and to advocate for improvements to their legal rights before and after the film was released.

Conclusion

1. These films include, for example, *ABC da greve* (ABC of the strike; directed by Leon Hirszman and released by Taba Filmes, Brazil, in 1990) and *Linha de montagem* (Assembly line; directed by Renato Tapajós and released by Tapiri Cinematográfica, Brazil, in 1982).

References

Acciari, Louisa. 2018a. "Brazilian Domestic Workers and the International Struggle for Labour Rights." *Engenderings* (blog), March 5, 2018. https://blogs.lse.ac.uk/gender/2018/03/05/brazilian-domestic-workers-and-the-international-struggle-for-labour-rights.

Acciari, Louisa. 2018b. "Paradoxes of Subaltern Politics: Brazilian Domestic Workers' Mobilisations to Become Workers and Decolonise Labour." PhD diss., London School of Economics and Political Science. http://etheses.lse.ac.uk/3839.

Agamben, Giorgio. 1998. *Homo Sacer: Sovereign Power and Bare Life*. Translated by Daniel Heller-Roazen. Stanford, CA: Stanford University Press.

Ahmed, Sara. 2017. *Living a Feminist Life*. Durham, NC: Duke University Press.

Alencastro, Luiz Felipe. 1997. "Epílogo." In *História da vida privada no Brasil*. Vol. 2, *Império: A corte e a modernidade nacional*, edited by Fernando A. Novais and Luiz Felipe de Alencastro, 439–440. São Paulo: Companhia das Letras.

Algranti, Leila Mezan. 1997. "Famílias e vida doméstica." In *História da vida privada no Brasil*. Vol. 1, *Cotidiano e vida privada na América portuguesa*, edited by Fernando A. Novais and Laura de Mello e Souza, 62–120. São Paulo: Companhia de Bolso.

Allemandi, Cecilia. 2015. "Niños sirvientes y 'criados': El trabajo infantil en el servicio doméstico (Ciudad de Buenos Aires, fines del siglo XIX —principios del siglo XX)." *Cuadernos del Ides* 30 (October): 11–38.

Allen, Alice. 2013. "Sites of Transformation: Urban Space and Social Difference in Contemporary Brazilian Visual Culture." PhD diss., University of Cambridge.

Ally, Shireen. 2015. "Domesti-City: Colonial Anxieties and Postcolonial Fantasies in the Figure of the Maid." In *Colonization and Domestic Service: Historical and Contemporary Perspectives*, edited by Victoria K. Haskins and Claire Lowrie, 45–62. London: Routledge.

254 REFERENCES

Almeida, Carlos Helí de. 2015. "Casa grande: Abismo social." Segundo caderno, *O Globo* (Rio de Janeiro), April 17.

Alves, Uelinton Farias. "Introdução." In *Diário de Bitita*, by Carolina Maria de Jesus, 7–11. São Paulo: SESI-SP Editora.

Anderson, Bridget. 2000. *Doing the Dirty Work? The Global Politics of Domestic Labour.* London: Zed Books.

Anderson, Bridget. 2003. "Just Another Job? The Commodification of Domestic Labor." In *Global Woman: Nannies, Maids and Sex Workers in the New Economy*, edited by Barbara Ehrenreich and Arlie Russell Hochschild, 104–114. London: Granta Books.

Andersson, Axel. 2014. "The Artifice of Modernity: Alienation by the Pool Side in the Cinema of Michelangelo Antonioni." In *The Cinema of the Swimming Pool*, edited by Pam Hirsch and Christopher Brown, 77–88. Oxford: Peter Lang.

Andrade, Márcio. 2017. "Eu sou o outro? —Notas sobre (auto)etnografias em doméstica, de Gabriel Mascaro." *Fronteiras—estudos midiáticos* 19 (1): 37–48.

Andrews, George Reid. 1991. *Blacks and Whites in São Paulo, Brazil: 1888–1988.* Madison: University of Wisconsin Press.

àngels barcelona. n.d. "Daniela Ortiz." http://angelsbarcelona.com/en/artists /daniela-ortiz/bio. Accessed April 8, 2021.

Anjos, Ana Paula Bianconcini, and Elen Doppenschmitt. 2008. "Autor e personagem." Caderno 2, *O Estado de São Paulo*, August 24.

Arias, Lola. 2010. *Mucamas* [Hotel maids]. https://lolaarias.com/es/maids/. Accessed February, 13, 2023.

Asamblea general de la República Oriental del Uruguay (Uruguay). 2006. *Regulación del trabajo doméstico 18065.* November 27, 2006. http:// www.impo.com.uy/bases/leyes/18065-2006.

Assis, Leandro, and Triscila Oliveira. 2020. *Confinada.* https://www .instagram.com/leandro_assis_ilustra/. Accessed January 23, 2023.

Aulestia Benítez, Ana Elizabeth. 2019. "Daniela Ortiz: Arte, migración y activismo." *Index, revista de arte contemporáneo* 8 (December): 160–166.

Badessich, Carlos A. 1992. "Testimonios: Voces de mujeres hispanoamericanas." In *Actas del X congreso de la asociación internacional de hispanistas: Barcelona 21–26 de agosto de 1989*, edited by Antonio Vilanova, 409–420. Barcelona: Promociones y publicaciones universitarias.

Badinter, Elisabeth. 1997. *XY: On Masculine Identity.* New York: Columbia University Press.

Baecque, Antoine de, Thierry Jousse, Jacques Derrida, and Peggy Kamuf. 2015. "Cinema and Its Ghosts: An Interview with Jacques Derrida." *Discourse* 37 (1): 22–39.

Baird, Vanessa. 2017. "Brazil's Soft Coup Hardens." *New Internationalist*, October 1. https://newint.org/features/2017/10/01/brazil-soft-coup.

Balloussier, Anna Virginia, and Guilherme Genestreti. 2015. "Histórias que nossas babás contavam." Illustrada, *Folha de São Paulo*, August 26, 2015.

Barbosa, Livia. 2008. "Domestic Workers and Pollution in Brazil." In *Dirt: New Geographies of Cleanliness and Contamination*, edited by Rosie Cox and Ben Campkin, 25–33. London: I. B. Tauris.

Barbosa, Zeli de Oliveira. 1993. *Ilhota: Testemunho de uma vida*. Porto Alegre, Brazil: UE Porto Alegre.

Baron, Jaimie. 2021. *Reuse, Misuse, Abuse: The Ethics of Audiovisual Appropriation in the Digital Era*. New Brunswick, NJ: Rutgers University Press.

Barrucho, Luis. 2016a. "Ex-empregada doméstica lança campanha nas redes sociais para denunciar abusos de patrões." #SalaSocial, *BBC Brasil*, July 21. http://www.bbc.com/portuguese/salasocial-36857963.

Barrucho, Luis. 2016b. "'I Am Housemaid, Hear Me Roar.'" *BBC News*, August 1. https://www.bbc.com/news/blogs-trending-36927502.

Barthes, Roland. 1993. *Camera Lucida: Reflections on Photography*. London: Vintage. First published in 1980.

Bartow, Joanna R. 2008. "Testimonial Literature." In *Latin American Women Writers: An Encyclopedia*, edited by María Claudia André and Eva Paulino Bueno, 504–509. New York: Routledge.

BBC News. 2018. "Eike Batista: Brazilian Ex-Billionaire Jailed for Bribery." July 3. https://www.bbc.com/news/world-latin-america-44703088.

Bentes, Ivana. 2003. "The Sertão and the Favela in Contemporary Brazilian Film." In *The New Brazilian Cinema*, edited by Lúcia Nagib, 121–138. London: I. B. Tauris.

Beverley, John. 1999. *Subalternity and Representation: Arguments in Cultural Theory*. Durham, NC: Duke University Press.

Bizzio, Sergio. 2004. *Rabia*. Barcelona: El Cobre.

Blank, Thais. 2012. "Do cinema ao arquivo: Traçando o percurso migratório dos filmes de família." *Revista digital de cinema documentário* 13:5–20.

Blankenship, Lisa. 2019. *Changing the Subject: A Theory of Rhetorical Empathy*. Logan: Utah State University Press.

Blofield, Merike. 2012. *Care Work and Class: Domestic Workers' Struggle for Equal Rights in Latin America*. University Park: Pennsylvania State University Press.

Brando, Oscar. 1997. "La narrativa uruguaya y sus fantasmas (1985–1997)." In *Papeles de Montivideo: Aproximaciones a la narrativa uruguaya posterior a 1985*, edited by Carlos Liscano, 10–33. Montevideo: Ediciones Trilce.

Bridikhina, Eugenia. 2007. "Las criadas y ahijadas: Servicio doméstico de los menores en La Paz a principios del siglo XX." In *Historia de la infancia en América Latina*, edited by Pablo Rodríguez Jiménez and María Emma Mannarelli, loc. 5129–5476. Bogotá: Universidad Externado de Colombia.

Brites, Jurema. 2007. "Afeto e desigualdade: Gênero, geração e classe entre empregadas domésticas e os seus empregadores." *Cadernos pagu* 29:91–109.

Brites, Jurema. 2014. "Domestic Service, Affection and Inequality: Elements of Subalternity." In *Domestic Work between Regulation and Intimacy*, edited by Encarnación Gutiérrez Rodríguez and Jurema Brites, a special issue of *Women's Studies International Forum* 46 (September): 63–71.

Bruzzi, Stella. 2006. *New Documentary*. 2nd ed. Abingdon, UK: Routledge.

Bunster, Ximena, and Elsa M. Chaney. 1985. *Sellers and Servants: Working Women in Lima, Peru*. New York: Praeger.

Burgos, Elizabeth. 1998. *Me llamo Rigoberta Menchú y así me nació la conciencia*. 15th ed. Coyoacán, Mexico: Siglo Veintiuno Editores. First published 1983.

Bustamante, Rodrigo. 2012. "Debate sobre clasismo en Chile por discriminación a nanas." *BBC,* January 18, 2012. https://www.bbc.com/mundo/noticias/2012/01/120118_chile_nanas_discriminacion_jgc.

CAITH (El centro de atención integral a las trabajadoras del hogar). n.d. Centro Yanapanakusun. https://www.yanapanakusun.org. Accessed January 29, 2019.

Campanella, Lucía. 2016. "Poétique de la domestique en France et au Río de la Plata, de 1850 à nos jours." PhD diss., Université de Perpignan, France, and Università degli Studi di Bergamo, Italy. https://halshs.archives-ouvertes.fr/tel-01409546v1/document.

Campanella, Lucía. 2018. "Retrato del artista como doméstica (y de la doméstica como artista)." In *Los de abajo: Tres siglos de sirvientes en el arte y la literatura en América Latina*, edited by María Julia Rossi and Lucía Campanella, 191–208. Rosario, Argentina: UNR Editora.

Canevaro, Santiago. 2020. *Como de la familia: Afecto y desigualdad en el trabajo doméstico*. Buenos Aires: Prometeo Editorial.

Canto, Cláudia. 2016. *Morte às vassouras*. São Paulo: Edicon.

Caraballo, Ramona. 1987. *La niña, el chocolate, el huevo duro: Historia verídica y real para personas formadas*. [Montevideo?]: Monte Sexto.

Caram, Bernardo. 2020. "Doméstica ia para Disney com dólar barato, 'uma festa danada', diz Guedes." Mercado, *Folha de São Paulo*, February 12. https://www1.folha.uol.com.br/mercado/2020/02/domestica-ia-para-disney-com-dolar-barato-diz-guedes-uma-festa-danada.shtml.

Carneiro, Karina. 2021. "Perfil da fortuna: Quem é João Moreira Salles e qual seu patrimônio?" *iDinheiro*, June 18. https://www.idinheiro.com.br/joao-moreira-salles.

Carneiro, Sueli. 2011. *Racismo, sexismo e desigualdade no Brasil*. São Paulo: Selo Negro.

CartaCapital. 2013. "PEC das domésticas é 'segunda abolição da escravatura,' diz liderança." *CartaCapital* (blog), March 27. https://www.cartacapital.com.br/sociedade/pec-das-domesticas-e-segunda-abolicao-da-escravatura-diz-lideranca.

Carvalho, Lenira. 1982. "Só a gente que vive é que sabe: Depoimento de uma doméstica." In *Cadernos de educação popular 4*, edited by Vozes and Nova, 9–78. Petrópolis, Brazil: Vozes.

Carvalho, Lenira, and Cornélia Parisius. 1999. *A luta que me fez crescer*. Recife, Brazil: DAD, Bagaço.

Castellanos, Rosario. 1957. *Balún-Canán*. Mexico, DF: Fondo de Cultura Económica.

Castillo, Debra. 2007. "The New New Latin American Cinema: Cortometrajes on the Internet." In *Latin American Cyberculture and Cyberliterature*, edited by Claire Taylor and Thea Pitman, 33–49. Liverpool: Liverpool University Press.

Chacón, Hilda. 2018. "Introduction." In *Online Activism in Latin America*, edited by Hilda Chacón, 1–30. New York: Routledge.

Chaney, Elsa M., and Mary Garcia Castro, eds. 1989. *Muchachas No More: Household Workers in Latin America and the Caribbean*. Philadelphia: Temple University Press.

Cleveland, Kimberly. 2019. *Black Women Slaves Who Nourished a Nation: Artistic Renderings of Wet Nurses in Brazil*. Amherst, MA: Cambria Press.

Conde, Maite. 2020. "Brazil in the Time of Coronavirus." *Geopolítica(s): Revista de estudios sobre espacio y poder* 11 (Especial): 239–249. https://revistas.ucm.es/index.php/GEOP/article/view/69349.

Cooperativa. 2014. "Ana Tijoux contestó a quienes intentaron insultarla llamándola 'cara de nana' en Lollapalooza 2014." *Cooperativa* (magazine), March 31. https://www.cooperativa.cl/noticias/entretencion/festivales/lollapalooza/ana-tijoux-contesto-a-quienes-intentaron-insultarla-llamandola-cara-de/2014-03-31/154324.html.

Cornwall, Andrea, Creuza Maria Oliveira, and Terezinha Gonçalves. 2013. "'If You Don't See a Light in the Darkness You Must Light a Fire': Brazilian Domestic Workers' Struggle for Rights." In *Organizing Women Workers in the Informal Economy*, edited by Naila Kabeer, Ratna M. Sudarshan, and Kirsty Milward, 149–180. London: Zed Books.

Corossacz, Valeria Ribeiro. 2017. *White Middle-Class Men in Rio de Janeiro: The Making of a Dominant Subject*. Lanham, MD: Lexington.

Correio Braziliense (Brazil). 2016. "Foto do Correio no Rio viraliza e expõe um país e uma web divididos." March 14. https://www.correiobraziliense.com.br/app/noticia/politica/2016/03/14/interna_politica,522052/memes-claudio-pracownik.shtml.

Cortázar, Julio. 1951. *Bestiario*. Buenos Aires: Editorial Sudamericana.

Coulson, Margaret, Branka Magas, and Hilary Wainwright. 1975. "The Housewife and Her Labour under Capitalism: A Critique." *New Left Review* 1 (89): 59–71.

Cox, Rosie. 2006. *The Servant Problem: Domestic Employment in a Global Economy*. London: I. B. Tauris.

Cox, Rosie. 2016. "Cleaning Up: Gender, Race and Dirty Work at Home."

In *Müll: Interdisziplinäre Perspektiven auf das Übrig-Gebliebene*, edited by Christiane Lewe, Tim Othold, and Nicholas Oxen, 97–116. Witten, Germany: transcript Verlag.

Crenshaw, Kimberlé. 1989. "Demarginalizing the Intersection of Race and Sex: A Black Feminist Critique of Antidiscrimination Doctrine, Feminist Theory and Antiracist Politics." *University of Chicago Legal Forum* 1989 (1): 138–168.

da Cunha, Olívia Maria Gomes. 2007. "Criadas para servir: Domesticidade, intimidade e retribuição." In *Quase cidadão: Histórias e antropologias da pós-emancipação*, edited by Flávio dos Santos Gomes and Olívia Maria Gomes da Cunha, 377–418. Rio de Janeiro: Editora FGV.

da Silva, Francisca Souza. 1983. *Ai de vós! Diário de uma doméstica*. Rio de Janeiro: Civilização Brasileira.

de Casanova, Erynn Masi. 2015. "'Como cualquier otro trabajo': Organizando a las trabajadoras remuneradas del hogar en Ecuador." *Revista Economía* 67 (106): 37–52.

de Casanova, Erynn Masi. 2019. "ROMA—Film Dossier." *Latin American Perspectives* (blog), February 24. https://latinamericanperspectives.com/roma.

de Jesus, Carolina Maria. 2014. *Diário de Bitita*. São Paulo: SESI-SP Editora. First published 1986.

de Jesus, Carolina Maria. 2021. *Quarto de despejo: Diário de uma favelada*. São Paulo, Brazil: Editora Ática. First published in 1960.

de Luca, Tiago. 2017. "'Casa Grande & Senzala': Domestic Space and Class Conflict in *Casa Grande* and *Que Horas Ela Volta?*" In *Space and Subjectivity in Contemporary Brazilian Cinema*, edited by Antônio Márcio da Silva and Mariana Cunha, 203–219. Cham, Switzerland: Palgrave Macmillan.

de Luca, Tiago, and Nuno Barradas Jorge. 2016. "Introduction: From Slow Cinema to Slow Cinemas." In *Slow Cinema*, edited by Tiago De Luca and Nuno Barradas Jorge, 1–22. Edinburgh: Edinburgh University Press.

Dennison, Stephanie. 2018. "Intimacy and Cordiality in Kleber Mendonça Filho's *Aquarius*." *Journal of Iberian and Latin American Studies* 24 (3): 329–340.

Dennison, Stephanie, and Lisa Shaw. 2004. *Popular Cinema in Brazil, 1930–2001*. Manchester, UK: Manchester University Press.

Derrida, Jacques. 1992. *Given Time*. Translated by Peggy Kamuf. Chicago: University of Chicago Press.

Dieleke, Edgardo, and Gabriela Nouzeilles. 2008. "The Spiral of the Snail: Searching for the Documentary—An Interview with Joao Moreira Salles." *Journal of Latin American Cultural Studies* 17 (2): 139–153.

Dijck, José van. 2013. *The Culture of Connectivity: A Critical History of Social Media*. New York: Oxford University Press.

Doane, Mary Ann. 2002. *The Emergence of Cinematic Time: Modernity, Contingency, the Archive*. Cambridge, MA: Harvard University Press.

Driscoll, Catherine. 2002. *Girls: Feminine Adolescence in Popular Culture and Cultural Theory*. New York: Columbia University Press.

Durin, Séverine, and Natalia Vázquez. 2013. "Heroínas-sirvientas: Análisis de las representaciones de trabajadoras domésticas en telenovelas mexicanas." *Trayectorias* 15 (36): 20–44.

Dutra, Delia. 2017. "Mulheres migrantes, trabalhadoras domésticas: Vulnerabilidades e violências." In *Mulheres e violências: Interseccionalidades*, edited by Cristina Stevens, Suzane Oliveira, Valeska Zanello, Edlene Silva, and Cristiane Portela, 341–356. Brasília, Brazil: Technopolitik.

Duvivier, Gregório. 2016. *Caviar é uma ova*. São Paulo: Companhia das Letras.

ECLAC (Economic Commission for Latin America and the Caribbean). 2020. "The Precarious Situation of Domestic Workers in Latin America and the Caribbean is Accentuated by the COVID-19 Crisis." United Nations ECLAC website, June 12. https://www.cepal.org/es/noticias/la-situacion-precariedad-trabajadoras-domesticas-america-latina-caribe-se-acentua-frente-la.

The Economist. 2008. "Fall of an Opportunist." The Americas, December 4, 2008. http://www.economist.com/node/12725169.

Ehrenreich, Barbara, and Arlie Russell Hochschild. 2003. *Global Woman: Nannies, Maids and Sex Workers in the New Economy*. London: Granta Books.

El Universal (Mexico City). 2019. "'Roma' Inspires Domestic Workers in the US to Seek Legal Protection." February 23. https://www.eluniversal.com.mx/english/roma-inspires-domestic-workers-us-seek-legal-protection.

El Universo (Guayaquil). 2007. "Protesta al impedir que empleadas se bañen en una playa." January 30. https://www.eluniverso.com/2007/01/30/0001/14/2ED5AEBC958B43EF83E04E64BC5EEE5D.html.

Excélsior (Mexico City). 2019. "Coincide López Obrador con Cuarón sobre racismo en México." February 25. https://www.excelsior.com.mx/nacional/coincide-lopez-obrador-con-cuaron-sobre-racismo-en-mexico/1298416.

Expósito, Marcelo. 2010. "D-O 1–5." *97 empleadas domésticas*, 49–54. Barcelona, Spain: Departament d'acció social i ciutadania, Secretaria de la joventut. Published in conjunction with an exhibition by Daniela Ortiz titled *97 empleadas domésticas* and presented at the Casa de la Mujer, Juana Francés Exhibition Hall, in Zaragoza, Spain. Internet Archive repository. https://ia600505.us.archive.org/21/items/97Empleadas DomesticasOrtizPublicacion/97_empleadas_dome%CC%81sticas_ortiz _publicacio%CC%81n.pdf.

Federici, Silvia. 2014. "The Reproduction of Labour Power in the Global Economy and the Unfinished Feminist Revolution." In *Workers and*

Labour in a Globalised Capitalism, edited by Maurizio Atzeni, 85–107. Basingstoke, UK: Palgrave Macmillan.

Fernández, Rosario. 2018. "Commodification of Domestic Labour, the Culture of Servitude and the Making of the Chilean Nation." *Österreichische Zeitschrift für Soziologie* 43 (1): 49–60.

Ferrero, Angel, and Iván Gordillo. 2008. "Lo que significa la jornada laboral de 65 horas." *Rebelión* (blog), June 19. https://rebelion.org/lo-que -significa-la-jornada-laboral-de-65-horas.

Flora, Cornelia Butler. 1989. "Domestic Service in the Latin American Fotonovela." In *Muchachas No More: Household Workers in Latin America and the Caribbean*, edited by Elsa M. Chaney and Mary Garcia Castro, 143–159. Philadelphia: Temple University Press.

Folha de São Paulo. 2016. "Justiça libera recursos de Daniel Dantas bloqueados na Satiagraha." July 4. http://www1.folha.uol.com.br/mercado/2016 /07/1788508-justica-libera-recursos-de-daniel-dantas-bloqueados-na -satiagraha.shtml.

Forbes Staff. 2019. "IMSS reconoce apoyo del equipo de 'Roma' a programa de trabajadoras domésticas." *Forbes México,* February 18. https://www .forbes.com.mx/imss-reconoce-apoyo-del-equipo-de-roma-a-programa -de-trabajadoras-domesticas.

Foucault, Michel. 2008. "Of Other Spaces." In *Heterotopia and the City: Public Space in a Postcivil Society*, edited by Michiel Dehaene and Lieven De Cauter, 13–29. Abingdon, UK: Routledge. First published in 1967.

Franco, Jean. 1999. "Going Public: Reinhabiting the Private." In *Jean Franco —Critical Passions: Selected Essays*, edited by Mary Louise Pratt and Kathleen Newman, 48–65. Durham, NC: Duke University Press.

Franco, Jean. 2013. *Cruel Modernity*. Durham, NC: Duke University Press.

Franco, Luiza. 2016. "Babá de foto polêmica diz ser a favor da manifestação." *Folha de São Paulo*, March 15. http://www1.folha.uol.com.br/poder/2016 /03/1750320-baba-de-foto-polemica-diz-ser-a-favor-da-manifestacao .shtml.

Freyre, Gilberto. 1963. *The Masters and the Slaves: A Study in the Development of Brazilian Civilization*. Translated by Samuel Putnam. New York: Alfred A. Knopf.

Freyre, Gilberto. 2003. *Casa grande & senzala: Formação da família brasileira sob o regime da economia patriarcal*. São Paulo: Global Editora e Distribuidora. First published in 1933.

Frota, Ana Maria Monte Coelho. 2007. "Diferentes concepções da infância e adolescência: A importância da historicidade para sua construção." *Estudos e pesquisas em psicologia* 7 (1): 147–160.

Furtado, Gustavo Procopio. 2019. *Documentary Filmmaking in Contemporary Brazil: Cinematic Archives of the Present*. New York: Oxford University Press.

G1 *Rio de Janeiro*. 2020. "Governo do RJ confirma a primeira morte por coronavírus." March 19. https://g1.globo.com/rj/rio-de-janeiro/noticia/2020/03/19/rj-confirma-a-primeira-morte-por-coronavirus.ghtml.

García Calvo, Cynthia. 2015. "Rodrigo Moreno, director de 'Réimon.'" *LatAm cinema*, June 25. https://www.latamcinema.com/entrevistas/rodrigo-moreno-director-de-reimon.

Genet, Jean. 1948. *Las criadas*. Translated by José Bianco and Silvina Ocampo. Buenos Aires: Sur.

Genet, Jean. 2001. *Les bonnes*. Paris: Gallimard. First published in 1947.

Gillam, Reighan. 2016. "The Help, Unscripted: Constructing the Black Revolutionary Domestic in Afro-Brazilian Media." *Feminist Media Studies* 16 (6): 1043–1056.

Giorgi, Gabriel. 2014. *Formas comunes: Animalidad, cultura, biopolítica*. Buenos Aires: Eterna Cadencia.

Goldsmith, Mary. 1989. "Politics and Programs of Domestic Workers' Organizations in Mexico." In *Muchachas No More: Household Workers in Latin America and the Caribbean*, edited by Elsa M. Chaney and Mary Garcia Castro, 221–242. Philadelphia: Temple University Press.

Goldsmith, Mary. 2013. "Los espacios internacionales de la participación política de las trabajadoras remuneradas del hogar." *Revista de estudios sociales* 45: 233–246.

Goldstein, Donna M. 2013. *Laughter Out of Place: Race, Class, Violence and Sexuality in a Rio Shantytown*. Berkeley: University of California Press.

Gonzalez, Lélia. 1984. "Racismo e sexismo na cultura brasileira." *Revista ciências sociais hoje*, Anpocs: 223–244.

Gramsci, Antonio. 2003. *Selections from the Prison Notebooks of Antonio Gramsci*. Edited by Quintin Hoare and Geoffrey Nowell-Smith. London: Lawrence and Wishart. First published in 1971.

Grant, Catherine, and Deborah Martin. 2021. *Rites of THE PASSAGE*. Video created for and shown at Vive le cinéma! / Critics Choice VII: On Positionality, International Film Festival Rotterdam, February–May, as part of the Vive le cinéma! Exhibition at Eye Filmmuseum, Amsterdam. https://vimeo.com/557508764?fbclid=IwAR3K8kanmA_lfteGSvyHiQjsXk0nXqRDRHrpMcjfV3VKEKIHzKVr49wLnVk.

Guimarães, Ligia, and Juliana Gragnani. 2020. "'Vai se isolar': Diaristas são dispensadas sem pagamento em meio à crise do coronavírus." BBC News Brasil, March 18. https://www.bbc.com/portuguese/brasil-51950880.

Gutiérrez, Ana. 1983. *Se necesita muchacha*. Mexico, DF: Fondo de Cultura Económica.

Gutiérrez-Rodríguez, Encarnación. 2010. *Migration, Domestic Work and Affect: A Decolonial Approach on Value and the Feminization of Labor*. New York: Routledge.

Guy, Donna J. 2002. "The State, the Family and Marginal Children in Latin

America." In *Minor Omissions: Children in Latin American History and Society*, edited by Tobias Hecht, 139–164. Madison: University of Wisconsin Press.

Hall, Stuart, ed. 1997. *Representation: Cultural Representations and Signifying Practices*. London: Sage.

Hardt, Michael, and Antonio Negri. 2004. *Multitude: War and Democracy in the Age of Empire*. New York: Penguin Books.

Harris, Anita. 2004. *Future Girl: Young Women in the Twenty-First Century*. New York: Routledge.

Haskins, Victoria K., and Claire Lowrie, eds. 2015. *Colonization and Domestic Service: Historical and Contemporary Perspectives*. London: Routledge.

Hirsch, Pam, and Christopher Brown, eds. 2014. *The Cinema of the Swimming Pool*. Oxford: Peter Lang.

Hoerder, Dirk, Elise van Nederveen Meerkerk, and Silke Neunsinger, eds. 2015. *Towards a Global History of Domestic and Caregiving Workers*. Leiden, Netherlands: Brill.

Holanda, Sérgio Buarque de. 2014. *Raízes do Brasil*. São Paulo: Companhia das Letras. First published in 1936.

Hondagneu-Sotelo, Pierrette. 2001. *Doméstica: Immigrant Workers Cleaning and Caring in the Shadows of Affluence*. Berkeley: University of California Press.

Huffington Post. 2018. "'Tenemos una deuda histórica con las trabajadoras del hogar', Alfonso Cuarón." Un mundo mejor, December 7. https://www.huffingtonpost.com.mx/2018/12/07/tenemos-una-deuda-historica-con-las-trbajadoras-del-hogar-alfonso-cuaron_a_23611775.

Human Rights Watch. 2012. "Uruguay: First to Ratify Domestic Workers Convention." May 1. https://www.hrw.org/news/2012/05/01/uruguay-first-ratify-domestic-workers-convention.

Hutchinson, Elizabeth Quay. 2010. "Many Zitas: The Young Catholic Worker and Household Workers in Cold War Chile." *Labor: Studies in Working-Class History of the Americas* 6 (4): 67–94.

Iglesias, Jovita, and Silvia Renée Arias. 2003. *Los Bioy*. Barcelona: Fabula Tusquets Editores.

Ikeda, Marcelo. 2012. "O 'novíssimo cinema brasileiro': Sinais de uma renovação." *Cinémas d'Amérique latine* 20 (December). https://journals.openedition.org/cinelatino/597#text.

ILO (International Labour Organisation). 2011. "Domestic Workers Convention, 2011 (No. 189)." June 16. http://www.ilo.org/dyn/normlex/en/f?p=NORMLEXPUB:12100:0::NO::P12100_ILO_CODE:C189.

ILO (International Labour Organisation). 2020. "Federaciones de trabajadoras del hogar de Perú demandan implementación efectiva del Convenio No. 189 de la OIT." May 25. http://www.ilo.org/lima/sala-de-prensa/WCMS_746871/lang—es/index.htm.

ILO (International Labour Organisation). n.d. "Ratifications of C189—Domestic Workers Convention, 2011 (No.189)." https://www.ilo.org/dyn/normlex/en/f?p=1000:11300:0::NO:11300:P11300_INSTRUMENT_ID:2551460. Accessed September 15, 2021.

IMDb. n.d. "Rio de Janeiro 'City of Splendor.'" https://www.imdb.com/title/tt0134935. Accessed August 26, 2021.

Institute for Applied Economic Research. 2016. *Initial Effects of Constitutional Amendment 72 on Domestic Work in Brazil.* Conditions of Work Employment Series no. 79. Geneva: International Labour Organization. https://www.ilo.org/wcmsp5/groups/public/—ed_protect/—protrav/—travail/documents/publication/wcms_506167.pdf.

Kantaris, Geoffrey, and Rory O'Bryen. 2013. "Introduction: The Fragile Contemporaneity of the Popular." In *Latin American Popular Culture: Politics, Media, Affect,* edited by Geoffrey Kantaris and Rory O'Bryen, 1–42. Woodbridge, UK: Tamesis.

Kratje, Julia. 2017. "Voces y cuerpos del servicio doméstico en el cine latinoamericano contemporáneo." *Revista de la asociación Argentina de estudios de cine y audiovisual* 15: 1–22.

Kratje, Julia. 2018. "En busca del tiempo perdido: Intervalos del ocio en *Réimon.*" In *Los de abajo: Tres siglos de sirvientes en el arte y la literatura en América Latina,* edited by María Julia Rossi and Lucía Campanella, 167–189. Rosario, Argentina: UNR Editora.

Krauze, Enrique. 2018. "Opinión | 'Roma': Una historia de amor y servidumbre." *New York Times* (Spanish ed.), December 14. https://www.nytimes.com/es/2018/12/14/opinion-roma-cuaron-krauze.

Kristeva, Julia. 1982. *Powers of Horror: An Essay on Abjection.* New York: Columbia University Press.

Kuznesof, Elizabeth. 1989. "A History of Domestic Service in Spanish America, 1492–1980." In *Muchachas No More: Household Workers in Latin America and the Caribbean,* edited by Elsa M. Chaney and Mary Garcia Castro, 17–35. Philadelphia: Temple University Press.

Lauderdale Graham, Sandra. 1989. "Servants and Masters in Rio de Janeiro: Perceptions of House and Street in the 1870s." In *Muchachas No More: Household Workers in Latin America and the Caribbean,* edited by Elsa M. Chaney and Mary Garcia Castro, 67–85. Philadelphia: Temple University Press.

Leaver, Tama, Tim Highfield, and Crystal Abidin. 2020. *Instagram: Visual Social Media Cultures.* Cambridge, UK: Polity.

Lehmann, David. 2008. "Gilberto Freyre: The Reassessment Continues." *Latin American Research Review* 43 (1): 208–218.

LePan, Nicholas. 2020. "Visualizing the Length of the Fine Print, for 14 Popular Apps." *Visual Capitalist,* April 18. https://www.visualcapitalist.com/terms-of-service-visualizing-the-length-of-internet-agreements.

Lins, Consuelo, and Cláudia Mesquita. 2008. *Filmar o real: Sobre o documentário brasileiro contemporâneo*. Rio de Janeiro: Jorge Zahar Editor.

Lispector, Clarice. 1964. *A paixão segundo G. H.* Rio de Janeiro: Sabia.

Lispector, Clarice. 2002. *A hora da estrela*. Lisbon: Relógio d'Água Editores. First published in 1977.

Locatelli, Piero. 2017. "Domésticas das Filipinas são escravizadas em condomínio de luxo." *CartaCapital* (blog), August 1. https://www.cartacapital.com.br/sociedade/domesticas-das-filipinas-sao-escravizadas-em-condominio-de-luxo.

Londoño, Ernesto. 2021. "'I Was Invisible': The Maid-Turned-Star Who's Taking On Racism in Brazil." *New York Times*, February 19. https://www.nytimes.com/2021/02/19/world/americas/brazil-racism-preta-rara.html.

MacDonald, Cameron Lynne. 2010. *Shadow Mothers: Nannies, Au Pairs, and the Micropolitics of Mothering*. Berkeley: University of California Press.

Magalhães, Ana. 2017. "Reforma trabalhista dificulta combate ao trabalho escravo." *CartaCapital* (blog), July 11. https://www.cartacapital.com.br/sociedade/reforma-trabalhista-dificulta-combate-ao-trabalho-escravo.

Maguire, Geoffrey, and Rachel Randall. 2018. "Introduction: Visualising Adolescence in Contemporary Latin American Cinema—Gender, Class and Politics." In *New Visions of Adolescence in Contemporary Latin American Cinema*, edited by Geoffrey Maguire and Rachel Randall, 1–33. Cham, Switzerland: Palgrave Macmillan.

Mancini, Adriana. 2018. "Variaciones entre criados y señores: Fani, *Sur* y Las Ocampo." In *Los de abajo: Tres siglos de sirvientes en el arte y la literatura en América Latina*, edited by María Julia Rossi and Lucía Campanella, 101–112. Rosario, Argentina: UNR Editora.

Marçal, Katrine. 2016. *Who Cooked Adam Smith's Dinner? A Story about Women and Economics*. London: Portobello Books.

Marks, Laura U. 2000. *The Skin of the Film: Intercultural Cinema, Embodiment, and the Senses*. Durham, NC: Duke University Press.

Marques, Leonardo. 2019. "Slavery and Its Economic Structures in Colonial Brazil." In *Oxford Research Encyclopedia of Latin American History*. Oxford University Press, online ed., December 23. https://doi.org/10.1093/acrefore/9780199366439.013.772.

Marsh, Leslie. 2011. "Taking Initiative: Brazilian Women's Film-Making before and after the Retomada." In *New Trends in Argentine and Brazilian Cinema*, edited by Cacilda M. Rego and Carolina Rocha, 257–270. Chicago: University of Chicago Press.

Martin, Deborah. 2016. *The Cinema of Lucrecia Martel*. Manchester, UK: Manchester University Press.

Martínez, Yolanda Bojórquez. 2011. *Modernización y nacionalismo de la arquitectura mexicana en cinco voces: 1925–1980*. Jalisco, Mexico: ITESO.

Marx, Karl. 2000. *Capital: A Critique of Political Economy*. Vol. 1. Translated by Samuel Moore and Edward Aveling. London: Electric Book Company. First published in 1887.

Marx, Karl, and Fredrick Engels. 1969. *Manifesto of the Communist Party*. Transcription of an 1888 English edition; translated by Samuel Moore and Frederick Engels; published in a later edition in 1969 by Progress Publishers in Moscow. Citations refer to page numbers in the transcription. https://www.marxists.org/archive/marx/works/download/pdf/Manifesto.pdf. First published in 1848.

Mascaro, Gabriel. 2021. "Q&A with Gabriel Mascaro." Lecture presented at the IV Congresso internacional da rede Europeia de Brasilianistas de análise cultural (REBRAC): O país do futuro, o futuro do país, March 19. University of Oxford.

Mas de Xaxàs, Xavier. 2020. "La artista Daniela Ortiz sale de España por una campaña de amenazas en las redes sociales." Cultura, *La Vanguardia* (Barcelona), August 2. https://www.lavanguardia.com/cultura/20200802/482579201722/daniela-ortiz-macba-centro-nacional-de-arte-la-virreina.html.

Massumi, Brian. 2002. *Parables for the Virtual: Movement, Affect, Sensation.* Durham, NC: Duke University Press.

Mata, Irene. 2014. *Domestic Disturbances: Re-Imagining Narratives of Gender, Labor, and Immigration.* Austin: University of Texas Press.

Melo, Max Miliano. 2016. "Empregada na cama e no fogão: Mães-pretas e mulatas no audiovisual brasileiro." Academia repository. https://www.academia.edu/51095028/Empregada_na_cama_e_no_fog%C3%A3o_M%C3%A3e_pretas_e_mulatas_no_audiovisual_brasileiro.%7D. Accessed February 17, 2023.

Merchant, Paul. 2022. *Remaking Home: Domestic Spaces in Argentine and Chilean Film, 2005–2015.* Pittsburgh, PA: University of Pittsburgh Press.

Merten, Luiz Carlos. 2007. "O mordomo e o filho do banqueiro." Caderno 2, *O Estado de São Paulo*, March 28.

Merten, Luiz Carlos. 2012. "Santiago, na trilha de Visconti." Caderno 2, *O Estado de São Paulo*, July 22.

Merten, Luiz Carlos. 2013. "As questões estéticas e sociais de doméstica." Caderno 2, *O Estado de São Paulo*, May 7.

Merten, Luiz Carlos. 2015. "Filme faz história." Caderno 2, *O Estado de São Paulo*, April 16.

Merten, Luiz Carlos, and Luciana Nunes Leal. 2015. "'Que horas ela volta?' Arma seus planos para o Oscar." Caderno 2, *O Estado de São Paulo*, September 11.

Migden Socolow, Susan. 2015. *The Women of Colonial Latin America.* New York: Cambridge University Press.

Milanich, Nara. 2005. "From Domestic Servant to Working Class Housewife:

Women, Labor and Family in Chile." *Estudios interdisciplinarios de América Latina y el Caribe* 16 (1): 11–39.

Monsiváis, Carlos, and Carlos Bonfil. 1994. *A través del espejo: El cine mexicano y su público.* Mexico, DF: IMCINE/El Milagro.

Montoya Robledo, Valentina, et al. 2020. "Invisible Commutes." On Invisible Commutes home page. https://www.invisiblecommutes.com/. Accessed February 17, 2023.

Moraña, Mabel. 2013. "Documentalismo y ficción: Testimonio y narrativa testimonial hispanoamericana en el Siglo XX." In *América Latina: Palabra, literatura y cultura*, edited by Ana Pizarro, 113–150. Santiago, Chile: Ediciones Universidad Alberto Hurtado.

Moreira, Daniel da Silva. 2009. "Reconstruir-se em texto: Práticas de arquivamento e resistência no *Diário de Bitita*, de Carolina Maria de Jesus." *Estação Literária* 3: 64–73.

MovieWeb. 2010. "'The Maid'—Exclusive: Director Sebastian Silva Interview" September 24. YouTube video, 10:33. https://www.youtube.com/watch?v=F0Wu96LwpUY.

Mullaly, Laurence. n.d. "Silvina Ocampo y Lucrecia Martel: Dependencias y promesas." Academia repository. https://www.academia.edu/30705718/SILVINA_OCAMPO_Y_LUCRECIA_MARTEL_DEPENDENCIAS_Y_PROMESAS. Accessed August 20, 2020.

Mulvey, Laura. 2006. *Death 24x a Second: Stillness and the Moving Image.* London: Reaktion Books.

Nagib, Lúcia. 2009. "Filmmaking as the Production of Reality: A Study of Hara and Kobayashi's Documentaries." In *Realism and the Audiovisual Media*, edited by Lúcia Nagib and Cecília Melo, 193–209. Basingstoke, UK: Palgrave Macmillan.

Obar, Jonathan A., and Anne Oeldorf-Hirsch. 2020. "The Biggest Lie on the Internet: Ignoring the Privacy Policies and Terms of Service Policies of Social Networking Services." *Information, Communication & Society* 23 (1): 128–147.

Ocampo, Silvina. 1962. *Lo amargo por dulce.* Buenos Aires: Emecé Editores.

Ocampo, Silvina. 1970. *Los días de la noche.* Buenos Aires: Editorial Sudamericana.

OECD (Organisation for Economic Co-operation and Development). 2020. "Stepping Up Digital Transformation in Brazil Could Reinforce Economic Recovery from COVID-19 Crisis." October 26. https://www.oecd.org/digital/stepping-up-digital-transformation-in-brazil-could-reinforce-economic-recovery-from-covid-19-crisis.htm.

Olcott, Jocelyn. 2011. "Introduction: Researching and Rethinking the Labors of Love." *Hispanic American Historical Review* 91 (1): 1–27.

Oliveira, Maurício Sellmann. 2020. "Beyond Tropes: Otherness and the Identity of the Brazilian Maid in *Domésticas—O Filme* and *Doméstica*." In

Domestic Labor in Twenty-First Century Latin American Cinema, edited by Elizabeth Osborne and Sofía Ruiz-Alfaro, 143–165. Cham, Switzerland: Palgrave Macmillan.

Oricchio, Luiz Zanin. 2009. "Santiago, um estudo sobre o tempo." Caderno 2, *O Estado de São Paulo*, April 5.

Oricchio, Luiz Zanin. 2015. "Filme ajuda a conhecer estruturas profundas do país." Caderno 2, *O Estado de São Paulo*, September 11.

Ortiz, Daniela. 2010a. *97 empleadas domésticas*, 1–49. Barcelona, Spain: Departament d'acció social i ciutadania, Secretaria de la joventut. Published in conjunction with an exhibition of the same title at the Casa de la Mujer, Juana Francés Exhibition Hall, in Zaragoza, Spain. Internet Archive repository. https://ia600505.us.archive.org/21/items/97Empleadas DomesticasOrtizPublicacion/97_empleadas_dome%CC%81sticas _ortiz_publicacio%CC%81n.pdf.

Ortiz, Daniela. 2010b. "P1–P2." On the àngels barcelona website. http:// angelsbarcelona.com/en/artists/daniela-ortiz/projects/p1-p2/220. Accessed April 8, 2021.

Ortiz, Daniela. 2011. "Habitaciones de servicio." On the àngels barcelona website. http://angelsbarcelona.com/en/artists/daniela-ortiz/projects /habitaciones-de-servicio/534. Accessed April 8, 2021.

Ortiz, Daniela. 2012. "Relat de Daniela Ortiz sobre el procés de realització de la publicació i la seva recepció." In *Cataleg d'art jove 2010–2011*, edited by Oriol Fontdevilla et al., 96–98. Barcelona: Sala d'art jove de la Secretaria de la joventut.

Ortiz, Daniela. 2013. "Carta abierta sobre 97 empleadas domésticas." *Kaos en la red* (blog), June 8. https://kaosenlared.net/carta-abierta-sobre -97-empleadas-dom-sticas-daniela-ortiz.

Osborne, Elizabeth, and Sofía Ruiz-Alfaro. 2020. *Domestic Labor in Twenty-First Century Latin American Cinema*. Cham, Switzerland: Palgrave Macmillan.

Page, Joanna. 2009. *Crisis and Capitalism in Contemporary Argentine Cinema*. Durham, NC: Duke University Press.

Parker, Richard. 2003. "Changing Sexualities: Masculinity and Male Homosexuality in Brazil." In *Changing Men and Masculinities in Latin America*, edited by Matthew C. Gutmann, 307–332. Durham, NC: Duke University Press.

Patai, Daphne. 1993. *Brazilian Women Speak: Contemporary Life Stories*. New Brunswick, NJ: Rutgers University Press.

Pateman, Carole. 1989. *The Disorder of Women: Democracy, Feminism and Political Theory*. Stanford, CA: Stanford University Press.

Paulino, Mauro, and Alessandro Janoni. 2015. "Longa 'Que horas ela volta?' retrata Brasil pré-crise política." *Folha de São Paulo*. September 13. https://www1.folha.uol.com.br/poder/2015/09/1681021-longa-que -horas-ela-volta-retrata-brasil-pre-crise-politica.shtml.

Paz, Octavio. 1950. *El laberinto de la soledad*. Mexico, DF: Cuadernos Americanos.

Peña, Milagros. 1994. "Liberation Theology in Peru: An Analysis of the Role of Intellectuals in Social Movements." *Journal for the Scientific Study of Religion* 33 (1): 34–45.

Perdigão, Gui. 2018. "The Cordial Maid: Representations of Servants in Brazilian Adaptations of Eça de Queirós." *Journal of Iberian and Latin American Studies* 24 (3): 391–400.

Pereira, Andrés. 2009. "La nana: Algunas consideraciones sobre esta ficción." http://www.lafuga.cl/la-nana/277.

Pereyra, Francisca. 2019. "'There's Always Someone Else': Argentina's Struggle to Improve Domestic Workers' Labour Conditions." *The Conversation*, June 11. http://theconversation.com/theres-always-someone-else-argentinas-struggle-to-improve-domestic-workers-labour-conditions-116702.

Pérez, Leda M., and Andrea Gandolfi. 2020. "Vulnerable Women in a Pandemic: Paid Domestic Workers and COVID-19 in Peru." *Bulletin of Latin American Research* 39 (S1): 79–83.

Pérez, Leda M., and Pedro M. Llanos. 2017. "Vulnerable Women in a Thriving Country: An Analysis of Twenty-First-Century Domestic Workers in Peru and Recommendations for Future Research." *Latin American Research Review* 52 (4): 552–570.

Pérez Zabala, Victoria. 2019. "Lucrecia Martel alza la voz." *La Nación*, October 6. https://www.lanacion.com.ar/espectaculos/lucrecia-martel-alza-voz-nid2294163.

Perrine, Alida Louisa. 2019. "The 'Audacity' of Visibility: Preta-Rara's Feminist Praxis." *Transmodernity: Journal of Peripheral Cultural Production of the Luso-Hispanic World* 9 (2): 21–43.

Pessoa, Gabriela Sá. 2015. "Domésticas se emocionam em pré-estreia do longa em SP." Ilustrada, *Folha de São Paulo*, August 26. https://m.folha.uol.com.br/ilustrada/2015/08/1673567-domesticas-se-emocionam-em-pre-estreia-de-que-horas-ela-volta.shtml.

Pinho, Patricia de Santana. 2015. "The Dirty Body That Cleans: Representations of Domestic Workers in Brazilian Common Sense." *Meridians* 13 (1): 103–128.

Pitasse, Mariana. 2018. "Milhares de pessoas marcham no Rio de Janeiro contra prisão do ex-presidente Lula." Geral, *Brasil de Fato* (São Paulo), April 6. https://www.brasildefato.com.br/2018/04/06/milhares-de-pessoas-marcham-no-rio-de-janeiro-contra-prisao-do-ex-presidente-lula.

Pite, Rebekah E. 2011. "Entertaining Inequalities: Doña Petrona, Juanita Bordoy, and Domestic Work in Mid-Twentieth-Century Argentina." *Hispanic American Historical Review* 91 (1): 97–128.

PNAD. 2010. "Pesquisa nacional por amostra de domicilios 2009." Rio de

Janeiro: Instituto Brasileiro de geografía e estatística. https://biblioteca.ibge.gov.br/visualizacao/periodicos/59/pnad_2009_v30_br.pdf.

Poblete, Lorena. 2015. "Modos de regulación del trabajo doméstico." *El trabajo doméstico: Entre regulaciones formales e informales (Cuadernos del IDES)* 30: 3–10.

Podalsky, Laura. 2011. *The Politics of Affect and Emotion in Contemporary Latin American Cinema: Argentina, Brazil, Cuba, and Mexico*. Basingstoke, UK: Palgrave Macmillan.

Poniatowska, Elena. 1980. *Fuerte es el silencio*. Mexico DF: Ediciones Era.

Poniatowska, Elena. 1983. "Presentación al lector mexicano." In *Se necesita muchacha*, edited by Ana Gutiérrez, 7–86. Mexico, DF: Fondo de Cultura Económica.

Poniatowska, Elena. 1988. *Nada, nadie*. Mexico, DF: Ediciones Era.

Poniatowska, Elena. 1994. *Luz y luna, las lunitas*. Mexico, DF: Ediciones Era.

Poniatowska, Elena. 1998. *La noche de Tlatelolco*. Mexico, DF: Ediciones Era. First published in 1971.

Poniatowska, Elena. 2016. *Hasta no verte Jesús mío*. Madrid: Alianza Editorial. First published in 1969.

Prates, Suzana. 1989. "Organizations for Domestic Workers in Montevideo: Reinforcing Marginality?" In *Muchachas No More: Household Workers in Latin America and the Caribbean*, edited by Elsa M. Chaney and Mary Garcia Castro, 271–290. Philadelphia: Temple University Press.

Presidência da república casa civil subchefia para assuntos jurídicos (Brasil). 2012. *Lei no. 12.711*. August 29. http://www.planalto.gov.br/ccivil_03/_ato2011-2014/2012/lei/l12711.htm.

Presidência da república casa civil subchefia para assuntos jurídicos (Brasil). 2015. *Lei Complementar Número 150*. June 1. http://www.planalto.gov.br/ccivil_03/leis/lcp/Lcp150.htm.

Preta-Rara. 2016. "Eu empregada doméstica." Facebook page, "About" section, July 20. https://www.facebook.com/euempregadadomestica/about/?ref=page_internal.

Preta-Rara. 2019. *Eu, empregada doméstica*. Belo Horizonte, Brazil: Letramento.

Pyle, Jean L. 2006. "Globalization, Transnational Migration, and Gendered Care Work: Introduction." *Globalizations* 3 (3): 283–295.

Rancière, Jacques. 2003. *The Philosopher and His Poor*. Durham, NC: Duke University Press.

Randall, Rachel. 2015. "Childhood, Movement and Play: An Analysis of Child Agency and Heterotopia in *Linha de Passe* (2008) and *Los Colores de la Montaña* (2010)." *Bulletin of Latin American Research* 34 (2): 214–228.

Randall, Rachel. 2017. *Children on the Threshold in Contemporary Latin American Cinema: Nature, Gender, and Agency*. Lanham, MD: Lexington Books.

Randall, Rachel. 2018a. "Cordiality and Intimacy in Contemporary Brazilian Culture: Introduction." *Journal of Iberian and Latin American Studies* 24 (3): 295–310.

Randall, Rachel. 2018b. "'Eu não sou o meu pai!': Deception, Intimacy and Adolescence in (the) *Casa grande*." In *New Visions of Adolescence in Contemporary Latin American Cinema*, edited by Geoffrey Maguire and Rachel Randall, 101–126. New York: Palgrave Macmillan.

Randall, Rachel. 2020. "Domestic Workers and COVID-19: Brazil's Legacy of Slavery Lives On." *Migration Mobilities Bristol—Latin America* (blog), August 6. https://mmblatinamerica.blogs.bristol.ac.uk/2020/08/06 /domestic-workers-and-covid-19-brazils-legacy-of-slavery-lives-on.

Renov, Michael. 1999. "Domestic Ethnography and the Construction of the 'Other' Self." In *Collecting Visible Evidence*, edited by Michael Renov and Jane Gaines, 140–155. Minneapolis: University of Minnesota Press.

Revista E. 2013. "Produção ativa." *Revista E.* (September): 16–21.

Ribeiro, Djamila. 2017. *O que é lugar de fala?* Belo Horizonte, Brazil: Letramento.

Rios, Sofia. 2015. "Representation and Disjunction: Made-up Maids in Mexican Telenovelas." *Journal of Iberian and Latin American Research* 21 (2): 223–233.

Rocha, Glauber. 1995. "An Esthetic of Hunger." In *Brazilian Cinema*, edited by Randal Johnson and Robert Stam, 120–127. New York: Columbia University Press.

Rohrer, Seraina. 2017. *La India María: Mexploitation and the Films of María Elena Velasco.* Austin: University of Texas Press.

Roman-Morfin, Raquel Diana. 2015. "Different Shades of Domesticity: Representations of Intersecting Power Relations in Latin American Literary and Visual Culture." PhD diss., University of California Irvine. https:// escholarship.org/uc/item/96q4v37w.

Romero, Macarena. 2021. "Migrant Domestic Workers in Argentina during COVID-19: Economic Violence and Access to Rights." *A-id* (blog), August 24. https://www.a-id.org/migrant-domestic-workers-in-argentina -during-covid-19-economic-violence-and-access-to-rights.

Romero, Mary, and Nancy Pérez. 2015. "Conceptualizing the Foundation of Inequalities in Care Work." *American Behavioral Scientist* 60 (2): 172–188.

Roncador, Sônia. 2007. "Histórias paranóicas, criados perversos no imaginário literário da belle époque tropical." *Estudos de Literatura Brasileira Contemporânea* 29: 127–140.

Roncador, Sônia. 2014. *Domestic Servants in Literature and Testimony in Brazil, 1889–1999.* New York: Palgrave Macmillan.

Ros, Ana. 2011. "Leaving and Letting Go As Possible Ways of Living Together in Jorge Gaggero's 'Cama Adentro/Live-in Maid.'" In *New Trends in*

Argentine and Brazilian Cinema, edited by Carolina Rocha and Cacilda M. Rego, 97–116. Bristol, UK: Intellect.

Rosen, Philip. 2001. *Change Mummified: Cinema, Historicity, Theory.* Minneapolis: University of Minnesota Press.

Rossi, María Julia. 2018. "La voz cantante: Esencia y excesos de las empleadas domésticas en Tania Kaufmann y Clarice Lispector." In *Los de abajo: Tres siglos de sirvientes en el arte y la literatura en América Latina*, edited by María Julia Rossi and Lucía Campanella, 113–133. Rosario, Argentina: UNR Editora.

Rossi, María Julia. 2020. *Ficciones de emancipación: Los sirvientes literarios de Silvina Ocampo, Elena Garro y Clarice Lispector.* Rosario, Argentina: Beatriz Viterbo Editora.

Rossi, María Julia, and Lucía Campanella, eds. 2018. *Los de abajo: Tres siglos de sirvientes en el arte y la literatura en América Latina.* Rosario, Argentina: UNR Editora.

Russell, Catherine. 1999. *Experimental Ethnography: The Work of Film in the Age of Video.* Durham, NC: Duke University Press.

Sá, Lúcia. 2018. "Intimacy at Work: Servant and Employer Relations in 'Que horas ela volta?' (The Second Mother)." *Journal of Iberian and Latin American Studies* 24 (3): 311–327.

Sacco, Victoria, and Verónica Panella. 2018. "*97 empleadas domésticas*: La representación / invisibilidad del trabajo del cuidado en Perú." In *Los de abajo: Tres siglos de sirvientes en el arte y la literatura en América Latina*, edited by María Julia Rossi and Lucía Campanella, 145–166. Rosario, Argentina: UNR Editora.

Sala de sesiones de la comisión legislativa permanente (Uruguay). 1934. *Código del niño Ley 9.342.* April 6. http://biblioteca.cejamericas.org/bitstream /handle/2015/4166/ur_cod_nino.pdf?sequence=1&isAllowed=y.

Salazar, Gabriel. 2006. *Ser niño huacho en la historia de Chile.* Santiago, Chile: LOM Ediciones.

Salem, Rodrigo. 2013. "Dependência de empregada." Ilustrada, *Folha de São Paulo*, May 1.

Salles, João. 2009. "The Difficulty with Documentary: A Filmmaker's View." In *Realism and the Audiovisual Media*, edited by Lúcia Nagib and Cecília Melo, 224–234. Basingstoke, UK: Palgrave Macmillan.

Sánchez Prado, Ignacio. 2018. "Special Dossier on Alfonso Cuaron's 'Roma': Class Trouble." *Mediático* (blog), December 24. https://reframe.sussex .ac.uk/mediatico/2018/12/24/special-dossier-on-alfonso-cuarons-roma -class-trouble.

Santiago Páramo, Andrea, ed. 2020. *Nuestras voces cuentan: Historias de trabajadoras del hogar durante la pandemia de Covid-19.* Ciudad de Mexico: Nosotr@s por la Democracia.

Schiwy, Freya. 2009. "Decolonizing the Technologies of Knowledge: Video

and Indigenous Epistemology." Academia repository. https://www
.academia.edu/42204048/DECOLONIZING_THE_TECHNOLOGIES
_OF_KNOWLEDGE_VIDEO_AND_INDIGENOUS_EPISTEMOLOGY.
Accessed February 16, 2023.

Schoonover, Karl. 2016. "Wastrels of Time: Slow Cinema's Labouring Body, the Political Spectator and the Queer." In *Slow Cinema*, edited by Tiago de Luca and Nuno Barradas Jorge, 153–168. Edinburgh: Edinburgh University Press.

Schuessler, Michael K. 2017. "Elenísima." *La Jornada* (Mexico City), February 25. https://www.jornada.com.mx/2017/02/25/deportes/a03a1cul.

Schwartz, Stuart. 2011. "The Iberian Atlantic to 1650." In *The Oxford Handbook of the Atlantic World, 1450–1850*, edited by Nicholas Canny and Philip Morgan, 147–164. Oxford: Oxford University Press.

Senado Notícias. 2019. "Aprovada em 2017, reforma trabalhista alterou regras para flexibilizar o mercado de trabalho." *Senado Federal,* May 2. https://www12.senado.leg.br/noticias/materias/2019/05/02/aprovada-em -2017-reforma-trabalhista-alterou-regras-para-flexibilizar-o-mercado-de -trabalho.

Shaw, Deborah. 1996. "Jesusa Palancares as Individual Subject in Elena Poniatowska's 'Hasta No Verte Jesús Mío.'" *Bulletin of Hispanic Studies* 73 (2): 191–204.

Shaw, Deborah. 2003. *Contemporary Cinema of Latin America: Ten Key Films*. New York: Continuum.

Shaw, Deborah. 2017. "Intimacy and Distance—Domestic Servants in Latin American Women's Cinema: La mujer sin cabeza/The Headless Woman and El niño pez/The Fish Child." In *Latin American Women Filmmakers: Production, Politics, Poetics*, edited by Deborah Shaw and Deborah Martin, 123–148. London: I. B. Tauris.

Shaw, Deborah. 2018a. "Serving the Master Text: Rethinking Digital Paratexts in the Social Issue Film 'Who Is Dayani Cristal?'" *Screen* 59 (2): 258–265.

Shaw, Deborah. 2018b. "Special Dossier on 'Roma': Children of Women? Alfonso Cuarón's Love Letter to His Nana." *Mediático* (blog), December 24. http://reframe.sussex.ac.uk/mediatico/2018/12/24/special-dossier-on -roma-alfonso-cuarons-love-letter-to-his-nana.

Shaw, Lisa. 2018. *Tropical Travels: Brazilian Popular Performance, Transnational Encounters, and the Construction of Race*. Austin: University of Texas Press.

Silva Santisteban, Rocío. 2007. "Perú: Se necesita muchacha (I)." *La Insignia,* March 16. https://www.lainsignia.org/2007/marzo/ibe_021.htm.

Simões, Mariana. 2020. "Primeira morte do Rio por coronavírus, doméstica não foi informada de risco de contágio pela 'patroa.'" *Agência Pública* (blog), March 19. https://apublica.org/2020/03/primeira-morte-do-rio-por -coronavirus-domestica-nao-foi-informada-de-risco-de-contagio-pela -patroa.

Simpson Lapp, Simca. 2019. "The Limits of Fictitious Kinship: 'Roma' Reveals the Need to Recognize Domestic Workers' Own Care Rights." *Work in Progress Sociology* (blog), February 19. http://www.wipsociology.org/2019/02/19/the-limits-of-fictitious-kinship-roma-reveals-the-need-to-recognize-domestic-workers-own-care-rights.

Sinembargo. 2019. "Cuarón y líder de trabajadoras domésticas aplauden plan del IMSS para darles seguridad social." Redacción, February 18. https://www.sinembargo.mx/18-02-2019/3538203.

Slimani, Leïla. 2018. *Lullaby*. London: Faber and Faber.

Smith, Paul Julian. 2018. "Special Dossier on 'Roma': Watching 'Roma' in Mexico City." *Mediático* (blog), December 24. https://reframe.sussex.ac.uk/mediatico/2018/12/24/special-dossier-on-roma-watching-roma-in-mexico-city.

Smith, Paul Julian. 2019. *Multiplatform Media in Mexico: Growth and Change Since 2010*. Cham, Switzerland: Springer International.

Sobreira, Vinícius. 2020. "Sindicato critica estados que incluíram domésticas em serviço essencial na quarentena." *Brasil de Fato* (São Paulo), May 25. https://www.brasildefato.com.br/2020/05/25/sindicato-critica-estados-que-incluiram-domesticas-em-servico-essencial-na-quarentena.

Sommer, Doris. 1988. "'Not Just a Personal Story': Women's Testimonios and the Plural Self." In *Life Lines: Theorizing Women's Autobiography*, edited by Bella Brodzki and Celeste Schenck, 107–130. Ithaca, NY: Cornell University Press.

Sommer, Doris. 1991. *Foundational Fictions: The National Romances of Latin America*. Berkeley: University of California Press.

Sosa, Cecilia. 2019. "Affective Architectures of the Real." In *Lola Arias: Re-enacting Life*, edited by Jean Graham-Jones, 196–199. Aberystwyth, Wales: Performance Research Books.

Soto, Héctor. 2011. "Sebastián Silva: Cautiverio infeliz." In *El novísimo cine chileno*, edited by Ascanio Cavallo and Gonzalo Maza, 93–102. Santiago, Chile: Uqbar Editores.

Souto, Mariana. 2018. "Invasores: Classe, território e perspectiva no cinema brasileiro contemporâneo." *Logos* 25 (1): 174–191.

Souto, Mariana. 2019. *Infiltrados e invasores: Uma perpsectiva comparada sobre relações de classe no cinema brasileiro*. Salvador, Brazil: EDUFBA.

Spinetto, Juan Pablo, Cristiane Lucchesi, and Alex Cuadros. 2013. "Brazil's Batista Loses Billionaire Status as Debts Mount." Bloomberg, July 26. https://www.bloomberg.com/news/articles/2013-07-25/brazil-s-batista-loses-billionaire-status-as-debts-mount.

Spivak, Gayatri Chakravorty. 1985. "Three Women's Texts and a Critique of Imperialism." *Critical Inquiry* 12 (1): 243–261.

Spivak, Gayatri Chakravorty. 1988. "Can the Subaltern Speak?" In *Marxism and the Interpretation of Culture*, edited by Cary Nelson and Lawrence Grossberg, 271–313. Urbana: University of Illinois Press.

Spyer, Juliano. 2017. *Social Media in Emergent Brazil*. London: UCL Press.

Staab, Silke, and Kristen Hill Maher. 2006. "The Dual Discourse About Peruvian Domestic Workers in Santiago de Chile: Class, Race, and a Nationalist Project." *Latin American Politics and Society* 48 (1): 87–116.

Staples, David. 2007. "Women's Work and the Ambivalent Gift of Entropy." In *The Affective Turn: Theorizing the Social*, edited by Patricia Ticineto Clough and Jean O'Malley Halley, 119–150. Durham, NC: Duke University Press.

Statista Research Department. 2020. "Brazil: Social Media Usage Rate 2017–2022, by Age." *Statista*, July 21. https://www.statista.com/statistics/1083577/brazil-social-media-usage-rate-age.

STHC (Sindicato de Trabajadoras del Hogar del Cusco). 1982. *Basta: Testimonios*. Cusco, Peru: Bartolomé de las Casas.

STHC (Sindicato de Trabajadoras del Hogar del Cusco). n.d. See the STHC website home page. https://sthcusco.webnode.es. Accessed January 29, 2019.

Stoll, David. 1999. *Rigoberta Menchú and the Story of All Poor Guatemalans*. Boulder, CO: Westview.

Suarez, Cristiano. 2020a. *Pandemia romântica n.1: covid-se*. May 4. https://www.instagram.com/p/B_xGYD1JKNm.

Suarez, Cristiano. 2020b. *Pandemia romântica n.2: live-se*. May 5. https://www.instagram.com/p/B_zv1LnJhH9.

Tapley, Kristopher. 2018. "Alfonso Cuarón on the Painful and Poetic Backstory Behind 'Roma.'" *Variety* (blog), October 23. https://variety.com/2018/film/news/roma-alfonso-cuaron-netflix-libo-rodriguez-1202988695.

Terraciano, Kevin. 2011. "Indigenous Peoples in Colonial Spanish American Society." In *A Companion to Latin American History*, edited by Thomas Holloway, 124–145. Malden, MA: Wiley-Blackwell.

Tierney, Dolores, and Olivia Cosentino. 2018. "Introduction to the Special Dossier on 'Roma' (Alfonso Cuaron)." *Mediático* (blog), December 24. https://reframe.sussex.ac.uk/mediatico/2018/12/24/introduction-to-the-special-dossier-on-roma-alfonso-cuaron.

Treré, Emiliano. 2018. "The Sublime of Digital Activism: Hybrid Media Ecologies and the New Grammar of Protest." *Journalism and Communication Monographs* 20 (2): 137–148.

Trezza de Piñeyro, Alicia. 2001. *La relación de trabajo doméstico*. Montevideo: Facultad de derecho, Universidad de la República.

Trigueiro, Edja, and Viviane Cunha. 2015. "The Maid's Room: A Tale of Unchanging Apartheid in a Changing Domestic Space." In *Housemaids: Anthology + Film*, edited by Victor Guimarães, 116–134. Recife, Brazil: Desvia.

UN (United Nations). 2021. "Domestic Workers Among Hardest Hit by COVID Crisis, Says UN Labour Agency." UN News, June 15. https://news.un.org/en/story/2021/06/1094022.

Valdes, Marcela. 2018. "After 'Gravity,' Alfonso Cuarón Had His Pick of Directing Blockbusters. Instead, He Went Home to Make 'Roma.'" *New York Times*, December 13. https://www.nytimes.com/2018/12/13/magazine/alfonso-cuaron-roma-mexico-netflix.html.

Valenzuela, María Elena, and Jacobo Velasco. 2019. "El trabajo doméstico remunerado en América Latina: Avances y retos para la protección de una ocupación eminentemente femenina." *Organización Internacional del Trabajo* (blog), December 13, 2019. http://www.ilo.org/santiago/publicaciones/reflexiones-trabajo/WCMS_732327/lang—es/index.htm.

Vargas Rojas, Vanessa. 2014. "María Emilia Tijoux: 'Acá nadie se imagina a una "nana" que no tenga rasgos de indígena.'" *El Desconcierto*, April 1. https://www.eldesconcierto.cl/nacional/2014/04/01/maria-emilia-tijoux-aca-nadie-se-imagina-una-nana-que-tenga-rasgos-de-indigena.html.

Vasconcelos, José. 2017. *La raza cósmica*. Mexico City: Porrúa. First published in 1925.

Vázquez, Karina Elizabeth. 2014. "Corre muchacha, corre: Estructura de clases y trabajo doméstico en 'La nana' (2009), de Sebastián Silva." *Chasqui* 43 (2): 161–178.

Vázquez Vázquez, María Mercedes. 2019. *The Question of Class in Contemporary Latin American Cinema*. Lanham, MD: Lexington Books.

Velho, Francianne dos Santos. 2017. "A (i)mobilidade da doméstica brasileira nos filmes 'Domésticas' (2001) e 'Que horas ela volta?' (2015)." Master's thesis, University of Leiden. https://openaccess.leidenuniv.nl/handle/1887/52288.

Véliz, Mariano. 2015. "Política doméstica en el cine latinoamericano." *Materia Artística* 1: 228–246.

Viezzer, Moema. 1999. *"Si me permiten hablar . . .": Testimonio de Domitila, una mujer de las minas de Bolivia*. Mexico, DF: Siglo veintiuno editores. First published in 1977.

Virno, Paolo. 2004. *A Grammar of the Multitude*. South Pasadena, CA: Semiotext(e).

Wade, Peter. 2013. "Articulations of Eroticism and Race: Domestic Service in Latin America." *Feminist Theory* 14 (2): 187–202.

Wells, Sarah Ann. 2016. "El trabajo en el cine brasilero." *Hispanófila* 177 (June): 101–114.

Wentzel, Marina. 2018. "O que faz o Brasil ter a maior população de domésticas do mundo." BBC Brasil, February 26, 2018. http://www.bbc.com/portuguese/brasil-43120953.

Wolfe, Cary. 2013. *Before the Law: Humans and Other Animals in a Biopolitical Frame*. Chicago: University of Chicago Press.

Xavier, Ismail. 2009. "Character Construction in Brazilian Documentary Films: Modern Cinema, Classical Narrative and Micro-Realism." In *Realism and the Audiovisual Media*, edited by Lúcia Nagib and Cecília Melo, 210–233. Basingstoke, UK: Palgrave Macmillan.

Xexeó, Artur. 2013. "Filmes e vozes." Segundo caderno, *O Globo* (Rio de Janeiro), September 4.

Yang, Guobin. 2016. "Narrative Agency in Hashtag Activism: The Case of #BlackLivesMatter." *Media and Communication* 4 (4): 13–17.

Yúdice, George. 1991. "Testimonio and Postmodernism." *Latin American Perspectives* 18 (3): 15–31.

Zelizer, Viviana A. 2009. *The Purchase of Intimacy.* Princeton, NJ: Princeton University Press.

Zotti, Mary Irene. 1990. "The Young Christian Workers." *U.S. Catholic Historian* 9 (4): 387–400.

Zuboff, Shoshana. 2019. *The Age of Surveillance Capitalism.* London: Profile Books.

Index

the abject, 25–26, 34, 82–84, 111–113, 115, 130, 222

activism, 3, 185, 196, 200, 213, 215, 218; digital, 17–18, 35, 184–185, 196–201, 213, 218; hashtag, 197; union, 37, 65, 199–200, 241n26. *See also* artivism

adolescents, 57, 59, 75, 91, 93, 123–124; in *Doméstica*, 124, 137, 153–155, 165–173, 194–195, 246n14, 247n33; and relationships to domestic workers, 89, 97–100, 124, 149, 165–171; and work in the domestic labor sector, 74, 241n33, 242n35

affective labor, 22–23, 26, 88, 160–161, 244n18. *See also* immaterial labor

affective value, 25–26

Afro-Brazilians: and childcare, 1–2, 116, 157–161, 186–187; and domestic work, 4–6, 30, 90, 99, 123, 161, 165, 196, 207, 213–214, 243n12; and domestic worker activism, 199–200, 202, 206, 213–214, 241n26; and enslavement, 4–5, 61–62, 120, 132, 148, 159–161, 165, 181, 196, 210; and feminism, 25, 241n26; and testimonios, 33, 35, 61, 85, 183, 196, 211–212, 220. *See also* Afro-descendant people; *mãe preta*

Afro-descendant people, 22, 40; and enslavement, 4–6, 8, 147; and paid domestic work, 28, 96, 112, 135; sexualization of, 9, 207; and wet-nursing, 8, 99, 162, 250n18. See also *mãe preta*

Ai de vós! Diário de uma doméstica (da Silva), 37, 44–46, 57–58

ambivalence: in films about domestic workers, 33–34, 88, 100, 119–120, 123, 129–130, 174–175, 217, 219–220, 222; and postcolonial nostalgia, 1–2, 119–120, 217; in testimonios, 56, 60–61, 75

appropriation, 3, 185, 194–195; and social media, 35, 192–194, 205, 224

Aquarius (Filho), 35, 113, 148, 178, 192, 219, 243n11

archive, 134, 156–159, 250n18

Argentina, 2, 35, 141, 145, 149, 184, 241n25; artists from, 29, 131, 133–134, 223; the Covid-19 pandemic in, 19, 20; domestic labor laws in, 11, 16, 18, 238n9; migration to, 244n3, 245n7; works made or set in, 34, 36, 103, 131–134, 142, 147, 222. *See also* Arias, Lola;

Cama adentro; *Las dependencias*; Martel, Lucrecia; *Mucamas*; Ocampo, Silvina; *Réimon*

Arias, Lola, 35, 184, 185, 189, 190, 196, 249n2, 249n11, 250n12

artistic labor, 3, 29, 30, 34, 132, 137–145, 174, 180–181, 185, 222, 249n3

artivism, 35–36, 183–184, 213, 215–216, 223–224, 225, 249n1

authoritarian rule. *See* dictatorship

babá. *See* nannies

Babás (Lins), 32, 34, 133, 136, 149, 168, 175, 186, 244n3, 245n11, 246n12; and experimental or domestic ethnography, 132, 150–155 157, 181–182, 194, 247n30; haunting in, 34, 132, 181, 219, 222–223; and the index, 132, 156–163, 192; interviews in, 134, 164–165; and the wet nurse, 153, 161–163, 189–190, 195. *See also* Lins, Consuelo

Bacurau (Filho), 35, 148

Balún-Canán (Castellanos), 9

Baron, Jaimie, 193–194, 195, 250n15

Barrios de Chúngara, Domitila, 25, 37, 42–43, 50–51, 85, 220, 239n7, 239n10. See also *"Si me permiten hablar . . .": Testimonio de Domitila una mujer de las minas de Bolivia*

Basta: Testimonios (STHC), 33, 44, 46, 50–51, 60, 66, 221, 240n21

Beverley, John, 41, 45, 52, 56, 73

"black mammy." See *mãe preta*

As boas maneiras (Rojas and Dutra), 34, 116, 219

Brazil, 2, 10, 27, 46, 58, 74, 135, 157, 197, 208–209, 237n2, 242n5, 244n3, 248n41; contemporary politics in, 20–21, 90–92, 117, 124, 127, 130, 202–203, 211; the Covid-19 pandemic in, 19–20, 22, 213–214; and domestic worker organizing, 11, 39, 65, 85, 198–200, 212–213, 216, 223–224, 241n26; and enslavement, 5, 34, 61, 91, 99, 116, 118–120, 132, 136, 148, 159–161, 174, 181, 196, 210, 217, 246n14; internet use in, 197, 205–206, 211, 250n21, 250n27; labor laws in, 11, 13–15, 18, 74, 93, 199–200, 238n9, 241n33; and live-in domestic work, 7, 105, 132, 207; and race, 1, 8, 25, 30, 99–100, 123, 162–163, 200, 206, 207, 243n12; terms for domestic workers in, 12, 237n6. *See also* Afro-Brazilians; cordiality; *mãe preta*; Northeast (of Brazil)

the butler, 27; in Marxist theory, 140; in *Santiago*, 135–136, 140–142, 164, 173–175, 177, 178, 180

Cama adentro (Gaggero), 31, 244n19

Campanella, Lucía, 29–30, 238n2, 246n19

capitalism, 3, 23–24, 27, 70, 106–107, 108, 110, 117, 140, 144, 246n20; and haunting, 3, 34, 36, 131, 132, 146, 180–181, 222. *See also* commodification; late capitalism; Marxism; surplus value; surveillance capitalism

care: chains, 22, 26; debt of, 109; relationships of, 3, 74, 89, 111, 123, 128–129, 136, 138, 146, 160–162, 222; work, 23, 24, 26–27, 35, 100, 130, 131, 132, 139, 184, 189, 190, 208, 212, 224, 225. *See also* childcare; migration

Carvalho, Lenira: and domestic worker organizing, 64–65, 67–68, 69, 72; life of, 62–63, 64, 76; theorization of the domestic worker's condition by, 26–27, 67, 75, 78–79, 80–81, 83, 84, 104, 110, 111, 112, 114, 125, 128, 164, 188, 212. *See also* "Só a gente que vive é que sabe"

casa grande, 5, 7, 170, 210. See also *Casa grande & senzala*

Casa grande (Barbosa), 22, 31, 33, 87, 88, 111, 123–124, 129–130, 148, 176; adolescent–domestic worker relationships in, 98–101, 102, 117–119, 219, 221; crisis of masculinity in, 126–128; mise-en-scène in, 106–108; plot and context of, 91–93; territorialization in, 103–106

Casa grande & senzala (Freyre), 5, 91, 99, 148. *See also* Freyre, Gilberto

"Casa tomada" (Cortázar), 113

Castellanos, Rosario, 9, 29

Catholicism, 28; and domestic worker organizing, 11, 38–39, 64–68, 85, 240n16, 241n27; in domestic workers' testimonios, 38, 45, 60, 64–67, 85, 220–221. *See also* liberation theology; Santa Zita; Young Catholic Workers organizations

childcare, 4, 12, 24, 42, 85, 107; in Brazil, 70, 116, 136, 159, 160; on screen, 87, 96. *See also* nannies

child labor, 6, 74–75, 207, 220, 242n34

Chile, 2, 4, 20, 94, 110, 111, 244n20; artists from, 21; domestic labor laws in, 11, 16–17, 18, 238n9; domestic worker organizing in, 11, 241n27; migration to, 17; works made or set in, 36, 93. See also *La nana*

La ciénaga, 98, 245n8

cine clasemediero. See middle-class cinema

class: consciousness, 54, 59–60, 66–67, 69, 70, 85, 166; and discrimination, 17, 61, 85, 198–199, 212, 219, 220; and domestic space, 7–8, 98, 102–107, 112–113, 209, 221–222, 242n2; guilt, 45–46, 136, 151; struggle, 84. *See also* dominant class; homes: and the bourgeoisie; middle-class cinema; working class

classism, 17, 20, 21, 30, 111, 163, 219. *See also* class: and discrimination

cleaning, 4, 12, 23, 85, 140, 145, 215, 223, 246n19; and dirt, 25–26, 55, 111–113; on film, 92, 96, 100, 107, 142–145, 169; in hotels, 35, 184, 189, 190, 215, 223, 224; in testimonios, 59, 80, 205

O clube dos canibas (Parente), 34, 103, 116, 242n2

colonialism, 185, 247n29; and corruption, 91; and ethnography, 150, 152, 154, 156, 169, 182, 223; and the home, 7, 99, 148–149, 170; and intimate relationships with domestic employees, 1–2, 9–10, 93, 106, 118–120, 130, 149–150, 170–171, 174; and paid domestic labor, 3, 8, 12, 35, 132, 137, 139, 181, 185, 187, 193, 195, 196, 216, 219, 222–223, 246n14; and race, 8, 43, 120, 241n30; in testimonios, 45, 85, 210

colonization, 4–5, 7, 9, 22, 61, 91, 98–100, 106, 132, 147, 162, 186. *See also* colonialism

commodification, 23, 128, 140, 160; of domestic workers, 84, 86, 88, 110, 129–130, 220, 222; of Raquel in *La nana*, 110, 115

Como é boa nossa empregada (Mello and Porto), 30–31, 118

Confederation of Domestic Workers of Latin America and the Caribbean (CONLACTRAHO), 14, 47

Confinada (Assis and Oliveira), 22, 36, 213–214, 224

consent, 3, 5, 194, 204; of domestic employees, 137, 171, 194; and social media, 184, 192, 205, 216, 224. *See also* ethics

cooking, 4, 23, 42, 80, 101, 143, 145, 187; and value, 84–85

cooks, 12, 55, 56, 59, 61–62, 92, 140, 149

cordiality, 10, 116–117, 174, 248n43

Covid-19 pandemic, 18–20, 22, 35, 36, 184, 187, 213–215, 216, 224, 225

criada, 12, 55, 75, 77, 112, 133, 237n5. *See also* child labor; fictive kin relationships: between domestic employees and employers

Cuarón, Alfonso, 17–18, 95–97, 121, 143, 218, 243n9, 243n15, 251n34. See also *Roma*

Cusco Union of Household Workers (Sindicato de Trabajadoras del Hogar del Cusco, or STHC), 33, 54, 69, 79; history of, 47–48, 65–68, 240nn15–17; and testimonios, 48, 49–51, 63, 67, 70, 71, 77–78, 221. See also *Basta: Testimonios*; Goutet, Cristina; Gutiérrez, Ana; *Se necesita muchacha*

debt: crises, 38; emotional, 97, 109, 129, 221; historical, 245n11. *See also* gifts

de Jesus, Carolina Maria: biography of, 58–59, 82, 239n3; and experiences of paid domestic work, 59, 80, 81–82; writings of, 33, 38, 43, 60–62, 85, 220, 238n2, 239n5, 242n36. See also *Diário de Bitita*

democratic transition, 2, 11, 13, 16, 37, 38, 57

Las dependencias (Martel), 29, 132, 144, 149, 157, 244n3, 245n4, 247n34; and haunting, 34, 137, 145–148, 181, 219, 222–223; and immaterial labor or products, 131, 145–146, 160, 180; Ocampo's domestic employees in, 133, 138–139

Diário de Bitita (de Jesus), 33, 37, 43, 58–59, 61–62, 82, 85, 220, 239n9. *See also* de Jesus, Carolina Maria

dictatorship, 2, 11, 16, 37, 38, 47, 58, 65, 127, 239n4

dirt. *See* the abject

Doméstica (Mascaro), 32, 143, 164, 174, 219, 222, 246n17, 246n14; adolescent camera people in, 124, 154, 155, 165–166, 195, 246nn15–16, 247n33; and comparisons with other Brazilian films, 34–35, 132, 134, 149–150, 153, 181–182; context of, 136–137; as experimental domestic ethnography, 151–153, 165, 169, 170–171, 194; the index in, 156–157, 172–173, 223; performativity in, 154–155, 166, 167–168

Domésticas—O filme (Meirelles and Olival), 31, 246n17

domestic service. *See* servants

domestic space. *See* homes

domestic work: informality/precarity of, 12–13, 18–20, 30, 38, 208, 215; paid hourly, 7, 18, 19, 81. *See also* care; cooking; domestic workers; dominant class: and relationships to domestic workers; ethics: of hiring a live-in domestic worker; housekeepers; housework; immaterial labor; reproductive labor; salaries; unproductive labor; "women's work"

domestic workers: children of, 22, 205–206, 211–212, 218; commutes of, 20, 144–145; and labor rights in Latin America, 10–18; Spanish and Portuguese terms for, 12–13, 237n7. *See also* commodification: of domestic workers; fictive kin relationships; homes: and domestic workers' isolation; housekeepers; the hypersexualized maid; maids; Mexico: terms for domestic workers in; nannies; payment-in-kind; servants

Domestic Workers' Convention No. 189, 14–15, 16, 17, 20, 96, 187, 218, 238n9

dominant class, 16, 34, 35, 55, 61, 91, 134, 147, 183, 248n37; and fears of working-class invasion or contamination, 8, 20, 28, 102–105, 113, 129, 188, 209–210, 221; and haunting, 181, 192, 222; and relationships to domestic workers, 9, 10, 25–26, 72, 73, 118–120, 157; as scribes, 33, 221. *See also* class

Los dueños, 99, 103, 124

enslavement, 4–5, 8, 9–10, 106, 119–120; abolition of, 4, 13, 58, 105, 116, 132, 148, 161, 218; legacy of, 3, 5, 61–62, 98–100, 132, 136, 159, 160–162, 165, 173, 181, 196, 210, 223. See also *Casa grande & senzala*; Freyre, Gilberto; modern slavery

ethics, 29, 144; and documentary filmmaking, 150, 153, 165, 171–172, 182, 195, 223, 224; of hiring a live-in domestic worker, 87, 160; and representations of the Other, 3, 33, 36, 144, 151, 184, 196; and social media, 35, 184, 192–195, 200–201, 204, 205, 212, 216, 224; and testimonios, 41, 56, 72,

86, 221. *See also* appropriation; consent

Eu, empregada doméstica (Preta-Rara), 2, 22, 35, 218; and activism, 90, 183–184, 196–200, 212–213, 215, 218, 223; and Facebook, 184, 200–203, 204–206, 224, 250n23; and race, 82, 196, 206, 207; and the testimonio tradition, 70, 183, 198, 200, 203–204, 216, 224; and theorizing the domestic worker's condition, 206–212. *See also* Preta-Rara

Facebook, 183, 196–197, 201–202, 211, 250n21, 250n23; business model of, 35, 184, 205, 216, 224; and privacy, 192–194, 204–205, 216, 224. See also *Eu, empregada doméstica*; *97 empleadas domésticas*; *Nuestras voces cuentan*; social media

feminism, 25, 51, 69, 72, 138, 198, 241n26; and Western individualism, 88, 126–129, 130, 222, 248n37

Fernandes, Joyce. *See* Preta-Rara

fictive kin relationships, 152, 243n15; between domestic employees and employers, 7, 74, 76–77, 86, 94, 105, 123, 207, 220, 251n30; between domestic employees and their employers' children, 92, 157. See also *criada*; *mãe preta*; "second mother" figure

Filho, Kleber Mendonça, 32, 35, 100, 113, 148–149, 178, 192, 219, 243n11

foundational narratives, 8–10, 33–34, 88, 96, 99, 120–123, 130, 163, 181, 217

Franco, Jean, 10, 28

Freyre, Gilberto, 5, 8–9, 91, 93,

99–100, 106, 117–120, 123, 130, 148, 162, 170, 210. See also *Casa grande & senzala*

Furtado, Gustavo Procopio, 32, 177, 178, 246nn15–16, 247n30, 248n41

"future girls," 127–128

ghosts, 120, 146, 147, 148, 190, 247n29; and the index, 156; and paid domestic work, 3, 34, 36, 131, 139, 143, 171, 180, 219; and the wet nurse, 163. See also *Babás*: haunting in; capitalism: and haunting; *Las dependencias*: and haunting; dominant class: and haunting; specters/spectrality

gift economy, 88, 109. See also gifts

gifts, 210; and domestic workers in film, 107, 108–110, 129, 221, 244n19; and payment, 208, 244n19. See also gift economy

Gonzalez, Lélia, 25

Goutet, Cristina, 33, 46–47, 51, 65–66, 67, 221, 239n13. See also Gutiérrez, Ana

Gutiérrez, Ana, 2, 33, 37, 62, 63; and interventions in *Se necesita muchacha*, 56, 86, 73, 240n21; life and work of, 46–51; religious beliefs of, 66, 221; and theorizing the domestic worker's condition, 68, 76, 79–80, 84. See also *Basta*; Goutet, Cristina; *Se necesita muchacha*

Gutiérrez-Rodríguez, Encarnación, 22, 23, 25–26, 139, 143

Habitaciones de servicio (Ortiz), 189

Hardt, Michael, and Antonio Negri, 26, 108, 139, 213. See also immaterial labor

haunting. See *Babás*: haunting in;

capitalism: and haunting; *Las dependencias*: and haunting; dominant class: and haunting; ghosts; specters/spectrality

Holanda, Sérgio Buarque de, 10, 116, 174. See also cordiality

homelessness, 6, 58, 62, 64, 80, 83

homes, 10, 32, 75, 78, 114, 125, 128, 187, 245n11; and allegory, 35, 135, 148–149; and the bourgeoisie, 12, 28, 70, 84, 102–103, 113, 116, 134, 148, 161, 209, 217; and childhood or adolescence, 33, 94, 96, 135, 146–147, 149, 153, 165–166, 245n10; in colonial Latin America, 4–5, 7, 93, 98, 170, 243n13; design of, 7, 92–93, 170, 189; and domestic workers' isolation, 13, 48, 67–68, 70, 79, 125, 160, 169, 213, 244n19; ownership of, 83, 123–125, 164, 248n37; reconstructed on screen, 7–8, 31, 87, 89, 90, 94–95, 96, 101–107, 125, 129, 143, 168, 176–178, 221, 242n2; and territorialization, 94, 103–104, 111, 117, 128, 209, 221; as workplaces, 6, 18–19, 20, 24, 49–50, 64, 68, 80–81, 102, 107, 137, 193, 207, 208, 210, 217, 241n30. See also dominant class: and fears of working-class invasion or contamination; housework; kitchen door; "maid's room"

home videos, 159, 177, 193; in *Babás*, 136, 153, 154, 157, 159–160, 192, 194; in Brazilian documentary, 134; in *Doméstica*, 154, 194; in *Santiago*, 154, 177, 178–179, 192

hotel cleaners. See cleaning: in hotels

housekeepers, 5, 172, 245n5; as characters, 28, 92, 100, 105; Spanish and Portuguese terms for, 12 housekeeping. *See* housekeepers

housework, 42, 107, 160. *See also* domestic work; reproductive labor; unproductive labor; "women's work"

the hypersexualized maid, 30, 100, 111, 118

Ilhota, 44, 83

immaterial labor, 3, 26, 29, 108, 109, 131–132, 139, 148, 224, 244n18; in *Babás*, 29, 34, 182, 185, 219, 222; in *Las dependencias*, 29, 34, 131–132, 145–146, 181, 185, 219, 222; in *Doméstica*, 29, 34, 182, 185, 219, 222; in *Réimon*, 29, 34, 131–132, 143, 145, 181; in *Santiago*, 29, 34, 131–132, 139–140, 142, 174, 181, 182, 185, 219, 222

immigration. *See* migration

the index, 132, 143, 150, 155–157, 165, 171, 181, 247n32. *See also Babás*: and the index; *Doméstica*: the index in; ghosts: and the index; *Santiago*: and indexicality

indigeneity, 50, 52, 64, 82. *See also* Mexico: race and domestic work in; Peru: domestic work and race in

International Labour Organization (ILO), 13, 14, 16, 17, 18, 20, 96, 187, 218, 238n9. *See also* Domestic Workers' Convention No. 189

intersectionality, 16, 25, 69, 82, 85, 129, 130, 171, 220, 222

Juventud Obrera Católica/Juventude Operária Católica. *See* Young Catholic Workers organizations

kitchen door, 7, 101, 104, 243n14

Kratje, Julia, 144, 146, 155

late capitalism, 36, 84, 106–107, 128, 137, 139

liberation theology, 11, 39, 64–67, 71, 85, 221. *See also* Young Catholic Workers organizations; Catholicism: and domestic worker organizing

Lins, Consuelo: and found-footage filmmaking, 157–159; and images of wet nurses, 161–162, 189, 195; influence of *Santiago* on, 131, 181, 223; and relationships to paid domestic workers, 132, 136–137, 155, 159–160, 163–165, 175, 244n3; and the use of voiceover in *Babás*, 152–154, 246n12. See also *Babás*

Lispector, Clarice, 28–29, 34, 112, 114, 209. See also *A paixão Segundo G. H.*

Lízia, Millena, 30, 246n19

Lula da Silva, Luiz Inácio, 21, 90, 127, 202

Lullaby (Slimani), 28

mãe preta, 8, 25, 99, 100, 120, 162–163. *See also* "second mother" figure; wet-nursing

maids, 27, 34, 107, 110, 165, 211; and protests in Brazil, 21, 90; stereotypes of, 30–31, 111, 118; terms in Spanish and Portuguese for, 12, 21, 25, 75, 94, 199; in testimonios, 46, 48, 50, 55, 68, 73, 84. *See also* the hypersexualized maid; "maid's room"; servants

"maid's room," 7, 189, 196, 209; in *A paixão segundo G. H.*, 28, 112, 114; on film, 101–102, 112, 149, 170, 173, 221. See also *Habitaciones de servicio*; homes: and territorialization; kitchen door; service areas

Martel, Lucrecia, 29, 34, 98, 131, 134, 147–148, 219, 243n17, 245nn8–9, 247n29, 247n34. *See also La ciénaga; Las dependencias; La niña santa; Zama*

Marxism, 11, 23, 26, 65–67, 85, 106, 145, 221, 247n24. *See also* liberation theology

Mascaro, Gabriel. *See Doméstica*

Me llamo Rigoberta Menchú y así me nació la conciencia (Burgos), 32, 40–41, 43, 73, 85, 220, 238n2, 239n5, 239n10

Menchú, Rigoberta. *See Me llamo Rigoberta Menchú y así me nació la conciencia*

mestiçagem. See mestizaje

mestizaje, 8–9, 25, 34, 36, 88, 99, 121–123, 130, 181, 217

Mexico, 4, 243n9; and the Covid-19 pandemic, 20, 214–215, 224; domestic labor laws in, 11, 17–18, 95–96, 238n9; domestic worker organizing in, 11, 95–96, 251n34; race and domestic work in, 30, 52–53, 97; terms for domestic workers in, 75, 237n7; works made or set in, 2, 36, 44, 51, 96–97, 121–122, 240n22. *See also Nuestras voces cuentan; Roma*

middle class. *See* dominant class

middle-class cinema, 3, 32, 90, 110, 134, 219

migration, 19, 24–25, 58, 116, 209, 225; international, 4, 14, 22, 26, 132, 142, 225, 244n3, 245n7; rural-urban, 16, 17, 22, 30, 62, 63–64, 83, 97, 121, 207, 242n35. *See also* care: chains

Mi nana y yo (Kahlo), 9

modern slavery, 14

Mucamas (Arias), 35, 184, 189, 190, 196

Muchachas No More (Chaney and Garcia Castro), 33, 47, 75

La mujer sin cabeza, 31, 243n17, 245n8

Muylaert, Anna, 22, 88–90, 118, 127, 128, 218. *See also Que horas ela volta?*

nana, La (Silva), 2, 22, 31–32, 33, 87, 88, 117, 219; adolescent–domestic worker relationships in, 98, 100; bestial imagery in, 112, 115–116; gift-related symbolism in, 109–110, 129, 221; plot and context of, 93–95; Raquel's breakdown in, 110–112; Raquel's field of vision in, 101–102, 123, 125, 130, 219; reproductive and productive labor in, 107–108, 129; Western individualistic feminism in, 125, 128, 222

nannies, 59, 80, 81–82, 136, 195, 250n18; artists' relationships to, 9, 55, 87, 89, 97, 159, 164, 177, 245n7; on film, 1, 27–28, 140, 153, 157–160, 168–169, 177, 179, 186, 248n36; and foundational narratives, 9, 162–164, 181; terms in Spanish and Portuguese for, 12. *See also* childcare; "second mother" figure

neocolonialism, 22, 24. *See also* colonialism; colonization

Netflix, 17, 96, 184, 243n9

La niña, el chocolate, el huevo duro (Caraballo), 37, 38, 239n6; Caraballo's biography in, 56–57, 239n3; and comparisons with other paid domestic workers' testimonios, 58, 59, 60, 61, 80, 84, 85, 220, 242n36, 242n38; religion in, 64, 67; sexual abuse in, 58, 78, 79

La niña santa (Martel), 34, 147, 245n8
97 empleadas domésticas (Ortiz), 35, 159, 178, 183–196, 205, 209, 215–216, 223, 249n4
Northeast (of Brazil), 5, 89, 99–100, 120, 128, 134, 149, 209
Nuestras voces cuentan (Santiago Páramo), 20, 36, 214–215, 224

Ocampo, Silvina, 245n9, 247nn27–28, 247n34; the literature of, 29, 34, 131, 133–134, 137–138, 145–146, 148, 181, 223, 245n6; and relationships to her domestic employees, 133–134, 137–139, 145–147, 181, 245n5, 245n7, 246n18. See also *Las dependencias*
Ortiz, Daniela: biography of, 185–186, 188; and the controversy sparked by *97 empleadas domésticas*, 192–193, 194–195, 196; works of, 35, 159, 178, 183–184, 187–192, 195–196, 216, 223, 249n4. See also *Habitaciones de servicio*; *97 empleadas domésticas*

A paixão segundo G. H. (Lispector), 28–29, 34, 112–114
Parasite (Bong), 27, 28, 113
paternalism, 45, 49–50, 67, 85, 106, 149, 170
patriarchy, 72, 91, 118; and the colonial household, 4, 5; and cordiality, 10, 116, 174; and paternalism, 67; and the public-private divide, 24–25, 105–106. See also cordiality; paternalism
payment. See salaries
payment-in-kind, 4, 13, 17, 27, 76, 208, 244n19. See also gift economy; gifts; salaries
PEC das domésticas, 13, 18, 199–200, 202–203

Peru, 20, 54, 63, 185, 188, 193, 196, 216, 240n20; colonial period in, 4, 186–187; domestic labor laws in, 11, 15–16, 74, 187, 238n9; domestic work and race in, 52–53, 187, 191; domestic worker organizing in, 11, 39, 47, 66, 85, 221, 240n16; impact of Covid-19 on domestic workers in, 19–20; workers' movements and land reforms in the 1960s in, 68–69, 241n30; works made or set in, 2, 32, 36, 37. See also *Basta: Testimonios*; Cusco Union of Household Workers; *97 empleadas domésticas*; *Se necesita muchacha*
Poniatowska, Elena, 69; and the prologue to *Se necesita muchacha*, 43, 47, 50–51, 52–56, 84; and the theorization of the domestic worker's condition, 75, 77, 97, 142, 145; works of, 240n22
pornochanchadas. See *Como é boa nossa empregada*
Preta-Rara, 74, 90, 185, 206, 214, 250n19; biography of, 196; as an influencer, 200–201. See also *Eu, empregada doméstica*
private space, 6, 19, 24, 102–107, 188, 126, 129, 217, 243n16. See also homes; public space
public space, 24, 102–107, 129, 174, 185, 188, 217, 243n16. See also private space
punctum, 158–159, 177, 191–192, 248n35

Que horas ela volta? (Muylaert), 2, 22, 31, 32, 33, 93, 94, 96, 105, 117, 118, 176, 212, 218, 242n2; adolescent–domestic worker relationships in, 97–98, 100; bestial imagery in, 112–113, 222;

employers' labor in, 108; gift giving in, 109, 129, 221; the home in, 103–104, 107, 129, 209; plot and context of, 87–91; self-sacrificing domestic worker in, 111; Val's field of vision in, 101–102, 123–125, 130, 219; Western individualistic feminism in, 126–128

La raza cósmica (Vasconcelos), 8–9, 123

Recife frio (Filho), 35, 100, 149

Réimon (Moreno), 30, 34, 131, 180, 247nn23–25; and slow cinema techniques, 142–145, 181

reproductive labor, 88, 100, 128, 129, 140, 180; and the abject, 111; devaluation of, 23–26, 43, 84, 107–109, 222; and foundational narratives, 163, 181; and haunting, 3. *See also* unproductive labor

Rio de Janeiro: City of Splendour (FitzPatrick), 1, 2, 187

Roma (Cuarón), 2, 22, 27, 32, 88, 99, 101; bestial imagery in, 112–113, 129–130, 222; depiction of the home in, 102, 104; and domestic workers' rights reform in Mexico, 17–18, 95–96, 130, 218, 222, 251n34; emotional ties in, 219, 243n15; employers' work in, 108; the foundational narrative in, 94, 120–123; plot and context of, 33, 87, 96–97, 109, 157, 184, 221; self-sacrificing domestic worker in, 111; and slow cinema techniques, 143; Western individualistic feminism in, 129. *See also* Cuarón, Alfonso

Roncador, Sônia, 29, 43, 44–45, 60, 73, 105, 238n2, 239n5, 239n12

Rossi, María Julia, 28, 29–30, 133, 245n6

Rousseff, Dilma, 13–14, 18, 21, 90, 127, 202–203

Russell, Catherine, 136, 150–151, 154

salaries, 23, 42, 89, 109, 140, 144; and domestic labor laws, 13–17; and emotions, 27; and precarity, 19, 38, 215; withholding of, 59, 74, 208. *See also* payment-in-kind

Salles, João Moreira: biography of, 135–136, 140, 164, 177, 245n10, 249nn46–47; and the theorization of documentary, 151–152, 154, 176. See also *Santiago*

Santa Zita, 65, 241n27

Santiago (Salles), 2, 131–132, 144, 244n3, 245n10, 247nn22–23; and comparisons with other Brazilian documentaries, 32, 34, 132, 160, 167, 172, 175, 219, 222–223; context of, 134–136; as domestic and experimental ethnography, 151–155, 175–176, 181; and indexicality, 149–150, 155, 157, 177–180, 192; and performance, 167, 173–174, 176, 181–182; and similarities to *Babás*, 34, 152–153, 159, 164–165; virtuosic labor in, 139–142, 181. See also Salles, João Moreira

Santiago Badariotti Merlo. See Salles, João Moreira; *Santiago*

scribes, 3, 33, 36, 39–40, 44–50, 86, 198, 200, 220, 221, 237n2. See also testimonios

seamstress, 133, 137–138

"second mother" figure, 34, 88, 122, 128, 162–163. *See also* fictive kin relationships: between domestic employees and their employers' children; *mãe preta*

Se necesita muchacha (Gutiérrez), 44, 220; and *Basta*, 51–52, 221;

and Catholicism, 64, 65–68, 85–86, 221; critical attention for, 43, 47; and domestic worker unionization, 2, 33, 37–38, 46–51, 62–69, 70, 71, 85, 198, 221; and Poniatowska, 50–56; role of the scribe in, 49–50, 86, 221; and theorizing paid domestic work, 73–80, 82–85, 111, 142. See also *Basta: Testimonios*; Cusco Union of Household Workers; Goutet, Cristina; Gutiérrez, Ana

servants, 11, 34, 119, 132, 140, 150, 157, 218, 219, 242n34; and artists, 131, 139, 181, 223; in colonial Latin America, 4–5, 237n5; in global culture, 27–28; in post-independence Latin America, 6–9, 94; in *Santiago*, 135, 142, 174, 219; terms in Spanish and Portuguese for, 12, 25; in the works of Lucrecia Martel, 147, 245n8; in the works of Silvina Ocampo, 29, 133, 138, 146–149, 245n6; in testimonios, 38, 41, 43, 44, 53, 57, 59, 62, 63, 73, 74, 75, 76, 238n2, 239n3. *See also* maids; service areas

service areas, 7, 101, 104, 113, 114, 146–147, 149, 189, 209. See also *Habitaciones de servicio*; homes: and territorialization; kitchen door; "maid's room"

sexism, 25, 30, 206

sexuality, 151, 163, 176

sex work, 100, 224–225

Shaw, Deborah, 31, 95, 98, 117, 243n10, 243n17, 245n8

"Si me permiten hablar . . .": Testimonio de Domitila una mujer de las minas de Bolivia (Viezzer), 32, 42–43, 50–51. See also Barrios de Chúngara, Domitila

slavery. *See* enslavement

"Só a gente que vive é que sabe" (Carvalho), 39, 70, 220; and Catholicism, 64–65, 67, 85–86, 221; and domestic worker unionization, 2, 33, 37–38, 62–63, 64–65, 68, 69, 71, 85, 198; the role of the scribe in, 46; and theorizing paid domestic work, 72–81, 83–84. *See also* Carvalho, Lenira

social media, 21, 90, 166, 193–194, 205, 243n10; campaigns, 17–18, 183–184, 201–202, 206; influencers, 3, 35, 70, 74, 90, 183, 200–201, 213, 216, 220; and representations of domestic workers, 35, 183, 185, 206, 213–214, 216; and terms of service, 250n14; use of in Brazil, 211, 250n21, 250n27. See also *Domésticas—O filme*; *Eu, empregada doméstica*; Facebook; *97 empleadas*

O som ao redor (Filho), 35, 100, 103, 105, 148

Sommer, Doris, 39–40, 69–70, 163

Souto, Mariana, 32, 103, 166, 171, 245n11, 248n39

specters/spectrality, 145, 181. See also *Babás*: haunting in; capitalism: and haunting; *Las dependencias*: and haunting; dominant class: and haunting; ghosts

Spivak, Gayatri, 46, 71–72, 204

Suarez, Cristiano. See *Confinada*

subalternity, 71–72, 108; and ethics, 3, 33, 36, 184, 195, 204–205, 216; and foundational narratives, 163, 181; and testimonios, 43, 44, 46, 51, 56, 73, 86, 167, 211–212, 224

surplus value, 23–24, 36, 107, 117, 140, 181, 246nn20–21. *See also* productive labor; unproductive labor

288 INDEX

surveillance capitalism, 184

telenovelas, 30, 144, 219
testimonios. See *Ai de vós! Diário de uma doméstica*; *Basta: Testimonios*; *Diário de Bitita*; *Eu, empregada doméstica*; *Me llamo Rigoberta Menchú y así me nació la conciencia*; *La niña, el chocolate, el huevo duro*; *Nuestras voces cuentan*; *"Si me permiten hablar . . .": Testimonio de Domitila una mujer de las minas de Bolivia*; *"Só a gente que vive é que sabe"*
Todos os mortos (Dutra and Gotardo), 35, 148, 219
Trabalhar cansa (Rojas and Dutra), 34, 116

unproductive labor, 23, 34, 108, 140, 143, 224; and domestic work, 23, 84, 106, 145, 221–222
upper class. *See* dominant class
Uruguay: domestic labor laws in, 11, 15, 18, 74, 238n9; domestic worker organizing in, 11; works made or set in, 2, 32, 36, 37, 56–57, 242n38. See also *La niña, el chocolate, el huevo duro*

Vázquez Vázquez, María Mercedes. *See* middle-class cinema

wages. *See* payment-in-kind; salaries

wet-nursing, 23, 100, 159, 190, 195, 250n18; in colonial Latin America, 4–5, 116; and foundational narratives, 1, 8–9, 98–99, 153, 161–163, 217. See also *mãe preta*; "second mother" figure
"women's work," 23, 100, 106, 108–109, 110, 139; in Latin American women's testimonios, 37, 43, 50, 84. *See also* childcare; cleaning; cooking; domestic work; immaterial labor; reproductive labor; servants; unproductive labor; wet-nursing
Workers' Party (PT), 13, 21–22, 90, 91, 117, 202, 211, 224
working class, 54, 57, 61–62, 94, 180, 188, 209, 211; and domestic labor, 16, 43, 104, 116, 207, 212; and migration, 4, 16, 132; and the Workers Party in Brazil, 21–22, 90, 91–92, 117, 211–212; and Young Catholic Workers organizations, 39. *See also* class

Young Catholic Workers organizations (Juventud Obrera Católica/ Juventude Operária Católica or JOCs), 11, 38–39, 64–65, 241n27. *See also* Catholicism: and domestic worker organizing

Zama (Martel), 34, 134, 147, 219